Cresap's Rifles

Cresap's Rifles

THE UNTOLD STORY OF THE RIFLEMEN WHO
HELPED SAVE GEORGE WASHINGTON'S ARMY

―――

Robert L. Bantz, Karen E. Cresap, Nina Cresap, and Champ Zumbrun

© 2018 Robert L. Bantz, Karen E. Cresap, Nina Cresap, and Champ Zumbrun
All rights reserved.

ISBN: 1974128822
ISBN 13: 9781974128822
Library of Congress Control Number: 2017912184
CreateSpace Independent Publishing Platform
North Charleston, South Carolina

Contents

Acknowledgments ... ix
Preface ... xi

Chapter 1   The Reluctant Rifleman ... 1
Chapter 2   The Light in the Stars ... 9
Chapter 3   Theatrics by Firelight ... 17
Chapter 4   A Parade through Pennsylvania ... 27
Chapter 5   Dark Moon Rising ... 35
Chapter 6   Back Door to Boston: The Upper Road ... 44
Chapter 7   Strangers to Fear ... 53
Chapter 8   Keeping the Wolf from the Door ... 64
Chapter 9   Snuffers of the Candle Come to Town ... 73
Chapter 10   Rebels in Roxbury ... 79
Chapter 11   Into the Storm: Washington Takes Ploughed Hill ... 88
Chapter 12   A Meeting with General Washington ... 98
Chapter 13   The Liberty Tree Falls ... 102
Chapter 14   A Farewell Parting of Comrades in Arms ... 105
Chapter 15   Days of Glory ... 110
Chapter 16   The Long Journey Home ... 120
Chapter 17   Beat No Drum ... 123
Chapter 18   Before There Was Glory ... 127

Epilogue ... 141
References ... 157
Appendix A ... 179
Appendix B ... 183

But hear, O ye swains ('tis a tale most profane), How all the tyrannical powers,
Kings, Commons, and Lords, are uniting amain To cut down this guardian of ours.
From the East to the West blow the trumpet to arms, Thro* the land let the sound of it flee:
Let the far and the near all unite with a cheer, In defense of our Liberty Tree.

Thomas Paine, "Liberty Tree," published in the Pennsylvania Magazine, July 1775[1]

---
1 A. Owen Aldrich, *"The Poetry of Thomas Paine." (January 1955). https://journals.psu.edu/pmhb/article/viewFile/41002/40723.*

Acknowledgments

THE AUTHORS ARE EXTREMELY GRATEFUL to our family and friends who have lent patience and support during the authors' journey through this narrative.

We also thank the many individuals we met who work or volunteer keeping records at libraries, museums, courthouses, historical societies, and old church buildings. We can honestly say we did not meet one person on the road who did not show enthusiasm for our project and were more than willing to help us in any way they could.

We are especially grateful to those unseen individuals who scan out-of-print books and post online rare historic materials so that researchers like ourselves have access to them. This book could have not been written in such factual detail without the internet, which allowed the direct access to the world's library and its unending primary resources.

We were amazed at the number of colonial era taverns that still stand en route from Brownsville, Pennsylvania to Boston, Massachusetts and we are indebted to owners past and present who have maintained these establishments over the years.

Many thanks to Keith and Patte Zumbrun for their support while accompanying us on our New England road trips.

A special thank you goes out to Jilla Allen Smith and Judy Allen O'Hara for the Michael Cresap House and Museum and for their father - the Reverend Irvin Allen - who had the foresight to recognize the importance of the historical home that stood before him – and who obtained and preserved this Oldtown, Maryland landmark. We are also mindful of their many years of devotion and tender loving care in the upkeep of the house and its artifacts, and for all their work over the years in the continued preservation of this vital piece of history, family lore, and the name of Michael Cresap.

We thank Lance Bell and Kathie Smith of Advertising Art Design, Inc. for spending a cold morning with us at the Irvin Allen/Michael Cresap Museum and who photographed the image that graces the cover of this book. With great attention to detail, Lance and Kathie delicately utilized the interior of the Michael Cresap House & Museum -- which stands today as a memorial to Michael Cresap.

Thank you to Holli and Lisa of Amazon's "Create Space" for their superb editing skills and their rapt attention to detail in advising and guiding the authors' manuscript to its fullest potential.

The authors express our gratefulness to Bobbi Dubins for her diligence and for her insightfulness in the excellent rendering of her drawings of maps of the Boston area and the route of Cresap's Rifles from Michael Cresap's starting point in Kentucky, to his company's trek through towns from Frederick, Maryland, to the military camps at Roxbury, Massachusetts.

A sincere thank-you to Louise Cresap Geubelle, direct descendant of Thomas Cresap and granddaughter of Joseph Ord Cresap (co-compiler of the HISTORY OF THE CRESAPS) for her sketch of a minuteman who has just been summoned from his work in the field to Revolutionary action.

We also remember John Jeremiah Jacob--confidante and friend of Michael Cresap-who penned "A Biographical Sketch of The Life of the Late Captain Michael Cresap" in the year 1826. His story captured the pioneer spirit of the Cresap family and prominent associates, while relating numerous family-involved activities on the Western Maryland frontier when Jacob was under Michael's tutelage. Jacob, probably the closest friend Michael Cresap had during that era, became father figure and caregiver to the Cresap family at Oldtown. In his early-day narrative, Jacob performed a most revealing and elegant undertaking of honoring Captain Michael Cresap.

We also acknowledge the caretakers at Trinity Episcopal Church in New York City who have kept tidy the landscaping around Michael Cresap's grave site in Trinity Churchyard - and who have carefully watched over and guarded against the deterioration of Michael Cresap's grave for nigh unto 250 years.

We also appreciate the staff and volunteers at the New York Historical Society for their reverent care of the original Michael Cresap tombstone over these many years. For the sake of preservation, the "Captain Michael Cresap" tombstone - removed from Trinity in 1867 and donated to the New York Historical Society by the rector and vestrymen - is on display for the viewing public. A replica of the original tombstone stands today at the Captain's grave site in Trinity churchyard.

We thank the Cresap Society and its members for materials published over the decades by its founders, and works continued by its current membership whose information and data regarding the Cresap families from the inception of the organization have proved extremely helpful to the authors in this labor of love.

Finally, we express our gratitude to all who have served in the military from the days of Cresap's Rifles and the American Revolutionary War, and to those who continue to serve in the United States Armed Forces in all branches around the globe.

Robert Bantz
Karen Cresap
Nina Cresap
Champ Zumbrun

May 14, 2018

Preface

At the dawn of the American Revolutionary War, the Continental Congress requested ten rifle companies from Pennsylvania, Virginia, and Maryland to join Washington and the continental forces outside Boston. Congress made this request on the auspicious date of June 14, 1775, which the US Army celebrates as its official birthday. In response to this request to join Washington's army, Michael Cresap's men made an epic march of more than 550 miles from Oldtown, Maryland, to Boston, Massachusetts, covering a marathon distance of more than 20 miles a day on the "Upper Road," a backdoor inland route to Boston that proved important to the success of the American Revolution.

Through the eyes of Captain Michael Cresap and other riflemen, this extraordinary story relates the invaluable contributions made by the elite riflemen who served as "George Washington's Continental Army Shock Troops."[2] These backwoods men saved Washington's army when unfavorable conditions threatened failure for the colonial troops, who were at their weakest militarily during the summer of 1775. *Cresap's Rifles* remembers, appreciates, and celebrates these long-forgotten men who helped change the course of American history and secured the freedoms and liberties we enjoy today as Americans.

During the writing of this book, the authors made numerous field trips that retraced the route Captain Michael Cresap took from the Ohio River near Pittsburgh, Pennsylvania, to Boston, Massachusetts. More than thirty photographs and maps accompany this story. The authors also drew information from the journals of riflemen and from hard-to-find contemporary sources as well as visiting and obtaining many historical documents from libraries across the eastern quadrant of the nation from Pittsburgh to Boston. The end result of these efforts is this narrative, which relates the compelling story of ten rifle companies that included Captain Michael Cresap and his company of riflemen during the summer of 1775. These patriots—many of their personal sacrifices grievously overlooked in the annals of history—helped save General Washington's army and, most importantly, aided in the winning of the American Revolution.

---

2 Charles P. Neimeyer, "Praise for Washington's Immortals," in *Washington's Immortals*, Patrick K. O'Donnell (New York: Grove Press, 2016).

CHAPTER 1

The Reluctant Rifleman

Along the Ohio River, Kentucky
June 14, 1775

HIS BROW DRIPPING WITH PERSPIRATION, his heart racing, the young rider spurs his horse westward, following the well-worn Braddock's Path. Authorities back at Oldtown, Maryland, had stressed upon him the importance of delivering a message that originated with officials from the Continental Congress. This information the rider is to impart must be delivered into Michael Cresap's hands. There is to be no handling of it through any secondary or intermediary. The horseman understands that this is the most important message he has ever delivered. On this most important day of his young life, he knows that failure to carry out this urgent task is not an option. As he prods his animal to hurry, hurry, the excited equestrian cannot predict how his friend will respond once he receives the message. He only knows that the situation at hand is critical. He mutters to himself, practicing what he will say, attempting to remain calm.

On April 19, 1775, when the battles of Lexington and Concord occurred, Michael Cresap was clearing land along the Ohio River in Kentucky. Around the same time, farther south in Kentucky, Daniel Boone, who works for Richard Henderson of the Transylvania Company, was clearing the Wilderness Road. Boone will found Boonsborough later this year.

Just before Cresap's trip back west into the Ohio River Valley in the early spring of 1775, an opportunity for a much-needed respite presents itself. Throughout the entire winter of 1774 to 1775, Cresap finds a rare block of time to spend a few months with his family at Oldtown. This period of rest begins in the late fall of 1774, when Lord Dunmore disbands his army after the Indian War.

However, by early in the spring of 1775, after hiring several young helper hands, Cresap has returned with his hired help to the Ohio River to resume surveying and claiming land. This task had begun in the spring of 1774 before he was so rudely interrupted by George Rogers Clark and Lord Dunmore's War. His work involves blazing trees, cutting timber, and laying a foundation for a cabin. Cresap does not stay on the land after this work is complete but continues scouting along the Ohio River for the best bottomland to survey and claim for himself.[3]

---

[3] Note: In 1774 and 1775, Cresap surveyed and cleared land on a one-thousand-acre tract along the Ohio River in present-day West Virginia, near and downstream from present Sistersville, West Virginia, on tracts of land extending three miles below Middle Island Creek and reaching below the mouth of French Creek. He also surveyed four hundred acres of land above Bull Creek, in present-day Waverly, West Virginia, and four hundred acres at the mouth of French Creek, near the present site of St. Marys, West Virginia.

Michael Cresap House (west side), Oldtown, Maryland

As he works on his new land claims along the Ohio River, Cresap has good reason to hope that his financial situation will soon take a turn for the better. Several months ago, on February 23, 1775, Michael Cresap secured the rights from a Virginia court to operate a ferry at Redstone to Indian Peter's land across the Monongahela River from the site of Redstone Old Fort at present-day Brownsville, Pennsylvania.[4]

The year before, Cresap had descended as far south along the Ohio River as the mouth of Sandy River at present-day Ravenswood, West Virginia. However, in 1775, once he finally finishes the job he began the prior year around Middle Island Creek on the Ohio River, Cresap goes into Kentucky territory, an area he has not surveyed

---

4 J. Percy Hart, Hart's History and Directory of Three Towns: Brownsville, Bridgeport, and West Brownsville, Pennsylvania (Cadwallader, PA: J. Percy Hart, 1904), 260. This ferry on the Monongahela River stayed active until 1820, when the National Road was completed. At this time, authorities moved the ferry operation upriver to Bridgeport, Pennsylvania. Here the ferry stayed active until 1833, when it ceased operation with the construction of a wooden bridge over the river.

before. Cresap continues the trek down the Ohio River with his hired hands to claim bottomland in Kentucky, this privilege now allowed following the recent signing of the Treaty of Chillicothe at the end of Dunmore's War.[5]

Cresap continues to survey and blaze trees until he senses that something is not quite right with his health. This perception begins with a feeling of illness, which soon becomes serious enough that he is not able to continue the work at hand. Harboring a nagging feeling of unrest, Cresap instructs several of his workers to continue the task of clearing the land in his absence. Then, leaving the Kentucky region with a helper named Thomas Hallam,[6] Cresap returns home to Oldtown with plans to rest and recover his health.[7]

While Michael Cresap is in Kentucky clearing land, the world seems to turn upside down following the battles of Lexington and Concord. The estimated population of the colonies in 1775 is about 2.4 million people. Of these, one third supports the revolution. Another third are Tories or loyalists who support the king. These two factions both believe they are patriots. The final third sit on the fence, supporting whoever is on the winning side.[8]

While the Continental Congress meets to ponder how the colonists will respond to the latest acts of violence perpetrated by the British, organizers hold conventions and form committees throughout the colonies. Among the men serving Congress as Maryland delegates are Thomas Johnson, Jr., William Paca, and Samuel Chase, men with whom Michael's father, Thomas Cresap—an early eighteenth-century immigrant from Yorkshire, England, and early-day pioneer on the western Maryland frontier—is very well acquainted because of Thomas's prior lengthy stint as a western Maryland delegate from 1757 to 1770.[9]

In early spring, while Michael Cresap works his way back to Redstone, George Washington is traveling from Mount Vernon toward Philadelphia to meet with the Continental Congress. On May 5, 1775, Washington, now holding the rank of colonel, reaches Baltimore, Maryland, and stays at the elegant Fountain Inn.[10] Washington's entrance into town is greeted with a great show of celebration by the people. Officials of the city lead Washington and other dignitaries to the courthouse, where a rousing toast is offered. They proclaim, "May the town of Baltimore flourish and the noble spirits of the inhabitants continue till ministerial tyranny be at an end."[11]

On June 14, the Second Continental Congress legislates and authorizes the raising of ten companies of riflemen, as well as initiating a plan to pay salaries to soldiers in the army.[12] Congress has resolved to raise six companies of riflemen from Pennsylvania and two each from Virginia and Maryland. Congress expects this "small body

---

5 Officials posthumously awarded to Michael Cresap Preemption Warrant #2686 on April 6, 1782. Cresap's heirs therefore received two tracts of land at Bull Creek, a one-thousand-acre tract and a four-hundred-acre tract. One of the provisions of the Land Law of May 1779, passed by the Virginia assembly, was the development of a land-patenting process for early Kentucky settlers. All persons who made improvements and planted a crop in present-day Kentucky prior to January 1, 1778, were entitled to a four-hundred-acre certificate of settlement. Under the preemption warrant, the family could purchase an additional one thousand acres adjacent to the certificate-of-settlement tract.

6 Thomas Hallam marched to the camps in Boston as one of Cresap's riflemen.

7 John J. Jacob, A Biographical Sketch of the Late Captain Michael Cresap (Cincinnati, OH: John F. Uhlhorn, 1866), 117–118; Lyman Chalkley, "Chronicles of the Scotch-Irish Settlement of Virginia, vol 2," US Gen Web Archives (1999), Accessed November 8, 2017, http://files.usgwarchives.net/va/augusta/court/2court23.txt.

8 David McCullough, "A Man Worth Knowing," Imprimis 35(5) (2006).

9 Other Maryland delegates who served in Congress at this time are Mathew Tilghman, John Hall, Robert Goldsborough, and Thomas Stone.

10 The Fountain Inn in Baltimore, Maryland, first opened its doors in 1773 near present-day Light and Redwood Streets. George Washington visited here on several more occasions: in 1781, en route to the Battle of Yorktown; in 1783, en route to Annapolis to resign his commission as commander in chief of the Continental army; and again in 1798, when he stood on the steps of the Fountain Inn to review the Maryland militia. The Fountain Inn was razed in 1871 and was replaced with another hotel. Digital Maryland, Cator Print 163: Fountain Inn, accessed September 26, 2017, http://collections.digitalmaryland.org/cdm/ref/collection/cator/id/65.

11 O'Donnell, Washington's Immortals, 12; Cator Print.

12 The Second Continental Congress's decisive action results in the birth of the US Army, which today our country celebrates every year on June 14.

of men…to be expert hands" at handling the long rifle. This will make the men serving in the rifle companies more "serviceable to the defense of America in the Continental Army near Boston."[13]

Congress requires that all riflemen be young men of good character and self-sufficient. They must have adequate means to pay for their own clothing, gear, and supplies, which include a rifle, shot pouch, powder horn, tomahawk, and scalping knife. A blanket and a knapsack are the only amenities that Congress will provide for each rifleman, as well as an allotment for each rifle company of two supply wagons and ten horses, each wagon pulled by four horses.[14]

Congress further states that it expects that the committee will quickly organize its rifle companies and have them ready to march toward Boston by July 1, 1775. With a confirmed date now approved and sanctioned, Congress sets the duration of the employment of men in the rifle companies at one year, with enlistments slated to end on July 1, 1776.

Once formed, say the powers that be, the rifle companies are to march independently with "all expedition" without need to "rendezvous" at any set location until they arrive at camp in the Boston area. Congress, still demanding more from the committees, desires that those men chosen in Maryland to lead the rifle companies be "experienced officers…the very best men that can be procured…to honor the Maryland Province."

When men from Massachusetts and the surrounding provinces learn that the southern men whom officials recruit must carry their own weapons, some northerners question the type of firing arms the riflemen carry. New Englanders are more familiar with muskets constructed with smooth barrels than they are with weapons that gunsmiths have created with rifled barrels.

Thomas Cresap and frontiersmen of his kind who reside around the areas of the Maryland-Pennsylvania border are members of the first generation to master the handling of the improved version of weaponry known as the Pennsylvania long rifle. Daniel Boone, born in the area of Reading, Pennsylvania, first learned how to handle the Pennsylvania long rifle as a teenager during the late 1740s and early 1750s. Forty years after Cresap and his kin appear on the Maryland and Pennsylvania wilderness, Boone will become renowned for traversing all over the land carrying his famous Kentucky long rifle.

The riflemen are very much on the mind of John Adams, the congressional delegate from Massachusetts. On June 11, 1775, in a letter sent from Philadelphia to their Massachusetts home, Adams imparts to his wife, Abigail, that Congress has just authorized ten southern companies and that they will carry with them a kind of weapon relatively unfamiliar in New England: "a peculiar kind of musket, called a rifle. It has circular…grooves within the barrel, and carries a ball with great exactness to great distances. They are the most accurate marksmen in the world."[15]

On June 18, in a letter to Elbridge Gerry, Adams writes that the riflemen "are said to be all exquisite marksmen, and by means of the excellence of their firelocks, as well as their skill in the use of them, to send sure destruction to great distances."[16]

In yet another letter on June 27 to James Warren, Adams writes: "We are sending you, Ten Companies of Riflemen. These, if the gentlemen of the Southern Colonies are not very partial and much mistaken, are very fine

---

13 Jacob, A Biographical Sketch of the Late Captain Michael Cresap, 118; John R. Maass, "June Fourteenth: The Birthday of the US Army," US Army Center of Military History (2013), accessed September 24, 2017, http://www.history.army.mil/html/faq/birth.html.
14 Constitutional Gazette, August 9, 1775.
15 Charles Francis Adams, Familiar Letters of John Adams and his Wife Abigail Adams during the Revolution (Cambridge, MA: Riverside Press, 1876), 65–6.
16 "Papers of John Adams, vol. III," The Adams Papers: Digital Collection, 25, accessed November 7, 2017, https://www.masshist.org/publications/apde2/view?mode=p&vol=PJA03&page=16#PJA03d052n4.

fellows. They are the most accurate Marksmen in the World: they kill with great Exactness at 200 yards Distance. They have sworn certain death to the ministerial officers.[17] May they perform their oath."[18]

James Madison also throws in his praise for the riflemen. To William Bradford, Madison writes the following accolades about these frontiersmen: "The strength of the Colony will lie chiefly in the Riflemen of the Upland Counties, of which we shall have great numbers. You will be astonished at the perfection this art is brought to. The most inexpert hands rec[k]on it an indifferent shot to miss the bigness of a man's face at the distance of 100 yards. I am far from being among the best & should not often miss it on a fair trial at that distance. If we come into an engagement, I make no doubt but the officers of the enemy will fall at a distance before they get within 150 or 200 Yards. Indeed I believe we have men that would very often hit such a mark at 250 Yds. Our greatest apprehensions proceed from the scarcity of powder but a little will go a great way with such as use rifles."[19]

To prove the point, had there been any question at all among these plotting colonial leaders regarding the utility of and need for additional men from the southern colonies, the Battle of Bunker Hill occurs outside Boston on June 17, three days after Congress authorizes the organization of the ten southern rifle companies. This battle will turn out to be the bloodiest day of the entire American Revolution.

On June 15, the day after Congress selects "expert riflemen" as the first members of the Continental army, members of this second congressional meeting vote unanimously to appoint George Washington to command this new and untried army. By authorizing ten rifle companies from the three southern colonies, Congress has created this "Continental" army as one that encompasses a much greater number of men than the New England militia, who now call themselves the Army of Observation.

Congress organizes the companies of the elite riflemen in the following manner. Each company will consist of one captain ($20.00 per month), three lieutenants ($13.33 each per month), four sergeants ($8.00 each per month), four corporals and one drummer ($7.33 each per month), and sixty-eight privates ($6.66 per month).[20] Six of the ten companies are to march from Pennsylvania, two companies from Maryland, and two companies from Virginia.[21]

The response to join is so great in Pennsylvania that Congress allows the colony to raise three additional companies. Three delegates from Congress, who represent each of the colonies, are responsible for organizing the units. These delegates rely on county committees to select skilled riflemen in their area. For example, in Virginia, the Committee of Correspondence selects Daniel Morgan and Hugh Stephenson to lead the two Virginia rifle companies.

On June 15, 1775, delegates representing Maryland in the Continental Congress send a letter from Philadelphia to the Committee of Correspondence in Frederick County, Maryland. This letter, yet one more link in the chain of events, has direct bearing on the direction Michael Cresap's life now takes. Three districts exist in Frederick County at this time: Fredericktown, Elizabethtown (present-day Hagerstown), and Oldtown. Serving on the

---

17 In this letter, John Adams distinguishes between the king of England and the British Parliament. Ministerial refers to representatives of British government who serve as ministers of Parliament responsible for carrying out the oppressive laws they impose on the colonies. In 1775, the colonists were still loyal to King George and hoped that he would come around to and sympathize with their plight; as this letter expresses, the sworn enemy of the riflemen was not the king. No, these frontiersmen reserved their hostility that knew no bounds for the ministers in Parliament. As late as September 1775, George Washington and his staff were lifting up their glasses in toasts to both King George and members of the Continental Congress. Young, "The Spirit of 1775: A Letter of Robert Magaw," 10.
18 "Papers of John Adams," 50; Young, "The Spirit of 1775: A Letter of Robert Magaw," 25.
19 Halbrook, The Founders' Second Amendment, 98–9.
20 Colonial soldiers considered their pay fair when it was compared to the pay of an ordinary civilian worker. In 1775, colonists accepted as a fair wage seven fifteenths of a dollar per day for common labor. Using this rate, a captain's monthly pay was worth forty-three days of common labor, and a private's monthly pay was worth fifteen days of common labor. Although not lavish, this pay was still better than the wages a British soldier received. Thomas Balch, ed., Papers Relating Chiefly to the Maryland Line during the Revolution: Daniel McCurtin. Journal of the Times at the Siege of Boston (Philadelphia: T.K. and P.G. Collins, Printers, 1857), 5; Young, "The Spirit of 1775: A Letter of Robert Magaw," 28.
21 Thomas John Chew Williams and Folger McKensey, History of Frederick County, vol. 1 (Baltimore: L. R. Titsworth and Co., 1910), 89.

Committee for Correspondence for the Oldtown District, Maryland, are Thomas Cresap, Thomas Warren, Ezekiel Cox, Thomas French, and Moses Rawlings.[22]

By June 21, 1775, in compliance with the resolution of the Continental Congress, the Committee of Observation makes its decision as to who will lead Frederick County, Maryland's two rifle companies. One of the men chosen is Thomas Price of Frederick County. Then, in an announcement that comes as no surprise to many, the man whom the members of the Committee of Frederick County choose to lead in the newly designated First Rifle Company of Maryland with the rank of captain is Michael Cresap and as officers under his command will serve 1st Lieutenant Thomas Warren; 2nd Lieutenant Joseph Cresap; and Ensign Richard Davis.[23]

Both Price and Cresap are residents of Frederick County. Thomas Price, who is ten years Michael Cresap's senior, served in 1759 as a captain representing Pennsylvania in the French and Indian War. Since 1763, Price has been quite active in the community, serving several terms as a justice and as delegate for the provincial government. Since 1768, Price has been making hats for a living and owns a hat store in Fredericktown. In 1774, Price served on the Committee for Correspondence and now serves on the Committee for Maryland Observation, the same committee that has now selected him to serve as a captain of one of the two Maryland rifle companies.[24]

Now that the captains of Maryland's rifle companies have been selected, how to get the word to Michael Cresap becomes the next order of business. Soon after June 21, authorities, likely at the behest of Thomas Cresap, utilize family friend and helpmate John Jacob as the messenger who will find Michael Cresap posthaste and notify him of his appointment as captain of one of the two companies that will march from Maryland to Cambridge, Massachusetts.

Jacob, the young rider from Michael's hometown, overcomes some of his anxiety as he espies Cresap traveling down the Allegheny Mountains eastbound on the Braddock Path on his way home to Oldtown.

Just as he feared, Jacob finds Cresap in very poor condition, tired and not feeling well and not very receptive to the message he delivers. Cresap is anything but joyous when he receives news of his appointment. In later years, Jacob will pen a biography in which he divulges that, upon hearing the news, Cresap "became pensive and solemn, as if his spirits were really depressed; as if he had a presentiment this was his death warrant."[25]

Jacob informs Cresap that if he refuses to accept the appointment, Thomas Cresap, now more than eighty years old, will march in Cresap's place at the head of the company. When Michael Cresap hears this, vowing to "let the consequences be what they might,"[26] he accepts the appointment on the spot. By accepting this offer, Cresap unknowingly reaps the distinction of being the leader of the first company in the newly formed army assembled west of the Allegheny Mountains.

---

22 American Archives: Documents of the Revolutionary Period, 1774-1776, "Frederick County (Maryland) Committee: June 21, 1775," accessed November 8, 2017, http://amarch.lib.niu.edu/islandora/object/niu-amarch%3A95917. On January 24, 1775, a county convention was held at Fredericktown, Maryland, during which a Committee of Observation was organized to execute resolves established by the Colonial Congress. One of the first tasks at hand was the proposal to raise funds to be used in the purchase of arms and ammunition. Following this crucial advisory, the Provincial Maryland Convention in Annapolis agreed that the province of Maryland would raise £10,000 by subscription to aid "their suffering brethren in Boston." Frederick County was assigned to raise £1,133 of the required £10,000. This amount was due by March 23, 1775. Three members of the Committee of Observation were Thomas Cresap and two men who would serve as officers with Captain Michael Cresap's riflemen: Moses Rawlings and Richard Davis, Jr., who faithfully carried out their part to raise £1,133 in the region surrounding Skipton (present-day Oldtown, Maryland). Williams and McKensey, History of Frederick County, vol. 1, 85.

23 Maryland State Archives. "Muster Rolls and Other Records of Service of Maryland Troops in the American Revolution." Archives of Maryland Online. http://msa.maryland.gov/megafile/msa/speccol/sc2900/sc2908/000001/000018/html/am18--28.html

24 Edward C. Papenfuse, Alan F. Day, David W. Jordan, and Gregory A. Silverson, eds., A Biographical Dictionary of the Maryland Legislature, 1635–1789: Thomas Price (1732–1795), vol. 1 (Baltimore: John Hopkins University Press, 1985).

25 Jacob, A Biographical Sketch of the Late Captain Michael Cresap, 120.

26 Ibid.

Michael Cresap then asks Jacob to continue to the "west side of the mountains" and find his "old companions in arms"[27] and notify them of his intentions to march and to ask them, if they are interested, to join him at Oldtown as soon as possible.

Jacob is successful in locating the men he seeks residing in the Allegheny Mountains at and near Redstone, presently Fayette County, Pennsylvania. He collects twenty-two frontiersmen who travel back with him to Oldtown. Jacob describes these colleagues of Michael's as being "as fine fellows as ever handled a rifle, and most, if not all of them, completely equipped with rifles."[28] These men cheerfully jump at the chance to serve again with Cresap. They march "voluntarily nearly one hundred miles [to Oldtown], leaving their families and all, merely from a message sent by a boy [Jacob] to join the standard of their old captain."[29]

When Michael Cresap marches east from Oldtown on his way to Fredericktown, he will acquire thirty-three more eager riflemen at Elizabethtown, Maryland. One of Cresap's lieutenants is Richard Davis, who resides in Elizabethtown and who helps the captain in the recruitment of the men from this town. This brings the size of Cresap's rifle company to fifty-five men before the captain even arrives at Fredericktown, where his father is training eighty more men.[30]

On June 22, 1775, from his home at Traveler's Rest in Virginia, Brigadier General Horatio Gates writes in a letter to George Washington, "The request for Riflemen was received well in this Province [Virginia] and in Maryland…Colonel Cresap told me on Monday morning that his son had eighty riflemen ready to march."[31] Gates writes this letter just three days after the Continental Congress appoints him to serve as brigadier general and adjutant general of the Continental army. Gates, who has the distinction of being the first adjutant general in the fledgling army, shares a history with Colonel Thomas Cresap. Both men served under General Edward Braddock during Braddock's ill-fated 1755 campaign.

Silas Deane serves as a delegate to the Continental Congress in Philadelphia representing Connecticut. From here, on June 29, 1775, Deane writes his wife, who resides in Connecticut. The content of the letter no doubt refers to a colorful and memorable letter that Horatio Gates received from one Colonel Thomas Cresap. Deane seems quite moved by the words Cresap has written, apparently the same words by Tom Cresap that Horatio Gates noted in his June 22 letter to George Washington. Gates evidently carried Cresap's letter with him and shared it with Silas Deane when he saw him in Philadelphia as Gates made his way north from Virginia to join Washington in the camps at Cambridge, Massachusetts.

And thus in the letter to his wife, Deane expresses a bit of emotion as he writes the following: "Riflemen are raising fast. A commission is given to one Mr. Cresop [sic] to command from Virginia. He being absent when it arrived the brave old Colonel Cresop [sic], now ninety-two years of age, took the command and determines to join the head, if his son should not arrive in season.[32] I saw a letter from him this morning, which exceeded anything I ever read."[33]

Silas Deane gives the letter addressed to his wife and dated June 29, 1775, to General Gates to carry and deliver to her during Gates's trip north to join General Washington's army.

---

27 Ibid.
28 Ibid., 121.
29 Ibid.
30 Young, "The Spirit of 1775: A Letter of Robert Magaw," 21.
31 National Archives, "To George Washington from Brigadier General Horatio Gates, 22 June, 1775," November 14, 2103, http://founders.archives.gov/documents/Washington/03-01-02-0011.
32 Deane overestimates the age of Thomas Cresap. In reality, the colonel was about eighty-one years of age, and Michael Cresap was from Maryland, not Virginia.
33 J. Hammond Trumbull, Collections of the Connecticut Historical Society (Hartford, CT: Press of Case, Lockwood, and Brainard, 1870), 274–5.

It is true. The eighty-one-year-old Thomas Cresap has vowed that if his son does not arrive soon, the father himself will march at the head of the company for the more than five-hundred-mile journey from Fredericktown, Maryland, to Cambridge, Massachusetts. Thomas Cresap organizes, prepares, and makes ready his son's rifle company, consisting of eighty riflemen from the Fredericktown area, while the father impatiently awaits word of his son's return from the western country.[34]

Thomas Cresap prepares the rifle company he trains in a manner similar to that which Silas Deane described after seeing another rifle company making ready for their march to Boston: they "exercise in neighboring groves…firing at marks and throwing their tomahawks; forming on sudden into one line, and then at a word, break their order and take their posts, to hit their mark…Each afternoon [the riflemen] collect, with a vast number of spectators" looking on.[35]

What Thomas Cresap does not know while he drills the Maryland riflemen is that Michael Cresap is on his way to Fredericktown with 55 additional men who will unite with the 80 men his father has readied for the march to join Washington's army. Before all is said and done, there will be more than 130 riflemen marching with Cresap from Fredericktown to Cambridge!

---

34 Apparently, Thomas Cresap had some assistance in the training of Michael Cresap's riflemen. Christian Orndorff "helped organize, equip, and train men including the first company west of Blue Ridge Mountain which was led by Captain Cresap." Orndorff's farm was part of the Joshua Newcomber Farm located along Antietam Creek near Sharpsburg, Maryland. Jacob Rohrbach Inn, "The Farmsteads of Antietam: Joshua Newcomer Farm." August 9, 2017. https://jacob-rohrbach-inn.com/blog/2017/08/the-farmsteads-of-antietam-joshua-newcomer-farm/.
35 Silas Deane Online, "Letter from Silas Deane to Elizabeth Deane, 3 June 1775," accessed November 24, 2017, http://www.silasdeaneonline.org/documents/doc12.htm.

CHAPTER 2

The Light in the Stars

Fredericktown, Maryland
July 1775

ONE WHO USUALLY HEADS WEST, Michael looks eastward now that he is committed to responding to his calling from Congress. From the Allegheny Mountains, Cresap travels on the Braddock Road, departing Redstone, Pennsylvania.

Summer has just begun. The leaves on the northern red oak, sugar maple, American chestnut, and black cherry are still fresh and green. The canopy of the surrounding forest provides welcome shade to this weary traveler. Shadows dance on the forest floor as the sun shines through branches overhead, where leaves flutter and whisper in the warm summer breeze.

Michael travels on top of the Appalachian Plateau along Braddock Road. He is still west of the Eastern Continental Divide, where all water flows into the Ohio River and then onward west to the Mississippi River before discharging into the Gulf of Mexico.

Cresap travels east along Braddock Road. From the Monongahela River at Redstone, he travels approximately twenty-five miles and camps at Great Meadows, the site of Fort Necessity. Continuing approximately ten miles eastward, the rifleman comes to Big Crossings on the Youghiogheny River. Approximately six miles east, the road passes Puzzley Run, near the site of the grave of the black frontiersmen on Negro Mountain. Michael fondly remembers this man of tremendous size, a Goliath sort of individual, who in 1756 sacrificed his life on this mountain to save Michael's father from certain death. Officials later named this mountain in honor of this free African American frontiersman. Four miles farther eastward is Little Crossings on the Casselman River, at present-day Grantsville, Maryland. Onward Cresap travels about four more miles to Little Meadows. He camps here on his second night, having traveled about fifty-three miles in two days since leaving Redstone.

The next morning, Cresap breaks camp and travels onward through the Shades of Death along the alignment of present Route 144, its never-ending dark recesses harboring an eeriness that, in his mind, foretells what is to come. He crosses the Eastern Continental Divide and leaves the Ohio Watershed near present-day Finzel, Maryland. He has now crossed over into the Chesapeake Bay Watershed. All water from here flows toward the Potomac River on into the Chesapeake and from there into the Atlantic Ocean. It is downhill from here toward Cumberland and Oldtown.

On Savage Mountain, he passes by the grave of his older brother, Thomas Cresap, Jr., killed at the age of twenty-three during the French and Indian War. At that time Michael was merely a lad of fourteen years old, and now he sadly remembers his brother Thomas Jr. and his premature demise in the spring of 1756 at the vicinity of Savage River near the western slope on Big Savage Mountain. It was here that young Thomas met with a tragic fate, being slain by members of an Indian war party. After pausing to pay his respects, Michael continues his travels down the Great Allegheny Front and descends into the Ridge and Valley Province of Maryland.

Cresap continues his travels east through a long narrow valley (present-day LaVale, Maryland), eventually passing through the Cumberland Narrows, where bald eagles fly overhead in their search for fish swimming and cavorting in Wills Creek. Cresap most likely stays in Cumberland on his third day of travel, being only fifteen miles away from Oldtown and his family.

Four days after leaving Redstone, Cresap arrives at Oldtown about July 3, 1775, the date George Washington, after traveling twelve days from Philadelphia to Cambridge, Massachusetts, formally takes command of the colonial army consisting of an estimated seventeen thousand men. At Oldtown, Cresap pauses and enjoys a much-needed rest, as he awaits the return of John Jacob with additional men recruited from the western country to join Cresap's company of riflemen.[36]

While Michael Cresap waits in Oldtown, John Dickinson, a representative in the Continental Congress, with earlier help from Thomas Jefferson, composes the Olive Branch Petition. This is an attempt by Congress to avoid a war with Britain and states the colonies' loyalty to the king. The writing of the Declaration of Independence is a still a year away.

On July 5, Congress approves the statements written in this petition addressed to King George III of England. The document expresses the colonists' hopes of reconciling with King George and Britain and asks his help to restore peace. In the interim, the colonies still hope to reconcile with their mother country and king.

The next day, on July 6, Congress issues the Declaration on the Causes and Necessity of Taking Up Arms. This document mentions that, since the French and Indian War ended and after England subdued its enemies, the British promptly began oppressing its friends. This became evident when Parliament began assuming unbounded power over the colonies of America, which had led to the recent Battles of Lexington and Concord. While still expressing loyalty to the king, the defiant colonial citizens make it known they would not tamely submit to slavery or cruel tyranny but that they would resolve to "die free men rather than live as slaves."[37]

Early in the week of July 27, during the dog days of summer, after Jacob returns to Oldtown with twenty-two veterans of Dunmore's War, Cresap and his men begin their journey to glory and legend—a more than five-hundred-mile march from Maryland to Massachusetts. They are a gallant lot of hardy men marching in defense of their country, many "educated in the frightful conflicts of Indian warfare…skilled in Indian warfare and hardened to Indian discipline, with remarkable skill in the use of their rifles."[38]

The riflemen most likely take the shortest route from Oldtown to Fredericktown, present-day Oldtown Road, located in Allegany County, Maryland, which is present-day Green Ridge State Forest. Cresap knows this road and the route to Fredericktown like the back of his hand. His father opened the Oldtown Road in 1758 to connect Fort Frederick and Fort Cumberland. The spectacular view at Point Lookout on present-day Carroll Road may serve as a good rest stop after about twelve miles of travel before continuing onward to the mouth of Fifteen Mile Creek.[39]

---

36 Arthur M. Schlesinger, Jr., The Almanac of American History (New York: Bramhall House, 1983), 119.

37 Yale Law School, "A Declaration of Representatives of the United Colonies of North America, Now Met in Congress at Philadelphia, Setting Forth the Causes and Necessity of their Taking Up Arms," http://avalon.law.yale.edu/18th_century/arms.asp.

38 John Allen Miller, "The Flying Camp Batallion," Emmittsburg Area Historical Society, October 4, 2013, http://www.emmitsburg.net/archive_list/articles/history/rev_war/flying_camp_battalion.htm.

39 Edward T. Schultz, First Settlements of Germans in Maryland (Frederick, MD: D. H. Smith, 1896. Cresap's most probable route from Oldtown toward Fredericktown took him through the present-day Green Ridge State Forest along Oldtown Road, the oldest colonial road in eastern Allegany County. For the purpose of connecting Fort Frederick to Fort Cumberland during the French and Indian war, Thomas Cresap blazed this road in 1758. This route took Michael Cresap and his men along Packhorse Road through Kirk Orchard before connecting to Purslane Road, not far from the intersection of Oldtown and Malcolm Roads. Continuing on the Oldtown Road, the riflemen turned at Lick Hollow, which comes out onto Carroll Road at the site of the landmark Carroll Chimney, built in 1836. They continued onward past Point Lookout Overlook, possibly the most spectacular view the riflemen would have on the entire route toward Boston. Reentering present Oldtown Road, the men turned toward Fifteen Mile Creek and then took a woods road that came out past St. Patrick's Church to Goodview Lane/St. Patrick's Road. From Little Orleans and Bill's Place, the riflemen proceeded onto High Germany Road, past another grand view of the Potomac River. Turning right at Ziegler Road, the riflemen then crossed Sideling Hill Creek, entering present-day Washington County, Maryland. From here, the riflemen continued east along Zeigler Road and possibly traveled by way of Woodmont Road to Old Route 40 and on to Hancock.

Point Lookout, Green Ridge State Forest, Flintstone, Maryland (Photograph courtesy of Steve Dean)

Michael Cresap will leave the Ridge and Valley Province east of present Hagerstown and cross over the Blue Ridge Mountains, connecting to another road his father had a hand in opening in 1733 for colonial travel, the Old Monocacy Road/Old Conestoga Road. This road takes Cresap across the Blue Ridge Province to the Piedmont Province, leading directly into the Monocacy River Valley and Fredericktown.

It takes Cresap about three days to reach Fredericktown, which lies about seventy miles east of Oldtown. Germans and English have settled into this well-established, bustling frontier settlement of about two thousand people. In 1775, Fredericktown exceeds the size of both Williamsburg and Annapolis.[40]

Fredericktown is located near two major inland routes, the north-south corridor of the Monocacy Road[41] and the east-west corridor of the Annapolis Road. Officials established this settlement as the county seat in 1748, three years after forming Frederick County in 1745. By the time Cresap arrives with his riflemen, Fredericktown is a thriving market town and political center. Another attractive attribute to the area is that well-laid-out farms surround the town. These farms have fertile soil that yields abundant crops of wheat, which not only enrich the inhabitants but also support nearby communities with important agricultural commodities. The late Daniel Dulany,

---

40 Although there has been no documentation found to prove the exact route they took from present-day Hancock to Frederick, the most probable route starting from Hancock would have taken Cresap along the Potomac River to Fort Frederick. From this military outpost, the riflemen may have continued on to Williamsport, a town known at this time as Conococheague, where Daniel Cresap, Michael's oldest brother, resided at the time. From Williamsport, Cresap marched along Route 63 on the Spielman Road to Downsville, where it intersected with Route 632. From here, he continued straight on Bakersville Road toward where it intersected with Route 65; then Cresap continued straight on Keedysville Road, crossing Antietam Creek where it intersected with Route 34. The riflemen then continued straight on Sumter Drive/Dogstreet Road to where it intersected with Route 67. From here, a road General Braddock traveled in 1755, Cresap and his men continued straight on Reno Monument Road through Fox's Gap to Bolivar Road/Marker Road where it intersected with Alternate Route 40 just before Middletown. The last leg of this part of the journey would follow Alternate Route 40 past Middletown to Frederick (Powell 1998, 55 -60).

41 *The general alignment of the Monocacy Road corridor heading eastward from Middletown, Maryland to Frederick likely followed alternative Route 40 until merging onto W. Patrick Street, then onward to N. Market Street through Frederick toward Walkersville, Maryland, where the road connects to present Route 26, leading to Route194 toward Taneytown, Maryland.*
(Henry Hamilton Pittar."Map of Frederick City, Frederick County, Maryland." 1853).

Sr. (1685–1753), once legal representative of Thomas Cresap during the 1730s and the Pennsylvania-Maryland Border war, founded Fredericktown on land that he owned. In fact, as fate would have it, Thomas Cresap had worked as Dulany's land agent and surveyor.

Fort Frederick, Fort Frederick State Park, Big Pool, Maryland (Photograph courtesy of the Committee for Maryland Conservation History).

When Captain Michael Cresap and his riflemen arrive in 1775, Fredericktown, its dwellings mostly stone and brick houses mixed in with wooden domiciles, presents a neat and tidy appearance. Three churches amid the residences represent the Anglican, Lutheran, and German reformed faiths. Taverns and inns are scattered throughout the city, including an inn-tavern on All Saints Street along Carroll's Creek that hosted a meeting held by General Braddock, Governor Sharpe, and George Washington in 1755.

On All Saints Street, within shouting distance of some town taverns—some might remark with amusement, "from folly to grace"—is located Michael Cresap's family church, All Saints' Parish. Michael's parents attended this church on special occasions, for their children's baptisms, and for other family religious concerns. Members of the Swearingen family—two of whose daughters married Michael Cresap's brothers, Daniel and Thomas, Jr.—also worship at All Saints' Parish. Indeed, Fredericktown is Michael Cresap's home away from home. This settlement considers Michael Cresap one of its own.[42]

Captain Cresap's company advances through Fredericktown a little less than two and a half weeks after the rifle companies of Captain Morgan, Captain Stephenson, and Captain Price. Morgan's rifle company passed through Fredericktown on July 17.[43] An observer of these events writes, "On Monday last Capt. Morgan, from Virginia, with his company of men, (all chosen) marched through this place [Frederick-town], on their way to

---

42 Schultz, First Settlements of Germans in Maryland, 54–5; Ernest Helfenstein, Historical Notes of All Saints Parish, Frederick, MD, 1742–1908 (Frederick, MD: Marken and Bielfeld, 1908), 9.
43 "Extract of a Letter from a Gentleman in Frederick-town to his Friend in Baltimore, dated July 19," Pennsylvania Packet, August 7, 1775, 2.

Boston. Their appearance was truly martial, their spirits amazing elated, breathing nothing but a desire to join the American army, and to engage the enemies of American liberty."[44]

Captain Price's rifle company marched through Fredericktown on July 18,[45] and Stephenson's rifle company did not lag far behind. Cresap, delayed by his extended excursion to Ohio, is not ready to march out of Fredericktown until the very end of July, but all folks in this neck of the woods and beyond know that he is preparing and on the move from Redstone heading toward Fredericktown.

A person in the know in Fredericktown on July 19 excitedly writes a letter to a friend in Baltimore informing him of the following news: "Captain Cresap…with his brave company, have marched. I need not say anything of Capt. Cresap's undaunted courage; not an American but knows him to be an intrepid warrior, and of course he knows his men, and has culled them from the many."[46]

An excerpt from an article written in Purdie's *Virginia Gazette* and published on August 4, 1775, affirms that these "chosen riflemen [are] eager to hazard their lives in their country's cause, and to follow the fortunes of their beloved Washington!"[47]

The good people of Fredericktown likely celebrate the arrival of Cresap's Rifles with the same pageantry that they rolled out for Captain Morgan and his riflemen when they approached town two weeks before. A few miles outside town, Cresap's rifle company is greeted and escorted into town by several companies of local militia and officers "amid the acclamations of all the inhabitants who attended them."[48]

The townsfolk know that over the last couple of weeks, they have been privileged to witness something special in the demeanor of the rifle companies. They know that "no finer companies [have been] raised in any other country more determined to conquer and die."[49]

On August 1, 1775, an anonymous gentleman in Fredericktown writes a letter to a friend in Philadelphia in which he records the general feelings of the townspeople and expresses his own elation at what, at least in his mind, must surely be a turning point in the fight for freedom.

The Fredericktown author begins his account, recording in detail what he witnesses from start to finish. At first glimpse, he is stunned at the sight of Cresap's company as it marches into town.

The riflemen's adoption of certain customs and dress from Indian culture gives them an unorthodox appearance. Their uniform is the distinctive dress of backwoods frontiersmen, which consists of hunting shirts, leather leggings, and moccasins. To the settlers of Fredericktown, the marching unit coming up before them is a wonder to behold! A gathering crowd finds itself looking at a people who come from a land highly populated with Native Americans. More impressive to bystanders is the fact that each rifle company passing through town has some unique feature to distinguish it from other rifle companies. For instance, one rifle company wears bucktails attached to their round hats. In the case of Cresap's company, beneath their round hats, many of the riflemen paint their faces the Indian way.

Recuperating from his initial shock, the writer swells with pride upon seeing Captain Michael Cresap marching at the head of a "formidable company, upward of 130 men from the mountains and backwoods."[50] This formation of frontiersmen is indeed a remarkable sight.

---

44 Ibid.
45 Ibid.
46 Ibid.
47 Purdue's Virginia Gazette, "PostScript Number 27," August 4, 1775, 7. Newspapers.com
48 "Extract of a Letter from a Gentleman in Frederick-town," 2.
49 Ibid.
50 Pennsylvania Gazette, "Extract from a Letter from Fredericktown, Aug. 1," August 16, 1775, 3.

According to news reports and stories bandied about the frontier, some of Cresap's men have traveled nearly eight hundred miles from the banks of the Ohio, and yet they march with vigor, their feet lifting light and easy as they march into Fredericktown, "not with less spirit than the first hour of their march."[51]

To the writer, Cresap and his men project nothing but "health and vigor"—this in spite of the trials and tribulations he knows the men have undergone during the recent Indian Wars. The crowd can readily see that these men are "intimate with hardship and familiar with danger."[52] Nothing distracts the riflemen from their mission and purpose amid all the chatter and excitement of the crowds.[53]

The crowd gathering along the street greets Michael Cresap and his company with an outcry of exhilaration. It is quite probable that they cheer the riflemen as saviors of sorts, for they understand the great cause for which these men stand, and they know the perils of the journey on which they are about to embark.

The formation that passes before the writer's eyes certainly seems to live up to stories he has read about them: "Their guns are rifled barrels, and they fight in the bush, five hundred provincials would stop the march of 5,000 regulars. And a whole army might be cut off, without knowing where the fire came from."[54]

This observer[55] serves as a personal attendant to Michael Cresap during the captain's stay in town. He is especially impressed with the behavior of the men and the respectful and attentive manner in which Cresap handles the men in his company.

While in Fredericktown, the attendant to the captain notes that Cresap listens intently to the wants and needs of his riflemen. If there is a complaint or request made by any one of the men, Cresap meets that grievance or solicitation with dignity as if he is not troubled at all by it, and he seems always to offer a satisfactory solution.

The newspaper commentator notices that the riflemen in the Maryland company look up to Cresap. The writer of the article also states that many appear to idolize him, observing that the riflemen's obedience to his every wish is evident as each command Cresap gives the men is swiftly carried out. The scribe observes that the men apparently view the captain not only as their commander but also as a father figure—or, at the very least, as their friend and confidante.

Out of deference to their captain, some of Cresap's men refer to him as "Old Mike," even though he is only thirty-three years of age. The moniker probably refers to his veteran status on battlefields when compared to many of the older but less experienced officers. One historian states this about the leadership style of Captain Cresap: "He was a strict disciplinarian, but not a martinet [not a rigid taskmaster]. His sense of discipline was "inherited from his father and confirmed by his own experience."[56] The respect Cresap commands from his men is evident in the overwhelming number of volunteers who join him.[57]

Near the end of the riflemen's stay in Fredericktown, officials supply them with a small amount of powder from the magazine, but the powder needs airing; in its present condition, it is unusable for their rifles. However, the conditions improve enough by evening so that the men of the company can give the crowd a demonstration,

---

51 Ibid.
52 Pennsylvania Gazette, "Extract from a Letter from Fredericktown," 3.
53 Ibid.
54 Charles *Royster, A Revolutionary People at War: The Continental Army and the American Character, 1775–1783 (Chapel Hill: University of North Carolina Press 1979), 34.*
55 The name of the observer who is mentioned in the August 1, 1775, edition of the Pennsylvania Gazette is unknown.
56 "Unveiling of Cresap Tablet: Logan Elm Park, October 1916," Ohio Archaeological and Historical Publications 26 (1916), 134-5.
57 Ibid.

one meant to display their shooting ability and dexterity. Primed with anticipation and curiosity, the people of the town turn out in great numbers to watch the show.[58]

The riflemen mark a white piece of paper the size of a dollar, attach it to clapboard they have put up as a target, and begin by firing offhand, to the surprise of the bystanders. Most of their shots land close to or on the paper. Next, some of the men lie on their backs or on their breasts or sides and shoot their mark, while still others run twenty or thirty steps while firing, equally certain of their mark even while on the move.

If the crowd thinks this is all there is to it and begins to disband, it is soon proved wrong, drawn back to the scene as a young man takes up the board in his hand and holds it by its side. His brother walks a distance and very coolly shoots directly into the white mark. Then, in a reversal of roles, he lays down his rifle, and his brother walks the distance and performs the same feat.

As if the observer of this amazing rifle exhibition has not had enough, the spectator stares in astonishment when one of the men takes the board, places it between his legs, and stands with his back to a tree. Another man drives a shot into the center of the mark. The newspaper reporter, after seeing the reaction of the crowd, remarks that the riflemen's feat, to the eyes and ears of everyone in attendance, is nothing short of unbelievable.[59]

If Lord North himself, prime minister of Great Britain at the time, had been present, Cresap's attendant declares, and if North believed that Captain Cresap could raise thousands more just like these men here today, North would very quickly have seen that the light in the stars of Great Britain had already begun to fade![60]

As the observer notes, "What would a regular army of considerable strength in the forests of America do with one thousand of these men, who want nothing to preserve their health and courage but water from the spring, with a little parched corn, and what they can easily procure in hunting; and who wrapped in their blankets, in the damp of the night, would choose the shadow of a tree for their covering, and the earth for their bed." [61]

On July 28, General Washington nervously awaits the arrival of the rifle companies from the south. Washington reports to General Schuyler from his headquarters at Cambridge, "Our Enemy Continues strongly posted about a Mile from us, both at Bunker's Hill and Roxbury…Part of the Rifle-men are come in and the rest daily expected."[62]

Ten days earlier, on July 18, General Putnam, veteran of the battle of Bunker Hill, assembles Washington's troops at the fort on Prospect Hill near Cambridge, where the authorities read to the troops the Declaration of Arms from Congress. For the first time, the troops officially hear the causes for and necessity of taking up arms against Britain. On that day, the reading is followed by a prayer, and upon conclusion, the troops applaud with great enthusiasm and shout with three cheers, "Huzzah! Huzzah! Huzzah!" The rebels immediately conclude the ceremony with a thunderous cannon blast from the fort.

---

58 *From the layman's study of the plot of three-acre ground off present Council Street in Frederick at the courthouse square, this location would seem to be the most likely spot where Cresap's Rifles performed their shooting demonstration in the summer of 1775. Ten years earlier, in 1765, citizens of the town gathered here to participate in the protest of the Stamp Act. All Saints Episcopal Church, occasionally attended by the family of Thomas Cresap family, was located on present W. Church Street, directly across the road from the courthouse. (Timothy L. Cannon, Tom Corsline, and Nancy F. Whitmore. Pictorial History of Frederick, Maryland: The First 250 Years, 1745-1995. Key Publishing, 1995. Chapter 1).*

59 Pennsylvania Gazette, "Extract from a Letter from Fredericktown," 3.

60 Ibid.

61 Pennsylvania Gazette, "Extract from a Letter from Fredericktown," 3.

62 John C. Fitzpatrick, ed., The Writings of George Washington from the Original Manuscript Sources 1745–1799, January 1770–September, 1775, vol. 3 (Washington, DC: US Government Printing Office, 1931. 375.

The men of this newfound army then raise a red banner, the universal symbol of defiance and a signal for battle. The spirits of the men are further elevated knowing that from Fort Prospect on the hill, the red banner can be seen by the redcoats in Boston!

The red banner flaps with a flourish in the wind. Embroidered gold letters on the banner herald the words "An Appeal to Heaven." The phrase is inspired by a letter from the Provincial Congress of Massachusetts written shortly after the Battle of Lexington, the content of which is addressed to Great Britain. A line from the missive includes the words "appealing to heaven for the justice of our cause, we determine to die or be free."[63]

Even as they raise the red banner, divine providence seems to be answering the prayers of the ammunition-poor colonial army. Responding to Congress and Washington's call, the southern rifle companies, including Cresap's men, steadily advance toward Massachusetts. The anxiously awaited riflemen from the south are marching northward on their jubilant jaunt to join Washington's army.[64] One spectator who has seen the riflemen march through Fredericktown writes, "God grant them a speedy and happy arrival there."[65]

---

63 Schuyler Hamilton, History of the National Flag of the United States of America (Philadelphia: Lippencott, Grambo, and Company, 1852).
64 In June 1775, along with their orders, authorities may have given Captain Cresap and the other nine captains of rifle companies copies of maps showing the route they were to take to Cambridge, Massachusetts. The original route maps are lost to history at this time.
65 "Extract of a Letter from a Gentleman in Frederick-town."

CHAPTER 3

Theatrics by Firelight

August 1, 1775, to August 6, 1775
Fredericktown, Maryland, to Lancaster, Pennsylvania

On August 1, 1775, Cresap's riflemen depart Fredericktown and march about twenty-five miles along the Monocacy Road to Taneytown, where they will camp. The road Cresap follows generally parallels upstream the east bank of the Monocacy River on present-day Route 194. Between Cookerley's Inn at present-day New Midway and Taneytown, they will cross both Little and Great Pipe Creeks, tributaries that flow into the Monocacy River, a body of water that George Washington will deem by its appearance as navigable. Here Washington will describe the lands as "remarkably fine…the farm houses are good, mostly of stone and the settlers compact with good Barns and meadows appertaining to them."[66]

Cookerley's Tavern, New Midway. Maryland

---

66 National Archives, "Washington Papers: Diary Entry 1 July, 1791," accessed September 25, 2017, https://founders.archives.gov/documents/Washington/01-06-02-0002-0006-0001#GEWN-01-06-02-0002-0006-0001-fn-0002.

The people of Taneytown are the first to see the full contingent of Cresap's Rifles enter their town. Cresap likely organizes his unit into formation just before the men enter this community, a procedure that the men likely repeat just before entering each town en route to Massachusetts.

Leading the parade of men now in formation, which makes up two or three orderly columns, is the celebrated Captain Michael Cresap. Cheers of excitement well up from the Taneytown citizens. Cresap smiles, nods, and tips his hat to those with whom he makes eye contact as enthusiastic onlookers on each side of the road jostle for the best possible viewing positions. Immediately behind Cresap comes the drummer, who times the pace of the slow march through the settlement with single taps of the drum. Next come the riflemen, all 130 of them—their steps light and muffled by the moccasins they wear. Sweeping the rear of the parade are two supply wagons, each pulled by four horses, and two horses tethered behind the last wagon. At the finale of this slow and deliberate procession, Cresap releases his men to set up camp in a nearby field, while the captain and his officers stay overnight in one of the town taverns.

Stone Tavern, Taneytown, Maryland

Cresap expects to pass a tavern every five to ten miles on the route toward Boston. These important places of business are set up to accommodate travelers, along with their horses and wagons. Taneytown boasts five taverns, which are located at or near each of the four corners on the town square. The Stone Tavern, constructed in 1760 of local fieldstone, is likely the oldest tavern in town. Immediately across the street stands the Adam Good Tavern, constructed of logs in the early 1770s. On its welcoming sign, this place boasts that it is "A Damn Good Tavern." Perhaps this sign has caught the eye of George Washington for when he visits Taneytown on July 1, 1791, he will select this tavern out of the five in which to stay overnight. Just before visiting Taneytown, Washington will visit Fredericktown. On his way toward Taneytown, Washington will travel also on the Monocacy Road and dine at Cookerly's, thirteen miles northeast of Fredericktown on present-day Route 194. From here, Washington notes that Taneytown is "only 12 miles further." On this trip, Washington also records that "Tawny town is but a small place with only a Street through w[hi]ch the road passes…The buildings are principally of wood."[67]

It is in camp at night after a long march that Cresap's men have a bit of time to let down their guard and relax. Like the campfire settings during Dunmore's War, "These [are] periods of great conviviality." After walking marathon distances each day, "in the evening, the sturdy foresters [bivouac] around a fire of huge logs, recount[ing] their hairbreadth adventures, or if perchance a violin or Jews-harp [is] possessed by the foresters, it [is] certainly introduced, and the monotony of the camp [is] broken by a boisterous 'stag dance.'"[68] During this jovial time, Old Mike may mingle and interact briefly with his men.[69]

On the morning of August 2, the riflemen depart Taneytown and march just a few miles before reaching Petersburg, present-day Littlestown, Pennsylvania. Because of the long distances between towns, to boost morale and promote camaraderie among the riflemen while on the march, Cresap likely relaxes protocol and formality at certain times. While on the move, the men are not required to walk in cadence and are permitted to quietly talk among themselves. During this time, perhaps Cresap's company members speak about their upcoming mission. Or maybe they will share their feelings about leaving family and friends behind at the old home place. As the men cross over into Pennsylvania and continue their banter, Cresap likely entertains not one single thought that he is leaving Maryland soil for the last time.

Ten years before, in 1765, Peter Klein established Petersburg, a town settled by German farmers. In 1791, while traveling on the Monocacy Road from Mount Vernon to Philadelphia, George Washington will describe Littlestown as "a good land" but "an insignificant place."[70]

Cresap continues past Littlestown on the Monocacy Road, and on the afternoon of August 2, after traveling a distance of about sixteen miles from Taneytown, he reaches McAllister's Town, at present-day Hanover, Pennsylvania. Pioneers laid out McAllister Town in 1762, and after a little more than ten years, more than five hundred individuals live here. Cresap likely stops at one or two of the more prominent taverns in town. In 1794 George Washington would describe this town as a place of "many log houses and brick buildings, presenting an attractive appearance."[71] In 1745, Richard McAllister built a two-and-a-half-story log tavern and inn -which also included a store - at the town crossroads at present-day Middle and Baltimore Streets. In 1755, Benjamin Franklin stayed here while traveling to Frederick County, Maryland, to meet with General Edward Braddock during the French and Indian War.

Another popular tavern and inn at McAllister Town is the Sign of the Horse, which Caspar Reinecker built in 1764. Thomas Jefferson will spend a night here on April 12, 1776, on his way from Monticello to Philadelphia, where the Continental Congress will meet. Two months after his stay at the Sign of the Horse tavern, Jefferson will write a draft of the Declaration of Independence. Jefferson will stay at Reinecker's Inn two more times: in September 1776, when returning home from Philadelphia, and again in 1783, when returning to the Continental Congress with his daughter Martha. George Washington will also visit and have breakfast at the Sign of the Horse on July 2, 1791.[72]

On August 3, after Cresap calls his men to muster, they march another twenty miles to York, Pennsylvania, where they once again set up camp. Here in York is the landmark Golden Plough Tavern, built in 1743 on the east side of

---

67 "Washington Papers"; Robert O. Bonnell, Edgar T. Bennett, and John J. McMullen. Report of State Roads Commission for Fiscal Years 1957–1958 (Baltimore: State Road Commission, 1958), 10–1.
68 Franklin Ellis, History of Fayette County, PA, with Biographical Sketches of Many of Its Pioneers and Prominent Men (Philadelphia: L. H. Everts and Co., 1882), 421–2.
69 Ibid; Jacob, A Biographical Sketch of the Late Captain Michael Cresap, 26–7.
70 Robert L. Bloom, History of Adams County, Pennsylvania: 1700–1990 (Gettysburg, PA: Adams County Historical Society, 1992).
71 Hanover (York County, PA) Centennial Committee, Official Program of the Centennial of Incorporation of the Borough of Hanover (Hanover, PA: E. L. Koller, 1915).
72 Hanover Area Chamber of Commerce, "Hanover's History," accessed September 25, 2017, http://hanoverchamber.com/wp-content/uploads/2014/10/HanoversHistory.pdf; Hanover Centennial Committee, Official Program of the Centennial of Incorporation of the Borough of Hanover, 10–1, 22; McGrew 1991).

Codorus Creek. Cresap likely stops here for refreshment and to gather important information he may need to know about the road ahead or to obtain news from Washington's camp. The Continental Congress will relocate to York, Pennsylvania, and conduct business here from September 30, 1777, to June 27, 1778. The Golden Plough Tavern will certainly become an important building where congressional members will meet to carry out some of their important political activities.

Golden Plough Tavern, York, Pennsylvania

Immediately adjacent to the Golden Plough Tavern is a building, built in 1751, that will later become known as the General Horatio Gates House. Here, in a little over two years, Lafayette will make a timely toast to congressional members to support George Washington during a time when some important figures within Congress were conspiring to replace him with General Gates, who will become very popular after his victory at Saratoga. Lafayette, knowing of the conspiracy, will say, "Gentlemen, there is but one you have forgotten." Lifting his glass, Lafayette will then say, "I propose a toast to our commander in chief, General Washington. May he remain at the head of the army until independence is won." These few words seem to kill any movement to replace Washington with Gates.[73]

Upon leaving York the next morning, Cresap's Rifles cross on a ferry over the Susquehanna River at present-day Wrightsville, Pennsylvania. Cresap and his company march with their usual fervor into Lancaster on the evening of Friday, August 4, 1775, their spirits buoyant. After their jaunt of twenty-five miles, the 130 men appear orderly as they step in time to the music of a patriotic air played by the fifer and drummer assigned to them. After traveling an arduous eighty-six miles from Fredericktown, Cresap's company sets up camp near the Lancaster courthouse town square.[74]

---

73 National Registry of Historic Places Inventory, "General Gates House and Golden Plough Tavern," July 1971, accessed November 10, 2017, http://www.dot7.state.pa.us/CRGIS_Attachments/SiteResource/H001123_01H.pdf.

74 "The Origin of the American Army," United States Army and Navy Journal 34 (1897): 558–9; Young, "The Spirit of 1775: A Letter of Robert Magaw," 22. The general road alignment that Michael Cresap's riflemen marched from Frederick, Maryland, to Lancaster, Pennsylvania, followed the present-day routes as follows. They went from Frederick on Route 15 to Route 26 to Route 194, past present-day Walkersville, Woodsboro, New Midway, and Keymar to Taneytown. From Taneytown, they took Route 194 over the Pennsylvania line to Littlestown and to Hanover. Then the path took them from Hanover to York, Pennsylvania, on Route 116 and from York, Pennsylvania, to Wrightsville, Pennsylvania, on Route 462, crossing over the Susquehanna River to Lancaster, Pennsylvania. The Old Monocacy Road was sometimes referred to as the Great Wagon Road to Lancaster and at other times as the Great Wagon Road to Philadelphia.

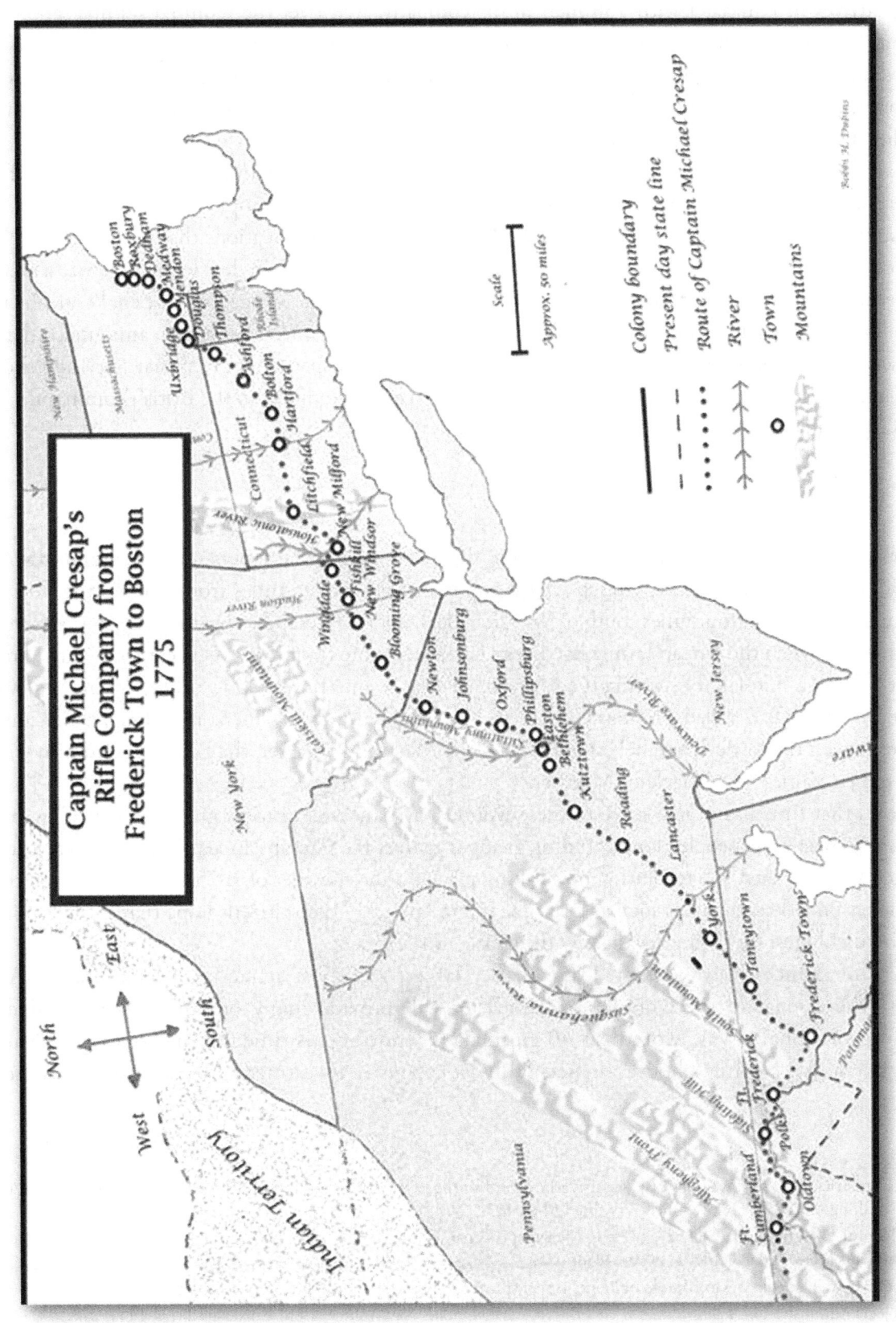

Cresap arrives in Lancaster with 130 men in his company, well over the required number approved by the Continental Congress. Unlike other rifle companies who turn men away, Captain Cresap does not refuse any qualified volunteer who clamors to travel with him, for reasons he does not reveal. Perhaps because most of these riflemen proved their abilities in the Indian War, Cresap does not deny their service or reject men whom his father prepared for the march during his own absence.[75]

In direct contrast to Cresap's decision-making process, other rifle companies kept the numbers of volunteers within the constraints Congress authorized. One newspaper account, for example, cited a captain from one of the frontier counties, possibly Frederick County, Maryland, who received applications that well exceeded the number of volunteers allowed by Congress. Not wanting to offend anyone, the captain decided to organize a shooting contest to determine which men to take with him on the march. The officer, using a piece of chalk on a board, drew a figure of a life-size nose and placed the target 150 yards from the applicants. The captain announced that he would enlist those shooters who hit the target nearest to the mark. The newspaper reported that sixty-odd shooters were successful in hitting the object and concluded the article with an admonition to the British commander in Boston: "General Gage, take care of your nose."[76]

By 1775, the town of Lancaster has existed for more than fifty years. The streets in the center of town were laid out in 1730, the same year Thomas Cresap settled approximately sixteen miles from here on the west side of the Susquehanna River, about four miles south of Wrightsville. Captain Cresap has heard many stories from his father recalling the time when the Cresap family lived near Lancaster more than forty years earlier. Many Lancaster citizens blamed Thomas Cresap for starting the Maryland-Pennsylvania Border War, calling it Cresap's War. At that time, Pennsylvanians had called Thomas Cresap "the Beast of Baltimore." Then, as he fought ferociously for the rights of settlers on the fortieth parallel established by the Maryland Charter, the Penns labeled him with an even more outrageous name: "the Maryland Monster."[77]

It appears that time has healed some of these wounds, as Lancaster citizens greet Thomas Cresap's son with courtesy and respect. The people's long-standing grudges against the Cresaps appear forgiven or at least temporarily set aside. After all, there is a revolution now taking place. In the summer of 1775, many persons in the colonies pin their hopes on rifle companies such as that of Captain Cresap. These citizens hope that the welcome riflemen can help to quickly resolve their grievances with British authorities.

At this time Lancaster is considered one of the "largest and most attractive inland cities in America."[78] Known as "the arsenal of the Colonies,"[79] Lancaster will provide many of the weapons used during the American Revolutionary War. More than 40 gunmakers reside at this time in Lancaster and throughout the surrounding county. Next to a house, the second most expensive investment a colonist makes is the purchase of a rifle.[80]

---

75 John C. Fitzpatrick, ed., The Writings of George Washington from the Original Manuscript Sources 1745–1799, January 1770–September, 1775, vol. 3 (Washington, DC: US Government Printing Office, 1931), 507.
76 Purdie's Virginia Gazette, Friday, July 21, 1775, 10. Newspapers.com; Frank Moore, Diary of the American Revolution from Newspapers and Original Documents (New York: Charles T. Evans, 1858), 111.
77 Kenneth P. Bailey, Thomas Cresap: Maryland Frontiersman (Boston: Christopher Publishing House, 1944), 31-55.
78 Work Projects Adminstration. *Pennsylvania: A Guide to the Keystone State.* New York: Oxford University Press, 1940. 247
79 *Ibid*, 29
80 "Pennsylvania Rifles are Born In Lancaster ." *Lancaster PA Changed America.* 2018. http://visithistoriclancaster.com/history_art/pennsylvania_rifles

Lancaster, originally known as Hickory Town, has a trading hub at the center of the town. The settlement is located on the former site of a stately hickory tree favored by the Indians who first settled here. Stores, street markets, homes, a drugstore, a tannery, a post office, a bank, even a hat store are just some of the buildings built here over time as the population has grown. To appease the varied interests of the residents who call Lancaster home, the community holds social gatherings around the courthouse square, as well as in private homes and nearby taverns.

In 1775, besides having the distinction of being places to meet and make merry and to offer toasts and sing patriotic songs, taverns and inns serve as important settings for receiving and sharing communications at a time when few weekly newspapers are published. Moreover, when things are moving at such a rapid pace, a week is too long to wait for valuable information.

To entice customers, tavern and inn owners hire local artists to design and construct colorful signs that hang near or over the entrances of their businesses. To welcome customers inside, the signs display images of portraits, animals, or other objects for which the business is named. One can only imagine the attractive array of signs that catch Cresap's eye as he enters the vicinity of the town of Lancaster and sees the following taverns: the Lamb, the Swan, Cross Keys, Cat Tavern, the Leopard, Fountain Inn, Shober House, Block House, Indian Queen, and Plough Tavern, just to name a few.

Most of the taverns are adjunct to impressive courtyards surrounded by stone fences. Innkeepers need the enclosures, sometimes a city block in size, so that they can quarter and shelter their customers' horses and wagons. Local leaders likely treat Captain Cresap to a tour, which no doubt includes the grandeur of the White Swan Hotel, a hotel General Washington will later visit.[81]

When passing through towns like Lancaster, Captain Cresap surely stops in at an occasional tavern for a bit of respite from his long journey and to catch up on the latest news. At some point during his three days in Lancaster, Cresap probably visits the Grape Tavern. This tavern, owned by revolutionary leader Adam Reigart, is the meeting place for the Committee of Correspondence and serves as Lancaster's Revolutionary War headquarters. Citizens with the same revolutionary mind-set as Cresap hang out here.

As he enters the Grape Tavern, the first item of note is a picture of a bunch of grapes painted on the sign above the door. Upon closer examination, Cresap's eye falls on the unique ornamental iron bracket supporting the sign, a masterpiece of wrought-iron work. Five years earlier, a Lancaster blacksmith specially designed this wrought-iron bracket, hammering into the metal impressions of grape clusters hanging on a vine adorned with lifelike leaves, featuring finely etched veins in the blades.

Cresap's observant eye appreciates this fine work of art, but today his mind is focused on more urgent matters. On this day, he must make certain that his company is fully supplied with guns, ammunition, and all manner of equipment and other goods before he reaches the camps at Cambridge. It is in establishments like the Grape Tavern that he takes time out to address this important business.

During his journey to Cambridge, Captain Cresap will spend $860.90 on supplies, of which $268.40 buys rifles to arm his company.[82] It is possible that Cresap purchases some if not most of the supplies in Lancaster at Joseph Simon's store, which fronts the courthouse square on King Street.

Joseph Simon established his store, located near Plough Tavern, twenty-one years earlier. His long-standing business has made Simon one of the wealthiest and most prominent merchants in the Pennsylvania province. Although

---

81 "Lancaster's Ancient Inns: Taverns Which Have Stood Since the American Revolution," New York Times, August 27, 1888, http://query.nytimes.com/mem/archive-free/pdf?res=F00E12F9395413738DDDAE0A94D0405B8884F0D3.

82 The Committee of Frederick County asked the Continental Congress to pay to Samuel Chase and William Paca, both future signers of the Declaration of Independence, $860.90 to reimburse the Committee of Frederick County for expenses Captain Cresap incurred purchasing supplies and rifles for his company. The Continental Congress took up this business on February 17, 1776. Peter Force, Peter Force's American Archives, 4th series, vol. 4. n.d., http://archive.org/stream/AmericanArchives-FourthSeriesVolume4peterForce/AaSeries4VolumeIv#page/n836/mode/1up.

he suffered financial hardship during the French and Indian War, Pontiac's War, and last year's Dunmore's War, Simon has managed to remain successful. His fortune has been due in part to his establishing a lucrative trade with the Indians in the Ohio Valley.

Simon's reach into the western frontier is vast. His trade empire starts at the fork of the Allegheny at present-day Pittsburgh and extends north to the Great Lakes, west to the Mississippi River, and south to the Cumberland and Tennessee Rivers. In fact, it was one of Simon's Indian traders who in June 1755, while returning from a trading excursion out west, encountered Braddock's army at Great Crossing on the Youghiogheny River. This party was the first to bring news of the progress of Braddock's forces back to citizens east of Carlisle, Pennsylvania.

Simon has known of Thomas Cresap and his Oldtown settlement for many years through business relations with many of his Indian traders, including Bernard and Michael Gratz, Alexander Lowrey, John Gibson, William Trent, and Evan Shelby. All traders in this region know the elder Cresap, as many have passed through Oldtown on their journeys back and forth through Indian country.

Joseph Simon partners and trades with William Henry, an established Lancaster gunsmith. Henry, who began making guns in the early 1750s to help supply the Indian trade, also helped to arm the expeditions of both Braddock and Forbes. Now Henry has hired more gunsmiths to help support the cause of the American Revolution.[83]

It would be quite natural for Michael Cresap, now in Lancaster, to visit Simon at his store. Besides having much in common, the two men would likely have a great deal to say to each other and many thoughts to share.

Underscoring the prowess of this collection of riflemen, another letter surfaces in a Pennsylvania newspaper on August 28, 1775. This observer pens the letter on August 7 in similar fashion to the Fredericktown letter written by Cresap's attendant. Although there are similarities in the descriptive content of the letters, no known personal connection exists between the two writers. In fact, the text of the Lancaster letter delves into a more detailed account of some of Cresap's activities in Pennsylvania. Furthermore, the writer concludes this account of events in Lancaster with an astonishing tale of rifle skills that closes with a grand and fiery finale.[84]

In his letter, the Lancaster author[85] particularly notes the physical appearance of the men. The spectator describes the marks, scars, and wounds perpetrated upon the men from their participation in the recent Indian wars. One warrior in particular, he records, bears the aftermath of four bullet wounds to the body. He writes, "They bear in their bodies the visible marks of their prowess and show scars and wounds, which do honor to Homer's Iliad…'Where the gor'd battle bled at every vein.'"[86]

The storyteller, realizing that these men were raised in harsh surroundings, largely in backwoods country, is aware that their battle scars are merely par for the course. He immediately detects that the men have known hardships from infancy. Yet he senses that the men, so long acquainted with tribulations and danger, have never felt the passion known as fear. They have faced all intervening threats with bravery and daring. Carrying their rifles at shoulder height, they appear formidable as a small army that assumes a kind of omnipotence over enemies.

In the future, the spectator will surely not shy away from sharing the seemingly mythic images he has just witnessed. Time after time, he will repeat this seemingly fantastic account of what he has seen long after Cresap's

---

83 LancasterHistory.org, "Sketch of Joseph Simon," October 24, 2013, http://www.lancasterhistory.org/images/stories/JournalArticles/vol3no7pp165_172.pdf.
84 "The Origin of the American Army," 558-9.
85 The name of the Lancaster reporter is unknown.
86 "The Origin of the American Army."

company has left town. Some who don't know him may think he tells tall tales, but he confidently knows that his story can be validated by many reputable spectators who witnessed the same marvels that he did that August weekend in Lancaster when Captain Michael Cresap's riflemen came to town.

The first spectacular event occurs when two brothers in the company take up a piece of board measuring five inches broad and seven inches long. The brothers nail a piece of white paper, about the size of a dollar, into the center of the board. While one man supports this board perpendicular between his knees, his brother, at a distance of up to sixty yards, shoots eight bullets successively through the board, just sparing his brother's thighs. Neither man requires a moment's rest or seems to have any qualms about the astonishing feat. This is just another ordinary day as a rifleman.

The show is just getting started. The men of Cresap's company have other tricks up their sleeves, one in which a rifleman holds a barrel stave perpendicular in his hand, with one edge close to his side, while one of his comrades, at the same distance, shoots several bullets through the stave. These men, as the brothers before them, seem to have no apprehension about the sure shots they are confident their fellow riflemen will deliver.

Captain Cresap, who narrates this phenomenal sideshow, explains to the crowd that at least fifty men in his company are able to perform the same feat. He tells them stories of the men's past heroic deeds and the way that each man in the company can without any doubt "plug nineteen bullets out of twenty," as he bluntly puts it, "within an inch of a ten-penny nail."[87]

The people continue to watch in wonderment—that is, until some of the men volunteer to stand with apples on their heads while other men undertake the task of shooting off the red targets of fruit. The crowd shies away, no doubt not wishing to witness the loss of a man's head. Yet the unbelievable accomplishments of these men so skilled with firearms will prove to be merely child's play compared to what is coming next.

After the good folks of the town partake of their evening meals and tend to their last chores of the day, many reconvene in town, where a strange picture begins to come together. As they arrive, the residents observe a cast of men already assembled in an outlandish yet uniform order on the town square. Night begins to cloak the site. The riflemen seem to be waiting for something—a more complete darkness. Then the observer and the townspeople know that their suspicions are correct, for they watch Captain Cresap and his men light a fire around a pole that they have planted in the square. Nightfall wreaths the scene as something bizarre yet sacred, a scene the likes of which these farmers and merchants of Lancaster have never before witnessed.

The fire sparkles and crackles and grows to a mammoth size. In this glowing, eerie firelight, the men's bodies become surreal, their forms seemingly disembodied under the half dark, half incandescent glow of the courthouse square. The men, the crowd sees, are all naked to the waist, and the riflemen are, in the reporter's words, "painted like savages."[88] They begin a war dance, an exhibition so perfectly executed that one would not know they were not the real "savages" the villagers have heard so much about.

Only the captain is not dressed in this manner. Cresap wears an Indian shirt during his presentation to the people. Captain Cresap exudes such an expertise and refined manner that the crowd can only stand or sit and stare at him and his men in amazement, feeling as if they have been magically transported to some surreal, majestic outdoor theater. Many of the people in the crowd likely understand that they are witnessing a once-in-a-lifetime experience.

When the war dance concludes, the riflemen begin the second phase of the show, demonstrating a realistic representation of Indians holding council as well as a dramatic portrayal of Indians going to war. Their lives and experiences on the frontier and the nature of their business allow Cresap's men to give presentations of ambuscades, just as they are conducted in the west. Next, in a scene that must seem frenetic, the frontiersmen defile, attack, and even feign the scalping of their pretend enemies.

---

87 "The Origin of the American Army."
88 Ibid.

As suddenly as it begins, the night on the square concludes in an almost unsettling quiet. The theatrics by firelight have ended. It is time for sleep and rest, for tomorrow the men will set out on their march to Cambridge. Cresap and his men have spent several very active days and nights in Lancaster. The riflemen have rested and restocked their supplies.

The people will long remember the riflemen and Captain Michael Cresap. The recording observer concurs, "The Captain's ability and expertness, in particular, in these exhibitions, astonished every beholder."[89]

---
89 "The Origin of the American Army."

CHAPTER 4

A Parade through Pennsylvania

August 7, 1775, to August 10, 1775
Reading, Bethlehem, and Easton, Pennsylvania

WHEN MORNING BREAKS, THE DATE is August 7, 1775. Cresap is now fully equipped with rifles and supplies. From Lancaster, he will pick up the pace with renewed purpose, temporarily putting aside shooting exhibitions for the townspeople. Captain Cresap, sensing the urgency to join Washington's army as soon as possible, fixes his sights on Cambridge.

Up to this point in the march to Lancaster, Cresap has been familiar with the towns and roads he has been traveling, for he has journeyed this way more than once when visiting the James Whitehead family in Philadelphia. The captain has most likely traveled this route to Lancaster, except that in 1764, the year he married Mary Whitehead, he would have continued eastward toward Philadelphia, where the couple exchanged wedding vows. Facts reveal strong ties between the Whiteheads and the Cresaps[90] that go back as early as 1749, but perhaps no fact is so revealing as the support Mary's father provides to the captain and his rifle company this summer.[91]

James Whitehead, Michael Cresap's father-in-law, who serves as a Philadelphia jail warden, has committed to Cresap's company £100, a value of about $267 in Pennsylvania currency. This generous donation will fund the purchase of woolen goods for clothing that Cresap's men will need to help them endure the cooler climate of New England.[92]

Now on August 7, 1775, as Captain Cresap sets out from Lancaster for Cambridge, he takes a new direction northeast, which leads him through unfamiliar towns and roads. The captain travels on the King's Highway, which opened in the 1750s in this part of eastern Pennsylvania. The King's Highway from Lancaster leads travelers through the towns of Adamstown, Reading, Kutztown, Bethlehem, and Easton. Cresap likely camps on August 7, at Adamstown, Pennsylvania after marching 24 miles.[93]

On August 8, the first settlement Cresap's company passes through after crossing the Schuylkill River is the village of Reading, a settlement with a population of two thousand people. Reading has steadily become a vital

---

90 More evidence to support the close connection between the Whitehead and Cresap families is that in 1773, Mary Whitehead's sister, Elizabeth Whitehead of Philadelphia, married Captain Michael Cresap's nephew, also named Michael Cresap, the son of Daniel Cresap, Sr. Also, Joseph Cresap, son of Daniel Cresap, Sr., married Deborah Whitehead, and in a second marriage, Joseph Cresap married Deborah's sister, Sarah Whitehead. (Cresap and Cresap).
91 William H. Rice, Colonial Records of the Upper Potomac, 1748–1750, vol. 3 (Parsons, WV: McClain Printing Company, 2013), 61.
92 Northern Illinois University Libraries, "Committee to Purchase Woollen Goods," November 14, 2013, http://lincoln.lib.niu.edu/cgi-bin/amarch/getdoc.pl?/var/lib/philologic/databases/amarch/. The £100 given by James Whitehead in 1775 is equivalent to $16,000 today.
93 "History's Headlines: Highway to the Past: The 18th Century Road Between Easton and Reading Was Once the Pathway to Patriots," WFMZ-TV 69 News, May 27, 2016, accessed November 13, 2017, http://www.wfmz.com/features/historys-headlines/historys-headlines-highway-to-the-past-the-18th-century-road-between-easton-and-reading-was-once-the-pathway-of-patriots/18286679.

source for the war effort.[94] In this area, which is the heart of gun-manufacturing country, many gunmakers reside in remote stretches along the Wyomissing Creek. Since 1732, gunmakers have produced long rifles here. Most of the long rifles in eastern Pennsylvania are crafted at Wyomissing Creek, just west of Reading, and throughout the Lancaster County region from Shillington to Mohnton to Adamstown.[95]

A minister of the Church of England who currently resides in America writes to the Earl of Dartmouth in England about the rifles and the quality of the men who use them:

> Rifles…are daily made in many places in Pennsylvania, and all the gun-smiths everywhere constantly employed. In this county, my lord, the boys, as soon as they can discharge a gun, frequently exercise themselves therewith, some a fowling and others a hunting. The great quantity of game, the many kinds and great privileges of killing, making the Americans the best marksmen in the world, and thousands support their families principally by the same, particularly riflemen on the frontiers, whose objects are deer and turkeys. In marching through the woods, one thousand of these riflemen would cut to pieces ten thousand of your best troops.[96]

Of the ten original rifle companies authorized by Congress to meet Washington at Cambridge, Massachusetts, Cresap follows behind nine other formations of troops, which have already passed through Reading. Captain George Nagel's rifle company, organized at Reading, is the first of the ten companies to reach the camps at Cambridge, having arrived there on July 18. Captain Cresap and his men, who got a late start, are destined to be the last rifle group of the original ten to arrive in Cambridge.

In 1734, when the Pennsylvania-Maryland border wars engulfed Thomas Cresap in conflict, a child named Daniel Boone was born near Reading. At that time Reading lay on the western edge of civilization in Pennsylvania.[97] Boone received his first rifle here at the age of twelve. Taught by local settlers and Lenape Indians, the lad quickly learned to hunt for food.[98] True, the famous legend of Daniel Boone began here at Reading, although twenty-five years prior to Captain Cresap's company passing through town, Boone's family had moved south to North Carolina. The paths of Michael

---

94 The Pennsylvania long rifle was a fascinating novelty to the New England townsfolk. The colonists lived in a world where technology had changed little over the past two thousand years. A rifleman wounded in battle could expect the same kind of medical treatment a Roman soldier received during the Roman Empire. In another example, riflemen marched to war much the same way the Spartans traveled to war—on their feet with support wagons following closely behind. In the 1730s, Thomas Cresap and other men of his generation who resided in the eastern Pennsylvania region were the first to master the long rifle. George Washington saw firsthand what Thomas Cresap and frontiersmen like him could accomplish with the use of these guns. Washington knew that a proficient rifleman could accurately shoot a round almost twice as far as with the more common smoothbore musket. The muskets of the colonists at Cambridge did not have the necessary range to reach the British soldiers under siege in Boston. In a strategic tack, Washington's Continental army kept the redcoats surrounded by land and contained inside the city. But now, as promised, the companies were arriving with their long rifles, possessing the range Washington urgently needed.

95 Young, "The Spirit of 1775: A Letter of Robert Magaw," 22. The long rifle's ancestry goes back to the 1500s, in the regions of Germany and Austria. Here, gunsmiths discovered that when several spiraled grooves were cut inside the barrel of a gun, it fired with significantly more accuracy and distance than a standard smoothbore gun. Americans called the rifled gun Jaeger, a word meaning hunter in German. The Jaeger was typically a .60 to .70 caliber gun about twenty-eight inches in length with seven rifled grooves. Skilled gunsmiths from Germany who immigrated to America brought with them the skills to make Jaeger rifles around 1710—the same year Thomas Cresap arrived on the shores of the Maryland colony.

96 Alexander Rose, American Rifle: A Biography (New York: Random House Publishing, 2008), 46.

97 Because of the fortunate seclusion of these sites during the revolution, the enemy presented no interference along the length of the Wyomissing Creek. When components of the British army overran the lower Schuylkill Valley in Pennsylvania, its leaders had no idea that their prized redcoats were so close to the men who manufactured the guns used against them.

98 Families living deep in the American wilderness far from civilization depended on the rifled gun for their survival to hunt game and to defend themselves against attacks by hostile Indians. To meet the unique needs of frontier life, gunsmiths continued to improve the accuracy and distance of the Jaeger rifle. Most of this work was done in Lancaster, Pennsylvania, or in nearby communities, such as Reading, Pennsylvania. By 1730, German gunsmiths in America had fashioned the Jaeger into a formidable weapon that came to be known as the Pennsylvania long rifle. The gunsmiths increased the barrel to forty inches in length and reduced the caliber to .4 to .6 inches, with the barrel rifled with six or seven grooves. With the Pennsylvania long rifle, a skilled marksman could shoot accurately up to three hundred yards, about three times farther than with the average smoothbore musket, the weapon commonly used by the British soldier. Kentucky Rifle Association, The Kentucky Rifle: A True American Heritage in Picture (Washington, DC: The Forte Group, 1985; George C. Neumann, The History of the Weapons of the American Revolution (New York: Bonanza Books, 1967), 134–5.

Cresap and Daniel Boone have crossed in the past. During Braddock's expedition, Daniel Boone served as wagonmaster for Braddock and camped with the army for two days on Thomas Cresap's fields at Oldtown in June 1755. It is likely that the thirteen-year-old Michael met, or at least laid eyes on, the twenty-one-year-old Daniel at this time.[99]

The area called Long Swamp lies among Reading and Allentown and Pottsville, Pennsylvania. The road the riflemen march passes on the east side of this large patch of low-lying scrub oak wetland, which proves to be an unsettled, unbroken wilderness. This time of year, the swamp teems with mosquitoes and horseflies. Ferries usually aid the riflemen in crossing larger rivers, but upon approaching smaller streams, like those found in this region, the riflemen must cross on foot. The men, already exhausted from their long, demanding march, now endure heat, humidity, bug bites, and wet feet as they pass through this region.[100]

The next memorable landmark they pass is Swan Hotel (present-day Kutztown, Pennsylvania) on the southwest side of Sacony Creek. The likeness of a swan is painted on the sign that hangs near the entrance of the business. Here on August 8, Cresap's Rifles likely camp after a 28 mile march from Adamstown.[101]

From Swan Hotel, it is another eighteen miles to Allen's Town (present-day Allentown), founded about 1762. This town is likely where Cresap and his men set up camp on August 9.[102] In 1770, James Allen, son of the town's founder, William Allen, built a hunting and fishing lodge along King's Highway in Allentown at present-day Walnut Street. Allen named the building Trout Hall for the high population of trout caught from the nearby Jordon Creek and Lehigh River.[103] James Allen is a British sympathizer, loyalties that will not bode well for him and will eventually have a negative impact on his personal wealth and freedom. In 1777, colonists will hide the Liberty Bell in the basement of a church in Allen's Town to keep the British from melting down this iconic symbol of liberty from which they could make ammunition.

Trout Hall, Allentown, Pennsylvania

---

99 "Gunmakers along the Wyomissing Produced Arms for Reading Riflemen Who Aided Washington: Local Troops Rushed to Commander's Assistance When War Started," Reading Eagle, September 23, 1934, http://news.google.com/newspapers?nid=1955&dat=19340922&id=4PIwAAA AIBAJ&sjid=k-EFAAAAIBAJ&pg=3724,4534628.1934.
100 "The Brobst Chronicles: A History of the Early Brobst/Probst Families in Pennsylvania," Rootsweb, November 17, 2013, http://homepages.rootsweb.ancestry.com/~brobst/chronicles/chap3.htm.
101 William Francis Harrity, Journal of Captain William Hendricks: From Carlisle to Boston, Thence to Quebec, 1775, 2nd series, vol. 15 (Harrisburg, PA: E. K. Meyers, 1890), 26; Kutztown Historical Committee, The Centennial History of Kutztown, Pennsylvania (Kutztown, PA: Kutztown Publishing Company, 1915), 43–4.
102 Harrity, Journal of Captain William Hendricks, 26.
103 Work Projects Administration. *Pennsylvania: A Guide to the Keystone State.* New York: Oxford University Press, 1940. 185

On the morning of August 10, 1775, the men are energized anew, largely because Cresap's preplanned directions take him through communities that offer refreshment and rest as his company moves ever onward toward Cambridge. On the east side of Allen's Town, Cresap's company crosses the River Jordon (Jordon Creek), a tributary of the Lehigh River. Not long after this, the riflemen set their bearings on the crossing of the Lehigh - which abruptly turns eastward, taking the men along the north side of the riverbank. Following the flow of this waterway leads the men to yet another watercourse – the Monocacy Creek – after when they cross, they come upon an impressive little town called Bethlehem.[104]

As one rifleman from another company describes the town, "Bethlehem is a small town pleasantly situated on the banks of the Lahay [Lehigh]. Here are beautiful gardens and all kinds of fruits and flowers, and also an elegant nunnery."[105] The Crown Inn, built in 1744 on the King's Highway, is located on the main road from the Lehigh River to Philadelphia. It sits directly on the highway of travel that all the southern rifle companies must pass in July and August of 1775 to reach the patriot camps at Cambridge. The inn with its welcoming tavern offers an ideal spot for the rifle companies to set up a temporary place to rest, and many take advantage of this opportunity. A sign, upon which some well-meaning artist has emblazoned an image of the crown of King George, hangs suspended on the portal of the tavern. If the captains had not instructed their men to be on their best behavior, the riflemen probably would have been happy to use this sign for target practice.[106]

As the riflemen pass through Bethlehem, their shadows fall on the Sun Inn, located along present-day Broad Street. Built around 1758, the Sun Inn is destined to entertain many leaders of the American Revolution in the coming years that include all the Presidents from Washington to Buchanan as well as distinguished personalities such as Richard Penn, Benjamin Franklin, John Hancock, and Lafayette. At the rear of this tavern patriots will temporarily hide the Continental Army's military stores when the British take possession of Philadelphia. [107]

The good people of Bethlehem have seen a parade of rifle companies come through their town. On July 21, three companies of mounted riflemen stopped here for several hours before moving on. On Monday, July 24, several more, including Captain Morgan's rifle company from Virginia, arrived in Bethlehem. Morgan's company stayed, and he requested a church service for his men the next day. Citizens later comment that Morgan's company was so quiet and orderly that one would not have known that a large group of soldiers was in town. On Tuesday, July 25, Captain Price's Maryland rifle company followed closely behind Morgan's company. Price and his men also rested here and attended an evening church service. Then on July 28, Stephenson's rifle company from Virginia came through town, and today, on August 10,[108] Cresap's Rifles pass through Bethlehem.[109] All will be quiet and peaceful in the little town of Bethlehem for several months after the last of the companies, the Bedford rifle company, finally marches by on August 13.[110]

---

104 Henry Melchior Muhlenberg Richards, "The First Defenders of the Revolution," in The Pennsylvania German in the Revolutionary War, 1775–1783 (Lancaster, PA: Pennsylvania-German Society, 1908), 19–20.
105 Harrity, Journal of Captain William Hendricks, 26.
106 Harrity, Journal of Captain William Hendricks.
107 Work Projects Administration. *Pennsylvania*, 191
108 Joseph Mortimer Levering, A History of Bethlehem, Pennsylvania: 1741–1892 (Bethlehem, PA: Times Publishing Company, 1903) 441–2.
109 Henry P. Johnston, The Campaign of 1776 Around New York and Brooklyn (Brooklyn, NY: Long Island Historical Press, 1878), 104–5.
110 Levering A History of Bethlehem, Pennsylvania, 441–2; Johnston, The Campaign of 1776 Around New York and Brooklyn, 104–5; Bethlehem, Pennsylvania Online, "History of South Bethlehem, Pennsylvania, Previous to Its Incorporation," 1913, accessed November 14, 2017, http://www.bethlehempaonline.com/sbethhistory.html.

Sun Inn, Bethlehem, Pennsylvania

After leaving Bethlehem, Cresap's company continues to parallel the north side of the Lehigh River until the unit reaches the town of Easton, where the Lehigh pours into the Delaware River. Easton is situated about eighteen miles east of Allentown.[111]

Captain Cresap has certainly heard of Easton before, for here parties signed the 1758 Treaty of Easton. This treaty was a legal form establishing permanent Indian hunting rights in the Ohio River Valley. The Cresap family frowned on this treaty, for it caused havoc to their plans as land speculators to promote settlements in the Ohio Valley.

Easton boasts a town circle that serves as the centerpiece of the community. The main roads lead to the town square, a central place for people to gather. Travelers usually find buildings such as courthouses and town halls in colonial town squares, and Easton is no exception. At sites like this in the center of towns near the courthouse are located "the pillories and whipping posts where culprits" are "punished in the manner prescribed by colonial law."[112]

The route to Easton takes Cresap's company past the steps of the courthouse, where in less than one year, on July 8, 1776, one of Easton's leading patriots, Robert Levers, will read the Declaration of Independence from the courthouse steps at the town square, making Easton one of the first of three towns privy to the document.[113]

Dr. Samuel Johnson (1709–1784), the English lexicographer, noted that, "There is nothing which has yet been contrived by men by which so much happiness is produced as by a good tavern and inn." Travelers will find taverns

---

111 Based on the calculation that Cresap's company traveled an average of twenty miles per day, since leaving Lancaster, Captain Cresap would have set up four overnight camps: likely south of Reading, Kutztown, Allentown, and Easton. The route that took Cresap's company of riflemen through Pennsylvania from Lancaster through Reading, Kutztown, Allentown, Bethlehem, and Easton followed the general alignment of modern-day Pennsylvania Route 222 and Route 22.

112 Work Projects Administration. *Pennsylvania, 211*

113 Philadelphia and Lancaster were the other two towns to first read the Declaration of Independence. Like Thomas Cresap, Robert Levers represented his county as a member of the Committee of Safety in 1775 as well as a member of the Committee of Correspondence. Ancestry.com.

and inns located near colonial town squares that serve not only as places for "food and drink" but also act as "inns, meeting places, political forums, and news outlets."[114]

In Easton, there are about twenty such taverns and inns from which to choose. One of these, located on present Northampton Street, is the Bachmann Publick House, built in 1753. Like many taverns of its times, it serves as the town social center. Since 1761, George Taylor, a future signer of the Declaration of Independence, has run the tavern. Other signers of the Declaration of Independence who will stay here are John Adams of Massachusetts, William Ellery of Rhode Island, and William Whipple of New Hampshire.[115] It is probable that Michael Cresap stepped inside the walls of this tavern to learn the latest news before traveling onward.[116]

Bachmann Publick House, Easton, Pennsylvania

On August 10, near the banks of the Delaware River, Cresap's company camps for the night.[117] Since leaving Lancaster, Cresap has marched about eighty-eight miles in four days, averaging a little more than twenty-two miles per day.

---

114 Wayside Exhibit in front of Bachmann Publick House in Easton, Pennsylvania, September 28, 2017.
115 Historians also believe that George Washington and Benjamin Franklin visited the Bachmann Publick House tavern, considered the oldest surviving structure in the city.
116 Wayside Exhibit, Bachmann Publick House, 2017; Sigal Museum, "Bachmann Publick House," acccessed October 7, 2017, https://sigalmuseum.org/bachmann/.
117 Harrity, Journal of Captain William Hendricks, 26–7.

When the rifle companies arrive in Boston, they serve under the direct command of George Washington in the role of light infantry. Washington warmly greets each rifle company as it arrives at Cambridge. Each rifle company is a self-contained unit of fighting men, many being veterans of Lord Dunmore's Indian War, a conflict fought the year before.

George Washington was present on June 14 when Congress selected the original ten rifle companies from Maryland, Virginia, and Pennsylvania. The next day, Congress selected Washington as chief officer to lead the newly formed fledgling continental forces. With this action, Congress created the US Army, its birthday celebrated on June 14 from that day forward.

In Washington's mind, the rifle companies from the south seem to symbolize the united cause of this fight against the British. To Washington, this conflict is not just a New England affair but one that concerns all the colonies.

One article gives a dire report that should concern every British soldier posted in Boston. The article says, "Congress have ordered one thousand Marksmen, or as we call them, Rifle-men…these men are to be divided into small parties and scattered through the [colonial] army for the purpose of removing [British] officers…A party of these men at a late review on quick advance placed their balls in poles of seven inches in diameter, fixed for the purpose at the distance of two hundred and fifty yards."[118]

The riflemen see their role as sharpshooters and skirmishers, who make sport to kill as many British "lobster coats" as possible—preferably officers. Once they establish their camps, the riflemen begin sneaking past the guards to stalk the outermost British fortifications. Once the victim is in range of the long rifle, the rifleman shoots, often with deadly accuracy.

Meanwhile in Boston, after a march of six hundred miles in twenty-one days, Daniel Morgan's rifle company from Virginia arrives in Cambridge on August 6, while Cresap's company is still in Lancaster. Daniel Morgan, like Cresap, is a veteran of Dunmore's War. Three days later, on August 9, Captain Price's rifle company from Maryland will show up in Cambridge while Cresap's company, still in Pennsylvania, is near Swan Hotel, just south of present-day Allentown.[119]

Morgan and Price both report to Washington at headquarters and receive a briefing of the current situation of the colonial army. The news they hear is dismaying. As they marched through Roxbury toward Cambridge, both Morgan and Price perceived a hint of how bad things were when they observed the drably dressed, poorly equipped colonial troops, but what the men hear at the briefing is nothing short of shocking.

Washington reported this desperate predicament to Congress one month earlier, just after assuming command of the continental forces. On July 3, the day he took command, Washington inspected his army at Roxbury and Cambridge and found a very unhappy condition overall. After his inspection, Washington penned to Congress that the army was "a mixed multitude of people…under very little discipline, order, or government." Washington wrote, "Confusion and disorder reigned in every department."[120] There have been only modest improvements of this situation since the arrival of Morgan and Price a little more than a month later.[121]

Headquarters staff briefs Morgan and Price that Washington's army presently consists of approximately sixteen thousand colonials, almost all of them lacking experience in the art of warfare. In the meantime, they face a British army of about six thousand highly trained regulars. Since the Battle of Bunker Hill, redcoats have controlled the heights at Bunker Hill and Breeds Hill next to Charlestown. The rest of the British army is under siege in Boston, surrounded on land by the Colonial army.

---

118 "London Intelligence," London Public Advertiser, August 5, 1775, 2.

119 Tucker F. Hentz, Unit History of the Maryland and Virginia Regiment (1776–1781): Insights from the Service Record of Capt. Adamson Tannehill (Richmond: Virginia Historical Society, 2007).

120 Hugh T. Harrington, "Patriot Riflemen During the Ammunition Crisis at the Siege of Boston in 1775," Americanrevolution.org, 2000, *http://www.americanrevolution.org/riflemen.html*.

121 Ibid.

At Cambridge, Captains Morgan and Price learn more about the nine-mile crescent-shaped siege line that the strategically placed colonial troops on the ground occupy around Boston. The line stretches along the west side of Boston Harbor, from Medford southward to Boston Neck at Roxbury. The captains at once realize Washington's problem. They understand that this long, thin alignment of troops makes the Colonial army vulnerable. An attack in the middle of the line by the British could divide Washington's army in two, severely weakening its effectiveness, or even destroy his fledgling forces.

Washington has made it clear that he believes that an attack by the British is imminent. What is worse, Morgan is informed that the Continental army has an ammunition crisis. The colonial units have no more than nine cartridges of ammunition per man, contrasted with the British army, which has an estimated sixty rounds per soldier. This fact must remain top secret. If the British discover the colonials' grim condition, they will immediately storm over Boston Neck at Roxbury and attack.

The one luminous highlight for Washington during this dark time is that the rifle companies he has requested are finally beginning to arrive in Boston. Some have already arrived from the south. Washington knows the riflemen will act as a kind of deterrent to the British, whose officers have warned their men about the deadeye aim of the riflemen. The fear instilled in the British army works to keep them from crossing over Boston Neck. Since the British have learned of the rifle companies' presence in Cambridge and Roxbury, they have laid low. A contemporary newspaper account states that the arrival of riflemen has "grown so terrible to the [redcoats] that nothing is to be seen of them over their breastworks but their hats."[122]

In the meantime, while Captains Morgan and Price camp and stand by in Cambridge awaiting further orders, Captain Cresap continues to propel himself and his men forward to the front, one mile at a time, bound for the center of disturbance at Boston to join his fellow riflemen, "the first defenders of our country in its struggle for Independence."[123]

---

122 "Extract of a Letter from a Gentleman in Frederick-town," 2.
123 Richards, "The First Defenders of the Revolution," 16–33.

CHAPTER 5

Dark Moon Rising

Passing through the Jerseys
August 11, 1775, to August 14, 1775

WITH THE ROAD UNDERFOOT ONCE again, Cresap departs Penn's Woods, leaving behind the serenity of Bethlehem and Easton. On August 11, within the babbling sounds at the forks of the Lehigh and Delaware Rivers, Cresap and his men board a ferry established by David Martin about 1739 and cross the Delaware River.[124] Cresap takes special note of the ferry operation to see what productive methods he might wish to apply to his own ferry operation at Redstone after he fulfills his enlistment obligation. However, for now, Cresap's back faces Oldtown and his family as he dutifully marches farther and farther from home.

Forks of the Delaware and Lehigh Rivers, Easton Pennsylvania

Once Cresap and his men cross the Delaware River with Pennsylvania at their back, they pass through the small village of Phillipsburg, allocated along the east bank of the Delaware River in the northwest section of New Jersey.

---

124 The ferry connecting Easton to Phillipsburg operated from around 1739 to 1806 and was located near the conjunction of the Lehigh and Delaware Rivers (the present-day site of Scott Park). The strategic location of the ferry, connecting Pennsylvania to New Jersey, made it very important to the colonial cause. Here, during the American Revolution, the ferry transported troops and supplies over the Delaware River.

Once in "the Jerseys,"[125] Cresap's company soon reaches the area of present-day Washington Township, where Dr. Peggy Warne resides. Warne is one of the best-known obstetricians in the region, but today she serves both citizens and soldiers who are in need of medical attention. Warne's medical services are especially valued now that most of the male doctors are away serving in the army. Many years before Florence Nightingale is born, Dr. Warne, who keeps a horse ready and saddlebag supplied with a variety of medicinal herbs, travels throughout the surrounding hills and valleys to care for the sick, no matter the weather conditions. If any of the men need medical attention, Dr. Warne, about four years younger than Captain Cresap, is the most likely doctor to attend their needs while Cresap's company is in this part of the country.

Shippen Manor, Oxford Township, New Jersey

At an intersection about eleven miles east of Phillipsburg,[126] Cresap's company takes the road north to Oxford Furnace, about eighteen miles from Easton. Cresap likely camps near the Oxford Meeting House.[127] Here, on his first night on New Jersey soil, a full moon lights the area around his encampment.[128] Several log cabins housing ironworkers surround the Oxford Furnace, a small village in Oxford Township in Warren County, New Jersey

---

125 During colonial times there were two geographical divisions of New Jersey: West Jersey and East Jersey. A detailed map showing the delineation of the two Jerseys can be found by referring to the source for "The Province of New Jersey."

126 About a year later, Washington's army retreated on a road passing through Washington Township after the Battle of Long Island. The road along which Washington retreated was along present-day Route 632, which follows the Asbury-Anderson Road. Al Frazza, "Revolutionary War Sites in Oxford, New Jersey," Revolutionary War New Jersey, 2013, accessed November 14, 2017, http://www.revolutionarywarnewjersey.com/new_jersey_revolutionary_war_sites/towns/oxford_nj_revolutionary_war_sites.htm.

127 Harrity, Journal of Captain William Hendricks, 27.

128 Apparently patriots, under the authority of the Continental Congress, instructed town leaders to support the patriot cause as best they could by providing for the needs of men in the rifle companies when they passed through their town (Harrity, Journal of Captain William Hendricks, 27; Jonathan Heart, Wilshire Butterfield, John Dickinson, and Josiah Harmar, Journal of Captain Jonathan Heart on the March with His Company from Connecticut to Fort Pitt (Albany, NY: Joel Munsell's Sons, 1885).

founded by Dr. William Shippen, Sr., in 1741. Dr. Shippen, a physician from Philadelphia who will serve in the Continental Congress representing Pennsylvania in 1778, owns the ironworks.

Oxford Furnace, Oxford Township, New Jersey

When Dr. Shippen comes to Oxford to oversee his business investment, he stays at the mansion he built in 1753 on his four-thousand-acre estate. This plush residence sits on a knoll overlooking the Oxford Furnace, which rises to a height of thirty-one feet. The furnace, which burns charcoal for fuel, is just downhill, about 150 yards from the impressive structure run by Shippen. Presently, the mill produces two tons of iron ore a day. Workers convert the ore into tools, musket balls, and grapeshot, items that Washington urgently needs to support his army. Before he finishes his medical practice, Dr. Shippen will count among his patients George Washington, Benjamin Franklin, John Hancock, General Gage, and Lafayette.[129]

On August 12, their second day in New Jersey, Cresap's company will march fifteen-miles to Johnsonburg, New Jersey. About twelve miles into their journey from Oxford, they pass through the Moravian Village called Hope.[130] Peace loving Moravians from Bethlehem, Pennsylvania, established this small village in 1774 on 1,000 acres that they purchased from an early settler of this area. Within no time, from native blue limestone, the Moravians built "substantial houses, two mills, a brewery, a tannery, a public inn, and a church – all that [is]

---

[129] John W. Barber and Henry Howe, Historical Collections of the State of New Jersey (New York: P. S. Tuttle, 1844), 501; Frazza, "Revolutionary War Sites in Oxford, New Jersey"; Kathryn Ptacek, "The Oxford Furnace Incident," New Jersey Skylands, December 9, 2013, http://www.njskylands.com/hsoxfordfurnace.htm.2013.

[130] On July 26, 1782, George Washington dined at Hope en route to Newburg, New York. The route Cresap's company traveled in northwest New Jersey was a primary travel corridor for military units during the American Revolution. Present-day Route 519 north took the riflemen through Hope. At High Street, Route 519 north makes a hard right and continues on toward present-day Newton, the same road alignment the riflemen traversed as they passed through Hope.

needed for a self-sustaining community."[131] Because Moravians refuse to participate as soldiers in the revolution, riflemen from companies who pass through this area at first suspect Moravians are Tories. The truth is, according to their religious beliefs, it goes against Moravians' conscience to go to war. But soon enough, Moravians redeem themselves in the eyes of American colonists for the generous care they will provide to sick and wounded soldiers who fight for the cause.

It is along this section of road that the riflemen first notice an oddity in the features of the terrain, which has become rockier than before. A rifleman from another company who passed through the area before Cresap's company noted in his journal "the barrenness of New Jersey."[132] The diarist has made a keen observation, for the riflemen have entered a new kind of landscape they have not walked before, a countryside carved and shaped by glaciers more than thirteen thousand years before.[133] The marchers might be surprised to know that icy glaciers of more than several thousand feet in height once blanketed these mountains and valleys.[134]

Upon arriving in the Boston area, an observant Pennsylvania rifleman will record his impressions of the landscape he viewed on his journey from the Appalachian Mountains through the New England landscape. He writes, "The country we passed through from Dellawar [Delaware River] to this place [Boston] is poor [,] hilly [,] sandy [,] and very Stony and in many places the Roads as bad as our mountains. The Country is well improved Notwithstanding [considering] the poverty of the Soil. Stone fences and neat Frame houses [are] almost always in view." [135]

Continuing from Hope, Cresap marches his company through Log Town, to present-day Johnsonburg where they likely camp during their second night in the Jerseys after a fifteen mile march.[136] Log Town, sometimes referred to as Log Goal (Jail), is so named because a judge holds court in a private home near a log building constructed for use as a jail. Not everyone is sympathetic to the patriots' cause. Just a few weeks before, members of a Pennsylvania rifle company staying overnight at Log Town "tarred and feathered one of the Ministerial tools who refused to comply with the resolves of the Continental Congress."[137]

Possibly the person the riflemen tarred and feathered was one of the sons of Samuel Green, the deputy colonial surveyor of New Jersey. Samuel is on record for having voted to build a log jail near the Dark Moon Tavern at Log Town.[138] The town judge, Jonathan Pettit, owns the Dark Moon Tavern. When Judge Pettit built the tavern, he placed a swinging sign painted with a black crescent moon near the door of the establishment. In the minds of more than one person, the sign foretells dark things to come. These unwelcome forebodings will eventually strike

---

131 Workers Project Administration, Federal Writers' Project. *New Jersey: A Guide to Its Present and Past.* 456

132 Balch, Papers Relating Chiefly to the Maryland Line during the Revolution, 11.

133 Over the years, farmers have converted many of the smaller stones left behind by the glaciers into stone fences that modern-day motorists can view throughout New England. The most southern terminal moraine of glacier deposits begins just north of Oxford, creating the rocky, barren landscape that the riflemen observed. Glaciers once covered the Kittatinny Mountains, the easternmost mountains of the Appalachians in New Jersey. Like Michael Cresap's home in Oldtown, the Kittatinny Mountains are located in the Ridge and Valley Province. These mountain ridges vary in elevation from about 1,400 to 1,600 feet. The highest point is High Rock at 1,803 feet. The mountains here are very similar in appearance and elevation to Green Ridge Mountain and Warrior Mountain near Michael's house at Oldtown, Maryland. Henry B. Kummel, "Map Showing Direction of Ice Movement in Northern New Jersey," Rutger's University Cartography Services, 2013, accessed November 15, 2017, http://mapmaker.rutgers.edu/HISTORICALMAPS/IceMovement_1902.jpg.

134 Balch, Papers Relating Chiefly to the Maryland Line during the Revolution, 11.

135 Young, "The Spirit of 1775: A Letter of Robert Magaw," 7.

136 Harrity, Journal of Captain William Hendricks, 27. Although Captain Jonathan Heart's march occurred ten years after Captain Cresap's through New Jersey, Heart's journal provides additional details of the route through New Jersey missing in Captain Hendricks's journal published in the book by Harrity.

137 Harrity, Journal of Captain William Hendricks, 27.

138 Also known as The Black Crescent Moon tavern, this building stood as of 2015 in Johnsonburg along Main Road/Black Crescent Moon Road, on the original road the rifleman walked. Main Road/Black Crescent Road reconnects with modern-day Route 219 just north of town, leading directly to Newton, New Jersey.

the family of Samuel Green when four of his five sons, who are sympathetic to the loyalists' cause during the war of the rebellion, are housed in the same jail Green supported building (Clark 2013).

Dark Moon Tavern, Johnsonburg, New Jersey

The next morning, on August 13, Cresap's rifle company continues their march through a great valley in the shadows of the Kittatinny Mountains, which lie nearby to the west.[139] As this is Sunday, Cresap and his men mentally ready themselves for an approximately ten-mile trek to the next small town, called Sussex (present-day Newton), where they will finish their march for the day, this decision works out well pace-wise, as the next favorable stop is more than twenty miles distant. Cresap's men camp in Sussex, New Jersey.[140]

Sussex, founded around 1761, is at this time a very small village containing a courthouse and several taverns, one bearing the colorful name the "Sign of Captain O'Blunder." Cresap may stop here to obtain information concerning the important affairs of the moment.

Sussex is strategically located in an intermountain area that provides support to military units like Cresap's that pass through this region. The road through town is also important for transporting supplies and communications between New England, Philadelphia, and the forts along the Hudson River.[141]

---

139 Both the Iron Furnace and the mansion stand today as noted historical sites. The modern-day highways that align the route Captain Cresap traveled are Route 57 from Phillipsburg to Washington, New Jersey, and Route 31 from Washington to Oxford. Cresap's riflemen followed the general present-day alignment of Route 519 north from Oxford through Hope, Johnsonburg, and Newton.
140 Harrity, Journal of Captain William Hendricks, 27.
141 On November 28, 1780, George Washington stayed at the Sussex courthouse while traveling through New Jersey to a military installation at New Windsor, New York. Citizens gutted the courthouse and constructed a new building on the site, using some materials from the original courthouse. Again on July 26, 1782, Washington traveled this part of New Jersey en route to Newburg, New York, and after visiting the court house likely dined at Thomas Anderson's house and stayed overnight at a tavern where the Old Cochran House once stood at Main and Spring Streets. Both the tavern and Anderson's house were located facing the town green .Workers Project Administration, Federal Writers' Project. New Jersey: A Guide to Its Present and Past. 462

Travelers passing through here more likely than not stay at the County Hotel, licensed in 1753. This is probably the place where Captain Cresap and several of his officers stay. However, sometimes travelers on official business reside at the ten-year-old Sussex courthouse. On the grounds of the Sussex courthouse, as is ordinary at courthouses in most colonial towns, is situated a grassy commons area, where citizens gather for public events and meetings and hold town elections and where the militia conducts military exercises.

The leading revolutionary patriot of Sussex is a lawyer named Thomas Anderson (about 1743–1805). On August 13, 1775, Anderson, who is about the same age as Captain Cresap, likely welcomes the Maryland native and his company when they arrive in town. Like Thomas Cresap of Frederick, Maryland, Thomas Anderson represents his county of Sussex regarding revolutionary matters. Anderson helped select the representatives from New Jersey to serve in the Congress that began to meet in Philadelphia, Pennsylvania, on September 5, 1774. Like Thomas Cresap, Anderson also served in 1774 on the Committee of Correspondence for his county. Presently, both Thomas Cresap and Thomas Anderson serve on the Committee of Safety for their respective home counties.[142]

On August 14, their fourth morning in New Jersey, Cresap's company reassembles at the Sussex courthouse. From here, they march about twenty-three miles northeast to Dr. John Hinchman's thirty-seven-room tavern at Hadestown.[143] Dr. Hinchman, one of the first surgeons to settle in the area located near present-day Vernon, serves the Sussex County, New Jersey, militia. During the revolution, General Washington will stay overnight at Hinchman's Tavern and will eat breakfast there the following morning. While her husband is apparently away serving in the militia, Dr. Hinchman's wife, Abigail, will kill thirteen bullocks and sixty sheep in one night to feed Washington and his troops.

Actions taken by Abigail Barton Hinchman during her husband's absence reveal that she is a true revolutionary patriot. When a man named James Hamilton escapes from his British and Tory captors, he seeks refuge at Hinchman's Tavern, his trackers in hot pursuit. Mrs. Hinchman hides Hamilton in a large barrel that she then covers with a spread of flax. When the British and Tories arrive at the tavern, Mrs. Hinchman serves the would-be-captors a very healthy dinner accompanied by many servings of cider. The well-fed pursuers depart Hinchman Tavern without ever detecting their fugitive prisoner hiding in the barrel near the table where they dined.[144]

Tavern owners are generally leaders in their communities. The owners of these businesses, who serve as doctors, judges, or officers in the local militia, are usually pillars of their settlements. Besides being important gathering places for the community, taverns offer convenient support sites for military encampments along these routes. Here, citizens conduct all manner of community business. Tavern owners frequently are responsible for the maintenance of the roads. Their knowledge of the area and connections to the local and outside community make it

---

142 Al Frazza, "Revolutionary War Sites in Newton, New Jersey," Revolutionary War New Jersey, 2017, accessed November 14, 2017, http://www.revolutionarywarnewjersey.com/new_jersey_revolutionary_war_sites/towns/newton_nj_revolutionary_war_sites.htm.; Kevin W. Wright, "Anderson House: 1785," NewtonNJ.net, 2000, December 10, 2013, *http://www.newtonnj.net/Pages/andersonhse.htm.2000*. The similarities between Colonel Thomas Cresap and Anderson did not stop here. As Thomas Cresap served in the role of commissary and agent to General Braddock's army in 1755, Anderson was destined to serve as General George Washington's assistant deputy quartermaster general. Beginning in January 1777, when Washington began his winter encampment at Morristown, New Jersey, Anderson played a key role in securing provisions for the continental troops. During this critical time, Anderson supplied to the Continental army "flour, chopped feed, hemp, and iron" at Trenton, New Jersey, and Morristown. Winthrop Sargent, The History of an Expedition against Fort Du Quesne in 1755 under Major General Edward Braddock, Lewisburg, PA: Wennawoods Publishing, 1997), 312–3).

143 Hinchman's Tavern is called Hinksman's Tavern in the journal of Captain Hendricks, who commanded a Pennsylvania rifle company that passed through the area before Captain Cresap and his company. Hinchman's Tavern, destroyed in a fire many years ago, was located at the present-day site of the intersection of Route 94 and Maple Grange Road, about six miles south of the New York boundary.

144 Jennie Sweetman, "Early Surgeon Remembered," New Jersey Herald, n.d.; Jennie Sweetman, "Hinchman Clan Has Vernon Ties," New Jersey Herald, June 8, 1980; Jennie Sweetman, "Sussex County Inns: Taverns Served Many Purposes," KWWL.com, December 10, 2013, http://www.kwwl.com/story/20512513/2013/01/05/sussex-county-inns-taverns-served-many-purposes; Ronald J. DuPont, Jr., Vernon 200: A Bicentennial History of the Township of Vernon, New Jersey, 1792–1992 (McAfee, NJ: The Friends of Dorothy E. Henry Library, 1992), 61.

standard protocol for captains like Cresap to meet the owners of these establishments and share information vital to the revolution.

Cresap's company likely camps at Hinchman's Tavern during their fourth night in New Jersey.[145] The riflemen are now about six miles south of the New York boundary line, their journey through northwest New Jersey having taken them sixty- six miles.[146]

George Washington himself will travel this very same route through New Jersey in the ensuing years of the revolution. It appears that the paths of Michael Cresap and Washington are predestined to cross now and then. Washington, ten years Michael Cresap's senior, has stopped at Cresap's childhood home on his travels into western Maryland since 1748 in his role as a surveyor, military officer, and landowner. On more than one occasion, Washington stayed overnight at Michael's home place, where he was entertained by and enjoyed the warm fellowship and hospitality of the Cresap family.

"Cresap's Rifles and Lady Liberty on the March: "Concept drawing by Bobbi Dubins for book cover consideration

---

145 Harrity, Journal of Captain William Hendricks, 27.
146 George Wyckoff Cummins, History of Warren County, New Jersey (New York: Lewis Historical Publishing Company, 1911), 33, 54. From Sussex, Cresap's company followed the general alignment northeast toward the state of New York along Route 94 through present-day Hamburg and Vernon, New Jersey, toward the New York boundary.

Onward Cresap marches, again destined to meet Washington, this time at Cambridge. If necessary, the men of the captain's company are prepared to fight to the death to defend the safety and dignity of Lady Liberty. "The Liberty Song," composed by fellow patriot John Dickinson soon after the successful repeal of the 1765 Stamp Act, stirs the hearts of the riflemen:

Come join hand in hand, brave Americans all.
By uniting we stand, by dividing we fall.
No tyrannous acts shall suppress your just claim
Or stain with dishonor America's name.

In freedom we're born, and like sons of the brave,
We'll never surrender but swear to defend her
And scorn to survive, if unable to save.[147]

On August 14, while Captain Cresap's company is likely camped at Hinchman's Tavern in New Jersey, a boisterous celebration is taking place near Washington's headquarters in Cambridge. This date commemorates the tenth anniversary of the repeal of the notorious 1765 Stamp Act. During this time, rioters protesting the Stamp Act burned several public buildings and homes of officials. This incident set in motion events that eventually led to the repeal of the British decree, which proved quite unpopular throughout the colonies. The Stamp Act united individuals throughout the colonies to fight against oppressive policies imposed on them by British authorities and stimulated the creation of secret societies, including the Sons of Liberty.[148] Among members of the Sons of Liberty in Massachusetts are John Adams, Samuel Adams, and Paul Revere.

The anniversary celebration in New England likely includes flying flags, music, firing of cannons, and, in a home or tavern, the raising of glasses with hearty toasts proposed between each drink. The toasts made this night at one officer's house captures the mind-set of the patriots Captain Cresap will meet when he arrives at the Cambridge battlefront:

- Here's to the Continental Congress!
- Here's to the success of our undertakings!
- Here's to the memorable August 14th, 1765!
- May American valor ever prove invincible to the attempt of ministerial tyranny to oppress them!
- Here's to the twelve united colonies![149]
- Here's to all our friends in Great Britain!
- Here's to liberty without licentiousness!
- Here's to a speedy and happy conclusion to the present unhappy disputes!
- Here's to April 19, 1775 [Battles of Concord and Lexington]!
- Here's to a speedy entrance, possession, and opening of the town of Boston!

---

147 Louis C. Elson, The History of American Music (New York: MacMillan Company, 1904), 140–3.
148 The protests against the Stamp Act spread like wildfire throughout the colonies in 1765. Colonel Thomas Cresap became one of the primary leaders of the Sons of Liberty in Maryland. Michael likely participated in his father's protests as a member of the Sons of Liberty. Ten years later, in 1775, the Stamp Act shaped the destinies of Maryland's Captains Price and Cresap in ways that they could not have imagined. The actions of these two patriots in 1765 identified them in the Maryland community as leaders and guardians of liberty.
149 Georgia had not yet sent representatives to the Continental Congress; therefore, only twelve of the thirteen colonies were in the fight at this time. Moore, Diary of the American Revolution from Newspapers and Original Documents, 127.

- Here's to the president of the Continental Congress [John Hancock]!
- Here's to General Washington and the other general officers of the Continental army!
- Here's to a speedy export of all enemies of America without any drawback!
- Here's to the immortal honor to that patriot and hero, Doctor Joseph Warren, and the brave American troops, who fought the Battle of Charlestown on June 17, 1775 [Battle of Bunker Hill]!

While Cresap's company pushes forward in New Jersey, Stephenson's Virginia rifle company arrives in Cambridge on August 11, 1775, joining Captain Morgan's and Captain Price's companies in Cambridge.[150]

Looking across the harbor from Cambridge toward Boston, the riflemen can see British soldiers operating close to the Boston shore, performing military exercises in small rowboats. British General Thomas Gage has apparently ordered his officers to build these rowboats, thirteen in all, each capable of carrying sixty people. At a summit near Cambridge, one can also hear and see detachments of up to eight hundred British regulars, some on horseback, practicing military exercises on the Charlestown common.

After observing these maneuvers, Washington's officers suspect that the British plan a possible attack by water supported by a simultaneous inland invasion from nearby Boston Neck and from Charlestown. All colonials are on edge, thinking that the British attack will come at any time.[151]

On August 13, Morgan and Stone receive new orders from headquarters. Together, the two companies march the six miles from Cambridge to their new duty station at Roxbury. Washington intends an intentional show of symbolism by combining the Maryland and Virginia rifle companies of Morgan and Price on their very visible march to Roxbury from Cambridge. The general hopes to convey to everyone that this war is not just about the siege at Boston and the colony of Massachusetts. He wishes it to be known to all that this army is a joint continental effort, that all twelve colonies are fighting together as one, united in battle against British tyranny.

The riflemen from Pennsylvania are doing a good job annoying the British regulars. To protect themselves from the deadly aim of the sharpshooters, the British build their breastworks higher at Boston Neck and at the foot of Bunker Hill.[152]

Newspaper accounts published throughout the colonies have tracked the progress of Cresap's company and the other southern rifle companies since they departed Fredericktown, Maryland, on their way to Boston. The articles, particularly those that focus on Captain Cresap's company, seem to exaggerate their incredible shooting abilities that the public witnessed in Fredericktown and Lancaster, the stories sounding more like tall tales or hyperbole. By the time Cresap reaches Boston, he will have captured the public's imagination. In this brief shining moment, Captain Cresap is one of the most talked-about riflemen in America.[153]

Not only do reports of the riflemen's shooting abilities spread throughout British-occupied Boston in the summer of 1775, but newspapers also transport their story all the way to London. The *London Chronicle* dated August 17 through August 19, 1775, states, "This province has raised 1000 riflemen, the worst of whom will put a ball into a man's head at a distance of 150 or 200 yards, therefore advise your officers who shall hereafter come out to America to settle their affairs in England before their departure."[154]

---

150 Hentz, Unit History of the Maryland and Virginia Regiment.
151 Moore, Diary of the American Revolution from Newspapers and Original Documents, 124; Richard Frothingham, Jr., History of the Siege of Boston (Boston: Charles C. Little and James Brown, 1851), 232.
152 Moore, Diary of the American Revolution from Newspapers and Original Documents, 124.
153 Ibid., 123; Robert G. Parkinson, "From Indian Killer to Worthy Citizen: The Revolutionary Transformation of Michael Cresap," The William and Mary Quarterly 63(1) (2006): 97–122.
154 Harrington, "Patriot Riflemen During the Ammunition Crisis at the Siege of Boston in 1775."

CHAPTER 6

Back Door to Boston: The Upper Road

New York
August 15, 1775, to August 17, 1775

ONE WOULD THINK THAT ON August 15, after more than two weeks of marching, the men in Cresap's rifle company would feel like hell warmed over as they leave Hadestown, near Hinchman's Tavern (near present-day Vernon, New Jersey). They have not rested since they left Lancaster, Pennsylvania, on August 7. Now six miles from the New York boundary line, the men reassemble with their gear in the morning to tread off again on yet another long day's march. The riflemen are keenly aware that they have about ten more days of this routine ahead of them before they reach their destination.

There is little doubt that the exceptional leadership of Captain Cresap keeps the morale of his men lifted. This is no small task, since his men must march a little less than the distance of a marathon each day. Today, if they travel the same distance that one other rifle company ahead of them has just covered, Cresap will march about twenty-two miles through Warwick and Chester, New York, following the general alignment of present-day Route 94.

On their first night in New York, the company camps near Brewster's Tavern[155] (present-day Blooming Grove), which presently serves as the government seat of Orange County, New York. Here, citizens of the town have held public meetings since 1765. During this time, churches and taverns serve as social centers for each community, and Brewster's Tavern is no exception. John Brewster, Jr., the innkeeper, proudly informs some of his customers that he is descended from an individual who came to America on the *Mayflower*.[156]

If Captain John Brewster is present when Cresap visits, the Maryland leader will certainly experience New England–style hospitality and undoubtedly hear the same story that John Adams notes in his journal around November 17, 1777 when Adams dined at the tavern: "Brewster's grandfather, as [Brewster] tells me, was a clergyman, and one of the first adventurers to Plymouth.[157] He died at ninety-five years of age, a minister of Long Island; left a son, who lived to be about eighty and died, leaving my landlord [tavern owner Brewster], a son who is now, I

---

155 Harrity, Journal of Captain William Hendricks, 27.

156 The riflemen would have been stricken with wonder had they been aware of the mysterious bones that lay concealed underneath the path upon which their footsteps fell. This landscape contained a large graveyard of mammoth-size fossilized Ice Age creatures. When individuals began to uncover these mysterious remains, no one knew initially what type of animals lay buried here. However, scientists soon identified these strange creatures as mastodons. In 1782, General George Washington, while encamped at nearby Newburgh, visited a farm near Brewster Tavern. The purpose of the general's visit was to inspect the startling discovery of the partial remains of a large fossilized animal found by a farmer in his field in 1780. While engaged in this endeavor, Washington became indebted to the farmer, who gave him a tooth from the skull of this curiosity. This tooth turned out to be the molar of a mastodon. In 1845, Nathaniel Brewster, a descendant of the family that owned the Brewster Tavern, found a complete, near-perfect skeleton of a mastodon on his farm in this region. Scientist named this specimen the Warren Mastodon, and it is presently on display at the New York Natural History Museum. Devine, Mastadons and Other Fossil Elephants.

157 Brewster's Tavern operated from about 1765 to 1799 and was visited often by George Washington when he passed through the area. John Brewster, Jr. (173?–1811) served as first lieutenant in Captain Tuthill's Regiment of Cornwall Militia during the American Revolution. Brewster's father, also named John Brewster (1702–1778), appears to be the one whom Adams quoted in his journal. Russel Headley, History of Orange County, New York (Middletown, NY: Van Deusen and Elms, 1908), 792; Roebling, 11–2; Brewster Family Genealogy Forum, Colonialamerica.com.

believe, between sixty and seventy. The manners of this family are exactly like those of the New England people, a decent grace [being conducted] before and after meat; fine pork and beef, and cabbage and turnip."[158]

On August 16, Cresap's company rouse themselves yet again for another day's march. They follow the present-day corridor of Route 94 to New Windsor, a settlement situated on the Hudson River, sometimes called the North River. The men are somewhat consoled by the fact that today's march to New Windsor is only about eleven miles, approximately half the distance they have ordinarily been covering in a day.

On the way to New Windsor, the men pass the Edmonston House near the location where five roads come together at the junction of Vail's Gate. This stone house, built in 1755, will serve as the future headquarters for Major General Horatio Gates and Major General Arthur St. Clair. Washington holds a fitting respect for St. Clair, who will accompany him during his famous crossing of the Delaware River in 1776. In 1782, during the last winter of the American Revolution, St. Clair will serve as part of General Washington's staff while the Continental army encamps at Newburgh, New York. Major General Gates has closer ties to the Maryland men who now march to Cambridge, for Gates is the man who corresponded with Michael's father, Thomas Cresap, during the organization of Michael Cresap's rifle company in June of 1775.[159]

Edmonston House, New Windsor, New York

Two of the major roads that intersect at Vails Gate are present-day Route 94 and the Old Forge Hill Road. Just south of this intersection that Cresap's company passes through stands the John Ellison House. This house, built in 1754, will serve as headquarters at various times during the war for Nathaniel Greene and Horatio Gates. Later on, during the winter of 1782–1783, the structure will serve as headquarters for Henry Knox, secretary of war, during the time when Washington's army is encamped with seven thousand soldiers and five hundred camp followers at nearby Newburgh, New York.

---

158 John Langdon Sibley, Biographical Sketches of Graduates of Harvard, vol. 1, 1642–1658 (Cambridge: Charles William Sever, 1873), 73.
159 Both the Edmonston House and Knox's headquarters still stand and are on the National Register of Historic Places. Workers constructed the Edmonston House about the same year Thomas Cresap built his two-story stone house at Oldtown, Maryland, known as Cresap's Fort. Edmonston House; Knox's Headquarters State Historic Site.

Cresap, as have the captains of most of the other rifle companies that preceded him, permits his men to rest at New Windsor after marching eleven miles from Brewster's tavern before they cross the "North or Hudson's River"[160] the next day. For the southern rifle companies, New Windsor is the halfway point to Cambridge. Cresap's men, "being weary marching in exceeding hot weather,"[161] like the men from other rifle companies that march before them will most likely take advantage of the welcome hospitality that they receive here from the townsfolk. At this friendly place, the men will take time to bathe, relax, and wash their linens.[162]

The towns along the way to Cambridge would have been overwhelmed had all the rifle companies appeared together at one time. The citizens of New Windsor have already hosted nine rifle companies. Cresap's company is in essence the sweep, the last of the original ten rifle companies selected on June 14 by the Continental Congress to pass through their town. More than one thousand men have already come and gone. With them in total were twenty-one wagons, each pulled by four horses, "which together with the horses the officers rode, [made] upward of a hundred"[163] animals that have passed through New Windsor from July 20 through July 26.[164]

It is not surprising that excitement stirs in the community as Cresap and his men enter the next gateway into this settlement on the road leading to Cambridge. The citizens organize and carry out plans to welcome and offer support to this group of long-awaited riflemen. On August 16, Captain Cresap finally appears, several weeks behind the last rifle company to have come through town.[165]

After a spell of relative quiet, the townsfolk receive Cresap's company with open arms. With their arrival, the town enters into another round of celebratory jubilation, cheering the men as they march to their encampment. Like the other companies before them, Cresap's 130 impassioned riflemen parade into town accompanied by the beating of drums and playing of fifes, their faces painted the Indian way, with some of the men howling an occasional Indian war whoop.

To the citizens, these riflemen appear invincible. They lift the hopes of all patriots who see them. Surely the men who march to join Washington's army, "all stout fellows [who] seem able to endure hardships,"[166] will overcome those British redcoats at Boston who have the audacity to trample on their liberties!

The warm, enthusiastic reception the riflemen receive in New Jersey and New York will become less warm and welcoming as they march farther northeastward. After arriving in the Boston area, one Pennsylvania rifleman records in a letter to a friend his thoughts concerning this matter: "We by no means experienced the same friendship and hospitality in Connecticut and Massachusetts which was shown to us in the Jerseys and N. York."[167]

The dampening enthusiasm of the crowds, a mood detected by this rifleman, might reflect the feelings of all the men. The cooler responses onlookers offer the rifle companies as they approach the more urban areas of the East Coast are possibly due to the men encountering a higher population of people more sympathetic to the Tory cause.

---

160 Harrity, Journal of Captain William Hendricks, 27.
161 Ibid.
162 Ibid.
163 Constitutional Gazette.
164 While Captain Cresap organized his men in Fredericktown in mid-July, other rifle companies had already departed for Cambridge. One astute observer recorded the dates of the following rifle companies as they arrived at New Windsor. On Thursday, July 20, Captains Smith, Loudon, and Nagel arrived with 330 men. On Saturday morning, July 22, Captain Morgan and his Virginia rifle company marched in, and on Sunday afternoon, July 23, came Captains Chambers, Miller, and Hendricks with 300 men. One day later, on Monday, July 24, Captain Price's Maryland company surfaced, and on Wednesday, July 26, Captain Stephenson's Virginia company made its appearance. *Constitutional Gazette, August 9, 1775.*
165 David Barclay, Old Houses and Historic Places in the Vicinity of Newburgh, NY (Newburgh: NY: Historical Society of Newburgh Bay and the Highlands, 1909), 198–9.
166 Young, "The Spirit of 1775: A Letter of Robert Magaw," 7.
167 Ibid.

It is about this time that stories that bend Cresap's ears begin to emerge. Some citizens in towns where Cresap stops entertain him by telling humorous Yankee yarns about some of the antics of his fellow comrades in arms. One story circulating in the taverns involves an Albany-bound sloop on the Hudson River. This single-masted sailing boat appeared on the river several weeks before, on the same day that the first three rifle companies arrived in town.

When the riflemen saw the sloop, the drummer boys beat their drums. This caught the attention of the men on the boat. After noticing that the riflemen had the liberty colors hoisted, the patriots in the sloop responded with three cheers that echoed over the Hudson River. The men from the three rifle companies followed again with the beating of their drums, playing their fifes and returning the favor with three more cheers. Then the riflemen and townsfolk yet again heard the reply of three boisterous cheers from the sloop. To conclude this memorable interaction, more than three hundred riflemen fired their pieces in the air as the craft sailed slowly away upriver, pushed along by a fine breeze. The men in the sloop drifted off to resume their part in the revolution.[168]

Another tale making the rounds of the taverns while Cresap is in town involves an imposter who tried to outsmart the town's ferry operator. This tale reveals an incident involving Captain Morgan's Virginia rifle company, which, before leaving town several weeks ago, conducted a "tarring and feathering frolic."[169]

The charlatan first stopped at William Edmonston's place and said that Captain Morgan was coming. Then the imposter went to William Ellison's home and falsely claimed that he was Captain Morgan. Unfortunately for the rascal, a rifleman who knew Captain Morgan was in town.[170] Almost immediately, authorities imprisoned the impersonator overnight. The next morning, Captain Morgan and the riflemen[171] "gave their pretended general a new fashion suit of tar and feathers" and then paraded him through town. After three cheers, the riflemen led the perpetrator back to the ferry landing. After dunking him in the Hudson River, Morgan "then sent [the impersonator] about his business."[172]

As the riflemen march and progress toward New England, noting the sharp increase in population along the way, they cannot help but compare this area to the much more sparsely populated region in which they were born and bred. To add one more novelty to their daily grind, the men note that people in this part of the country speak with a different accent, which is somewhat foreign to them.

On August 17, a drummer boy from Cresap's company beats the drum that reassembles the men to begin the second half of their journey. In the morning, the women of the community offer the same amenity given to all the other rifle companies that have previously passed through town, distributing freshly baked bread for the men to carry with them on their journey. The warm reception the riflemen received at New Windsor sends the men of Cresap's company off in high spirits.

---

168 Young, "The Spirit of 1775: A Letter of Robert Magaw," 7.
169 Charles Sealsfield, Life in the New World (New York: J. Winchester, 1844), 336.
170 Headley, History of Orange County, New York, 389.
171 Captain Morgan was a man of "powerful frame and stalwart courage." Most of men in Morgan's rifle company were of Irish descent. Across their hunting shirts were written "Liberty or Death." Ruttenber and Clark write, "Wonderful stories of the [riflemen] went to England. The written record of their service forms one of the brightest pages of American history." Edward Manning Ruttenber and Lewis H. Clark, History of Orange County, NY (Philadelphia: Everts and Peck, 1881), 228.
172 Edward Manning Ruttenber, History of the Town of New Windsor (Newburgh, NY: Historical Society of Newburgh Bay and the Highlands, 1911), 67. New Windsor was a community full of patriots and claimed as one of their own native-born Thomas Young, leader of the Boston Tea Party. During the revolution, not only would the Continental army use the site of New Windsor as a major military depot, but the army would also host a large medical department here. While Washington was encamped at Newburgh near New Windsor, on August 7, 1782, five years after Michael Cresap's company marched through the area, the general established the Badge of Military Merit, later known as the Purple Heart. Barclay, Old Houses and Historic Places in the Vicinity of Newburgh, NY, 199.

They cross over the Hudson River on a ferry, the river being nearly a mile wide at this point. As Cresap looks south down the river, he sees steep bluffs. In January 1778, on one of these precipices on the west side of the river, colonial soldiers will occupy for the first time a newly constructed fort known as West Point. The ferry transports Cresap's company across the Hudson River to the landing at Fishkill, on the east side of the Hudson River at present-day Beacon, New York, where they disembark.[173]

Fishkill, strategically located on the main Upper Road to Connecticut and surrounded by an area of seemingly inaccessible mountains, will soon grow into an important depot supporting the revolution. Here, provisions and munitions needed to supply Washington's army will be stored. In addition, hospitals and workshops will be an important part of this newly built military infrastructure.[174]

Both sides covet control of the Hudson River. If the British gain control of the waterway, they will divide the New England colonies from the southern colonies. Washington will do whatever he can to prevent this, and thus he constructs the fort at West Point, which not only protects the Hudson River but also helps him control the Upper Road corridor, the backdoor road that allows him to skirt around British forces.

Once West Point is constructed, the Upper Road becomes the primary inland military road over which to transport and store large amounts of supplies to and from the Fishkill area during the revolution. General Washington establishes this site as his main depot to stockpile military munitions and supplies as well as a location for repairing armor and manufacturing gunpowder. The Upper Road will gain even more importance once the British take control of New York City, about sixty-five miles south of New Windsor, in 1776. At this time the British will have command of the Hudson River south of West Point as well as the Lower Road, a coastal route that leads to New York City. The Lower Road will then become an unsafe passageway for the movement of Washington's men and supplies. For General Washington and his army, the strategic importance of West Point and the Upper Road becomes even more evident in 1780, when Benedict Arnold will attempt to betray Washington and surrender his command at West Point to the British.[175]

Like the colonial roads Thomas Cresap opened for colonists in Maryland, the Upper Road in New York follows an old Indian trail used originally by Wappinger Native Americans. The Upper Road is now the main east-west inland route connecting Fishkill and the Hudson River to Hartford, Connecticut.[176]

Now at Fishkill Landing, Cresap's company travels on Madam Brett's Road through her property, Brett's home being situated about one and a half miles east of the ferry landing. Madam Brett and her husband established a gristmill on lower Fishkill Creek in 1708 and built a home that same year. During a storm, Brett's husband drowned in the Hudson River while shipping supplies from New York to Fishkill Landing. Widowed at the age of thirty-one while raising three children, Madam Brett very successfully managed the business and property on her own. The section of toll-free road Madam Brett laid out through her property is now part of present-day Route 52.[177]

---

173 Ruttenber, History of the Town of New Windsor, 32–4; Ruttenber and Clark, History of Orange County, NY, 110–1, 218.
174 Donna P. Hearn, "Brief Overview of the Town of Dover's History," Town of Dover, New York, January 30, 2014, http://townofdoverny.us/Town_History.cfm 2014.
175 Piers Mackesy, The War for America: 1775–1783 (Cambridge, MA: Harvard University Press, 1964), 98.
176 Mackesy, The War for America: 1775–1783.
177 *Madam Brett died in 1764, her house later becoming the residence of her granddaughter and her granddaughter's husband, Major Henry Schenck. During the American Revolution, their family home will serve as a storage facility. Historians will later write that notable personalities, such as General Washington, Marquis de La Fayette, and Baron Von Steuben, visited the building.* The Madam Brett Homestead is the oldest building still standing in Dutchess County, New York, and is on the National Register of Historic Places (Madam Brett Homestead, Beacon, NY).

Madam Brett Homestead, Beacon, New York

From Fishkill Landing, Cresap travels northeastward on the Upper Road through Fishkill, East Fishkill, Hopewell, and Beekman, where Colonel James Vanderburgh lives. What Colonel Cresap, Michael's father, is to Frederick County, Maryland, Colonel Vanderburgh is to Dutchess County, New York. Both are colonels in their county militias, and individually, each is among the most influential and respected men of his region.[178]

Fishkill Landing, Beacon, New York

---
178   Frank Hasbrouk, History of Dutchess County, NY (Poughkeepsie, NY: S. A. Matthieu, 1909), 180–5.

Colonel Vanderburgh lives in a substantial mansion built of stone and wood, located about a quarter mile from Poughquag. During the revolution, he will command the Fifth Regiment Dutchess County Militia. General George Washington will dine at Vanderburgh's home several times while his army camps nearby in the highlands. Colonel Vanderburgh will also entertain Major General Marquis de Lafayette in his home. While dining there, the colonel will likely amuse his distinguished guests with colorful stories about how his wife saved the day when Tories try to kill him in his own home. Over glasses of wine, his guests will all likely chuckle when they hear how the colonel's loyal spouse frustrated the Tories' evil plot by barricading the mansion so effectively that they gave up in despair and ran off. Colonel Vanderburgh likely greets each of the rifle companies, including Captain Cresap's, as it passes near his house.[179]

Not far past Beekman on the Upper Road is the Morehouse Tavern. Exhausted after a twenty-seven-mile march on August 17, Cresap's men set up camp near this tavern (present-day Wingdale, Dutchess County, New York).[180] Foreign dignitaries like Rochambeau, traveling in the colonies during the revolutionary period, will later stay at Morehouse's Tavern.[181]

Taverns exist to serve the local community. In Captain Cresap's world, taverns are the heart and soul of a community, where people can feel the town's pulse. Taverns function much like modern-day office buildings, banks, or post offices. At taverns, people buy land, sell lumber, quarry stone, form new companies, induct men into militias, conduct auctions, get on and off stagecoaches, and send and collect their mail. It is from the bustling interiors of these edifices that most of a town's business takes place. As a rule, the most prominent citizens operate taverns, including those individuals who hold high public status within their communities and serve as politicians, church deacons, or militia leaders.

A French general traveling with Rochambeau notes in his journal, referring to Colonel Morehouse, "Nothing is more common in America than to see an innkeeper a colonel. They are in general militia colonels chosen by the militias themselves, who seldom fail to entrust the command to most esteemed and creditable citizens."[182] These perceptive comments could easily apply to Captain Michael Cresap's father, Colonel Thomas Cresap, well-known for taking in travelers at Cresap's Fort in Oldtown, Maryland.[183]

---

179 J. H. Beers, Commemorative Biographical Record of Dutchess County, New York (Chicago: J. H. Beers and Co., 1897), 424; Philip H. Smith, History of Dover, New York: General History of Dutchess County, 1609–1876 (Pawlings, NY: published by the author, 1877), 140-1. The people of Beekman razed the mansion of Colonel James Vanderburgh (1729–1794) around 1860. The family graveyard with the colonel's tombstone still stands near where the mansion stood in Beekman.

180 Harrity, Journal of Captain William Hendricks, 28.

181 Smith, History of Dover, New York, 160-4. Several years later, Benedict Arnold had his last friendly conversation with George Washington at the Morehouse Tavern. As the Revolutionary War progressed, many officers of the Continental army were entertained and stayed at the Morehouse Tavern. In addition to Rochambeau, Washington, and Arnold, guests included Gates, Putnam, Heath, Parsons, and Lafayette. Hasbrouk, History of Dutchess County, NY, 180-5, 289.

182 Smith, History of Dover, New York, 161.

183 Cresap's company followed the Upper Road along the general road alignment from Fishkill Landing at present-day Beacon, New York, to the Morehouse Tavern at present-day Wingdale, New York. From Fishkill, the route Cresap took on the Upper Road generally followed Route 52 to Route 82 at Brinkerhoff. From here, the route followed Route 82 toward Hopewell Junction. After passing through Hopewell Junction, the riflemen marched along present Beekman Road to Poughquag. At Poughquag Cresap's riflemen then followed Clove Valley Road. Here, at a junction, they took a turn eastward on present-day Wingdale Road (Route 21) straight on to Pleasant Ridge Road and to the existing town of Wingdale. The Morehouse Tavern was located at the present-day intersection of Route 22 and Route 55 across the road from the present-day Wingdale town library. The riflemen's entire passage through New York, from the New Jersey line to the Connecticut border, was about sixty-one miles, a distance Cresap's company covered in three days. Mackesy, The War for America: 1775–1783, 97–8.

The riflemen who arrive in the Boston area before Cresap, many of them veterans of Indian warfare, quickly realize that this is going to be a different kind of fight requiring a new set of tactics and strategies. The men find themselves occasionally dodging solid iron cannonballs the British throw at them, the heavy round projectiles always accompanied by the shout of cannon thunder. To keep the colonists on edge, the British mix up the ammunition hurled from the cannon. At the beginning, the balls, bombs, and grenade shells sometimes flung by the British from cannons on flotillas are strange and shocking to the riflemen. At other times the British fill the canisters with grapeshot, which simulates a superpowered shotgun blast.[184]

Cannonballs generally range from three to twelve pounds in weight. It can be supposed that the most terrifying moment for a colonial soldier is the instant he sees an oncoming cannonball traveling in his direction about three feet above the ground at nine hundred feet per second. The continuous artillery cannot only cause great physical harm but can also wreak havoc on the nerves.[185]

At four hundred feet, the cannonball starts bouncing on the ground and continues to bounce and roll for another four hundred feet. Until the force of the cannonball's momentum has run its course, it will seriously injure —or worse —kill anyone in its path. Injuries may include loss of limbs and blood, along with broken bones.[186]

Cannons are so named by the weight of the ammunition they fire. For example, a six-pounder cannon fires a six-pound cannonball. The cannon is not very accurate at 1,200 yards, hitting its target on average once out of every five times. However, when shot at 520 yards, cannon fire is often very accurate. Over several weeks at Roxbury, the riflemen endure a continual barrage of cannonballs launched in their direction. Fortunately, the British fire the cannonballs from a great distance, causing damage to buildings but little loss of life to the soldiers. By the end of summer, the riflemen will develop a war-hardened, callous disregard for these iron balls that bounce around them day after day.[187]

On August 4, long before Cresap's company arrived in town, Washington, in order to conserve precious ammunition, issued a stern directive, possibly to enforce discipline among the first couple of rifle companies to have arrived from Pennsylvania. Washington told them not to be overambitious and waste gunpowder by taking futile shots. Washington wanted the ammunition saved for the British attack expected to come any day.

The truth is that the arrival of the rifle companies gives George Washington a much-needed psychological edge over the British. By late August 1775, with the arrival of Captain Cresap's company, about six percent of Washington's army will consist of these elite forces of riflemen. Yes, the British have their cannons, but Washington will have his riflemen when all the southern companies finally arrive at the front. More than a thousand sharpshooters will be on hand by the end of August. Never before have this many expert riflemen been assembled in one place at one time.

Not having before seen the likes of these riflemen, who can accurately shoot any object larger than an orange at a distance of more than two hundred yards, witnesses of their shooting abilities are astounded. Richard Henry Lee, one of George Washington's generals, observes these men in action firsthand. Under the criteria mentioned above, Lee asserts, "Every shot is fatal."[188]

Lee praises the "spirit of frontiersmen" with their "amazing hardihood," stating that these men "for their number make the most formidable light Infantry in the world." These veterans of war are extremely self-sufficient. These mighty hunters have a proven record of accomplishment illustrated by their ability "of living so long in the

---
184 Balch, Papers Relating Chiefly to the Maryland Line during the Revolution, 13.
185 Allen C. Guelzo, The American Revolution (Chantilly, VA: The Teaching Company, 2008).
186 Ibid.
187 Ibid.; James Thacher, Military Journal During the American Revolutionary War (Boston: Richardson and Lord, 1823), 37.
188 Richard Henry Lee, The Letters of Richard Henry Lee, vol. 1, 1762-1778 (New York: Macmillan, 1911), 130.

woods without carrying provisions…[their] exceeding quickness with which they can march to distant parts, and above all, the dexterity…in [their] use of the rifle gun."[189]

The riflemen bask in the respect they receive from members of the Continental army. A Pennsylvania rifleman notes this in a letter to a friend: "You will think me Vain should I tell you how much the Riffle men are esteemed [in] their Dress, their Size [,] their Strength [,] and activities [,] but Above all [,] their Great eagerness to [Attack] the Enemy entitle them to the first Rank [.] The hunting Shirt is like a full suit at St. James [.] A Riffle man in his Dress may pass [Sentinels] and go Almost where He pleases while officers of the other Regiments are [stopped]. Since we [came] here, the Enemy Dare not show their heads."[190]

Instead of attacking Washington's army, to avoid their heads being served as targets for the riflemen, the redcoats keep their heads down, under cover. At this crucial time when Washington is low on ammunition, the riflemen seem to act as a deterrent, discouraging a full-scale British attack on Washington's army, when it is most vulnerable. The British put off a major confrontation for another day, but every man on the front is most certain that the showdown will come soon.[191]

---

189 Ibid., 129–30.
190 Young, The Spirit of 1775: A Letter of Robert Magaw," 7.
191 Douglas Southall Freeman, Planter and Patriot, vol. 3 of George Washington: A Biography (New York: Scribner, 1951), 431–435, 522–526.

CHAPTER 7

Strangers to Fear

August 18, 1775, to August 20, 1775
Western Connecticut

ONCE THEY ARE IN Connecticut, it appears that Cresap's Rifles pick up the pace as they near Cambridge. Following an old Indian trail that is now a colonial road, they will travel about twenty-five miles today. From the Morehouse Tavern at Wingdale, Cresap's company resumes its march, traveling along present-day Route 55. About two miles northeast of the Morehouse Tavern, Cresap's company approaches Ten Mile River. Here they veer right, walking along the river's south bank until they come to present-day Dog Tail Corners Road. They follow this road to the New York-Connecticut boundary into western Connecticut. From here, they continue, following Bull's Bridge Road then cross the Housatonic River by way of Bull's Bridge.[192]

Bull's Bridge, South Kent, Connecticut

---

[192] During the revolution, Washington crossed over Bull's Bridge at least three times. A little less than six years from Cresap's march, on March 3, 1781, General Washington recorded in his journal a somewhat harrowing experience that occurred during one of these crossings. Local legend stated that a horse in Washington's party slipped on a loose plank while being walked across the bridge and fell into the river. At this time Washington was traveling to meet French officials to discuss important matters that involved their helping the American war effort by using their naval support against the British who occupied New York. In such an unfortunate situation, the army would ordinarily leave a poor stranded horse behind. However, that would not be the case in this incident. The fact that the army took the time to rescue the animal lends credence to the legend that the horse might have been one of Washington's personal favorites. The fallen horse possibly bore the name Nelson, a sorrel the general preferred to ride in battle because the animal was less skittish during cannon fire and other sounds of battle. Or perhaps this frightened horse was Blue Skin, a whitish-colored horse that Washington liked to ride in parades. The general's entry in his journal following this incident revealed his willingness to expend an inordinately large sum to rescue this highly prized animal: "Getting a Horse out of Bull's Bridge Falls, $215.00." George Washington's Dates and Places, March 29, 2014, https://sites.google.com/site/gwdatesplaces/dates.

After they cross Bull's Bridge,[193] the lay of the land requires Cresap's men to again cross the Housatonic River, this time fording the river at the location of Bull's Iron Works. The orientation of the Berkshire Mountains, which lie immediately to the east, temporarily forces Cresap for the first time on this journey to veer southeast instead of the preferred northeast direction. This road now leads Cresap from Bull's Bridge through New Milford to their destination at Baker's Tavern,[194] near Roxbury, Connecticut.

The riflemen parallel the Housatonic River downstream on the Upper Road for about eight miles from Bull's Bridge until they reach New Milford, the first town they come upon in Connecticut. The town is situated along the Housatonic River. Pioneers first settled here around 1707. New Milford now has about 2,776 inhabitants, of whom 285 men will fight in the revolution.

At New Milford, Cresap's company passes by an ancient oak tree. After the Revolutionary War, local citizens will call this tree the Washington Oak. During the war, according to local lore, Washington, on one of his trips through New Preston, will conduct a staff meeting under the welcome shade of this oak. On another occasion, while traveling between Hartford and New York, Washington will again find himself under this tree. This time Washington, joining officials in the shade under a canopy of long-reaching limbs, will discuss with Marquis de Lafayette the need to increase French support for the revolutionary cause.[195]

At the center of New Milford, Cresap passes a store at the town square established in 1750 by former town resident Roger Sherman, a future signer of both the Declaration of Independence and the US Constitution. Sherman, who lived in New Milford from 1742 to 1761 before moving to New Haven, Connecticut, mirrors some of the same accomplishments as Michael's father, Thomas Cresap. Both men established the first stores in their communities, were leading surveyors of their areas, and were entrusted by their respective communities with important community business that required much of their personal time and attention.[196]

From New Milford, Cresap continues southeast, passing over Second Hill where, because of its commanding view, Connecticut militia stand watch to detect enemy movements. Cresap trudges on until he crosses the Shepaug River. On August 18, after marching twenty-five miles, Cresap comes to Baker's Tavern,[197] wherein he stays while his men camp on the nearby fields, marked by a lone, white oak tree that grows near Roxbury. From this point, Cresap's route to Cambridge will take him north toward present-day Washington, Connecticut. .[198]

---

193 A little more than two years after Cresap's journey, around late October 1777, after a colonial victory at the battle of Saratoga, the Continental army transported in its custody British officers of General John Burgoyne's army along with the redcoats' family members across Bull's Bridge en route to Fishkill Landing.

194 Harrity, Journal of Captain William Hendricks, 28.

195 Joe Hurley, "New Milford Loses Historic Oak," Danbury News-Times, April 4, 2003. http://www.gaylordsville.org/DNT_APR16_TREE.html.

196 Lewis Henry Boutell, The Life of Roger Sherman (Chicago: A. C. McClurg and Company, 1896).

197 Remember Baker (1737–1775), born at present-day Roxbury, Connecticut, He was a first cousin to Ethan Allen and was likely related to the Bakers, where Cresap camped. Another first cousin to Remember Baker was Seth Warner (1743–1784), who also was born at present-day Roxbury. Baker and Warner were members of Ethan Allan's Green Mountain Boys. Both cousins participated in the French and Indian War, and in 1775, serving under Ethan Allen, they took part in the capture of Fort Ticonderoga. After the mid-1760s, Baker and Warner lived in present-day Vermont. On August 22, only days after Cresap camped at Baker's birthplace, Indians killed Remember while Baker was scouting on a military endeavor in Quebec. Richard B. Warner, "A Band of Cousins," Connecticut Society of the Sons of the American Revolution, March 24, 2014, https://www.connecticutsar.org/patriots/cousins.htm; Connecticut American Revolution, "Ethan Allen: The Green Mountain Boys and the Arsenal of the Revolution," March 24, 2014, *http://www.ctamericanrevolution.com/maps/1_Ethan_Allen_January_2013.pdf.*

198 On August 18, while Cresap's Rifles camp in the fields near Baker's Tavern, all six of the original Pennsylvania rifle companies authorized on June 14 by the Continental Congress arrived at Cambridge. Three additional Pennsylvania rifle companies, which Congress authorized after June 14, also arrived. The nine Pennsylvania rifle companies were under the command of Colonel William Thompson's Battalion of Riflemen from Pennsylvania, who reported to Cambridge headquarters on August 17 Thomas Lynch Montgomery, Colonel William Thompson's Battalion of Riflemen, in Pennsylvania Archives, vol. 2 (Harrisburg, PA: Harrisburg Publishing Company, 1906), 6.

Once he crosses the Shepaug River to Roxbury, Cresap marches from New Milford along the general alignment of present-day Route 67. After his first night spent at Baker's Tavern, Cresap shepherds his men northward along the alignment of present-day Route 199 toward present-day Washington, Connecticut.[199]

On August 19, Cresap continues on a steady course, leading his riflemen to present-day Washington, Connecticut. An estimated 270 families now live in this area, first settled in 1734. Industry here consists of farms, small mills, ironworks, quarries, and factories powered by the Aspetuck and Shepaug Rivers. In 1779, citizens will name part of this community Washington, in honor of General Washington, who will pass through this area several times during the revolution.

If time permits, Cresap will certainly stop to rest and see what news stirs at Major William Cogswell's Tavern. Established in the early 1760s, Cogswell's Tavern is located along the Old Litchfield Turnpike. The Cogswells have been in the community for a long time. In 1746, Cogswell's father secured permission to mine ore in New Milford. On May 25, 1781, General Washington will stop in at Squire Cogswell's Tavern on his way to visit Rochambeau at New Windsor. Cogswell—a citizen-soldier and politician of outstanding character and importance, much like the Cresap family in Oldtown, Maryland—has been awarded a license to operate a tavern because he is so highly regarded in his community. Furthermore, to add to his credentials, Cogswell is destined to become the first elected town official of Washington, Connecticut.[200]

Cogswell's Tavern, Washington, Connecticut

Cresap's company may pause in the area of Cogswell's Tavern in New Preston near the shore of Lake Waramaug, the second-largest natural body of water in Connecticut. Here, Cresap's men will likely refresh themselves, perhaps bathing in the lake before they continue the arduous journey still ahead. Cresap then marches about ten more miles to the northeast until he reaches Litchfield, where he may stop again for a short rest before continuing ahead.[201]

---
199 The general alignment that Cresap followed from Washington to Litchfield was present-day scenic Route 47 and Route 202.
200 Connecticut Society of the Sons of the American Revolution. "Governor Oliver Wolcott Branch #10." March 25, 2014. http://www.connecticutsar.org/branches/wolcott.htm.
201 "Cogswell Tavern," RevolutionaryCT.com, March 25, 2014, http://www.revolutionaryct.com/cogswell-tavern-private-residence/.

The captain's course has led him through Fishkill, New York, and now Litchfield, Connecticut, towns where General Washington will locate his priceless storehouses of ammunition and powder, the arsenals of the revolution.[202]

First settled around 1720, Litchfield is a bustling little New England town situated among the Litchfield Hills, about eleven hundred feet above sea level. Like Oldtown, Maryland, Litchfield originally served as an outpost and trading center for the new frontier. Community leaders raised a regiment, inducting soldiers from here and from nearby communities during the French and Indian War. Litchfield also sent regiments to Bunker Hill as reinforcements.

Because of Litchfield's strategic inland location with extensive agriculture production, the town will become increasingly important after the capture of New York by the British in 1776. The Upper Road, upon which Cresap's men tread through Litchfield, will become, from 1776 to 1780, "the principal military artery to Boston… and a depot for military stores and provisions."[203]

Cresap most likely visits Sheldon's Tavern in Litchfield, a fifteen-year-old business establishment built for the owner, Elisha Sheldon. His sixteen-year-old son, Samuel Sheldon, runs the tavern in 1775, as his father now serves under General Washington as a colonel over a cavalry unit known as Colonel Sheldon's Dragoons.[204]

Sheldon's Tavern, Litchfield, Connecticut

---

202 Here at Litchfield, Cresap entered another Connecticut town where lived one more "strong pillar of the American Cause" and future signer of the Declaration of Independence, Oliver Wolcott. He, too, hosted George Washington in his home. Oliver Wolcott likely was not in town when Cresap's company arrived, as it is more probable that Wolcott was in Cambridge serving under Washington. By early 1777, Washington had commissioned Wolcott as brigadier general, commanding fourteen regiments. Wolcott's wife and several of their sons and daughters, along with other Litchfield women, later greatly helped the revolutionary cause when they manufactured 42,088 bullets from a four-thousand-pound statue of King George III. Well-intentioned rebels rudely knocked the leaden sculpture of the British monarch from its pedestal and transported it to Litchfield. Those Litchfield women in Wolcott's backyard surely understood and enjoyed the irony of making the much-needed lead for Washington's army from the image of King George. Charles A. Goodrich, Lives of the Signers to the Declaration of Independence (Hartford, CT: R. G. H. Huntington, 1841), 179–82.

203 Workers of the Federal Writers Project, American Guide Series: Connecticut: A Guide to Its Roads, Lore, and People (Boston: Houghton Mifflin Company, 1938), 193–6.

204 Historic Buildings of Connecticut, "Sheldon's Tavern (1760)," July 8, 2008. March 31, 2014. http://historicbuildingsct.com/?p=859. Tradition has it that George Washington later stayed overnight in the northeast bedroom of Sheldon's Tavern on May 24, 1781, while passing through town.

Five years from now, in 1780, Washington's spies will uncover an attempt by the traitor Benedict Arnold to surrender to the British army the fort Arnold commands at West Point. During this appalling discovery, Washington's men will detect papers containing valuable intelligence information found on the person of British spy John Andre. Washington's officers will intercept these documents, which will expose Arnold's treacherous intentions to undermine Washington's war effort, before the papers can fall into the hands of British officers. These documents will also reveal that Sheldon's Cavalry is one of the colonial units guarding West Point.[205]

Born in 1741, Colonel Elisha Sheldon is just one year older than Captain Cresap. Colonel Sheldon cuts a figure at Litchfield much like Colonel Thomas Cresap does at Oldtown. Both men prominently command the business, social, military, and political pursuits within their communities, their establishments being where most of the towns' activities occur. Both know George Washington, and both have hosted the eminent Virginian as an overnight guest in their homes on several occasions.[206]

In a tavern such as this, Cresap can catch up on any news that has trickled in. Here, Cresap likely hears the latest Tory tale, one that occurred just three weeks before on August 3, involving Captain Price's Maryland company. Captain Cresap's ears perk up, for he personally knows well several of the men in Price's rifle company, including Otho Holland Williams,[207] who is a close family friend.

Captain Cresap learns that it was here at Litchfield that Captain Price's company caught up with Captain Hendricks's Pennsylvania rifle company. In Price's custody, was a Tory "ministerial tool,"[208] whom the captain had caught near New Milford. The Captain compelled the Tory to walk with his company, forcing him to carry his own geese the more than eighteen miles to Litchfield. Captain Hendricks records in his journal that the men of Captain Price's company then "tarr'd and feathered the Tory at Litchfield," making the man pluck his own goose, after which the riflemen "bestowed the feathers upon him." The Maryland rifle company then "drummed [the Tory] out of town" but not before making him "kneel down, confess acknowledgments" of his shortcomings, and thank the [riflemen] for their leniency."[209]

In most of the larger townships where riflemen stop, citizens respond with rousing and enthusiastic greetings. Wherever they go, crowds are fascinated and drawn like magnets to these charismatic, rustic-looking "buckskin buccaneers."[210]

---

205 H. B. Whitney, "History of the Town of Sheldon," Rootsweb, 2004, March 24, 2014, http://www.rootsweb.ancestry.com/~vermont/FranklinSheldon.html.

206 Litchfield was also the birthplace of Ethan Allen (1738–1789), Revolutionary War hero best known for his capture of Fort Ticonderoga, his leadership of the Green Mountain Boys, and his legend as a pioneering settler of present-day Vermont. The much-needed cannons and armaments that Ethan Allen seized from the fort later helped Washington break the siege at Boston. The British captured Ethan Allen and took him as prisoner in September 1775, during the Colonial army's invasion of Quebec. The British released Allen in a prisoner exchange in May 1778. It was the aforementioned Colonel Elias Sheldon of the Light Horse Cavalry who escorted the newly freed Allen from New York to General Washington's headquarters at Valley Forge, Pennsylvania. Whitney, "History of the Town of Sheldon,"; Connecticut American Revolution, "Ethan Allen: The Green Mountain Boys and the Arsenal of the Revolution. (The Upper Road in the Bull's Bridge region is mapped in this source.)

207 In 1776, Captain Cresap's friend, Otho Holland Williams, found himself imprisoned in a four-foot-by-four-foot cell with Ethan Allen after Williams was captured by the British following the Battle of Fort Washington in New York. Because of his rank as an officer, Williams at first had permission from British command to roam free on parole in New York City. This privilege did not last long after Williams's reply to an impertinent British officer, who asked what the prisoner's vocation was before the war. Williams responded that he was "bred in that situation which taught him to rebuke and punish insolence, and [the British officer] would have ample proof of his apprenticeship on a repetition of [the questioner's] offense." Not long after that comment, Williams found himself locked up in a sixteen-square-foot cell with Allen. One would think that Captain Cresap, known more as man of action than of words, would certainly have responded to the British officer in the same succinct manner as his friend Williams, had he found himself in similar circumstances. Osmond Tiffany, A Sketch of the Life of and Services of Otho Holland Williams (Baltimore: John Murphy and Co., 1851).

208 Harrity, Journal of Captain William Hendricks, 28.

209 J. W. Lewis, History of Litchfield County, Connecticut (Philadelphia: J. W. Lewis and Company, 1881), 451.

210 George W. Bruns and Thomas W. Blackburn, "The Ballad of Davy Crockett," 1954.

The wives and children of Litchfield likely witness and participate in the excitement of the colorful arrival of Cresap's company to their town. After all, the Litchfield natives know that these frontiersmen have come the longest distance from a faraway world to lend their help alongside their community's militia, who are also fighting the cause.

The riflemen also note "the unfair number of fine ladies"[211] in this region, to them their beauty "exceeding every part of America." One traveler who recently passed through the region notes that he had never before seen in "such a small collection of women so many beauties."[212] Captain Cresap wisely keeps his company moving through settlements like Litchfield, perhaps to help keep order among his young men, who are in the prime of life. The riflemen would certainly, if they could, "find themselves strongly disposed to stay here a few days for the pleasure" [213] of conversing with these women.

In New England, as the company approaches closer and closer to Cambridge, the soldiers take notice of the absence of men. In fact, most of the able-bodied men are now with General Washington's army participating in the siege line around Boston.

America's first law school, the Tapping Reeve Law School, just opened at Litchfield in 1775. Aaron Burr, Tapping Reeve's brother-in-law, is the school's first student. However, the Battle of Lexington interrupted Burr's law education. When Cresap arrives in Litchfield,[214] Burr is no longer in town, as he, like many of the men of this community, has joined General Washington's army at Cambridge, leaving families and many single women behind.[215]

Cresap's company continues its march away from Litchfield. The men travel along a twenty-year-old stagecoach line that connects Litchfield to Hartford, Connecticut. From Litchfield, the road-weary riflemen continue east on present-day Route 118 to Route 4 at Harwinton - a modest hamlet that lies just downhill from Litchfield. On August 19, after traveling about twenty-nine miles,[216] the riflemen camp their second night in Connecticut at Harwinton, first settled in 1731. The settlement takes its name from the combination of the words *Hartford*, *Windsor*, and *town*.[217]

On August 20, their third day in Connecticut, they launch the journey anew. This time, the riflemen will travel from Harwinton to Hartford, a distance of about twenty-two miles along a well-worn stagecoach road established before 1755.[218]

---

211 Balch, Papers Relating Chiefly to the Maryland Line during the Revolution, 11.

212 Ibid.

213 Ibid.

214 Litchfield became an important armory depot for military stores and provisions, which supported General Washington as the Revolutionary War progressed. One historian writes that "night and day" during the war, Litchfield was a bustling village, resounding "with the creak of loaded carts, the pounding of hammers, and the tramping of marching feet." Workers of the Federal Writers Project, American Guide Series: Connecticut, 194.

215 American History from Revolution to Reconstruction and Beyond, "Aaron Burr Jr. (1756–1836)," accessed November 21, 2017, http://www.let.rug.nl/usa/biographies/aaron-burr-jr/.

216 Harrity, Journal of Captain William Hendricks, 28.

217 On September 20, 1780, Washington and his entourage passed through Harwinton. Before he continued on his way, the general stopped for refreshments at the home of Abijah and Hanna Cook Catlin. Hannah was the granddaughter of Captain Joseph Wadsworth, a man who gained fame in 1687 when he hid a document sacred to the province in the hollow of an oak tree growing in Hartford, Connecticut. This document, the Connecticut Charter, served to elevate the status of the tree, which later became known as the Charter Oak. The Catlin House was located in Harwinton at the present intersection of Burlington Road (Route 4) and Harmony Hill Road. Claghorn, Charles Eugene III, "Washington's Travels in New England: A Chronological Itinerary," Florida Society, Sons of the American Revolution, last revised August 4, 2003, accessed November 21, 2017, http://archive.today/wOpmB.

218 Harwinton Historical Society, "The Stage Coach Ride from Hartford to Litchfield," March 25, 2014. http://www.harwintonhistory.com/Stagecoachroad.html.

Once the road dips into the valley, it parallels Farmington Creek, where the trail leads the men to Farmington, a community replete with patriots who gained military experience during the French and Indian War (1754–1763). Thomas Cresap and three of his sons—Daniel, Thomas, Jr., and a young Michael Cresap—also participated in the French and Indian War.

Since the Boston Tea Party in 1773, feelings of patriotism have run strong in Farmington. Upon hearing of the exchange of gunfire at Lexington and Concord, in support of the revolution, the town responded by sending soldiers, including two Indians from the Tunxis tribe and fourteen African Americans, along with an array of much-needed supplies to the siege line in Boston.[219]

On this August day, Cresap and his men travel on present-day Route 4, an old Indian trail converted into a colonial road. Cresap and his men continue onward through the West Woods, at present-day Burlington, Connecticut. Many Tories who live in this region call this area West Britain. During the revolution, many Tories will hide from patriots in a natural cave just southwest of the area.[220]

Farmington is a "village of pretty houses,"[221] as later described by George Washington, who will pass through here several times during the revolution. First settled in 1640, Farmington now contains the tenth-largest population in the colonies.

An observant rifleman who marches to Cambridge with a different company notes in his journal that there are but a few Tunxis Indians still residing in Farmington. By 1775, most of the Tunxis Indians have left Farmington for good to join a tribe at Stockbridge, Massachusetts, while others have joined a tribe at Oneida, New York. Those few friendly Tunxis Indians who have chosen to remain behind have integrated and blended into the Farmington community, where they attend the town's churches and schools. Some Tunxis living in Farmington have become teachers and ministers.

Presently, it is Cresap's turn to take command of this well-trampled high road. As he pilots his men eastward from Farmington making headway toward Boston, Cresap's company passes by the 120-year-old Elm Street Inn, owned by Phinehas Lewis.[222] Painted on one side of the Elm Tree Inn tavern sign is a house; on the reverse side is the image of a scantily clad "goddess, armed with a helmet, spear, and shield, in apparel better befitting the heat of summer than the blasts of winter."[223]

---

[219] Sam Houston State University, "Black Americans in Defense of Our Country," 1985, March 26, 2014, http://www.shsu.edu/~his_ncp/AfrAmer.html. The Mohican Stockbridge Indians and the Oneidas were the only two Native American tribes to fight with the colonists against the British, participating in the Siege of Boston, the Battle of Saratoga, and the Battle of Monmouth. Captain William Hendricks, leader of a rifle company from Carlisle, Pennsylvania, wrote the following in his journal: "Marched through Farmington to Tunis." It is probable that Hendricks misspelled "Tunxis" as there are no records of the existence of "Tunis," Connecticut. During the length of the American Revolution, five thousand of the three hundred thousand men who served in the Continental army were black soldiers. African Americans participated in most of the major battles of the revolution, eliciting honor and praise from their military leaders. Harrity, Journal of Captain William Hendricks, 28; Sam Houston State University, "Black Americans in Defense of our Country"; Lion G. Miles, "The Mohicans of Stockbridge," BerkShares, Inc., March 4, 2014, http://berkshares.org/heroes/mohican.

[220] Burlington Historical Society, "A Brief History of Burlington, Connecticut," March 28, 2014, http://www.burlington-history.org/historyof.html. After the Revolutionary War, as partial compensation for his service as a spy for General Washington, the Connecticut Revolutionary Government awarded Captain Benjamin Tallmadge a tract of land in the Burlington, Connecticut, area, land that had been confiscated from a well-known local Tory. Officials named a section of the road George Washington Turnpike (present-day Route 4 between Burlington and Farmington) in remembrance of the three times General Washington traveled through this area.

[221] James Galvin, "Washington Rides Through, Farmington Historical Society, March 29, 2017, http://fhs-ct.org/1781/01/10/the-village-of-pretty-houses-2/.

[222] On one of his several visits through Farmington, Washington traveled westward, traversing from Farmington to Litchfield on the High Road, the inland road also known as the Upper Road in western New York. While in front of the Elm Tree Inn, Washington overheard a young boy say, "Why, he's nothing but a man." Washington is said to have replied, "That's right, my lad, I am nothing but a man." Brooke E. Martin, "History of Farmington, Parts 1–3." Farmington Historical Society, March 24, 2014, http://www.farmingtonhistoricalsociety-ct.org/fh_histsources.html.

[223] Arthur M. Brandegee and Eddy H. Smith, Farmington, Connecticut: The Village of Beautiful Homes (Farmington, CT: Arthur M. Brandegee and Eddy H. Smith, 1906), 199.

Elm Tree Inn, Farmington, Connecticut

In his haste to move as quickly as he can, Cresap marches onward ten miles through Farmington and on to Hartford.[224] Since August 7, nine companies of riflemen from Virginia, Maryland, and Pennsylvania have passed through Hartford on their way to Washington's headquarters in Cambridge. A recent Hartford newspaper account describes the riflemen as "an exceeding fine body of soldiers…determined to defend their rights and privileges in conjunction with their Brethren of the Northern Colonies against those who attempt to barbarously… deprive us of them." In addition to these increasingly justified fears and open threats from foreigners, the citizens of Connecticut are deeply concerned that the British are actively trying to recruit "savage" Indian tribes to "take up the axe against the colonies."[225] The sight of the rifle companies encourages the citizenry that there is hope of prevailing against these evil British tyrants.[226]

On Saturday, August 5, Colonel Thompson of the Pennsylvania Regiment of Riflemen, having marched from Philadelphia, arrived in Hartford. After a pleasant one-day respite there on Sunday- where Thompson rested himself and his men - on Monday, August 7, Thompson's regiment began to proceed onward to Cambridge. Traveling with Thompson were "a number of fine gentlemen volunteers," including a friend of Captain Cresap from Philadelphia by the name of Jesse Lukens.

The colony of Connecticut has thus far raised three companies of recruits who have marched through Hartford to join the "forces of the United Colonies." A regiment of "respectable senior men near 60," just sixteen miles south of Hartford in Middletown, Connecticut, [has] just "formed themselves into a company for attaining the military art." What is even more remarkable, "their drummer is upward to 80 years of age and as much engaged and alert as any young man." These aged men mirror the character of Captain Cresap's father, Colonel Thomas Cresap. Like

---

224 Through western Connecticut, Cresap's Rifles traveled on the following general road alignment: from Bull's Bridge to New Milford on Route 7, from New Milford to the north of Roxbury on Route 67, to Baker Road to Route 199, from Route 199 to Route 47 just south of Washington, Connecticut, on Route 47 north through Washington to the east side of New Preston on Route 202, and then east to Litchfield, from Litchfield east on Route 118, and then Route 4 to Harwinton, and along the Harwinton east through Burlington, Farmington, to Hartford on Route 4.
225 Connecticut Courant, August 7, 1775.
226 Ibid.

Thomas Cresap, these elderly kindred spirits are "resolute and determined to preserve the liberty of their country at the hazard of their lives."[227]

Hartford, first settled in 1635 by settlers from Cambridge, Massachusetts, is the "chief town of Connecticut government." Captain Hendricks, a rifleman from Carlisle, Pennsylvania, notes in his journal that Hartford "is pleasantly situated on the Connecticut River" with "seven very elegant Presbyterian parish churches."[228]

Early on, the citizens adopted a constitution that set forth a radical principle: "The foundation of the authority is in the free consent of its people."[229] For this revolutionary concept, many of Hartford citizens have returned to the land of their ancestors at Cambridge to join General Washington's army during the Siege of Boston. It is in Hartford where community leaders, including Silas Deane, the same man who recently was so impressed with Colonel Cresap's spirited letter, planned the successful expedition of Fort Ticonderoga, a plan carried out the previous May by Ethan Allen, Silas Warner, and Remember Baker.[230]

As they travel through the town of Hartford, Cresap and his men walk toward Ferry Way, a lane that takes them to the landing by which they will take the ferry across the Connecticut River.

The ferry crossing lies just downhill about 150 yards, directly in front of the courthouse and in sight of the town commons. When Cresap's company enters the busy settlement, as has been the case with the rifle companies that came before him, it is customary for the men to gravitate toward the commons in the center of town, sometimes called the village green. Most public commons consist of a large open stretch of green area, usually containing a few large trees - the last surviving remnants of a virgin forest that was present before the settlement of the town.

The commons serve colonial communities in several ways: as a parade ground for local militia, as a place for citizens to gather to celebrate and hold galas or festive events, and as a site to meet and conduct public business. A tavern, meetinghouse, church, store, courthouse, and dwelling houses usually surround the green at the town square.[231]

Here at the commons, officials publicly punish and humiliate violators of the law at the whipping post - or by confining their hands and ankles in wooden stocks in front of a jeering, cheering public. Large crowds hasten to the commons to witness these events when officials administer justice, often turning them into celebratory affairs. However, when officials are not discharging discipline to lawbreakers, the whipping post and stocks serve as convenient advertisement boards where townsfolk post notices of town meetings, events, and other public business.

---

227 Ibid.
228 Harrity. Journal of Captain William Hendricks, 28.
229 Less than a mile south of the town commons grows the ancient Charter Oak, a large white oak tree estimated to be more than five hundred years old. Legend states that in 1676, Captain Joseph Wadsworth, ancestor of Elijah Wadsworth, hid Connecticut's 1662 charter in the cavity of this tree when a new English royal governor attempted to confiscate the original document, intending to replace it with one that eliminated many liberties that Connecticut people had long appreciated. The citizens of Hartford treasured the 1662 charter as it guaranteed the people a degree of autonomy not enjoyed elsewhere. The Connecticut Charter supported the rights of individuals and allowed freemen to elect their magistrates in secret ballots. It specified the powers of government but, more importantly, defined its limits. Our founding fathers adopted several of the principles found in the Connecticut Charter into the US Constitution. The 1662 Connecticut Charter adopted language from the 1639 Fundamental Orders of Connecticut. Historians claim that the 1639 Fundamental Orders was the first constitution to impose limits on government power and "the first American Constitution of government to embody the democratic idea." The Charter Oak became a symbol of American independence, representing those very principles of liberty that Cresap and his riflemen fought to defend. Captain Cresap and his men might have been privileged to view the tree as they ferried over the Connecticut River, probably not realizing the significance of the stately old oak. The Charter Oak, which was located at the intersection of present-day Charter Oak Avenue and Charter Oak Place in Hartford, fell during a storm in 1856. (William DeLoss Love, The Colonial History of Hartford (Hartford, CT: William DeLoss Love, 1914), 79, 153; Bartleby, "The Fundamental Orders of Connecticut, 1639, May 13, 2014; Workers of the Federal Writers Project, American Guide Series: Connecticut, 29, 170; Connecticut History, "The Charter Oak Fell—Today in History: August 21," May 13, 2014, http://connecticuthistory.org/the-charter-oak-fell/.
230 Workers of the Federal Writers Project, American Guide Series: Connecticut, 173.
231 Barbara Wells Sarudy, 2014. The colonial village green, usually located in the center of town, was a parcel of land that the entire township shared in ownership. Here, individuals in a town could publicly graze their animals without fear of repercussions from a private landowner. The colonial commons represented the nation's first public land, a concept that eventually evolved into the establishment of the nation's first state and federal parks and forests owned and shared by all Americans.

Here, on August 20, Cresap will camp on his third night in Connecticut, this day having covered twenty-two miles.[232] Along the west bank of the Connecticut River, Cresap rests his company of riflemen for the night. The popular William and Jannet Knox Tavern is nestled on the west side of the waterway near the ferry landing. Lieutenant William Knox controls the operation of this strategically located ferry.

While in Hartford, Cresap and his men may have stopped at some of the other popular taverns in town. Jennet Collier's Tavern is also a well-known establishment where men of revolutionary persuasion can gather without drawing any suspicion of Tory sentiment. It is here at Collier's that Washington and Rochambeau will meet and dine in 1781. Cresap's men may visit the Moses Butler Tavern located on Main and Elm Streets, where men like to gather to hear the news of the day. Cresap could also stop in the Austin Tavern, managed by Seth and Seymour Austin. About two months before, on June 30, 1775, while traveling to Cambridge, Massachusetts, to assume command of the Continental army, Washington visited and was served lunch at the Austin Tavern.[233]

The Old Red Tavern, operated by Captain Israel Seymour, is another favorite spot for revolutionary soldiers to visit on Capitol Hill in Hartford. A lightning bolt will strike and kill Israel at the front door of his tavern in August 1784, giving him little time to enjoy the fruits of liberty after the end of the war.[234]

"The Farmer/Soldier" by Louise Cresap Geubelle: concept drawing for book cover consideration

---

232 J. Hammond Trumbull, The Memorial History of Hartford County, Connecticut: 1633–1884 (Boston: Edward L. Osgood, 1866), 182; Harrity, Journal of Captain William Hendricks, 28.

233 Love, The Colonial History of Hartford, 236–8; James Little, "Ancestors of Elizabeth 'Betsy' Collier Little," California Littles, May 13, 2014, http://www.californialittles.com/betsycollier/a8.htm#i751; Claghorn, "Washington's Travels in New England"; Connecticut History Illustrated, "Moses Butler Tavern, Hartford, October 2, 1893," May 19, 2014, http://www.cthistoryonline.org/cdm/singleitem/collection/cho/id/829/rec/6.

234 Connecticut History, "The Old Red Tavern on Park Street, Hartford," May 19, 2014, http://connecticuthistoryillustrated.org/islandora/object/40002%3A19983. The cause of the shocking, sudden death of Captain Seymour (1735 (?)–1784) was described in the Connecticut Courant. A lightning bolt "struck the chimney," forcing its way through the garret stairs into a closet…traveled along a stud directly over the front door where the captain was standing…then into Seymour, killing him instantly." Find a Grave. "Captain Israel Seymour," May 13, 2014, http://www.findagrave.com/cgi-bin/fg.cgi?page=gr&GRid=10485534; Constance Neyer, "Authors Tell Graveyard History," Hartford Courant, October 31, 1994, http://articles.courant.com/1994-10-31/news/9410310177_1_gravestones-cemetery-unmarked-graves.

Cresap's journey takes him straightaway to a dark land under the overpowering shadow of tyranny. The riflemen aim to do their part to contribute their time, their talents, and the meager endowments they possess, at the risk of their lives, to defend their just rights and liberty from a belligerent, tyrannical king who threatens to impose absolute slavery upon America.

Amos Wadsworth closed his Farmington, Connecticut shop after hearing of the Battle of Lexington and Concord to join Washington's army. Wadsworth's letter to his brother near Boston perhaps captures the mind-set of Cresap's riflemen who soon will join and reinforce General Washington's siege line around Boston. Wadsworth writes, "the Army are in high spirits and appear to be perfect strangers to fear…better to die a freeman than to live as a slave." The motto inscribed on the sword of Farmington resident Colonel Fisher Gay, who now serves under General Washington in Boston, perhaps captures this sentiment best in three short words: "Freedom or death."[235]

---
235 Arthur and Smith, *Farmington, Connecticut: The Village of Beautiful Homes*, 115.

CHAPTER 8

Keeping the Wolf from the Door

Eastern Connecticut
August 21, 1775, to August 22, 1775

ON THE MORNING OF AUGUST 21, Cresap's company assembles at the town square near the fifty-five-year-old Hartford State House (present-day site of the Old Hartford State House built in 1796) then move uniformly toward the ferry crossing (located at the present-day site of Founder's Bridge).[236] Cresap's rifle company then crosses the Connecticut River by way of Knox's Ferry the distance of eighty perches, the width of the river at this point being a little more than 1,320 feet.[237]

Cresap has crossed several rivers by ferry on the way to Boston: the Susquehanna, the Delaware, the Hudson, and now the Connecticut. These river crossings have sparked ideas in his mind as to how he might best manage his business once he returns home. If the opportunity presents itself, Cresap might speak to William Knox about Knox's boat enterprise, the Maryland captain seeking to absorb any bit of helpful information that might be applied to his own awaiting ferry enterprise on the Monongahela River at Redstone.[238]

Cresap and his company set out by way of the Boston Middle Post Road, the shortest and fastest route from Hartford to Boston. Before the revolution, rebels used this road as their primary route to flee from British tariffs and taxes. During the war, this road will serve as the main corridor to deliver troops and supplies to Washington's Continental army.[239]

Today, Cresap's company will march another twenty-five miles, passing through Bolton and head toward Coventry. And onward the soldiers march, carrying their modest worldly belongings in their haversacks. Only the occasional sparse chatter among these comrades breaks the sound of their moccasins treading the road that brings them nearer to the battleground. [240]

East of Hartford on the Boston Middle Post Road following the general route of the present-day Middle Post Road on Route 44, Cresap's company comes upon Bolton, founded about 1720. A traveler passing through this area about this time describes Bolton as a small town with "many scattered houses, some clustered around the meeting house on a spacious but low plateau." The visitor states that Bolton is a very important agricultural area for "cattle, wheat and every kind of commodity." The wayfarer goes on to describe Bolton as being

---

236 Builders constructed the old Hartford State House at the Hartford town square in 1719. To make way for the construction of a new state house, citizens moved the old state house to another nearby location. It survived two hundred years at this new location; citizens eventually razed the building in 1920.
237 Harrity, Journal of Captain William Hendricks, 28–9; Love, The Colonial History of Hartford, 221–3.
238 William Knox (1732–1787) was an Irish immigrant who lived in Hartford for more than twenty years. During the American Revolution, his tavern housed British prisoner-of-war soldiers. The epitaph on Knox's tombstone warns of man's fragile existence and mortality, perhaps capturing a more callous view of death that existed at this time: "Behold my friend as you pass by./As you now are so once was I./As I am now, so must you be./Prepare for death and follow me." Kim Knox Beckius, "Wander Around an Ancient Burial Ground: Here Lies William Knox." TripSavvy. Last revised May 16, 2017, http://gonewengland.about.com/od/hartfordattractions/ig/Ancient-Burying-Ground/Here-Lies-William-Knox.htm.
239 Wikipedia, The Free Encyclopedia, s.v., "Boston Post Road Map," Accessed August 7, 2013, http://upload.wikimedia.org/wikipedia/commons/e/e7/Boston_Post_Road_map.png; Harrity, Journal of Captain William Hendricks, 2019.
240 Harrity, Journal of Captain William Hendricks, 29.

"unquestionably the most fertile province in America, for its soil yields everything necessary to life. The pasture is so good here that the cattle are of truly excellent quality. The beef is exceptionally good. The poultry and game are exquisite."[241]

This backcountry road corridor is especially important to the revolution because of its remote interior location away from naval ports and its distance from any large assemblage of British troops. Despite the fact that the British discourage intercolonial trade, rebels use this route to conduct "illegal-interior colonial commerce."[242] This inland route will prove to be the safest route for the deployment of troops and the transporting of supplies to support the revolutionary cause.[243]

The White Tavern, located at present-day 2 Brandy Street, built prior to 1750, began operating soon thereafter as a tavern in Bolton. Colonial Connecticut governance requires that each town establish at least one tavern to entertain strangers.

Captain Joel White runs the Oliver White Tavern in Bolton. This establishment is a favorite stopping place for military officers passing through, such as Captain Cresap and his company on this day.[244] White plays a role similar to that of Michael's father, Colonel Thomas Cresap, in Frederick County, Maryland. Both militia leaders serve as justices of the peace and have experience serving as county representatives in their respective state legislative bodies. Also like Colonel Cresap, White has donated and raised funds to help support the expenses of the American Revolution.[245]

Oliver White Tavern, Bolton, Connecticut

---

241 Hans Depold, *Bolton Historic Tales: America Chronicles* (Charleston, SC: History Press, 2008), 61–74.
242 Ibid.
243 Don Costello, "The Settling of Bolton," Bolton Historical Society, October 1995, May 19, 2014, http://www.boltoncthistory.org/specialedition.html.
244 *Guests at White's Tavern paid for bed space and not for an entire room. It was not unusual for a room that contained two beds to have four strangers sleeping in the same room. Strangers and friends alike ate at the same eating table. Once a visitor fell asleep, on occasion the landlord might enter the room with a candle in hand, bringing yet another nameless roommate to share one's bed until morning dawned. If any person objected to a unknown newcomer as a bedfellow, that complainer was seen as unreasonably fastidious, or worse--was labeled intolerable! Captain Joel White--a Bolton Justice of the Peace, Town Treasurer, and representative to the state legislature, lent 3,000 pounds to the State of Connecticut and the United States. On September 5, 1774, White is on record as being the town meeting moderator. During that year, with ongoing rumors of war, White sent two community leaders to Hartford to discuss a possible boycott of British goods, an action that seemed to trigger one of the first steps leading the colonies to American Independence. Hans DePold. "The Oliver White Tavern." Bolton Historical Society, Bolton, Connecticut. http://www.boltoncthistory.org/oliverwhitetavern.html.*
245 DePold, 2006.

Just last April, Captain Jonathan Birge led sixty minutemen from Bolton along with forty-five men from Hartford and rode out to Lexington after hearing the alarm for assistance. Captain Cresap now marches on the same road through Bolton that Birge did, a part of the Boston Middle Post Road.

The riflemen should feel right at home in the Bolton region for the thoroughfare on which the men stride is similar to the roadways back in their native region: "frightful, with mountains and very steep slopes." The characters of the people who cheerfully welcome the riflemen remind the soldiers of their friends and family back home. A French officer will later describe the general attributes of Bolton's senior people, traits that could also characterize the hospitality of the people of western Maryland. The officer writes,

> We have seen old people here of both sexes who enjoy perfect health at a very advanced age. Their old age is gay and amiable, and not all burdened with the infirmities that are our lot [the French people] in our declining years. The people of this province are very hardworking, but they do not labor to excess as our peasants do. They cultivate only for their physical needs. The sweat of their brow is not expended on satisfying the extravagant desires of the rich and luxury loving; they limit themselves to what is truly necessary. Foreigners are cordially welcomed by these good people. You find a whole family bustling about to make you happy.[246]

The road on which Cresap's riflemen march now directs them past the present-day Bolton Heritage Farm near the center of town, where visitors and soldiers traveling through are welcome to rest and to pitch a tent overnight.[247] From Bolton, Cresap presses forward to Coventry,[248] first settled around 1709. Just over two thousand people live in this settlement. On August 21, after marching about 25 miles from Hartford "for the relief of Boston, ... Captain Michael Cressup's (sic) company of Maryland rangers, making up more than "125 half-naked men, painted like Indians and brandishing tomahawks and rifles, burst into" the town of Coventry. The riflemen stay at a tavern owned by Amos Richardson, a patriot and leading pillar of the community. Captain Cresap quarters overnight in the tavern while his men camp outdoors in tents.

---

246 DePold, Bolton Historic Tales: America Chronicles, 61–74.
247 On March 4, 1781, General Washington, traveling with Alexander Hamilton, will pass through Bolton and partake of lunch at Reverend Colton's House at the present site in 2017 of the Heritage Farm House. On June 21 to 24, 1782, Rochambeau, with four regiments containing a total of five thousand men, will also travel through Bolton on the same road that Cresap now takes. Rochambeau, after camping for several days on the same farm where Washington dined over a year earlier, will likewise stay at Colton's house, (Hans DePold, "225th Anniversary of Rochambeau's March through Bolton," Bolton Historical Society, June 2006, May 19, 2014, http://www.boltoncthistory.org/rochambeaumarch.html; Hans DePold, "The Oliver White Tavern," Bolton Historical Society, February 2006, May 19, 2014, http://www.boltoncthistory.org/oliverwhitetavern.html; Hans DePold, "Bolton's Historical Moments During the American Revolution," Bolton Historical Society, last revised September 2013, May 15, 2014, http://www.boltoncthistory.org/historicmoments.html; Hans DePold, "Rediscovering the Minister's House," Bolton Historical Society, December 2005, May 19, 2014, http://www.boltoncthistory.org/ministershouse.html; Hans DePold, "The Changing Face of Bolton's Heritage Farm House," Bolton Historical Society, October 2007, accessed November 25, 2017, http://www.boltoncthistory.org/heritagefarmhouse.html.
248 Coventry was the birthplace of Nathan Hale (1755–1776), recognized today as a "symbol for youthful patriotism and as a martyr," who sacrificed his life at the age of twenty-one during the American Revolution. Hale traveled many times back and forth on parts of the road that Cresap walked, in particular as a student attending Yale College in New Haven, Connecticut. In September 1775, possessing the same "ardent of glow of patriotism" as Cresap's riflemen, Lieutenant Hale, under the command of Colonel Knowlton from Ashford, Connecticut, traveled this same route northeastward to join Washington's army. Hale then united with an estimated sixteen thousand other rebels, including Cresap's company, in the siege to help keep the British army penned in at Boston. After the Continental army retreated from Long Island on August 27, 1776, Hale volunteered to serve as a spy for Washington and went bravely behind enemy lines to the British encampment on Manhattan Island. Here, Hale worked to gain vital information regarding the British army's plans for the future. When Hale prepared to leave after obtaining the necessary information, his relative, a fugitive and British supporter, recognized him and revealed his identity to the British. The British arrested and hanged Hale the next day, on September 22, 1776, and buried him in an unmarked grave on Manhattan Island. Accounts state that at his hanging, Captain Nathan Hale said, "I regret that I have but one life to lose for my country." John Warner Barber, Connecticut Historical Collections (New Haven, CT: Durrie and Peck and J. W. Barber, 1836), 545–46; Edward Everett Hale, "Captain Nathan Hale (1755–1776)," The Connecticut Society of the Sons of the American Revolution, May 15, 2014, http://www.connecticutsar.org/patriots/hale_nathan.htm.

Bolton Heritage Farm, Bolton Connecticut

Here, in northeastern Coventry, the rifle company passes by the Brigham home, which in 1778 will become licensed as a tavern. Washington will breakfast here in 1789.[249]

Brigham's Tavern, Coventry Connecticut

---
249 Claghorn, "Washington's Travels in New England"; Brigham Tavern, 2014.

67

Richardson supplies the riflemen with "125 rations" of food. Apparently, something in the New England air causes a rare lapse of discipline in Cresap's riflemen, possibly while they perform a shooting demonstration for the community. Their boisterous misbehavior during the evening causes undisclosed destruction on the tavern property to such an extent that the owner will submit "a bill against the state for considerable damages." Perhaps the damages Cresap's riflemen incur are similar to those caused by a different rifle company that several days later damaged a building and "shot the tavern sign to pieces" during their stay at a nearby tavern belonging to Uriah Brigham. [250]

On August 22, Cresap's company moves on once more, and soon crosses the Willimantic River. Today, on their fifth and last full day in Connecticut, the men will march through Ashford, a village founded in 1714 that now consists of a population of 2,241 people. Cresap marches on the old Connecticut Path, the primary highway through this town. Numerous taverns that supply the needs of travelers and wagoners are located here, while communities such as these provide the riflemen fresh food and supplies. While in this area, Cresap may visit Esquire Isaac Perkins' Tavern to garner the most recent news. This tavern is the same establishment in which George Washington will stay on November 7, 1789. [251]

Over the long stretch of miles during lulls, or when there was a time for loneliness - the men's thoughts no doubt turn to family and friends that they have left behind. Since the war began, there are few able-bodied men to do the necessary work the riflemen once performed to keep the wolf from the door. One historian describes the character of the brave revolutionary women who maintain the home front: "Strong and courageous, they were not only inciters to patriotism, but most ardent workers in its cause. They accepted privation and sacrifices as a pleasure, and took up the burdens imposed on them with a cheerfulness that made them light…the women planted and harvested, then had their merry husking, pulled flax and hatched it, and had their spinning bees; thus aiding and encouraging each other."[252]

The revolutionary spirit runs strong in Ashford. The people of Ashford were quick to send supplies to Boston after the British closed its harbors to colonial trade. Captain Thomas Knowlton (1740–1776), a native of Ashford, led seventy-eight men of his militia from Ashford, Mansfield, and Windham to the scene of Lexington soon after he heard of the battle. Knowlton's unit was the first sister colony to assist Massachusetts. Two months later, Captain Knowlton commanded two hundred men in a fatigue (work) party constructing defense structures on Bunker Hill. During the Battle of Bunker Hill, Knowlton and his men manned the rail fence near the top of the hill and bravely stayed behind to cover the retreat of the patriots forming the rear guard on Breed's Hill.[253]

---

[250] Brook Messier; Janet Sutherland Aronson, The Roots of Coventry, Connecticut (275th Anniversary Comm.: Coventry CT., 1987) 64
[251] Richard M. Bayles, History of Windham County, Connecticut (New York: W. W. Preston and Company, 1899), 220.
[252] Bayles, History of Windham County, Connecticut, 84–5. Washington intended to visit Israel Putnam on this trip, but upon learning that Putnam lived about five miles off the main road, Washington proceeded westward eight miles to Ashford, where he stayed overnight at the Perkins Tavern. Unfortunately, this was Washington's last opportunity to visit with old Putnam, as the Pomfret hero passed away the next year in 1790. If Washington had to do it over again, he might have wished he had retired for the night at Putnam's, as Washington's stay in Ashford did not go as well as expected. The general arrived in Ashford late Saturday as the town prepared for the Sabbath. Because of this town's strict religious observances, Washington's greeting by town leaders was somewhat restrained, very different from the fanfare the general was accustomed to receiving. Washington ventured out to church the next morning, but otherwise, he spent a very quiet extra day in Ashford because the state considered travel on Sundays "contrary and disagreeable." Perkin's Tavern was located at the present-day intersection of Route 44 and Route 89 in Ashford. Richard Kollen, "Washington's Dinner at Munroe Tavern," Lexington Historical Society, March 2011, May 16, 2014, http://lhsoc.weebly.com/uploads/6/5/2/1/6521332/washingtons_dinner_at_munroe_tavern-d.pdf; diary entry 2014; Susan J. Griggs, Folklore and Firesides in Pomfret, Hampton, and Vicinity (1950) (Salem, MA: Higginson Book Company, 1992), https://archive.org/stream/earlyhomesteadso00grig#page/n0/mode/1up.
[253] "Lt. Colonel Thomas Knowlton, Connecticut's Forgotten Hero," The Connecticut Society of the Sons of the American Revolution, May 15, 2014, http://www.connecticutsar.org/patriots/knowlton_thomas.htm; Bayles, History of Windham County, Connecticut, 1023. Washington promoted Knowlton to lieutenant colonel on August 12, 1776. In 1776, Knowlton's Rangers formed under Washington's command as America's first intelligence unit. Nathan Hale was among the men who served as a spy under the command of Knowlton. At the Battle of Harlem Heights on September 16, 1776, Knowlton received a mortal wound. When Knowlton's men removed him from the battlefield to prevent his capture by the British, Knowlton is reported to have said, "You see, my son, I am mortally wounded. You can do me no good; go fight for your country." The next day, after hearing that Knowlton had fallen, Washington said, "The gallant and brave Colonel Knowlton, who would have been an honor for any country, having fallen yesterday while gloriously fighting."

The next town Cresap marches through in Connecticut is Pomfret, established around 1713. The Pomfret townsfolk who greet Cresap's company are very proud of one of their own, Israel Putnam (1718–1790). General Washington has recently promoted Putnam to major general, one of the first three officers to hold that rank in the newly formed Continental army. As Cresap passes through Pomfret, Putnam commands the center of the siege line at Cambridge.[254]

Cresap and his men soon come upon the Grosvenor farm. The owner, Thomas Grosvenor, is not home. After serving as a minuteman in one of the first of seven regiments recruited for the revolution in Connecticut and after fighting and suffering wounds at Bunker Hill, Grosvenor is presently on the siege line around Boston.[255]

From Pomfret, Cresap follows the general alignment of the route that leads from the town through Putnam and turns northward toward Thompson and East Thompson. By the time Cresap arrives at the town of Thompson, first settled as early as 1693, the riflemen will have traveled another thirty-three miles in one day, perhaps the longest distance they traveled in a day since they began their journey.[256] The town is named after one of its largest landholders, Sir Robert Thompson of Middlesex, England. The Red Tavern, built about 1716, is the earliest establishment constructed to serve travelers on the main road between Hartford and Boston. In 1774, the community erected a new meetinghouse on Thompson Hill at the fork where Oxford and Boston Roads meet.[257]

Cresap's riflemen pass on East Thompson Road the friendly patriotic institution known as Jacobs's Halfway House Inn, so named because it is halfway between Hartford and Boston. John Jacobs, owner of the inn, and three of his sons are patriots who support the revolutionary cause.

On August 22, on the fifth evening in Connecticut, Cresap likely camps at Thompson[258] in the northeast corner of the colony. Just several months before, at the green in the town center where Cresap's men now camp, Connecticut militia mustered to respond to the Lexington alarm. Near the green, atop the crest

---

[254] Some historians claim that Putnam, who served as one of the leading commanders at Bunker Hill and Breed's Hill, said at that battle, "Don't fire until you see the whites of their eyes." Putnam also receives credit as the man who killed the last wild wolf in Connecticut in the winter of 1742 to 1743. Further accounts mention the "reckless courage and fighting spirit" that Putnam demonstrated while serving as an officer with Rogers's Rangers during the French and Indian War. Indeed, it seems that America's "dense woods and stony soils" have a tendency, both in Maryland and Connecticut, to spring forth "hardy folks of firm principles," who are well represented in men like Maryland's Michael Cresap and Connecticut's Israel Putnam. Israel Putnam Wolf Cave, the site where Putnam killed the wolf, is located at Mashamoquet River State Park. Jill Knight Weinberger, "Touring the Quiet Corner," New York Times, June 2, 2002, http://www.nytimes.com/2002/06/02/travel/touring-the-quiet-corner.html.

[255] Thomas Grosvenor will later take part in the battles of Long Island, Trenton, Princeton, Brandywine, Germantown, and Monmouth. After Valley Forge, Washington will commission Grosvenor as lieutenant commander, commandant of the First Connecticut Regiment. On November 7, 1789, as president of the United States, Washington watered his horses at the Grosvenor farm while he traveled from Boston to Hartford. In his travels in the northeast, Washington stopped at inns and residences of patriots supportive of the revolution. In the famous John Trumbull painting of Bunker Hill, one can view Grosvenor in the foreground on the right side of the painting accompanied by a servant. (Claghorn, "Washington's Travels in New England"; Connecticut History, "George Washington Slept Here (Just Perhaps Not Well)," May 16, 2104, http://connecticuthistory.org/george-washington-slept-here-just-perhaps-not-well/.

[256] Harrity, Journal of Captain William Hendricks, 29.

[257] Cresap's Rifles followed the Middle Post Road toward Boston along the general present-day road alignment of Route 44, starting from Hartford eastward through the towns of Bolton, Coventry, and Pomfret and toward Putnam. Just north of Putnam, Cresap's men turned north to Thompson, traveling on the general present-day road alignment of Route 21 to Route 193.

[258] Harrity, Journal of Captain William Hendricks, 29.

of Thompson Hill, which rises to 625 feet above sea level, Cresap's men can view a scenic fifty-mile panorama of the surrounding New England woodland landscape.[259]

In June, Silas Deane saw a company of riflemen who were preparing to march to Boston. The unique clothing of the riflemen obviously made a memorable impression in the mind of Deane. In a letter to his wife, Deane writes, "The Riflemen…dress is hard to describe. They take a piece of tow cloth…it has the shade of a dry or fading leaf. Then they make a kind of frock out of it, reaching down below their knee, open before, with a large cape. They wrap it around them tight, on a march, and tie it with a belt; in which hangs their tomahawk."[260]

Silas Deane remarks that it would be well "that they [New England] would imitate their uniform, as it is cheap and light."[261] Not long after this, Deane will send a hunting shirt to his wife with a note saying, "I send on what is called the shirt uniform or rifle dress, as a sample or pattern, and wish it may be adopted."[262]

The "back country hunting shirt garment," a piece of apparel that is "synonymous with the American frontier,"[263] is unknown in New England before the companies of Captain Morgan and Captain Cresap and other rifle companies arrive from the south to Cambridge. Not to pin the business of fashion trendsetting on George Washington and Thomas Cresap - the reality is that the hunting shirt started in the backcountry of Virginia, Pennsylvania, and western Maryland where Washington, Cresap, and roving ranger militias operated during the French and Indian War. The hunting shirt languished as a backwoods Appalachian fashion west of the Blue Ridge Mountains; "however with the outbreak of the American Revolution in 1775, the garment becomes the symbol of American liberty and independence."[264]

This mode of dress of the Virginia frontier riflemen has left a lasting and positive impression on George Washington. His high regard for the frontier style is propelled even higher as the riflemen begin appearing in Cambridge. Washington's hopes lift as company by company of these men from Pennsylvania, Virginia, and Maryland arrive clothed in their homespun shirts. One of the Virginia rifle companies exhibits the words "Liberty or Death" sewn onto their hunting shirts. Members of other companies also have this slogan emblazoned in bold letters on their necessity bags.

When Daniel Morgan's Virginia rifle company appears on August 6, Washington notes, "The Troops of the Southward are come in very healthy and in good Order."[265] The riflemen are dressed in hunting shirts made from osnaburg linen, or some of which are made of Lindsey-Woolsey fringed on every edge. It would seem that Washington is referring to what he perceives as a relatively simple mode of dress—specially tailored with

---

259 Workers of the Federal Writers Project, American Guide Series: Connecticut, 536; Weinberger, "Touring the Quiet Corner"; Bayles, History of Windham County, Connecticut, 1003, 1023; Mary Caroline Crawford, Among Old New England Inns (Boston: Colonial Press, 1907), 185. Historic records document that well-known persons of distinction passed through Thompson as this oasis was located along a prominent road of travel. Accomplished leaders stopped at Jacob's Inn, including Lieutenant Nathan Hale, who breakfasted at the inn in 1776 while on his travels to join Washington's army at Cambridge. Lafayette also rested at Jacob's Inn for a brief respite. On his inaugural presidential tour, Washington breakfasted there on November 7, 1789, en route to Pomfret. On a more disparaging note regarding this handy place of repose, Washington was not pleased with his breakfast at Jacob's Tavern and later writes in his journal, "not a good House." Connecticut History, "George Washington Slept Here"; Claghorn, "Washington's Travels in New England"; diary entry, 2014.
260 Silas Deane Online, "Letter from Silas Deane to Elizabeth Deane, 3 June 1775." http://www.silasdeaneonline.org/documents/doc12.htm.
261 Neal Thomas Hurst, "Kind of Armour Being Peculiar to America: The American Hunting Shirt," BA thesis, College of William and Mary, 2013, May 13, 2014, http://www.academia.edu/3336557/_kind_of_armour_being_peculiar_to_America_The_American_Hunting_Shirt, 24.
262 Ibid.
263 Ibid., 13–14.
264 Ibid.
265 Fitzpatrick, The Writings of George Washington from the Original Manuscript Sources, vol. 3, 424.

color-coded shirts and cuffs, the stylish feature that denotes to which regiment these impressive Virginians belong. Colonel William Woodford, who commands the second regiment of Virginia, sometimes calls his men "shirt-men," referring to the hunting shirt the riflemen wore.[266]

Washington's comment is in stark contrast to the notation that he made less than one month before on July 10 concerning "the army in general and the troops raised in Massachusetts in particular, [who] are "very deficient in necessary Clothing."[267]

With the practical dress of riflemen still fixed in his mind, the general, after commanding the new army for just one month now, desires to transform his presently shabbily attired men holding the rank of private into the practical dress of the backwoods riflemen. To achieve this aim, as early as August 4, General Washington requested a large batch of "Tow Cloth," a coarse heavy linen, from which to make "Indian or Hunting Shirts" for his enlisted men, "many of whom are destitute of Cloathing," the material being "both cheap and Convenient."[268]

Washington writes that he is "of the opinion that a number of hunting Shirts, not less than 10,000, would in a great Degree remove the difficulty in the cheapest and quickest manner."[269] Washington also believes that the hunting shirt uniform would have a "Happy Tendency to unite the men and abolish those Provincial distinctions which lead to Jealousy and Dissatisfaction"[270]

The general sends authorities a pattern of the hunting shirt that he expects Congress to support and finance. In addition to providing them "Shirts, Shoes, Breeches, and Stockings"[271] and coats, Washington desires his enlisted men to look even more like riflemen by wearing "Indian Boots or Leggins…instead of stockings; as they are not only warmer, and wear longer, (but by getting them of a colour) contribute to uniformity in dress."[272]

The hunting shirt universally worn by the rifleman is truly an original American invention. By the time of the American Revolution, the outfit consists of two distinct pieces, a hunting shirt and a cloak, which is a kind of overcoat. The loose-fitting, oversize hunting shirt resembles a smock. Some of the hemlines of the shirts reach halfway down the thighs. If the rifleman wishes, he can shorten the length of the frock and create pockets by hanging the extra linen, sometimes up to a foot of material, over the waistband. Inside this handy pocket, the rifleman can place a "chunk of bread, cakes, jerk, tow for wiping the barrel of the rifle, a wallet containing money, or any other small necessity." The styles of the hunting shirts, with their varying lengths and shades of color, differ with each rifle company. For instance, the hunting shirts of Captain Morgan's company are "pepper and salt colored cotton cloth," short in length and open at the front with string ties.[273]

The long, baggy sleeves of the shirt allow the rifleman's arms to move about freely and unrestricted. Over his shoulders, the rifleman often wears a cloak made of a heavier material, like wool, sometimes fringed on the edges with material of a different hue. The cloak protects the shoulder area from soaking rain or snow. With their painted faces, rounded felt hats, long rifles, scalping knives, and tomahawks, these hardened combat veterans of the Ohio Indian War are indeed a unique sight for New England folks. One historian later noted that their appearance made them look like "a band of Assassins"[274] on a mission.

---

266 SecondVirginia, "The 2nd Virginia Regiment: Recreating the 2nd Virginia Regiment," April 17, 2010. https://secondvirginia.wordpress.com/2010/04/17/hunting-shirts/.
267 Fitzpatrick, The Writings of George Washington from the Original Manuscript Sources, vol. 3, 325.
268 Ibid., 389.
269 Ibid., 387.
270 Ibid., 325.
271 Ibid., 446.
272 Ibid., 404.
273 Hurst, "Kind of Armour Being Peculiar to America: The American Hunting Shirt," 25.
274 Hurst, "Kind of Armour Being Peculiar to America: The American Hunting Shirt," 21.

Washington will not fully realize his request to uniform his army in hunting shirts until around July 1776. In a general order about the new hunting shirt uniform written on July 24, 1776, Washington will recognize the significant role played by the presence of the sharpshooting riflemen, who act as a deterrent and create fear in the minds of the enemy at the Siege of Boston during the summer of 1775.

The general "earnestly encourages the use of Hunting Shirts, with long Breeches made of the same Cloth, Gaiter fashion about the Legs, to all those yet unprovided. No Dress can be had cheaper, nor more convenient, as the Wearer may be cool in warm weather, and warm in cool weather by putting on under Cloaths which will not change the outward dress, Winter or Summer—Besides which it is a dress justly supposed to carry no small terror to the enemy, who think every person (so dressed) a complete Marksmen."[275]

In June 1775, with the first steps the southern rifle companies take toward Cambridge, the hunting shirt began its inaugural journey to New England on the backs of men like Michael Cresap. Upon arrival, the riflemen influence the uniform dress of the entire Continental army,[276] creating a fearsome appearance in the eyes of the British enemy.[277]

Resolute, courageous, and determined, Cresap's men stay firmly on course. The riflemen set their "face like flint"[278] toward Cambridge, as unyielding as the flint that reposes in the locks of their long rifles. Come what may, Cresap's men step forward, undaunted by the challenges that they know lie before them.

Cresap's Rifles, the last of the original ten rifle companies selected on June 14 by the Continental Congress to pass through the final remaining towns, march along their designated route before they reach Cambridge. Most of the younger men from these towns who are able to fight have already joined Washington. The people in the settlements who come out to greet and cheer Cresap's company are primarily women and children or older men.

The excitement of these spectators almost overshadows the parade of these men dressed in Indian-like garb—a high-spirited unit surrounded and encompassed by rousing songs of patriotism. The tumultuous clamor of the crowd rises with each moccasin-clad step of the soldiers.

One spectator enamored of the sight of the rifle companies excitedly writes the following: "Mars the Great God of Battle is now honored in every part of this spacious Colony…every Presence is warlike, every sound is Martial! Drums beating, fifes and Bag-pipes playing, and only sonorous and heroic tunes—Every Man has a hunting shirt, which is the uniform for each company. Almost all have a cockade and Bucks Tale in their Hats to represent that they are hardy, resolute and invincible Natives of the Woods of America."[279]

The people throughout New England treated to the appearance of the men who make up Cresap's Rifles will long remember the grand spectacle of seeing these rugged frontiersmen march through their towns.

---

275 John C. Fitzpatrick, ed., Writings of George Washington, vol. 5 (Washington, DC: US Government Office, 1932), 336.
276 By late summer of 1775, word had circulated throughout the colonies for their armed militia to adopt the dress of the hunting shirt. For example, from Princeton on August 31, 1775, a directive came from the Committee of Safety of New Jerseys. The directive stated the following: "Resolved, That the several Officers and Privates who embody themselves as Minute Men in this province, be, and they hereby are directed, for the sake of distinction and convenience, to adopt, as their uniform, hunting frocks, as near as may be similar to those of the Rifle Men now in Continental service." Pennsylvania Packet, September 4, 1775, 3.
277 Fitzpatrick, The Writings of George Washington from the Original Manuscript Sources, vol. 3, 325, 387, 389, 404, 415, 422; Hurst, "Kind of Armour Being Peculiar to America: The American Hunting Shirt"; J. Lloyd Durham, "Outfitting an American Revolutionary Soldier." NCpedia, 1992. May 16, 2014. http://ncpedia.org/history/usrevolution/soldiers.
278 This paragraph and the use of the word flint inspired by the Bible, Isaiah 50:7.
279 Hurst, "Kind of Armour Being Peculiar to America: The American Hunting Shirt," 19.

CHAPTER 9

Snuffers of the Candle Come to Town

Entering Massachusetts
August 23, 1775, to August 24, 1775

IT IS A FINE MORNING for a march. In late August, the New England summer mist dampens the skin and clothing. The men of the rifle company arise, pack their gear, and ponder the latest news—compliments of their captain. Cresap leads the men in a rousing cheer. The group rallies and assembles into formation to depart Thompson, and as the men grow nearer to their target of joining their commander, General Washington, the talk of war and revolution grows more intense among their ranks.

On August 23, the day Captain Cresap and his rifle company enter Massachusetts, neither Congress, General Washington, nor Captain Cresap knows that the colonies are now officially at war with England. Today, King George III has rejected the conciliatory Olive Branch Petition drafted by John Dickinson, an appeal approved by the Second Continental Congress on July 5. King George today issues a proclamation declaring the American colonies in a state of open rebellion. In addition, the monarch calls on all his British subjects to help put an end to this turbulent rebellion. The king's proclamation makes it treasonous for any British subject to defend in any way the cause of the American colonists.

Cresap, who has not heard this woeful news, remains hopeful that a short war and quick reconciliation with the mother country will occur. The king's proclamation guarantees that the war will last beyond this year. Congress itself will not receive news of the British monarch's rejection until November 9.[280]

The first town in Massachusetts the riflemen come upon is Douglas, first settled in 1715. The road Cresap's Rifles march is the Middle Boston Post Road in Douglas on present-day Southwest Main Street.[281] People in this part of Massachusetts also know this road as the "Colony Road" - which is "the only road through this part of the province through the town of Mendon to the Boston market."[282] A short distance away lies Wallum Lake. A swampland, steeped in a strange and savage natural beauty, drains into this large fresh body of water. The men behold the Atlantic cedar, a tree they have not seen in western Maryland.

George Washington will pass by this area on November 9, 1789. He will not hold a high opinion of this section of the country, writing in his journal, "First stage, with a small exception is intolerably bad road, and a poor and uncultivated country covered chiefly by woods—the largest of which is called Douglass, at the foot of which, on the east side, is a large pond."[283] Cresap's men do not allow annoying mosquitoes from this wet area or the summer

---
280 Schlesinger, The Almanac of American History, 118; Bailyn, 1993, 1058; Revolutionary War and Beyond, "The Olive Branch Petition," July 22, 2014. http://www.revolutionary-war-and-beyond.com/olive-branch-petition.html.
281 The course from Thompson, Connecticut, through Douglas wends its way through present-day Douglas State Forest, a very remote section of Massachusetts. Officials did not pave the public road through the state forest until 2002.
282 William A. Emerson, History of the Town of Douglas, Massachusetts (Boston: Frank W. Bird, 1879), 243.
283 Benson J. Lossing, The Diary of George Washington from 1789–1791 (New York: Charles B. Richardson and Company, 1860), 50.

heat to break their spirits. The riflemen are in war-footing mode, ready to make sacrifices as needed for the good of the country.[284]

The road eastward through the backwoods of Massachusetts takes the riflemen to Uxbridge, first settled in 1662. An elderly sixty-three-year old widow named Lydia Chapin Taft[285] may be quietly watching as Cresap and his company march through the northern side of town.[286] History remembers Lydia Taft as the first woman known to have legally voted in America.[287]

Cresap passes near the Tavern owned by Seth Reed (1746–1797). Uxbridge resident Reed saw action in the Battles of Lexington and Concord and Bunker Hill. Historians credit Seth Reed for successfully petitioning the Massachusetts court in 1786 for a franchise to mint coins inscribed with the slogan "E Pluribus Unum" ("From Many, One"). The treasury still includes this motto on US coinage. The phrase alludes to the unity of the states at the inception of the country of America.[288]

---

[284] Using 2017 road designations, Cresap marched east from the Douglas town line on the present-day general road alignment of Route 16 for about two miles. Cresap's men then followed eastward along Hartford Road West, where the road intersects Route 16. Temporarily departing the Route 16 road alignment, the riflemen continued straight eastward on the present-day Hartford Road west to where the road intersects Route 122 (North Main Street) on the north side of Uxbridge. The road just east of Uxbridge crosses Blackstone River near the present-day site of Canal Heritage State Park. Cresap continued on Hartford Road until it intersects again at present-day Route 16. At this intersection, the riflemen proceeded about one mile to Mendon, marching along Route 16. (Emerson, History of the Town of Douglas, Massachusetts, 243.

[285] Lydia Taft was a trailblazing pioneer for the women's suffrage movement that will come many years later. Taft placed her historic vote on October 30, 1756, when town leaders requested that she vote in place of her recently deceased husband, Captain Josiah Taft. At that time, Josiah Taft was one of the highest-paying taxpayers in Uxbridge. The vote involved the issue of whether or not Uxbridge should support the French and Indian War effort. Taft cast her vote in favor of supporting the war 164 years before American political leaders in 1920 amended the US Constitution to allow women to vote. Carol Masiello, "Uxbridge Breaks Tradition and Makes History: Lydia Chapin Taft," Blackstone Daily, July 26, 2014, http://blackstonedaily.com/Journeys/cm-lt.htm.

[286] Cresap's riflemen, the forerunners of the US Army, clad in hunting shirts, marched on the north side through Uxbridge, a town that became the largest maker of woolen uniforms manufactured for the US military. In 1810, the Bernat Mill, later called the Bachman Uxbridge Worsted Company, manufactured uniforms for the American Civil War, World War I (khaki overcoats), and World War II (US Army uniform). In 1950, the mill received a contract to manufacture the US Air Force uniform in the color known as Uxbridge blue. Wikipedia, The Free Encyclopedia, s.v., "Bernat Mill," July 22, 2014, http://en.wikipedia.org/wiki/Bernat_Mill.

[287] By 1778, Samuel Taft, the grandfather of future US president William Howard Taft, operated the Taft Tavern in a building constructed in 1774 at present-day Sutton Avenue. At the tavern entrance, a sign bearing the painted image of an eagle greeted all visitors to the business. General Washington traveled along this same road and stayed at the Taft Tavern on November 6, 1789, while returning to New York following a presidential tour of New England. The president originally planned to stay in Mendon at an inn, built in 1745, owned by a Colonel Ammidon, a Revolutionary War veteran whom Washington knew personally. However, a maid of Ammidon's made a foolish, unauthorized decision and denied the presidential party lodging at Ammidon's tavern, forcing Washington and his entourage to travel an additional distance of five miles on a cold and rainy day to seek quarters at Uxbridge. When Ammidon and his daughter heard of the mishap involving George Washington and that he had traveled on to the Taft Tavern, they traveled to Uxbridge to try to persuade Washington to return to Mendon. The flustered Ammidon found Washington retired for the night. However, Washington momentarily left his room, attired only in a dressing gown, nightcap, and slippers, to greet Ammidon. They talked briefly, but the disappointed Ammidon could not persuade Washington to backtrack to Mendon and stay with him. At the end of their conversation, Washington turned to Ammidon's daughter and said, "Allow me to ask you one question. You have come a good ways to see an old man; how far would you have gone to see a young one?" Having resolved the dilemma of his resting place and feeling relieved to have soothed Ammidon's feelings, Washington returned to his room for the night. The president so enjoyed the hospitality he received at the Taft Tavern that when he arrived in Hartford, Washington wrote a letter and enclosed several pieces of chintz, a brightly colored fabric, one for each of Taft's daughters. The general also provided an additional gift of money for one of the daughters, who had gone beyond the call of duty to serve food and drink and provide whatever necessities Washington requested to make his stay a more agreeable one. Frank E. Best, The Amidon Family (Chicago: Frank E. Best, 1904), 30; Works Progress Administration, Massachusetts: A Guide to Its Places and People (Cambridge, MA: The Riverside Press, 1937), 605; Henry Chapin, Address Delivered at the Unitarian Church, Uxbridge, Mass., in 1864 (Worcester, MA: Press of Charles Hamilton, 1881), 41; D. Hamilton Hurd, History of Norfolk County, Massachusetts, with Biographical Sketches of Many of Its Pioneers and Prominent Men (Philadelphia: J. W. Lewis and Co., 1884), 106–7.

[288] US Department of the Treasury, "Resource Center: Portraits and Designs," last revised December 5, 2010. July 22, 2014, http://www.treasury.gov/resource-center/faqs/Coins/Pages/edu_faq_coins_portraits.aspx; Paul Hutchinson, "George Washington's Presidential Trail," July 23. 2014, http://www.paulhutch.com/brv_nhc/gw_presidential_trail.htm.

Taft Tavern, Uxbridge, Massachusetts

When the riflemen finally reach the village of Mendon, settled in 1660, they face a mere thirty-seven miles to reach Boston. For the redcoats, this is ill-boding news, for this means that the last of Washington's ten original crack-shot rifle companies will soon join and strengthen the general's siege line at Boston.

For the men of Cresap's rifle company, reaching Mendon is something akin to an anticlimax. All along the way, people have watched these riflemen, and likewise the Maryland marchers have watched back, intrigued and even at times astonished by these people of a different culture who exhibit a uniquely different accent. And now the last of the ten original companies of riflemen the townsfolk have so long awaited has finally arrived. Through each town they had passed, people stared at, cheered, admired, and revered these frontiersmen so different from them that they seem to have come from another world. Was it possible that the riflemen were truly nearing the end of their far-reaching, arduous journey?

Beginning at Thompson's Meeting House, Connecticut, earlier that morning, Cresap's Rifles have put twenty-one more miles behind them. On August 23, Cresap's men set up camp in the village of Mendon at the present-day site of Founder's Park.[289] The men of Mendon mustered at this same site in the spring when they heard news of the Battle of Lexington. From here, the men joined their fellow patriots in Boston, taking the Middle Post Road eastward, the same road Cresap's company now travel. The location of Mendon along the Middle Post Road makes

---

289 Harrity. Journal of Captain William Hendricks, 29.

this town a popular stopping place for military units.[290] Just across the street from where Cresap camps sits Colonel Philip Ammidon's Tavern where in 1776, Captain Nathan Hale, traveling with his company, will eat breakfast.[291]

Ammidon Tavern, Mendon, Massachusetts

Alexander Scammell, born in a part of Mendon known today as Milford, will become Mendon's most famous son of the revolution. He will participate in many of the major battles of the war and will become part of George Washington's inner circle.[292]

On the morning of August 24, Cresap's company breaks camp and proceeds southeast along the Old Mendon Road on the Middle Post Road. From Mendon, the riflemen travel along present Providence Road to Hartford Road East. At Bellingham, the Marylanders cross the upper headwaters of Charles River for the first time, following Hartford Road East until the road joins present-day Route 126 East. Along this section of road, the riflemen

---

290 Paul Revere took this route on the Old Mendon Road to convey the Suffolk Resolves to the Continental Congress in Philadelphia. Nathan Hale also traveled on this road.

291 Richard Grady and John Trainor, "Patriots Day: Mendon's Role in the American Revolution," Mendon, Massachusetts, July 23, 2014, http://hope1842.com/mendonamerrev.html; Richard Grady, "Mendon Walking Tour," Blackstone Daily, July 23, 2014, http://www.blackstonedaily.com/mendon.pdf. The general route Cresap's Rifles marched from Thompson, Connecticut, to Mendon, Massachusetts, followed East Thompson Road through Douglas State Forest to Douglas, Massachusetts. From Douglas, traveling on Route 16, they continued on Hartford Road West to just before where the road intersects with the 146 Worcester-Providence Turnpike. From here, they continued on Hartford Avenue West to just north of Uxbridge, where Route 122 intersects. From here, Cresap's company continued onward on Hartford Road East until the intersection with Route 16 just before Mendon. From here, the riflemen continued on Route 16 a short distance before they reached Mendon.

292 At Valley Forge, Washington would appoint Scammell to adjutant general. This deserved promotion is not the Mendonite's only claim to fame. Scammell, whose humor on occasion proffered some much-needed release of tension, became part of Washington's inner circle, whose members enjoyed Scammell's easygoing nature. Doling out his amusing stories and jokes, Scammell was one of the few officers who could make Washington laugh. In the fall of 1780, Washington would appoint Scammell to oversee the execution of John André, a cunning English officer caught up in the spy business for the British when he teamed up with the treasonous Benedict Arnold. During the Siege of Yorktown, Scammell received a fatal wound and died shortly afterward, thus becoming the highest-ranking officer Washington lost at Yorktown. Grady, "Mendon Walking Tour"; George F. Partridge, History of the Town of Bellingham, Massachusetts 1719–1919 (Bellingham, MA: Town of Bellingham, 1919), 197.

are encouraged by a mile marker and its inscription: "Thirty-one miles from Boston, RS, 1767."[293] The *RS* on the mile marker stands for *Royal Service,* as the postal service is at the time under the authority of the King of England.[294]

The riflemen continue on this course until it intersects with present-day Village Street (Old Mendon Road) on the west side of the Medway settlement. Here the men march on Village Street through the New England town. To the north sprawls the Great Black Swamp, a mucky body of water that separates the towns of Medway and Millis. In Medway, Village Street parallels the nearby Charles River.[295]

At Medway, Cresap passes by Clark's "Ordinary," a place of public entertainment that serves both "man and beast"[296] on the Middle Post Road (present-day Village Street). This portion of the road is located halfway between Dedham and Mendon, thus the name Midway. Cresap's men also march by the Moses Richardson Tavern (circa 1720), also on Village Street on the far east side of town.[297]

As is true of other New England towns where the patriotic spirit runs deep, most of the able-bodied Medway men are serving on the siege line at Roxbury and Cambridge. To further perpetuate this spirit, the town takes an active role in boycotting any products made by the British.[298] On April 19, 1775, as soon as they heard the Lexington alarm, at least thirty-seven townsmen marched this very road under the command of John Partridge. The men are fated to serve under Washington for the next eight months in Cambridge until the siege ends.[299]

The riflemen travel about six and a half miles on Village Street, crossing the Charles River by way of the Great Bridge (present-day Dover Road Bridge) before reaching the settlement of Medfield. From Medfield, the company continues east about five more miles on present-day Route 109 before reaching Ellis's Tavern,[300] at present-day 549 High Street, Westwood, Massachusetts. The tavern, built about 1732, also serves as a stagecoach stop, community-center store, and post office. The community uses the upstairs hall for dances, meetings, and other types of entertainment. Fire will destroy this building in 1887.[301]

When traveling westward on this road from Boston, settlers at this time refer to this corridor as the Road to the Wilderness. However, the riflemen continue eastward, walking through the town of Medfield until they finally

---

293 This mile marker that was on Route 126 is now displayed at the Ernie Taft Memorial Historical Center in Bellingham, Massachusetts. This part of the road through Bellingham was laid out in 1670 to connect Medfield to Mendon. The road became part of the Middle Post Road that connected Boston to New York by way of Hartford. In the early eighteenth century, travel was light on this section of road. A one-way stagecoach trip from Boston to New York using the Middle Post Road took two weeks. Ken Hamwey, "Bellingham Historical Museum Could Use a Helping Hand," Bellingham Bulletin, November 2009, accessed November 26, 2017, http://www.bluetoad.com/display_article.php?id=253829; Partridge, History of the Town of Bellingham, Massachusetts, 47–8.

294 Partridge, History of the Town of Bellingham, Massachusetts, 68–9; Hamwey, "Bellingham Historical Museum Could Use a Helping Hand."

295 Partridge, History of the Town of Bellingham, Massachusetts, 68–9; E. O. Jameson, The History of Medway, 1713–1885 (Providence, RI: J. A. and R. A. Reid, 1886), 56.

296 Francis D. Donovan, The Middle Post Road in Medway (Medway, MA: Francis D. Donovan, 1991), 6-7.

297 Hurd, History of Norfolk County, Massachusetts, with Biographical Sketches of Many of Its Pioneers and Prominent Men, 442, 543.

298 In January 1775, Medway town officials voted for thirty pounds "'to encourage the enlisting of a number of able-bodied men…to complete and hold themselves in readiness to march at the shortest notice." These were called minutemen. Hurd, History of Norfolk County, Massachusetts, with Biographical Sketches of Many of Its Pioneers and Prominent Men, 552; Jameson, The History of Medway, 411.

299 Gary Richardson, "Richardson Tavern, Millis, Massachusetts," Rootsweb, 2005, July 24, 2014, http://archiver.rootsweb.ancestry.com/th/read/RICHARDSON/2005-06/1117744546; Jameson, The History of Medway, 214; Francis D. Donovan, The New Grant: A History of Medway (New York: Mill River Press, 1976); Hurd, History of Norfolk County, Massachusetts, with Biographical Sketches of Many of Its Pioneers and Prominent Men, 552; Works Progress Administration, Massachusetts: A Guide to Its Places and People, 442.

300 Harrity, Journal of Captain William Hendricks, 29.

301 "Westwood Public Library Historic Photograph Collection," Historic Photographs of Westwood, Massachusetts, dcrapbook, March 2015; Liz Taurasi, "Historical View of Westwood: Ellis Tavern," Westwood Patch, July 25, 2012, July 23, 2014, http://westwood.patch.com/groups/goodnews/p/historical-view-of-westwood-ellis-tavern.

stop in present-day Westwood, the site of Ellis Tavern.[302] Here, on August 24, Cresap camps the last night of his journey, having traveled twenty-three miles this day.[303]

Since most of the able-bodied men are serving on Washington's siege line, it is mostly women, children, and the elderly who line the streets to witness the parade of fast-moving riflemen dressed in their signature hunting shirts, breechcloth pants, and moccasins and carrying their distinctive long rifles. One would expect the riflemen to be trudging forward with heavy feet after walking these many miles from western Maryland. However, Cresap's company marches light-footed through Westwood, moving as if their feet are not touching the ground. The townsfolk gaze in amazement at these high-spirited patriots who, as they understand it, have the capability with their rifles of "snuffing the candle" or "driving the nail" with perfect aim from the unbelievable distance of two hundred yards.[304] Reports state that Washington's riflemen can "hit a card nine times out of ten"…at 150 yards… The destruction they make of officers is dreadful."[305]

Because of this influx of riflemen, who will ultimately number more than one thousand, the British must readjust their safety zone to a distance farther away from General Washington's siege line. Since Bunker Hill, the British regulars have felt trapped within the confines of Boston, harboring fears that a rifleman lurks behind every tree, rock, and barricade, waiting for the opportunity to shoot with deadly effect. Captain Thomas Pinckney of the Continental forces has heard that the British "apprehend that a Rifleman grows naturally behind each Tree and Bush on the Continent."[306] After witnessing several of their comrades fall from the aim and fire of the sharpshooters, some of the redcoats have begun to refer to these wilderness men in frontier dress as "shirt tail men, with their cursed twisted (rifled) guns, the most fatal widow and orphan-makers in the world."[307]

With each passing day, as Cresap's company strides closer and closer to Boston, the British experience deadly fire from riflemen in companies already on site, the results of which cause havoc in the British ranks. Just recently, "riflemen killed three men on board a ship at Charlestown Ferry at a distance of half-a-mile!"[308] Unfortunately for the redcoats, this is just the beginning of their woes. In a few days, the worst fears of the British will become a reality. The increasingly anxious redcoats are about to witness firsthand the remarkable shooting abilities of Cresap's Rifles - and those coats of red are the targets!

---

302 From Mendon, Cresap followed along the Old Mendon Road, laid out around 1670, and onward on present-day Hartford Avenue East until reaching Bellingham. The riflemen took the general alignment along present-day Route 126, crossing present-day Interstate 495. They then picked up Route 109 and continued east through Medfield to Westwood, following the original Old Boston and Hartford Middle Post Road.

303 Orion T. Mason, The Handbook of Medway History: A Condensed History of the Town of Medway, Massachusetts (G. M. Billings, 1913), 79; Town of Millis, Massachusetts, "Historical Geography of Millis," July 26, 2014, http://millispd.net/index.cfm?pid=12334; Donovan, The New Grant: A History of Medway, 16–31; Ernest A. Taft, Bellingham: Images of America Series (Charleston, SC: Arcadia Publishing, 2003), 38. Harrity, Journal of Captain William Hendricks, 29.

304 Roger D. McGrath, "The American Riflemen in the Revolutionary War," New American, September 3, 2010, http://www.thenewamerican.com/culture/history/item/4786-the-american-rifleman-in-the-revolutionary-war.

305 Jeremy Black, War for America: The Fight for Independence, 1775–1783 (Phoenix Mill, GB: Sutton Publishing Limited, 1991), 60.

306 Charles Royster, A Revolutionary People at War: The Continental Army and the American Character, 1775–1783 (Chapel Hill: University of North Carolina Press, 1979), 33.

307 Donald R. McDowell, "Those Tall American Patriots and Their Long Rifles," Revolutionary War Archives, 1988, July 25, 2014, http://www.revolutionarywararchives.org/longrifle.html.

308 Ibid.

CHAPTER 10

Rebels in Roxbury

Roxbury, Massachusetts
August 25, 1775

ON THE FINAL DAY OF their march, Cresap impels his men forward one last time. The captain's leadership over the long hike has sustained the riflemen's fighting spirit, which is as strong as—if not stronger than—when they left Fredericktown twenty-five days ago.

On August 25, starting from Ellis Tavern and traveling generally along present-day Route 109, Cresap's Rifles cover the final ten-mile leg from Dedham to Roxbury. Around midmorning, Cresap passes through the town of Dedham. This settlement is located approximately halfway between Ellis Tavern and Roxbury. It is here that Maryland's gallant troops enter into the land of the Massachusetts Sons of Liberty. This brotherhood shares a righteous cause and has much in common with the men of Cresap's Rifles. They are men who are willing to leave their families and livelihoods behind and sacrifice their earthly goods "to establish Justice, insure domestic Tranquility, provide for the common Defense, promote the general Welfare, and secure the blessings of Liberty [for themselves] and [for] Posterity."[309]

Cresap's company passes Mother Brook Canal,[310] probably the first man-made waterway constructed in America. Townsfolk constructed the canal sometime before 1640 in order to connect the Charles and Neponset Rivers, a project that supplies power to operate the settlement's corn mills.

At the Dedham church green, the company passes a granite base inscribed with the words "Pillar of Liberty." In 1766, the Sons of Liberty built a ten-foot classical column topped with a bust of William Pitt. These patriots built the monument to honor leaders in Parliament who had successfully repealed the 1765 Stamp Act with its unjust taxes. The text inscribed in Latin on the stone base of the monument states that Pitt and parliament saved "America from impending Slavery." Colonists believe that the support of Pitt saved the colonies from the "jaws of hell"[311] resulting from British tyranny and overreach. However, on May 11, 1769, angry colonists destroyed the shrine after Parliament imposed new burdensome taxes on the colonies without their representation. On this morning of August 25, 1775, as Cresap and his riflemen march through town, only the granite base remains.

Most of the able-bodied men of Dedham are now serving on General Washington's siege line outside Boston. From this town populated by nearly 2,000 people, 672 men have left their families, homes, oxen, and plows to serve in the American Revolution. Forty-seven of these men will never return home.[312]

---
309 The Preamble to the US Constitution, 1787.
310 The grandson of Michael Cresap, Michael Cresap Sprigg (1791–1845), served as the president of the Chesapeake and Ohio Canal in Maryland in 1841–1842. Joseph Ord Cresap and Bernarr Cresap, The History of the Cresaps (Gallatin, TN: The Cresap Society, 1987), 259, 278.
311 David Hackett Fischer, Liberty and Freedom: A Visual History of America's Founding Ideas (New York: Oxford University Press, 2005), 99.
312 Fischer, Liberty and Freedom: A Visual History of America's Founding Ideas, 99; Dedham Historical Society, "A Capsule History of Dedham," September 10, 2014, http://web.archive.org/web/20061006081231/http://www.dedhamhistorical.org/history.php.

Cresap may stop at the Woodward Tavern[313] standing near the former Pillar of Liberty. Here, just about a year before in September 1774, patriots held the Suffolk Convention, which produced the Suffolk Resolves. This document "lighted the match that kindled the mighty conflagration of the American Revolution."[314] Language in the Suffolk Resolves later influenced the writers of the Declaration of Independence. The Resolves stated that the recently British-imposed Intolerable Acts were unjust and deprived the colonists of the basic rights to which they were entitled "by laws of nature, the British Constitution, and the Charter of the Province [Massachusetts]."[315] The Suffolk Resolves encouraged towns to organize militias "to protect the rights of the people."[316] The convention also appointed a committee to report and publish the name of any person caught drinking the recently banned tea. Paul Revere speedily delivered the Resolves to the Continental Congress, which quickly adopted this document.[317]

Captain Cresap, who received some of his childhood formal education in Baltimore, Maryland, passes this morning through a settlement that boasts the first tax-base-funded free school in America. Dedham, the town that first planted "the seed of American education,"[318] had authorized this school in 1644. Descendants of the first students who attended this public school will become presidents of Dartmouth College, Yale University, and Harvard University.

After marching more than five hundred miles since leaving Fredericktown, Captain Cresap leads his men to the battlefront at Roxbury.[319] With Cresap's Rifles present, all ten original southern rifle companies selected by Congress on June 14 are present on site, just outside Boston.

Newspapers express amazement at the quick response of the rifle companies to march long distances and defend Lady Liberty: The riflemen "had marched…[up] to 700 miles…all this was performed in less than two months, without a farthing of money being advanced by the continental treasury."[320]

Along the way from Dedham to Roxbury, Cresap and his men begin seeing signs of Washington's ragtag army. The riflemen walk into Roxbury with verve and confidence. Marching light-footedly, they see the harbor near the Boston Neck area for the first time. After a march of more than 550 miles, the riflemen exhibit little sign of wear, showing about as much stamina and panache as they had when they began their journey. One rifleman from Price's Maryland company, after marching the same route Cresap has just come, perhaps captures the esprit de corps of all the riflemen. This man, after three weeks of continuous marathon distance walks covering 550 miles, states that the jaunt was "pleasant."[321]

However, the above comment disguises the fact that some of the rifle companies suffered casualties along the road to New England. The same rifleman who describes his hike as pleasant also notes in his journal that his unit experienced four desertions, five illnesses, and one death along the way. Even in his haste to arrive in Boston, Captain Price still took the time to arrange that the body of the deceased be transported home to Maryland. One may speculate that Cresap's company has also experienced losses along their journey to the front lines.[322]

---

313 The Woodward Tavern was located where the Norfolk County Superior Court now stands.
314 Works Progress Administration. Massachusetts: A Guide to Its Places and People, 219.
315 Wikipedia, The Free Encyclopedia, s.v., "Suffolk Resolves," September 10, 2014, http://en.wikipedia.org/wiki/Suffolk_Resolves.
316 Ibid.
317 Works Progress Administration, Massachusetts: A Guide to Its Places and People, 217–22.
318 Dedham Historical Society, "A Capsule History of Dedham."
319 James McIntyre, "Separating Myth from History: The Maryland Riflemen in the War of Independence," Maryland Historical Magazine, June 2009, 111, 117.
320 "Extract from a Letter from Cambridge," Pennsylvania Packet, August 28, 1775, 6.
321 Balch, Papers Relating Chiefly to the Maryland Line during the Revolution, 12.
322 Ibid.

The riflemen arrive in war-torn Roxbury around noon.[323] Although other southern rifle companies have been present for several weeks, Roxbury citizens now see Cresap's Rifles for the first time. At first glance, the townsfolk sense something unique about Cresap's company. Several of the riflemen seem like giants - some of the men in the unit stand over six feet tall. These stout and hardy men are dressed in white frocks—sometimes called rifle or hunting shirts—and buckskin breeches, and on their heads, they wear round hats. The backwoods mountain men outlandishly paint their faces the Indian way. Their feet are clad in soft but serviceable moccasins, which, to the untrained eyes of the masses, make the men appear shoeless. For weapons, the riflemen carry tomahawks along with the famed long rifle, symbol of frontier independence.[324]

The senses of Cresap's men are overwhelmed with the sights and sounds of the Boston battlefront and the hustle and bustle of the business at hand: the hodgepodge of campsites spread all about and the comings and goings of a wide array of troops milling about in all directions. In the summer air, the men detect a strange odor. It soon becomes apparent that they are catching a whiff of decaying seaweed wafting inland from the Boston Harbor and the nearby briny sea. The squawking of seagulls overhead is also a new experience for the frontiersmen, many of whom have never seen an ocean, much less the large amassing of such noisy flying creatures.

Near Boston and the surrounding military confines, the riflemen cross a fine line between a world of relative calm along the long road they traveled and a world of chaos and unfamiliarity. The men of the company are at first taken aback by the barking orders of officers speaking in a New England dialect. Forced to waste no time in becoming acclimated to their new surroundings, the men occasionally step off the road to let wagons, horses, and troops pass. All this military activity in an urban environment, unlike their experiences on the Ohio frontier the previous summer during the Indian War, is alien to Cresap's men. Adding to the pandemonium, the company must adjust to the noise of ear-piercing cannons that bellow round after round from the ranks of both British and Colonial forces.

With tensions running high, Cresap does not report immediately to Washington's headquarters in Cambridge but alights in the Roxbury area, remaining on the right wing of the siege line. Roxbury is located near Boston Neck and is perhaps the most vulnerable section of Washington's long protective line girding Boston. Major General Artemas Ward, second in command only to George Washington - with Ward's more than five thousand men – oversees the right wing of the line at Roxbury covering Boston Neck and Dorchester Heights.

Captain Cresap reports to General Ward, who briefs the captain on the current state of affairs.[325] Ward brings the captain up to date on the rifle companies that have already reported, the placement and duties of officers and men, and all other vital information pertaining to the situation at hand. From this valuable intelligence, Cresap also learns about the arrivals and stations of the other rifle companies.

---

323 The general alignment Cresap's Rifles took on the last leg of their journey from Westwood brought them to an eastbound path on present-day Route 109 to Common Street and then to Dedham. From Dedham, they continued on Washington Street to Roxbury.

324 Thacher, Military Journal During the American Revolutionary War, 37–8.

325 General Ward's headquarters at Roxbury, built in 1723, were located next to the present-day site of the Redemptorist Mission Church on Mission Hill, at the intersection of Tremont and Alphonsus Streets. Captain Cresap probably reported to Major General Ward's headquarters to receive orders and briefings on more than one occasion throughout the summer of 1775. The mansion sat "in the midst of a large domain of park and wooded hills, and presented a picture of grandeur and stateliness not common in the New World." From this vantage point, Ward's view of Boston presented a grand and luxurious panorama, in stark contrast to the nearby war-torn town of Roxbury. Captain Cresap would have seen an elegant building containing colonnades and a vestibule with large mahogany doors studded with silver. The front door opened into a wide hall, where floors sparkled with different colors cast from the light that beamed through richly painted glass windows. Underneath the dome in the large room, two carved wooden cherubs with extended wings supported an enormous chandelier of cut glass. On the floor just underneath the dome stood a marble column surrounded by a divan splashed with materials of gorgeous coloring. The surrounding panel work on the walls consisted of intricate carvings fashioned in Europe. Highly detailed paintings of birds, fruits, and flowers abounded. Persian rugs carpeted the staterooms, and on the walls hung elaborate tapestries hued with silver and gold. Charles Martyn, The Life of Artemas Ward (New York: Artemas Ward, 1921), 167–8; Sam Bass Warner, Jr., Street Car Suburbs: The Process of Growth in Boston (1870–1900) (Boston: President and Fellows of Harvard College, 1978), 95.

During this briefing, Cresap learns that Captain George Nagel[326] from Reading, Pennsylvania, reported on July 18 and commands the first rifle company to arrive at Washington's headquarters in Cambridge. Captain Michael Doudel from York, Pennsylvania, arrived on July 25.

Only several weeks into his command, Washington has anxiously awaited the arrival of all the southern rifle companies. This is indicated when he writes from his Cambridge headquarters on July 28, "Part of the Rifle-Men is come in and the rest daily expected."[327] The general is not the only one awaiting the arrival of the remaining rifle companies to report for duty. A letter from a person in the area written soon after the arrival of Nagel's company notes, "The Reading company of rifles [Nagel] got into camp last Tuesday [July 18]; the rest are hourly expected and much wanted."[328]

Over time, the rifle companies drifted into town in waves. Much like the water riffles lapping the Boston harbor, one round of men after the other emerged from the south. Captain James Chambers from present-day Franklin County, Pennsylvania, reported to headquarters on August 7. Next Captain Daniel Morgan, starting from Winchester, Virginia, arrived in Cambridge on August 8. Following Morgan, both Captain Thomas Price from Frederick County, Maryland, and Captain William Hendricks from Carlisle, Pennsylvania, proceeded into Cambridge on August 9. Two days later, on August 11, Captain Hugh Stephenson from Shepherdstown, Virginia, reported to General Washington.[329] On August 17, Colonel William Thompson's battalion reported to headquarters at Cambridge. All nine rifle companies from Pennsylvania, including the three Pennsylvania rifle companies that Congress approved after June 14, were present when Captain James Ross[330] from Lancaster County, Pennsylvania, arrived at Cambridge headquarters on August 18.

On August 25, with Cresap's Rifles in town, Washington now has available to him thirteen rifle companies, making up more than thirteen hundred expert sharpshooters present and fit for duty.[331] The last of the ten original rifle companies authorized by Congress on June 14 to join Washington's army, Cresap and his men hold the distinction of having marched the longest distance. And one other astounding fact on this day is noted by his superiors—out

---

326 Captain George Nagel was the great-uncle of the future president Abraham Lincoln by way of Nagel's marriage to Rebecca Lincoln, the sister of President Lincoln's great-grandfather. Patrick H. Hannum, "America's First Company Commanders," Infantry 4 (2013): 12–9, accessed December 19, 2017, http://www.benning.army.mil/infantry/magazine/issues/2013/Oct-Dec/pdfs/Hannum.pdf.

327 Fitzpatrick, The Writings of George Washington from the Original Manuscript Sources, vol. 3, 375.

328 Chris Hueneke, "The Abrahams," Umstead Family Genealogy Central, 2007, September 14, 2014, http://www.umstead.org/abraham%20md%20time%20line.html.2007; Waymarking.com, "Captain Michael Doudel's Company, York, PA: US Revolutionary War Memorials," posted by Math Teacher, April 2, 2013, September 10, 2014, http://www.waymarking.com/waymarks/WMGR0M_Captain_Michael_Doudels_Company_York_PA. 2013; George R. Prowell, Continental Congress at York, Pennsylvania: York County in the Revolution (York, PA: York Printing Company, 1914); Richards, "The First Defenders of the Revolution," 22.

329 The ninety-eight volunteers of Captain Hugh Stephenson's rifle company promised each other that if they were still living in fifty years, they would meet for a reunion at present-day Shepherdstown, West Virginia. This was where, on July 17, 1775, the Virginia riflemen began their six-hundred-mile "bee-line" march to Boston. In the spring of 1825, only two of the five surviving riflemen were able to keep their pledge to reunite at the designated spot: Major Henry Bendinger of Berkeley County and George Michael Bedinger of Kentucky. Coughlin Bill, "The Spirit of 1775," Historical Marker Database, April 15, 2011, September 9, 2014, http://www.hmdb.org/marker.asp?marker=41708.

330 Captain James Ross (1753–1808) was the son of Colonel George Ross (1730–1779), a signer of the Declaration of Independence. David J. Hooker, "Colonel James Ross," September 9, 2014, http://www.djhooker.com/26/10990.htm; Francis B. Heitman, Historical Register of the Officers of the Continental Army: April 1775 to December 1783 (Washington, DC: The Rare Book Shop Publishing Company, 1914); Montgomery, Colonel William Thompson's Battalion of Riflemen, 1906.

331 Richards, "The First Defenders of the Revolution," 20–3; Balch, Papers Relating Chiefly to the Maryland Line during the Revolution, 12.

of all the rifle companies now present at Cambridge, Cresap's company, with 130 men, contains the largest number of battle-ready men.[332]

The geography of Boston appears as a peninsula-shaped like a head with a long neck. Water surrounds the head except at the neck, mapped out as a thin strip of land that connects Boston to the mainland. The harbor surrounding British-occupied Boston protects the city in the same way that a moat protects a castle. The town of Roxbury lies two miles directly south of Boston on the opposite side of Boston Neck.

Between Boston and Roxbury, at the southern end of Boston Neck, lies the colonial fort at Lamb's Dam.[333] The construction of the fort is still underway when Cresap arrives in Roxbury. Well before the outbreak of hostilities with the British, Boston residents built a dam to prevent the tide from overflowing the marshes of Boston Neck. Although musket men are working on building a protective trench at Lamb's Dam, the fort is still inadequate to protect the men on "fatigue duty," a military term for jobs that do not require arms. Cannonballs fired from British cannons continually disrupt the men from their labors as they build the trench. The workers are forced to "cover themselves in the daytime from the cruelty of the cannonballs"[334] that the British hurl at them. This fort—located less than a mile from the redcoats' fortification in Boston — is the closest colonial entrenchment to British forces on the siege line. Several of the nearby hills at Roxbury also contain forts recently built by the colonials.

Cresap and his men see that Roxbury was at one time "a pleasant place,"[335] a settlement of beauty and charm that probably showered long-lasting warm memories upon its residents and visitors. However, the siege has taken a devastating toll on this once-bucolic town. Roxbury is now a "desolate"[336] war zone. With every day the colonials and the British exchange cannonball fire, the village becomes further damaged and degraded. Since peaceful citizens have abandoned their homes to escape harm's way, family abodes now serve as barracks for colonial soldiers.

The combination of British shrapnel and gunfire riddling the sides of homes and businesses with bullets and gaping cannonball holes has turned some homes into mere burned-out shells. The appalling downward-spiraling disintegration of the town will continue throughout the summer of 1775.

After a relentless but ardent twenty-five-day hike from Maryland to Boston, Captain Cresap and his men have earned a much-needed break. However, downtime is not in the cards for Cresap's Rifles today. A full-fledged assault is now being launched from Castle William—a fortification that sits on a small island just east of Dorchester Heights and serves as a British stronghold during the siege. The cannonade from Castle William has provided a continuous bombardment into Roxbury day and night for the past four days.[337]

---

332 Young, The Spirit of 1775: A Letter of Robert Magaw," 22. In 1775, people knew Ward's headquarters as the Pierpont Castle or Brinley Place. In 1809, years after the Revolutionary War, General Henry Dearborn (1751–1829) became the owner of the house. Dearborn fought under John Stark at Bunker Hill and was a participant in the War of 1812. In 1869, the Redemptorist Fathers purchased the property. A stroke of bad luck followed in 1876, when a fire destroyed part of the house. However, the house continued to accommodate Redemptorists until 1902. At this time leaders of the flock razed the house to build a brick-and-stone rectory next to the existing Mission Church. Martyn, The Life of Artemas Ward, 167–8; Warner, Street Car Suburbs: The Process of Growth in Boston, 95.
333 Boston Revolutionary War historian J. L. Bell notes that Lamb's Dam extended from the present junction of Hampden and Albany Streets to a point near present Walnut Place, following very closely the present line of Northampton Street. The construction of the fort was completed by September 1775 and was located just upland from the dam. The fort's breastworks and entrenchments extended across the present highway.
334 Balch, Papers Relating Chiefly to the Maryland Line during the Revolution, 13.
335 Ibid., 12.
336 Balch, Papers Relating Chiefly to the Maryland Line during the Revolution, 12.
337 Castle William sat on land that is said to be the oldest continuously fortified site of English origin in the United States. The military had fortified the site since 1634. Today, Castle William is a Massachusetts state park.

About the same hour that Cresap arrives in Roxbury on Friday, August 25, the Colonial army is propelled into high alert after receiving an alarm that the British may soon land their boats on shore at Dorchester Point just east of Roxbury. Soon after the alarm sounds around noon on Friday, a major movement of troops and artillery causes quite a stir in and around the camps. Along with this orderly yet frantic exodus of men, it may justifiably be assumed that Cresap's men and several other units are now proceeding to the alarm port, a breastwork near Roxbury that provides cover and safety from incoming cannonballs.

From the alarm port, assuming that Cresap's Rifles participate, his men march a short distance east from Roxbury to Dorchester Point. Upon arrival, the riflemen see that Continental musketeers, so called by the riflemen because the musketeers carry smoothbore rifles, have effectively driven the British boats far from the shoreline. In fact, the redcoats are so far out of range of the sharpshooters that the British pose no further threat today.[338]

With the British threat thusly allayed, Cresap reports to General Artemas Ward. Perhaps while he meets with command staff, the captain orders his officers to take their company of riflemen and join up with Captain Price and his Maryland rifle company, who have "wheeled about" from Dorchester Point and are marching "into the country for to supple [his men's] "joints and make [them] healthy."[339]

As the men of Captain Price's company wind down their field exercises and prepare to return to camp, the British "[throw] a bomb in Roxbury which accidentally [fall} upon [its] fuse in the soft ground, and [sinks] in so far the fuse [cannot] not get air, which made it die out." A riflemen who witnessed this later recorded the following in his journal: "Then our men went to the place and dug [the bomb] out, which [we] weighed, and it was 190 pounds. It fell 1½ miles from where the Regulars threw it from."[340]

Headquarters staff briefs Cresap that Washington's army presently consists of up to sixteen thousand colonials, and with the exception of the men in the rifle companies, almost all of the men lack experience in the art of warfare. Meanwhile, the colonials face a British army thought to contain six thousand British regulars, all highly trained.

Because at this time the British control the heights of Bunker Hill and Breeds Hill next to Charlestown, General Washington—with valid reason—believes that an attack from Boston could come at any time. What is worse, Cresap is informed that the Continental army is faced with an ammunition crisis.[341] Washington's troops have no more than nine cartridges of ammunition per man, contrasted with the British army, which possesses an estimated sixty rounds per soldier. This fact must remain top secret. If the British discover the Continental army's true condition of its armaments, there could be an immediate attack from the enemy.[342]

Captain Cresap learns more about the nature of the nine -mile, crescent-shaped line of Colonial troops extending along the west side of the Boston Harbor from Medford southward to the neck at Roxbury. All of Washington's officers know that this long, thin alignment makes their army very vulnerable; an attack in the middle of the line could divide his army, causing a dangerous breech and severely weakening the effectiveness of the siege.

---

338 Balch, Papers Relating Chiefly to the Maryland Line during the Revolution, 14.

339 Ibid.

340 Ibid.

341 Major General Philip Schulyer highlighted the ammunition shortage in a letter to the President of Congress dated July 11, 1775: "Scarcity of ammunition subsists, no powder yet come to hand; not a gun carriage for the few proper guns we have, and as yet very little provisions…troops… badly, very badly, armed indeed, and one poor armorer to repair their guns." Fitzpatrick, The Writings of George Washington from the Original Manuscript Sources, vol. 3, 375.

342 *The shortage of ammunition was so desperate that Washington issued a general order on July 23, 1775 for his soldiers to construct a type of armament used by the military in medieval times. This unsophisticated weaponry was composed of thirteen foot long pikes of two handed spears made from the wood of trees that happened to be plentiful in the region just outside the camps. (Fitzpatrick, The Writings of George Washington from the Original Manuscript Sources vol. 3, 338; 357)*

History does not record Captain Cresap's thoughts about or reaction to what he hears at his first headquarters briefing. If he stops to ponder too much, such thoughts will naturally lead to concerns for all those back home who are counting on Cresap's leadership to complete their mission and to return the men of his company safely home to their families.

Though he disguises it well from the public, since late spring when he left Kentucky, Cresap has suffered from an illness that leaves him in a state of exhaustion. Now that he is in the Boston vicinity, considering the slow means of Colonial travel, Cresap may as well be half a world away from his home at Oldtown, Maryland; his beautiful pregnant wife, Mary; and their four children: Maria, nine years old; Elizabeth, seven years old; Sarah, five years old; and James Michael, two years old. Mary is very far along in her pregnancy and is due to deliver her baby in two months. The staff at Washington's headquarters believes this siege will end soon. If his superior officers' estimates are correct, as Cresap hopes, he can return home before Mary gives birth to their baby.

Washington stations the riflemen along the siege line as they arrive.[343] Proof of the effectiveness of the riflemen in Boston is immediate. One American patriot gleefully writes, "They [the riflemen] are now stationed on our lines, and their shot have proved fatal to British officers and soldiers who expose themselves to view, even at more than double the distance of the common musketshot."[344]

Military personnel follow suit with their own opinions. Rifle company captain James Chambers writes on August 13, just a little less than two weeks before Captain Cresap arrives, that since the first rifle companies reported for duty beginning July 18, the British have on a daily basis fired their cannon at the Colonials but that miraculously they "have not yet killed a man."[345] However, the British are not so fortunate. During this same period, the Colonial army, with the help of the riflemen, has killed forty-two redcoats and taken thirty-eight prisoners, "twelve of the latter Tories."[346] Among those killed are four British captains, one the son of a lord.

Thompson writes that General Washington allows "the riflemen go where they please" and that they keep the British "regulars in continual hot water."[347] While many along the front and throughout the colonies beam with pride and gratitude for these gallant men who appear to them as well-cast heroes, not all who espy these marching saviors are impressed with the riflemen's colorful attire and cavalier manner. Captain Smyth, a British loyalist, is inspired to write the following scathing lyrics titled "The Rebels," about the rifle companies in Washington's army. Both the redcoats and loyalists sing Smyth's derogatory verses to "Black Joke," an old Colonial melody. "The Rebels" will become the most popular loyalist song sung in taverns patronized by redcoats and loyalists during the American Revolution.

> Come listen a while, and I'll sing you a song.
> I'll show you those Yankees are all in the wrong.
> Who with blustering look and a most awkward gate

---

[343] General Washington divided his nine-mile siege line into three sections: Major General Artemas Ward commanded the right wing of the line centered at Roxbury; Major General Charles Lee, with about five thousand men, commanded the left wing of the line near Winter Hill and Ploughed Hill, guarding the roads coming out of British-occupied Charlestown; and Major General Israel Putnam, with about five thousand men, commanded the center wing of the line, operating from the fortifications at Prospect Hill near Cambridge, where Washington's headquarters were located. The thirteen rifle companies, making up an additional estimated thirteen hundred men, arrived in the summer of 1775 to join the Siege of Boston and contributed additional manpower to Washington's Continental army, bringing the total to about sixteen thousand men. Kennedy Hickman, "American Revolution: Brigadier General Daniel Morgan," ThoughtCo, accessed April 4, 2017, https://www.thoughtco.com/brigadier-general-daniel-morgan-2360604; Young, The Spirit of 1775: A Letter of Robert Magaw," 7–8.
[344] Thacher, Military Journal During the American Revolutionary War, 38.
[345] John Blair Linn and William H. Egle, Pennsylvania, War of the Revolution: Battalions and Line (Harrisburg, PA: Lane and Hart, 1880), 5.
[346] Ibid.
[347] Ibid.

> 'Gainst their lawful Sovereign dare for to prate,
> With their hunting shirts and rifle guns.[348]

Although meant to insult, Captain Smyth unintentionally pays the highest compliment to the riflemen. The song shows that the riflemen have made a deep impression on the minds of the king's military. Verse after verse, the song drags the names of the riflemen through the mud. The riflemen are "arch-rebels, barefooted tatterdemalions [dressed in rags] [who forgot] the mercies of Great Britain's King that saved their forefathers' necks from a string."[349]

The slander of the riflemen continues, "Their pasteboard dollars prove a common curse"—this alluding to the paper currency they attach to boards for target practice and public shooting demonstrations. Smyth's lyrics state the riflemen "renounce their allegiance and take up their arms; [that they] assemble like hornets in swarms; [and that] carrion crow follows them wherever they go."

As if that is not enough, the British and loyalists sing that the riflemen carry "the standard of Satan [patriotic banners] and that the riflemen are "perjured banditti [criminals that] now ruin this land, with their hunting shirts and rifle guns." The last verse of the song ends with hopes that the riflemen go to "oblivion" in hell, "fed with hot sulpher from Lucifer's kitchen."

The riflemen couldn't care less what derogatory songs their rivals sing about them, for the feeling is mutual. Let the British regulars sing their hearts out as long as it distracts them and they remain embedded in Boston. This allows General Washington more time to organize his army, obtain more ammunition, and strengthen his fortifications.[350]

Notwithstanding the somewhat misguided British perception that the Yankees are "perjured banditti,"[351] Cresap's men observe that the colonial soldiers along the siege line are in general good health and high spirits, and in a highly charged state of readiness. Morale is lifted even higher when word reaches the Maryland men that British deserters report that "the enemy are much terrified on account of the riflemen." Upon arrival at the battle-front, these riflemen are gratified to hear oft-repeated reports that since the presence of the rifle companies, "the enemy dare not show his head."[352] To add to their plucky mood, daily activity is eased by the riflemen's method of dress, the frontier style that easily distinguishes them from New England soldiers. Their unique appearance allows each man clothed in such manner of dress to "pass by sentinels and go almost where he pleases while officers of the regiments are stopped."[353]

Around the Roxbury military camps, veterans of Concord, Lexington, and Bunker Hill, no doubt entertain Cresap's men with war stories regarding the audacity of the British foe. Their colorful tales disclose dastardly deeds of redcoats who "plundered houses" in both Cambridge and Roxbury and "rendered them unfit to use," forced "women in childbed "from their homes "naked on the streets," and shot dead "old men" lying about "peaceably in

---

348 Arthur. F. Schrader, *American Revolutionary War: Songs to Cultivate the Sensations of Freedom*, Folkway Records no. FH 5279, album, 1976. Includes "The Rebels" and "The Liberty Tree."

349 The verse that the riflemen are "arch-rebels, barefooted tatterdemalions [dressed in rags] [who forgot] the mercies of Great Britain's King that saved their forefathers' necks from a string" rings true in the case of Michael Cresap, whose father, Thomas, led a rebellion against the king's Stamp Act in 1765.

350 Schrader, *American Revolutionary War: Songs to Cultivate the Sensations of Freedom*. The Pennsylvania Ledger published Captain Smyth's lyrics to "The Rebels" on January 7, 1778.

351 Ibid.

352 Young, "The Spirit of 1775: A Letter of Robert Magaw," 7–8.

353 Ibid.

their homes." These enlightening but sobering stories serve only to strengthen the riflemen's resolve to the rightness of their rebellious cause.[354]

At Roxbury, Cresap's Rifles are in close proximity to British fortifications. Here, where pandemonium could break loose at a moment's notice, riflemen prepare for battle. The next phase in their sojourn in this New England town leads them into a realm of the unknown, yet they revel in anticipation of what comes next.

Colonists note in their journals that since General Washington took charge on July 3, not one American on the colonists' siege line has been killed by British cannons or gunfire. With Cresap's company now present, the general's forces are as strong as they will be for the near future. Washington is anxious to make something happen to break the stalemate.

Devising a tactic meant to surprise the British, Washington draws up a plan—his first aggressive military move against the British since he assumed command of the Continental army. After sunset on August 26, the general will order his troops to seize a strategically located rolling mound called Ploughed Hill, about one half mile from Bunker Hill on Charlestown Neck. Washington's blueprint proposes that his army take possession of this low-rising plot of ground overlooking Charlestown and Boston one day after Cresap makes his presence known to headquarters. The stage is now set. On August 26, for the first time, in the heat of Boston's summer of 1775, the gates of hell are about to open!

---

[354] US National Park Service, "Roxbury during the Siege of Boston April 1775–March 1776," Boston National Historical Park, February 27, 2013, http://www.nps.gov/bost/forteachers/upload/roxbury.pdf.

CHAPTER 11

Into the Storm: Washington Takes Ploughed Hill

Roxbury and Ploughed Hill
August 26, 1775, to August 28, 1775

GENERAL WASHINGTON TRIES HIS BEST to end the stalemate that has lasted most of the summer. With the exception of a few minor skirmishes, the British have been relatively inactive since the southern rifle companies began arriving in late July.

Gage has good reason for his idleness this summer. The Battle of Bunker Hill has taken a severe toll on the forces he has available to fight. He lost 43 percent of his men who fought at Bunker Hill. Of the original 3,500 troops the British general had stationed in Boston last June, Gage engaged 2,300 of them in the fight at Bunker Hill, while the others remained in Boston to defend the city. Of the redcoats in the Battle of Bunker Hill, 228 were killed outright, and 828 others were wounded. Of that number, 250 died from their wounds within three weeks. As if that statistic is not bad enough, Gage also lost 92 of his 250 officers at Bunker Hill, many of them longtime, experienced veterans. As it stands, 2,000 British troops fit for duty remain in Boston while 2,000 more remain stationed on Bunker Hill. Making matters worse for the British is the hard fact that it takes three months to receive supplies and reinforcements from across the Atlantic; thus, any fresh resources are unfortunately three thousand miles away.[355]

Washington is not yet aware, but if the general only had spies in place, that mode of intelligence would have revealed that Gage is now extremely vulnerable. The British officer has only two thousand redcoats fit for duty. In the meantime, Washington has Gage trapped inside Boston within a semicircle of up to sixteen thousand of his colonial troops. Of these continentals, at least twelve hundred are sharpshooters serving in the rifle companies now stationed in the area.

Since the rifle companies began arriving, both officers and privates on the British side have been brought down by rifle fire when redcoats exposed themselves to the deadly aim of riflemen - who seem to harass the British as sport. And in so doing, the riflemen have also managed to capture and take prisoner British soldiers who grew slack while standing guard duty.

On August 13, while confusion and procrastination continue to occur, Robert Magaw, a major in command of a Pennsylvania rifle company, writes the following in a letter to the Committee of Correspondence located at Carlisle, Pennsylvania:

[I]t was Diverting some Days ago to stand on our Ramparts on prospect Hill and see half a Dozen Riffle men go Down to the Water side and from behind stone walls, Chimney's, etc. pop at [the British's] floating

---
[355] "Newport, Sept. 4," Rind's Virginia Gazette, September 28, 1775.

Battery's at About 300 [yards] Distance. [Tis] said we Killed several [.] A few Shotts from the Riffles always [brought] on fire from the floating Batteries and bunker Hill where the Enemy are [e]ntrenched but Without any Effect than to Afford us Amusement as they Seldom knew Where to fire and When they did their Great Guns [throw] the balls so Wild and uncertain that there is very little Danger. Our people went often in search of the Cannon balls and brought some into Camp…Gage has no hole to Creep out of but by the Sea. [I]f the God of Armies be but with us the Libertys of America are safe.[356]

After the conflict at Bunker Hill, Gage has gained a newfound respect for the "rebels." In a letter he writes during this time period, the British general states that the "trials we have had show that the rebels are not the despicable rabble too many have supposed them to be. In all their wars with the French they never showed so much conduct, attention and perseverance as they do now, and I find it owing to a military spirit … joined with an uncommon degree of zeal and enthusiasm, that they are otherwise. When they find cover, they make a good stand, and the country naturally strong, affords it to them, and they are taught to afford its natural strength by art."[357]

As Washington tries to provoke the British to come forth and fight, he is sorely cognitive of the fact that Congress struggles to pay his army. The alarming knowledge that ammunition remains scarce looms over the general's head. Washington desperately wants to put an end to this contest before winter arrives. Although he has learned that delivery of ammunition is forthcoming from New York, New London, and a few other places, none has yet arrived. The colonists cannot be proactive and launch a major offensive against the British chiefly because of the deficit of munitions the troops urgently need. Under these greatly challenging conditions, Washington does not know how long he can hold his army together.

However, Washington learns from deserters that the redcoats in Boston are also suffering, due to the British army's lack of fresh provisions and clothing. Because of the shortage of food and supplies, the British are pillaging nearby islands, and stealing farmers' sheep and cattle. The British are also destroying Boston homes to obtain anything usable for firewood, a resource in short supply for these invaders now dug in on American soil. By the end of the siege, the redcoats will raze almost all of the homes made of wood in Boston.

---

356 Young, "The Spirit of 1775: A Letter of Robert Magaw," 7–8; Hardy, 2015.
357 . Gage, General. "Extract of a Letter From General Gage to Lord Dartmouth." June 25, 1775.

Boston 1775

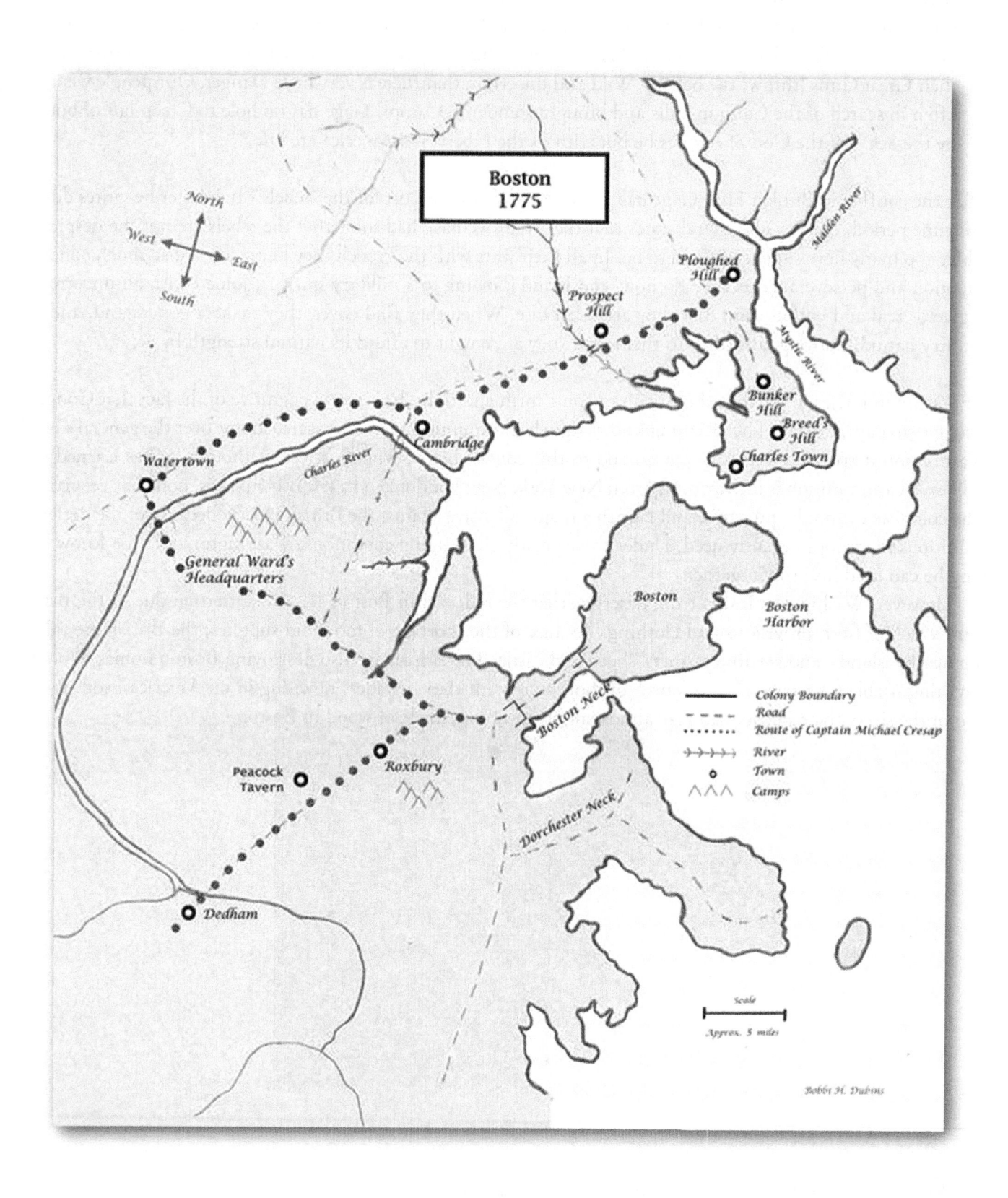

In the interim, as he attempts to calculate the next movement by the enemy, Washington presumes that the British must be waiting for reinforcements. He anticipates that once their reinforcements arrive, the British will most assuredly attack. During the month of August, even as Cresap was marching toward Boston, Washington's primary focus has involved efforts to strengthen fortifications at strategic places along the siege line, work that is now in the last stages of completion.

The Virginia general continues to hear rumors that the British boast of their intention to visit Washington and his army on "August 25"[358] somewhere along the siege line. Further news arrives that General Gage has put Brigadier General Earl Percy in command of the British lines at Boston Neck. Stories allege that authorities have put the British officer in charge so that he can "exhibit...proofs of his military abilities" and restore the honor that he lost in the recent "Lexington affray"[359] last April. However, the attack over Boston Neck at Roxbury does not occur on the rumored date of August 25. Now that all his rifle companies are present with Cresap's arrival, Washington plans to preempt the British and take possession of Ploughed Hill the next day. The day after Captain Cresap reports for duty at Roxbury, on the night of August 26, Washington initiates his first major offensive action as commander of the Continental army. The mission is to advance his lines and gain possession of the high point on Ploughed Hill (present-day Mount Benedict), a strategic middle ground between Winter Hill and the British-occupied Bunker Hill.[360]

General Washington has assigned the six original Pennsylvania rifle companies under Colonel Thompson to the left wing of the siege line. This grouping serves under the command of Major General Charles Lee situated on Prospect Hill near Cambridge. Washington stations the four rifle companies of Virginia and Maryland under Colonel Artemas Ward on the right wing of the siege line at Roxbury.

Never before at Roxbury has such an assembly of elite riflemen from two southern colonies gathered in one place. Among this roster of men is Daniel Cresap, Jr., who serves under his uncle Michael Cresap in Cresap's Independent Rifle Company, and Lieutenant Otho Holland Williams, who serves in Price's rifle company. The Maryland rifle companies work side by side with the two Virginia independent rifle companies under the commands of Captain Daniel Morgan and Captain Hugh Stephenson. This strategically placed pattern of defenders composes a true Continental unit, just as General Washington envisioned.[361]

General Washington hurries to align his plans, determined that he will take Ploughed Hill first. To accomplish this, on the night of August 26, Washington employs General Lee and Brigadier General John Sullivan to oversee a twelve-hundred-man working party supplied with shovels and picks. The workers carry gabions (baskets filled with earth and stones) and fascines (sticks used to build fortresses) and build a fort overnight on top of Ploughed Hill.

Most of the Pennsylvania riflemen under Colonel Thompson serve with General Lee's unit on Prospect Hill. To protect the working party, Washington assigns an additional twenty-four hundred guards, who, not to alarm the enemy, march quietly after nightfall without beat of drum to within three to four hundred feet of the redcoats'

---

358 Frothingham, History of the Siege of Boston, 233.
359 Ibid.
360 Balch, Papers Relating Chiefly to the Maryland Line during the Revolution, 14; Fitzpatrick, The Writings of George Washington from the Original Manuscript Sources, vol. 3, 453. Ploughed Hill, sixty-two feet above sea level, is about one mile north of Cambridge in East Somerville. Massachusetts. Today, Ploughed Hill is a tightly packed residential area known as Mount Benedict, located on Benedict Avenue off Broadway in East Somerville. Looking from Benedict Street on top of the hill to the east, one can easily see the Bunker Hill monument and, to the north, Mystic River. No monument exists on Ploughed Hill to indicate the site's historical significance; however, on the grounds of the town library about a mile from the site, a historical marker commemorates the events that occurred on Ploughed Hill. Albert L. Haskell, Haskell's Historical Guide of Somerville, Massachusetts (Somerville, MA: Haskell, n.d.).
361 Wikipedia, The Free Encyclopedia, s.v., "List of Continental Army Units (1775), accessed September 10, 2017, http://en.wikipedia.org/wiki/List_of_Continental_Army_units_(1775); Hentz, Unit History of the Maryland and Virginia Regiment.

strongest fortifications. Among the men who guard the workers at Ploughed Hill are the Pennsylvania rifle companies under the command of Captain Smith and Captain Nagle.

On August 26—their first full day of manning their post at Roxbury—Cresap's men can hear from six miles away the occasional sound of the British lobbing cannonballs onto Prospect Hill. During a lull in activity—knowing that keeping his men occupied serves to promote order and discipline—Captain Cresap may have decided to accompany Captain Price's rifle company to conduct field exercises away from the battlefront.

To shake things up a little, the British manage to fire into Roxbury a cannonball that seems to bear the names of the men serving in the two Maryland rifle companies. As the men parade and exercise in an apple or-chard, the cannonball lands near the riflemen and bounces "through an apple tree and cut[s] one of the large boughs…so far that it [breaks] down to the ground, which cause[s] the shaking of a great quantity of apples that [are] not ripe." Two riflemen are so startled that they break rank and run for shelter.[362]

On the evening of Saturday, August 26, Washington orders the combined forces of his army and men from the Virginia and Maryland rifle companies to stand by at Roxbury and keep British regulars from pouring over Boston Neck and interfering with Washington's Ploughed Hill operation several miles to the north.

After sunset on the evening of August 26, the time arrives to put Washington's Ploughed Hill plan into effect. At Roxbury, sixty of Price's riflemen, along with Cresap's Rifles, go "to Lamb's Dam to lie,"[363] patiently awaiting nightfall. It is obvious to anyone who sees ghostly silhouettes darting about in the dark or hears muted scrambling noises in the nearby brush that something is afoot.

Under the cover of darkness, the rifle-bearing men proceed along Boston Neck, slithering along as noiselessly as possible, soft moccasins treading dirt, glinting steel of their rifles pointed and ready. Their intent is "to fire upon the [British] sentries" in the haze of evening, but as luck would have it, the early night is clear. The British sentries detect the riflemen advancing toward them. The redcoats fire on the riflemen with "no damage" to the men. The riflemen "return…the compliment," firing back at the redcoats and then quickly retreat to Lamb's Dam.[364] However, the surefooted frontiersmen and their rifles are not finished. The night is still young.

Rifleman Henry Bedinger records the following in his journal: "Saturday Night, 26th Captain Creasop [sic], Who Came in the Night before,[365] agreed to go and fire on the Centries. About Thirty of our Company, Our Captain, Lieut. Scott, and Lieut Sheperd went along, they Borrowed Musketts, Loaded them with Ball and about fifteen Swan Shott. They all Creap Down along a ditch that passes the Chimneys, and so By the side of the Breastwork."[366]

Sometime around midnight, the riflemen sneak to within ten rods [165 feet] of the British line. Using tactics they learned on the frontier, the riflemen silently creep undetected in "Indian file"[367] on their "hands and knees"[368] up Boston Neck until they are directly along the sides of the British breastworks. This well-thought-out position places an estimated two hundred redcoats well within reach of Cresap's sharpshooters and the other riflemen. A fight begins with a hailstorm of firing from both sides. To add to the mayhem, a ferocious weather front accompanied by wind, lightning, and thunder moves into the area.[369]

362 Balch, Journal of the Times at the Siege of Boston Since Our Arrival at Cambridge, Near Boston, 14. 363 Balch, Journal of the Times at the Siege of Boston Since Our Arrival at Cambridge, Near Boston, 14. 364 Ibid.
365 *This source confirms that Cresap's Rifles arrived in Roxbury, Massachusetts on August 25, 1775.*
366 McIntyre, "Separating Myth from History," 111, 117.
367 Prowell, Continental Congress at York, Pennsylvania, 160.
368 Ibid.
369 Balch, Journal of the Times at the Siege of Boston Since Our Arrival at Cambridge, Near Boston, 14–5.

Later, as the men recall the evening of August 26, when they kept the British forces at bay on Boston Neck, their most impressive memory will be the sight of their dauntless leader, Captain Cresap, in action. Others record the composed but daring behavior of Cresap, who flawlessly executed his plan on Boston Neck while Washington took possession of Ploughed Hill.

Daniel McCurtin, of Price's Maryland rifle company, writes in his journal his impressions shortly following that night on Boston Neck: "Afterward came Captain Cressep [sic] up…accompanied with great thunder and lightning [with more] than the firing before from the British."[370]

In the throes of the storm, Cresap maneuvers about, shoots a precisely aimed shot, then seeks cover and quickly reloads his rifle. He shouts out a command or two to his company and dashes back out into the field of fire to seek another vantage point. Finding a target, Cresap again takes aim at the foe and shoots. To add to the infernal uproar, it must seem to Cresap's men that the booming thunder and firebolts of lightning that shadow Cresap's battlefield actions are purposely induced by heaven this day!

The riflemen kill ten British regular soldiers on Boston Neck the night of August 26 without any losses on the colonial side.[371] In the aftermath of the battle, many soldiers seem to share similar testimony regarding the success of this event. Caleb Haskell, a soldier in a Newburyport, Massachusetts company, writes in his journal shortly after this incident, "Our Riflemen and Indians[372] killed and wounded a number of the enemy today."[373]

The British soldiers are baffled by the tactics of the riflemen they have witnessed on Boston Neck. One dejected British officer writes home the following account of the riflemen's field maneuvers he recently observed:

> [T]he outposts [on Boston Neck] are universally considered as so many forlorn hopes. No sooner does [our] detachment appear at any of these stations [then] a party of forty to fifty riflemen instantly advance and take [us] off like so many rooks upon a tree. If a larger party be sent out to support [our Regulars], the riflemen retire by slow degrees, till they have drawn [us] into an ambush of 500 or 1,000 more [riflemen], than destroy our whole corps. In this manner it is that incredible numbers of our Regulars have been cut off; and should this petite war continue, it is not doubted that the [riflemen] will go near to destroy [us] all. [I] escaped [myself] by miracle![374]

The men labor building entrenchments on Ploughed Hill nonstop throughout the late night of August 26 and the early morning of August 27. The British finally respond to Washington's act of aggression on Sunday morning, August 27, at nine o'clock, but only after the Continentals have built a substantial fort overnight—much to the amazement of the British. In addition, the Continentals have added several valued "pieces of fine cannon"[375] to withstand the expected onslaught of enemy cannonade. From their vantage point on Ploughed Hill, the colonists

370 Balch, Journal of the Times at the Siege of Boston Since Our Arrival at Cambridge, Near Boston, 15.
371 Ibid., 14. In the late evening of August 26, almost exactly at the same time that Captain Cresap and his riflemen began their attack on Boston Neck, a tropical storm front, influenced by an off-shore Atlantic hurricane, blew into New England accompanied by lightning and thunder. Because the hurricane occurred at the dawn of the American Revolution, the massive tempest became known as the "Hurricane of Independence 1775" and is ranked as the eighth most destructive Atlantic hurricane in American history. http://www.revolutionary-war-and-beyond.com/independence-hurricane-hits-american-colonies.html#gallery[pageGallery]/0/.
372 The Indians were from the Oneida and Mohican Stockbridge tribes. They were two of only a few Native American tribes who participated in the American Revolutionary War. The Oneidas were a part of the Iroquois Nation, who lived in central New York state around Oneidas Lake. The Stockbridge Indians lived along the Housatonic River in the Berkshire Mountains of western Massachusetts. In addition to their participation in the Siege of Boston, these Indian tribes fought alongside the Americans in the Battles of Saratoga and Monmouth. Captain Michael Cresap and his men shared many experiences in western Maryland, interacting with members of the Shawnee and Delaware tribes. Now in New England, the riflemen intermingled and fought alongside the Oneidas and Stockbridge tribes. Stockbridge-Munsee Community, "Origin and Early Mohican History," November 17, 2014, http://www.mohican.com/originearlyhistory/; Sam Houston State University, "Black Americans in Defense of Our Nation."
373 "Newport, Sept. 4."
374 London Public Advertiser, 12 September 1775.
375 Balch, Journal of the Times at the Siege of Boston Since Our Arrival at Cambridge, Near Boston, 12.

can in relative safety "play upon"[376] the British "with great ease."[377] The redcoats do not disappoint them. The British on Bunker Hill fire cannonball after cannonball during the day, engaging in this action until nightfall. This punishing bombardment will continue for the next two weeks.

On Sunday, August 27, the British send two floating batteries up the Mystic River to fire onto Ploughed Hill. A nine-pounder cannon fired by the colonials wreaks havoc on the two armed British batteries. The British boats on Mystic River become as helpless as sitting ducks. Washington's cannons prove so effective that the Continentals sink one British battery ship while the other boat is cast asunder by a direct hit on its sail mast. British boatmen are at first stunned and then humiliated by the pounding they receive from the summit above. Resounding "huzzahs" echo through the air as the patriots see the British boats floundering in the water below.[378]

On Sunday, August 27, Cresap marches his company from Roxbury to Ploughed Hill, the hill lying closest to British-occupied Bunker Hill. Excitement stirs as groups of civilian onlookers along this route witness Cresap and his riflemen on the move.

Cresap's company marches toward the heavy British cannon fire on Ploughed Hill. General Washington places Cresap's rifle company with several other "Parties of Riflemen who [are] involved in firing upon the advanced Guards on Charlestown Neck."[379] Once on site, Cresap's Rifles join several other rifle companies stationed at the foot of Ploughed Hill facing Bunker Hill, "three or four hundred yards from the enemy's strongest works to cover the musketmen entrenched [on top of] Ploughed Hill."[380]

An August 28 newspaper account provided by an elated witness at Watertown, Massachusetts, informs the engaged New England readership of the latest news about Washington's Ploughed Hill campaign and Captain Cresap's company:

Watertown, August 28, 1775

Yesterday [Sunday, August 27], another company of Riflemen, commanded by Captain Michael Cressop [sic], arrived in town[381] in their way to join the Grand American Army.—Some of this company, we hear, have traveled from the Mississippi.[382]

On Monday, August 28, Washington observes additional British troops coming over from Boston and falling into formation at Charlestown, seemingly preparing for battle. Washington also observes a British man-o'-war coming up the Mystic River. All these signs indicate that the British are about ready to make a bold attack on Ploughed Hill.

---

376 Ibid.
377 Ibid.
378 Historians have left us with the false impression that General Washington did not have many cannons before Knox brought them to him in Boston from Fort Ticonderoga in early 1776. An October 1775 inventory conducted by Colonel Richard Gridley of the artillery regiment tells us otherwise. During the summer of 1775, Washington had forty-one cannons at his disposal, varying in size from two-and-a-half pounders to twenty-four pounders. He also had available to him ten mortars. J. L. Bell, "How Many Cannons Did Washington Have in 1775?" Boston 1775, January 21, 2013, accessed December 6, 2017, http://boston1775.blogspot.com/search/label/Richard%20Gridley; Frothingham, History of the Siege of Boston, 233–4; Haskell, Haskell's Historical Guide of Somerville, Massachusetts; Balch, Journal of the Times at the Siege of Boston Since Our Arrival at Cambridge, Near Boston, 13.
379 "Cambridge, August 31," Hartford Courant, September 4, 1775, 2.
380 Linn and Egle, Pennsylvania, War of the Revolution: Battalions and Line, 6.
381 This source places Cresap's Rifles passing through Watertown, Massachusetts, on August 27, en route toward Ploughed Hill.
382 TimeandDate.com, Calendar for Year 1775 (United States), accessed December 6, 2017, http://www.timeanddate.com/calendar/index.html?year=1775&country=1.13;" "Watertown, August 28," Pennsylvania Gazette, September 6, 1775.

This British cannonade on Ploughed Hill between August 27 and August 28 will prove to be the most intense bombardment the Continental army endures during the entire Siege of Boston, a blockade that will last until March of 1776.

On Monday, August 28, a new contest between the two armies seems imminent. Washington expects and hopes that the British will attack at high tide. The Continental army waits and waits in "awful silence."[383] The Continental officers know they are in a "terrible situation"[384] as regards their severe shortage of gunpowder. One colonial officer states that "the word gunpowder sets all [the men] on tiptoe."[385] Yet under these dire circumstances, the British army does not attack.

By three that afternoon, it is apparent to Washington that "the enemy has declined" his "challenge."[386] Perhaps recent memory of the staggering British losses at the Battle of Bunker Hill weigh heavily on the minds of the redcoats. The British also know that the Ploughed Hill fortifications are much stronger than the ones colonial forces built at Bunker Hill. Perhaps the British do not attack because of the several hundred riflemen who are posted on the front line at the foot of Ploughed Hill. Whatever the reason, to Washington's great dismay, the British withdraw from combat formation. The general is greatly disappointed at his futile attempts to goad the British into action. The battle between these two defiant forces, a match that might have ended this war before winter sets in, will not occur today.[387]

With the successful taking of the summit, Washington, in his own words, states that his troops are in "point blank" range "of "the enemy's lines on Charlestown Neck."[388] However, the general is forced to submit to the "insult of the cannonade…not daring to make use of [his] artillery on account of the consumption of powder,"[389] presently a scarce commodity.[390]

A reporter briefly summarizes the event for his newspaper:

Watertown, August 28, 1775

"Last Saturday night [August 26] about 2,000 of the United Troops of this Continent, entrenched on what is called Plough Hill, within point blank shot of the enemy; and notwithstanding a continual fire from them almost all yesterday [Sunday, August 27] we only had two killed, and two wounded…We have not heard how many the enemy lost, though it is said one officer and several men were seen to fall."[391]

The British cannonade kills four of Washington's men and wounds four others. General Washington judges that two of the four unfortunate souls —during a lapse of discipline in the field - died due to their own "folly."[392] These men constitute the first battle casualties Washington experiences since taking command on July 3.

---

383 "Extract from a Letter from Prospect Hill, dated August 31," Pennsylvania Gazette, September 21, 1775.
384 William Abbott, "The Relation of New Hampshire Men To the Siege of Boston," Magazine of History with Notes and Queries 6(2) (August 1907), 63–85.
385 Ibid., 76.
386 Abbott, "The Relation of New Hampshire Men To the Siege of Boston," 76.
387 One historian notes the following concerning the refusal of the British to engage Washington's army: "The poor state of the Revolutionaries' munitions in 1775 suggests that had the British army been able to act more vigorously in the early stages of war, instead of being confined to Boston, then they might have seriously checked their opponents." Black, War for America: The Fight for Independence, 1775–1783, 49.
388 Fitzpatrick, The Writings of George Washington from the Original Manuscript Sources, vol. 3, 453.
389 Ibid., 453, 462
390 Freeman, Planter and Patriot, 519.
391 "Cambridge, August 31," 2.
392 Fitzpatrick, The Writings of George Washington from the Original Manuscript Sources, vol. 3, 453.

Of the four fatalities during this campaign, two of the men in Washington's army suffered the loss of their heads, compliments of direct hits by British cannonballs. One of the unlucky souls proved to be a staff officer, Isaac Mumford, from Varnum's Rhode Island regiment. Also among the four killed is a Native American, whose name is unfortunately lost to history.[393]

One could argue that the first combat casualty since George Washington assumed command is William Simpson, who served in Captain Smith's Pennsylvania rifle company from Lancaster. On August 27, a British cannonball rips off Simpson's foot during the taking of Ploughed Hill. All means are taken to save the man's life, including the amputation of a part of his leg. General Washington and many of his officers visit and console Simpson over the next two days, but Simpson sadly succumbs to his injury on August 29.[394] During this time, word spreads along the siege line from Cambridge to Roxbury of Simpson's injury and death, becoming "a theme of common sorrow" among Washington's troops.[395]

Ploughed Hill Marker, East Somerville, Massachusetts

---

393 National Archives, "From George Washington to Richard Henry Lee, 29 August 1775," November 21, 2014, http://founders.archives.gov/documents/Washington/03-01-02-0270.

394 Before returning to Roxbury from Ploughed Hill, like Washington and other officers, Captain Michael Cresap may have trekked over to the Cambridge hospital to provide company and comfort to the mortally wounded William Simpson, injured by a cannonball during the taking of Ploughed Hill. Simpson served in Captain Smith's rifle company from Lancaster, Pennsylvania. Unfortunately, Simpson died on August 29. Historians consider Simpson General Washington's first battle casualty since taking command of the Continental army on July 3. Linn and Egle, Pennsylvania, War of the Revolution: Battalions and Line, 6–7; Hannum, "America's First Company Commanders"; "Gunmakers Along the Wyomissing"; Frothingham, History of the Siege of Boston, 233–4.

395 Linn and Egle, Pennsylvania, War of the Revolution: Battalions and Line, 6–7; Hannum, "America's First Company Commanders"; "Gunmakers along the Wyomissing"; Frothingham, History of the Siege of Boston, 233–4.

The British continue to fire more than three hundred shells on Ploughed Hill until September 10, 1775. They only cease catapulting these frightful cannonballs when they realize that the cannonade has little effect stopping Washington's men from successfully building trenches and fortifications on the summit.

The riflemen do not yet know it, but in this recent fracas, they are first-hand eyewitnesses to Cresap's last appearance on the battlefield. They have certainly heard of his past exploits in the Indians Wars, but for many of the young men, this is the first time they have seen their captain executing the widely acclaimed skills gained from his experiences in past wars.

George Washington "commends the spirit" of the captains of the rifle companies and their "brave men, who though they just arrived after a very long march, offer[ed] to execute [the general's] plan immediately."[396]

Captain Cresap also applauds the heroism of his riflemen, not yet fully recuperated from their more than five-hundred-mile march from Fredericktown, Maryland—although they have only been present at the battlefront for several days. After defending Boston Neck, they went beyond the call of duty and marched six miles to Ploughed Hill in the midst of heavy cannonade. They have represented Maryland well and have made a good account of themselves among their peers. Their tenacity contributed to the fact that there would not be another battle such as Bunker Hill this day. The British lack the will to attack and take possession of Ploughed Hill. Their want of motivation might well be attributed to the presence of these companies of riflemen who stare down their enemy—their long rifles ready and willing. Michael Cresap and his men have proved their fighting prowess in the thick of these events—seemingly heralding enough potential thunder and trepidation to deter the British yet one more time.[397] These battle-hardened Maryland riflemen have done their part to preserve Washington's army to fight another day.[398]

---

396 Prowell, Continental Congress at York, Pennsylvania, 160.
397 A parody was later published in a London newspaper addressing the problem of the British soldiers who were unwilling to confront Washington's army in Boston for fear of the riflemen. The satirically written article addressed to both houses of Parliament begin with the line "To fight or not to fight—that is the question…Which side will conquer—must give us pause. There's the respect—that gives rebellion such a lengthened life, for who would brook [the colonials] Insolence unpunished, but that the Dread of rifle—barrel'd Guns Puzzles our Officers—and makes them rather stay in Boston Town Than seek the Enemy." London Public Advertiser, November 3, 1775, 2.
398 In the mind of Benjamin Franklin, who met with General Washington in October 1775 at Cambridge, the forces of the Continental army taking Ploughed Hill reversed the success of the British at Bunker Hill. Franklin wrote to a friend in England in October 1775, "Britain, at the expense of three millions, has killed a hundred and fifty Yankees this campaign. Which is 20,000 [pounds] a head; and at Bunker Hill she gained a mile of ground, all of which she lost again by our taking post at Ploughed Hill. During the same time, 60,000 children have been born in America." Using this information, Franklin asks his friend to calculate "The time and expense necessary to kill us all and conquer the whole of our territory." Horace E. Scudder, A History of the United States of America (New York: American Book Company, 1901), 151.

CHAPTER 12

A Meeting with General Washington

Cambridge, Massachusetts
August 29, 1775

IN A REPORT TO CONGRESS, Washington states that the cannonade and bombardment on Ploughed Hill by the British occurred "with little Spirit on their side or Damage to ours." Things are rather anticlimactic and have settled down a bit since Washington's successful taking of Ploughed Hill and the "great throwing of bombs from Bunker's Hill" on August 27 and 28. Washington knows that "unless very large [British] reinforcements arrive, there will not be another engagement this year, as the [colonial army] have vastly superior numbers. At present the [British] lie terribly still, except disturbing [Washington's forces] at night with their bombs."[399]

On August 29, Cresap has the opportunity to report to General George Washington at his headquarters in Cambridge.[400] Cresap is obligated to do so under the stipulations of the Continental Congress dictating that the ten original rifle companies selected on June 14 are independent units serving directly under the command of General Washington. To Washington's mind, this Maryland unit with its standout leader is one of the more well-known companies the general has called to bear arms against the British.

From an objective outsider's view on a rather ironic set of events, Washington, a man about ten years Michael's senior, greets with professional decorum and courtesy—even while in war mode—the thirty-three-year old Captain Michael Cresap. After all, when Michael was just a six-year-old lad, Washington had the occasion to stay in Oldtown, at the house of Michael's father, Thomas Cresap, when the general performed a surveying mission as a young man in 1748.

As Cresap enters headquarters, he probably sees Washington's horse tethered to an outside post, the animal appearing expectant and ready to be mounted at a moment's notice. Washington is not attired in the frontier garb that Cresap has seen the Virginian wearing in the past around Oldtown.[401] Today, the general seems a different person than Cresap remembers. On this momentous occasion, the commander wears a "blue coat with buff colored facings, a rich epaulette on each shoulder, buff under-dress, and an elegant sword." The general also shows

---

399 "Extract from a Letter from Prospect Hill"; Fitzpatrick, The Writings of George Washington from the Original Manuscript Sources, vol. 3, 450, 453.

400 Washington's headquarters were the former home of John Vassall, a British loyalist. Vassal fled from Cambridge at the start of the revolution, abandoning the two-story stone home. The Vassall house, built in 1759, became Washington's first official headquarters as commander of the American Revolutionary War. Washington's headquarters in Cambridge, Massachusetts, still stand, now known as the Longfellow House—Washington's Headquarters National Historic Site at 105 Brattle Street. The noted American poet, Henry Wadsworth Longfellow, later owned this home, living here from 1843 until his death in 1882.

401 George Washington's relationship with Michael Cresap went back to an important time in the general's military career. In 1754, Washington passed through Oldtown and visited with Thomas Cresap and twelve-year-old Michael Cresap just before Washington encountered the French at Jumonville, Pennsylvania, the site where "the volley fired by the young Virginian [Washington] in the backwoods of America set the world on fire," an incident that historians note as the beginning of the French and Indian War. Military History Now, "The Shot That Set the World On Fire: How George Washington Started History's First 'World War,'" February 17, 2016, accessed December 7, 2017, http://militaryhistorynow.com/2016/02/17/the-shot-that-set-the-world-on-fire-how-george-washington-started-the-first-world-war/.

off a "black cockade in his hat." This Washington who now stands before Cresap is "tall and well-proportioned," making a "truly noble and majestic personal appearance."[402]

Feathers of various colors are used to indicate an officer's rank - the feather secured to the hat with a band of ribbon or silk ornamentation wrapped around the brim of the hat. To distinguish himself as a captain, Cresap likely wears in his round hat a yellow or buff-colored cockade in accordance to an operational order issued by General Washington just a little more than a month ago, on July 23: "As the Continental Army have unfortunately no Uniforms, and consequently many inconveniences must arise, from being able to distinguish the Commissioned Officers from the Non Commissioned Officers, and the Non Commissioned from the private it is desired that some Badges of Distinction be immediately provided; for Instance, the Field Officers may have red or pink colour'd Cockades in their Hatts, the Captains yellow or buff: and the Subalterns green. They are to furnish themselves accordingly."[403]

Inside headquarters, Washington and Cresap, out of respect for each other, remove their hats and face one another. A still silence in the room is broken by words finally spoken, greetings to break the ice, and then a parley that exudes civility and courteousness as the two men begin to discuss the urgent business of the day.

On August 29, 1775, possibly just before or after the meeting with Cresap, Washington writes the following to Richard Henry Lee, serving in the Continental Congress: "As we have now completed our Lines of Defense, we have nothing more, in my opinion to fear from the Enemy, provided we can keep our men to their duty and make them watchful and vigilant." In this same letter, Washington for the first time informs the Continental Congress that he has advanced his line and taken Ploughed Hill, throwing the British into "great consternation," with the British responding by a continuous "bombardment without any effect, as yet."[404]

The "as yet" unknown, there is much left to do, and the general knows that he can rely on Cresap to carry out his part. Washington perhaps mulls over in his mind the seasoned appearance of Michael Cresap, the noted Indian fighter who presents himself to the general in the attire of a backwoods frontiersman. This Marylander who exudes confidence and now wears a yellow cockade in his hat is by no means a Yankee Doodle, as some on the other side might call him.

To add further complexity to the history between these leaders of men, two separate land issues somewhat strain the relationship between Washington and Cresap. Before the business of the present rebellion, Washington engaged Michael Cresap and his father, Thomas, in an ongoing land dispute in which the Cresap family and Washington claim a valuable tract of bottomland on the Ohio River. In addition, Thomas Cresap and George Washington both claim yet another tract of land near Fort Cumberland. Although this is still a contentious issue, each party knows that there is a much more pressing matter at hand, and that is the persistent crisis of the revolution now before them.

In the end, nothing else really matters. If the colonials lose this war, all bets are off as to who will own the land, if anyone. In the hands of the British, any question regarding property ownership could prove to be a moot point of debate. If the British emerge victorious, there is a high probability that Washington will hang for treason, and this punishment would likely befall all his officers as well. For now, the two warriors must put the land dispute issue off for another day.

---

402 Thacher, Military Journal During the American Revolutionary War, 37.
403 Fitzpatrick, The Writings of George Washington from the Original Manuscript Sources, vol. 3, 357. The British sang the satirical song "Yankee Doodle" to mock the Continental soldier. Doodle means simpleton or fool. Referring to the cockade, in the lyrics "stuck a feather in his cap and called it macaroni," macaroni means effeminate. Around campfires, the Continental soldiers quickly developed their own lyrics to the melody to mock the redcoats.
404 Fitzpatrick, The Writings of George Washington from the Original Manuscript Sources, vol. 3, 450, 453.

For a final touch of irony in the aftermath of Ploughed Hill, George Washington and Thomas Gage, the British governor of the Province of Massachusetts Bay, glower at each other from their respective posts across Boston Harbor. In what now seems an eternity ago to both Washington and Gage, in the year 1755, these two tenacious and heroic men served together in the Braddock campaign. In May of 1755, it is highly likely that Michael Cresap interacted with both men as a young twelve-year-old when his father, Thomas Cresap, entertained General Braddock and his officers in their Oldtown, Maryland, home. At this juncture in Michael's young life, he was apt to have been quite awed to see one entire unit of Braddock's army camped in Thomas Cresap's fields for two days.[405]

At Cambridge, Cresap's men familiarize themselves with the environs of this quaint town. While Captain Cresap visits General Washington, Cresap's more than one hundred riflemen set up camp on the church commons opposite Harvard College in Cambridge. This camp is soon made ready just a little farther than a block south of Washington's headquarters on Watertown Road.

The town of Cambridge and its charm would most assuredly have been appreciated by the Maryland frontiersmen. The men who gaze upon the artistically well-proportioned architecture here are especially impressed, as noted by one rifleman who makes mention in his journal of the "elegant building[s]" on the grounds of the university. The surrounding structures where the "collegians" formerly stayed "make the town appear very beautiful to the eye."[406]

In the same month that this crucial meeting takes place between Washington and Cresap, a rifleman from a Pennsylvania company describes in a letter to his hometown his impressions of Cambridge, "besides the College is a Very large pile of Building[s] Ab[out] 3 times as big as that of Phila[delphia's] Meeting house and church. This town is situated on a Beautiful Plain—irregular and Scattered everywhere [are] Ave[nues] of fine Tall Locust Trees [,] all planted. Some of the most elegant Buildings I ever saw tho framed [are here.] The best of these the General Officers are in possession of—There is scarcely a good house in the Town or Neighbourhood that is not the property of the Tories who have fled and left Room for the Sons of Liberty."[407]

Similarly, a rifleman from Captain Price's Maryland company records in his journal a compliment that this town might have received in better days: "It makes me believe that [Cambridge] was a flourishing town in the time of peace."[408] However, the Siege of Boston, much like the calamity that has befallen Roxbury, has deteriorated the appearance of the buildings. The comely college campus has been transformed into a military camp occupied by soldiers.

From their vantage point at Cambridge, Cresap's men enjoy a broad view of Prospect Hill, which—gauging the distance from Cresap's camp site—is situated a short distance north of town. On Prospect Hill is a "fine large fort containing several pieces of fine cannon with fort spears and other implements fitting for war."[409] Stationed here are four thousand colonial soldiers. This array of military personnel and infrastructure constitutes the left-wing division of the siege line, under the command of General Charles Lee. Some of Cresap's men will have the distinct honor of being on hand when on January 1, 1776, the colonials will raise the first official American Flag, the Grand Union Flag, which represents for the first time a banner showing the colonies united as one.

---

405 Cresap and Cresap, The History of the Cresaps; Thacher, Military Journal During the American Revolutionary War, 37; Wikipedia, The Free Encyclopedia, s.v., "Yankee Doodle," December 15, 2014, http://en.wikipedia.org/wiki/Yankee_Doodle.
406 Balch, Journal of the Times at the Siege of Boston Since Our Arrival at Cambridge, Near Boston, 14.
407 Young, "The Spirit of 1775: A Letter of Robert Magaw," 80.
408 Balch, Journal of the Times at the Siege of Boston Since Our Arrival at Cambridge, Near Boston, 12.
409 Ibid.

North of town also lie the Cambridge commons. It was here that on July 3, a little less than two months before, acting under the authority of the Continental Congress, George Washington allegedly positioned himself near a large elm tree and officially took command of the Continental army.[410]

Even though General Washington has imposed strict orders to conserve ammunition, to enhance morale, he occasionally allows his riflemen to show off their skills with their long rifles. In spite of the harried schedule of the past few days, Cresap's riflemen take time to perform another shooting demonstration in Cambridge.[411] Dr. James Thacher, who works in the hospitals set up at Cambridge, is an eyewitness to the riflemen's shooting exhibition.[412]

Thacher records the following in his journal: "August 1775. These [riflemen] are remarkable for their accuracy of their aim, striking a mark with great certainty at two hundred yards distance."[413] Clearly overcome with amazement, Thacher records the jaw-dropping spectacle he witnesses regarding these men who walk around town light footed and easy in their moccasins: "While on quick advance, [the riflemen] fired balls into object of seven inches diameter at a distance of two hundred fifty yards."[414]

The doctor also records accounts he is hearing around the campfire regarding the sharpshooters' impact on the redcoats: "[The riflemen] are now stationed on our lines and their shot have frequently proved fatal to British officers and soldiers, who expose themselves to view even at more than double the distance of a common musket shot."[415]

Nearby, the Charles River flows into Boston Harbor. From the shore, the riflemen can see the town of Boston across the harbor. The riflemen confirm with their own eyes what they have been told — that detachments of up to eight hundred British regulars practice daily military exercises on the Charlestown common. The riflemen—who sport a more unembellished fashion—are now close enough to see for themselves the military exercises of the British soldiers. If the riflemen were to take time to think about it, the British probably present a much more professional appearance in their brightly colored red uniforms. And all this maneuvering and carrying on by their opponents surely raise questions in the minds of Cresap's men. Something is obviously afoot![416]

Cresap's men watch the British soldiers continually practice rowing small boats near the Boston shore. The riflemen must wonder what the British are up to. Are these red-coated men planning their next attack using small boats to reach the mainland? If they do, on which part of the mainland will they land and begin their invasion? Now that Washington has agitated the British by taking Ploughed Hill, tension prevails along the siege line, each man harboring his own personal thoughts and concerns that the British will soon attack. But the question remains in the minds of all, when and where and how will the strike occur?[417]

---

410   J. L. Bell, "An Earlier Allusion: Beneath the Venerable Elm…," Boston 1775, July 18, 2010, http://boston1775.blogspot.com/2010/07/earlier-allusion-beneath-venerable-elm.html.

411   *The perception that General Washington assumed command under the shade of the Cambridge Elm Tree may be fact or fiction. The safest historical comment one can state is that the legendary Cambridge Elm Tree grew at the southwestern corner of the Cambridge Commons where Washington assumed command of the Continental Army. The Cambridge Elm also likely witnessed the shooting exhibition presented by Cresap's Rifles on the Cambridge Commons, where the riflemen's shooting demonstration also likely occurred. J. L. Bell, "An Earlier Allusion: Beneath the Venerable Elm…," Boston 1775, July 18, 2010; It Has Stood Like a Watchman." Boston 1775, July 5, 2010. December 12, 2014.*

412   Although Thacher does not mention the rifle company by name, all signs in his journal point to the fact that he is referring to Cresap's company. This rifle company Thacher writes about shows the same modus operandi as Cresap's Rifles—while at a run, the men shoot at a seven-inch board 250 yards distant. These distinct particulars mirror the exact shooting techniques that Cresap's rifle company used at Fredericktown, Maryland, and Lancaster, Pennsylvania.

413   Thacher, Military Journal During the American Revolutionary War, 38.

414   Ibid.

415   Ibid.

416   Frothingham, History of the Siege of Boston, 232.

417   Bell, An Earlier Allusion: Beneath the Venerable Elm…"

CHAPTER 13
The Liberty Tree Falls

Boston, Massachusetts
August 31, 1775

IN LIGHT OF THE IMPORTANT work the riflemen still need to accomplish, Cresap receives orders from General Washington to return to Roxbury to cover Boston Neck against the impending attack expected at any time on the mainland.

En route to Boston Neck from Cambridge, Cresap and his company cross the Charles River, continuing southward six miles on a road that parallels the west side of Boston Harbor. The road they walk is muddy and wet. Much to the chagrin of the men, since the taking of Ploughed Hill, the weather remains soggy and overcast with an occasional shower until clearing on September 1.[418]

When Cresap's company was organizing at Fredericktown in response to Washington's call to arms, a poem about a liberty tree appeared in print in several newspapers around the colony. The poem speaks of how evil foreign powers seek to cut down the tree. It tells of adversaries, both "Kings and Lords," who maintain the perceived notion that the symbolic fruits produced by this tree threaten their very existence and their intent to rule:

> But hear, o ye swains, ('tis a tale most profane)
> How all the tyrannical powers,
> Kings, commons, and Lords, are uniting amain,
> To cut down this guardian of ours [the Liberty Tree]:
> From the east to the west, blow the trumpet to arms,
> Thro' the land let the sound of it flee,
> Let the far and the near—all unite with a cheer,
> In defense of our liberty tree.[419]

A copper-plated plaque attached to the bark boasted large gold letters, proclaiming this large elm tree in Boston the Liberty Tree. Since the 1765 Stamp Act, this tree has served as an iconic American patriotic symbol.[420] Under its branches, the Sons of Liberty in the Boston area met to protest the oppressive policies of the Stamp Act imposed by the British. In the hearts and minds of these colonists, the first fruits of liberty were born on this site.

---

[418] Balch, *Journal of the Times at the Siege of Boston Since Our Arrival at Cambridge, Near Boston*, 15.
[419] Schrader, *American Revolutionary War: Songs to Cultivate the Sensations of Freedom*.
[420] After 1765, inspired by the symbolism of the Boston Liberty Tree, American patriots established liberty trees in all thirteen colonies. These liberty trees came to symbolize the colonial resistance movement against the British that led to the American Revolution.

Scion of original St. John's College Liberty Tree, St. John's College, Annapolis, Maryland

The Boston Liberty Tree was still standing when Thomas Paine, the attributed author of "Liberty Tree," published this poem in the *Pennsylvania Magazine* in July 1775 when Michael Cresap was preparing to march to Boston. The words speak of how the Goddess of Liberty brought this tree from the heavens as a gift, a "tangible symbol of her love of American patriots to sit beneath, to worship under, and to rally round."[421]

On September 4, a newspaper publishes the story of the demise of the Boston Liberty Tree, the word spreading quickly throughout the body of Washington's troops. The men of Cresap's Rifles probably first hear about this dastardly deed while either standing guard at Lamb's Dam or off duty in camp at Roxbury.

Armed with axes, "Laughing and grinning, sweating and foaming with malice diabolical,"[422] loyalists furiously attack the defenseless elm. When the felling of the Liberty Tree accidentally kills a Tory soldier, an unsympathetic American patriot composes a poem detailing this incident:

A tory soldier, on its topmost limb—
The Genius of the Shade looked stern at him,
And marked him out that same hour to dine

---
421 Schrader, American Revolutionary War: Songs to Cultivate the Sensations of Freedom.
422 "Cambridge, August 31," 2.

Where unsnuffed lamps burn low at Pluto' shrine.
Then tripped his feet from off their cautious stand:
Pale turned the wretch-he spread each helpless hand,
But spread in vain-with headlong force he fell,
Nor stopped descending till he stopped in hell![423]

The Liberty Tree had grown to maturity in South Boston, several miles across Boston Neck[424] from Roxbury, the site that quarters Cresap's Rifles. The riflemen are so close to the tree that if they strained their ears, they might have heard it groan in rebellion as it crashed to the ground.

The following sentiments, published in a newspaper on September 4, 1775, no doubt capture the feelings of Michael Cresap, a Maryland Son of Liberty: "Be it known to this infamous band of traitors [loyalists] that the Grand American Tree of Liberty," symbolically planted in the "centre of the united colonies of North America, [still] flourishes with unrivaled increasing beauty." The seeds of the Liberty Tree are planted deep in the hearts of the Sons of Liberty, who are "numerous and disbursed"[425] throughout the American colonies. Be assured, we as patriots will continue to bask under the ever-growing "wide-spreading branches"[426] of the Liberty Tree whose fruits reside within the hearts of all the Sons of Liberty.[427]

Americans are deeply angered over the loss of the Liberty Tree. With this malicious act, the British mock the cause of liberty for which the patriots fight. In the end, anger over the willful destruction of the Boston Liberty Tree turns to positive action. Patriots soon make regimental flags bearing the image of the Liberty Tree with the slogan "Appeal to Heaven." Liberty Tree flags begin to appear in future American Revolution battlefields. Now that King George III has decided to ignore the patriots' numerous appeals for justice and liberty, they are putting the king and British soldiers on notice that the colonies will go higher up in the chain of command and will petition the ultimate highest power, God almighty himself, for justice and liberty.[428]

With September coming on, Captain Michael Cresap, one of the more famous Maryland Sons of Liberty, will soon face his most serious challenge. Even the seeds of the Liberty Tree that are planted deep in his heart will not be able to sustain him in the challenge he is about to endure. The aftermath of this event will astonish the people and shake to the core one of the largest cities in the colonies.[429]

---

[423] Abraham Tomlinson, Lemuel Lyon, and Samuel Haws, The Military Journals of Two Private Soldiers: 1758–1775 (Poughkeepsie, NY: Abraham Tomlinson, 1855), 68, https://archive.org/stream/militaryjournals00tomliala#page/n7/mode/2up.

[424] A plaque on a building at 630 Washington Street in Boston marks the former site of the Boston Liberty Tree. It is one block east of Boylston Station (green line) and the Boston Common, at the intersection of Washington and Essex streets.

[425] "Cambridge, August 31," 2.

[426] "Cambridge, August 31."

[427] Ibid.

[428] The Maryland Liberty Tree was located at St. John's College in Annapolis, about a block away from the legislative state house. Under this liberty tree in 1765, Thomas Cresap, a Maryland state delegate for many years, met with other Maryland patriots to protest the Stamp Act. One of these patriots was Samuel Chase, a future signer of the Declaration of Independence. This tulip poplar was destined to be the last surviving original liberty tree, falling victim to Hurricane Floyd in 1999. Today, officials continue to collect seed from a graft of the original Maryland Liberty Tree and plant the heritage/legacy tree seedlings at public patriotic events.

[429] Ironically, the authors of this chapter penned the story of the felling of the Boston Liberty Tree during the week of the Boston Marathon terrorist act that occurred on Patriots Day, April 15, 2013. The explosions occurred near the historic site of the Boston Liberty Tree. Terrorists and other ill-intentioned individuals still threaten our liberties more than 238 years after the British loyalists chopped down the Boston Liberty Tree near the very same location in Boston. Yet one surprising twist of history relates to the Liberty Tree. In 1765, on the now-iconic date of September 11, Boston patriots attached the identifying copper-plated plaque to the Boston Liberty Tree.

CHAPTER 14

A Farewell Parting of Comrades in Arms

Roxbury, Massachusetts
September 1, 1775, to September 10, 1775

CONSIDERING THE LAYOUT AND TOPOGRAPHY of the whole affair, one might surmise that Captain Cresap stays at the Roxbury Continental Officers Headquarters while his men lodge in the town's abandoned homes now used for Washington's army. Wherever the officers and riflemen lay their heads or take their daily meals, they are not out of harm's way from the enemy's cannonballs. With this constant threat looming, it is difficult for the men to relax.

One rifleman in Captain Price's Maryland company illustrates the difficulty for the men seeking peaceful repose when they are off duty. In a journal entry dated August 18, a rifleman quartered in a Roxbury home notes that while he was taking breakfast, the British fired four thirty-two-pounders at the house. The mammoth cannonballs "rushed through an upstairs room" where the rifleman sat at a table with three other men in his company. Amid a fit and frenzy of noise, the cannonballs "dashed out one side of the chimney [and] broke two partitions." The men's breakfast "dishes [were now filled] with plastering, ceiling, and bricks."[430]

The morning cannonade surprised "the four young heroes."[431] His adrenalin flowing, the rifleman ran down two sets of stairs in "three strides without a fall." Once out the door, the man ran in great haste to a nearby breastworks, the designated place for safety. One man in his company looked at the rifleman in "amazement," no doubt stunned with wonderment as to just how the intended victim escaped the house alive without injury, not to mention the fate of his unfinished breakfast.[432]

Apparently, the incident disturbed one of the other riflemen so much that, on the next day, he deserted to the British side.

However, in these tense hours that seem to last a lifetime, no attack occurs, and the rain keeps falling. The soggy weather finally abates, and at last on September 1,[433] the weather clears. For the next week, things remain relatively quiet in Roxbury. Only the occasional daily discharge of cannonballs breaks the haunting silence that surrounds Roxbury.

When not on guard duty, the men spend downtime in their quarters. Some write letters home or update their journals. Others catch up on news and gossip.

---

430 Balch, Journal of the Times at the Siege of Boston Since Our Arrival at Cambridge, Near Boston, 13.
431 Ibid.
432 Ibid.
433 Ibid., 15.

On August 30, William Norris, one of Captain Price's riflemen, dies following a long illness.[434] Under less than ideal conditions, his compatriots bury Norris "in as genteel a manner as [they] could get it done."[435] On the same day, two British regulars carrying a flag of truce over Boston Neck desert to the Continental army. In a twist of irony, it is from defectors that Washington obtains valuable intelligence concerning the true conditions and plans of the British in Boston.[436]

As if in retaliation for these traitorous acts of abandonment, almost immediately following the desertion of the British regulars, the Lobsters fire thirty cannonballs into Roxbury. This brash incident kills at least two colonial musketeers and slightly injures a rifleman serving in one of the allied rifle companies. This latest cannonade causes great alarm among the line of colonial soldiers stationed at Roxbury. On pins and needles, these anxious men place themselves in high readiness, anticipating that the redcoats will come storming across Boston Neck at any moment.[437]

Miraculously, even though there have been several near misses, cannonball fire has not injured any of Captain Cresap's or Captain Price's riflemen. On September 8, a private in Captain Price's rifle company gratefully notes this fact in his journal: "Blessed be the Lord, being so good and merciful that not one of our men was in the least hurted ever since our arrival till now."[438]

Just as one of Captain Price's riflemen defects to the British, a private from Cresap's company, whose name is lost to history, also deserts across Boston Neck into Boston just one week after the Ploughed Hill conflict. A British officer in Boston notes the following in his journal: "2 September: At 10 o'clock a Rifle Man came in from them, by Name_____, Servant to Capt. Cresap, Captain of the Company, they come from about Fort Pitt and are near 130 strong. He says the Rebels talk of starving us out, but is a Stupid Lad, an Englishman born in Oxfordshire."[439]

---

434 In the non-battle fatality category, epidemics from unsanitary conditions in the military camps caused the death of about 20 percent of Washington's soldiers. Dysentery caused by the consuming of contaminated water in the military camps made up the remaining 80 percent of soldiers in this category. From 1775 through 1781, the span of the American Revolutionary War, 210,000 men served in the army. The largest number serving under Washington's command at one time added up to 35,000 in November 1778. In sixteen major battles and twenty-two hundred skirmishes, the British killed 8,900 colonial soldiers in actual battle, 15 to 20 percent suffering death from bayonet wounds. Even more shocking is the fact that of the 80,000 soldiers who died during the war, more than 90 percent of Washington's army died from illnesses they contracted rather than from battle wounds. This means that fewer than 10 percent of the casualties actually died from battle-caused injuries. David C. Jahntz, "A Look at Late Eighteenth Century Medical Practices," BAHR No Products, 2012, April 11, 2016, http://www.bahrnoproducts.com/PDF/A%20LOOK%20AT%20LATE%2018TH%20CENTURY%20MEDICAL%20PRACTICES.pdf; David Dary, Frontier Medicine: From the Atlantic to the Pacific (New York: Alfred A. Knopf, 2008).

435 Balch, Journal of the Times at the Siege of Boston Since Our Arrival at Cambridge, Near Boston, 15.

436 Ibid.

437 Ibid.

438 Ibid., 16

439 J. L. Bell, "Lt. Colonel Kemble's Catalogue of Deserters," Boston 1775, May 15, 2012, January 21, 2015, http://boston1775.blogspot.com/2012/05/lt-col-kembles-catalogue-of-deserters.html.

Cresap and Price will not be the only captains of rifle companies to suffer desertions from their ranks. Between July 25 and September 8, at least four other riflemen, several from Virginia and Pennsylvania rifle companies, also desert or turn traitor and defect to the British in Boston.[440]

Headquarters of American Officers during the Siege of Boston, Roxbury, Massachusetts

On September 9, Michael Cresap and Daniel Morgan, longtime comrades in arms, part ways. Two of Washington's most iconic and charismatic rifle company captains, Cresap and Morgan are about to meet with two very different destinies, neither of which could have been predicted by anyone.

The histories of Daniel Morgan (1736–1802) and Michael Cresap go back a long way. Cresap and Morgan display much of the same character and courage—two frontiersmen bonded by numerous shared experiences dating back to the French and Indian War more than twenty years earlier. In May 1755, Cresap was just fourteen years of age when Morgan, along with his cousin Daniel Boone, served as wagoners under General Braddock. It was at

---

440   Ibid. An advertisement was placed in the Hartford Courant newspaper seeking to recover three deserters from two Pennsylvania rifle companies stationed in Cambridge, Massachusetts: "Deserted from Capt. Nagel's company, the second regiment of foot, in the Continental army, commanded by Col. William Thompson, viz. Elias Ruger (sp.), a thick, well made man, about 5 foot 6 inches high, swarthy complexion, black hair, had on a hunting shirt and trowsers, and took with him a rifle and shot pouch. Michael Mayer, about 18 years of age, 5 feet 5 inches high, swarthy complexion, short fair hair, had on likewise a hunting shirt and trowsers. He took with him an Indian blanket, a good rifle, and shot pouch—they took with them other clothes, and may probably change their dress. Likewise is with them, John Perree (sp.), of Captain Smith's Company, about 5 feet 10 inches high, of a swarthy complexion, with a large crooked nose, took with him an Indian blanket, a hunting shirt and trowsers of an ash colour, a good rifle, powder horn and shot bag. Whoever apprehends the said deserters, and secures them, a reward of thirty shillings, lawful money for each, and all reasonable charges paid by Geo. Nagel, Captain." Hartford Courant, September 11, 1775, 2.

this time that both Morgan and Boone camped with Braddock's army at Oldtown, Maryland, on fields owned by Michael's father, Thomas Cresap.[441]

Interactions between Morgan and Cresap's family were not all positive in nature. Sometime between 1758 and 1763, Thomas Cresap accused Daniel Morgan of stealing Cresap's horse. Apparently due to lack of evidence, when the case went to court, nothing ever came of this charge. The fact that Michael Cresap was later able to travel and fight alongside Morgan in Lord Dunmore's War showed that in a frontier setting, where people depended on one another for survival, there was a willingness to forgive, move on, and let the past remain in the past. That Cresap trusted Morgan was also evident by receipts for supplies that Michael advanced to Daniel Morgan from Cresap's commissary in Redstone.[442]

Cresap was in the company of Morgan at the successful conclusion of Dunmore's War in the fall of 1774. At that war's end, before departing for their homes, officers made a vow that later proved to be a foretelling of great magnitude. Both Cresap and Morgan kept that vow in the summer of 1775, living up to their promise as follows: "We an army victorious formed ourselves into a society pledging our word of honor to each other to assist our brethren of Boston in case hostilities should commence."[443]

Within ten months of that vow, the frontiersmen kept their word. Reunited once again in the summer of 1775, since arriving in the Boston area, Cresap and Morgan, along with the other southern rifle companies, have terrorized the redcoats. After Bunker Hill, the British army let their guard down, feeling that they had positioned themselves at a safe distance from the musket fire of Continental army regulars. However, once the rifle companies began arriving with their long-range, grooved-barrel shooting rifles, the sharpshooters immediately began "picking off sentries and stragglers and sending dignified officers for cover."[444]

The British were not used to tactics employed by riflemen such as Cresap and Morgan, who had adopted the woodland Indian style of fighting that involved methods of "ambush, hit-and run, mobile detachments, and personal marksmanship." By comparison, the technique of British combat involved open field fighting while standing or moving "close together [in] rank and file." Because the rebels shot from "behind cover and specifically marked out officers for annihilation," the redcoats thought of their foe as "white barbarians or semisavages."[445]

The 1763 Treaty of Paris, ending the French and Indian War, transferred Canada from French rule to British rule. As of 1775, Canada has been a British colony for twelve years. But Congress now believes that if Washington can take Montreal and Quebec from the British, the Continental war effort will be greatly benefited three ways: being the first to gain a great amount of new territory, obtaining valuable needed resources, and establishing control of the Hudson River. With the taking of Canada by the armed forces, Washington would significantly decrease the ability of the British to use the Hudson River as a backdoor approach to attack his forces in Boston.

On May 27, 1775, Congress sent an open letter to the Canadians saying, "We yet entertain hopes of your unit-ing with us in defense of common liberty." Congress feels optimistic that its cause for liberty is so righteous that

---

441 Paul Wallace, Daniel Boone in Pennsylvania (Harrisburg, PA: Commonwealth of Pennsylvania Historical and Museum Commission, 1967), 17.

442 Public Service Claims, 1775. A Public Service Claims Record dated October 26, 1775 states the following: "To Mich.l Cresap for advances to Capt. Morgan/John Jacobs."

443 Reuben Gold Thwaites and Louise Phelps Kellogg, Documentary History of Dunmore's War (Madison, WI: Wisconsin Historical Society, 1905), xxv.

444 Don Higginbotham, Daniel Morgan: Revolutionary Rifleman (Chapel Hill: Omahundro Institute of Early American Culture and the University of North Carolina Press, 1979), 25.

445 Don Higginbotham, The War for American Independence: Military Attitudes, Policies, and Practices, 1763–1789 (New York: The Macmillan Company, 1971).

it will inspire not only Canada but also Newfoundland, Nova Scotia, Georgia, east and west Florida, and Ireland to join their revolution against British tyranny.[446]

But first and foremost, if the situation is warranted, Congress is willing to take Canada by force. In its estimation, Canada poses a dire and immediate threat. There is still the ever-threatening possibility that the British will attack Washington's vulnerable forces in Boston from the north—thus the reason Congress saw fit to authorize the invasion of Canada on June 27, 1775.

Supporting General Washington's line of thinking is John Adams, Massachusetts Continental Congress member, who will declare, "Canada must be ours; Quebec must be ours."[447] Indeed, Congress greatly desires Canada to be the fourteenth American colony.

Benedict Arnold, a name synonymous with treason or traitor, is at his post in Cambridge, a mere six miles from Cresap's company stationed at Roxbury. In the summer of 1775, Arnold is still a trusted member and confidante of Washington's inner circle. At Cambridge, Arnold converses with Washington as to the best plan of attack on Quebec City, both men foreseeing an approach to the city charted through the Maine wilderness.

In a carefully planned strategy developed during the summer of 1775, Washington places Benedict Arnold in charge of a one-thousand-man force instructed to depart from Cambridge "to penetrate into Canada by way of the Kennebec River [Maine], and [north]…to Quebec."[448]

The growing concern regarding the British in Canada and that country's importance to the thirteen colonies cause Cresap and Morgan to separate and follow different pathways, with one more twist of fate to follow.

Washington calls on Daniel Morgan[449] and his Virginia rifle company, along with Captain Hendricks's Pennsylvania rifle company, to join Benedict Arnold's campaign. Captain Morgan's company departs Roxbury on September 9, and on September 13, under Arnold's command, the companies leave Cambridge to begin the colonial expedition to Canada. During this phase of army business combined with an old friend's departure, Captain Cresap and his rifle company remain behind at Roxbury to support the blockade at Boston Neck.

Historians do not record the final conversation between these two men. They certainly must wish each other well and a safe passage as each goes about his upcoming endeavors. Morgan marches off with Benedict Arnold, unknowingly assisting the efforts of a man who will later betray both the cause of the American Revolution and the safety of George Washington himself.

The lives of Cresap and Morgan now reach a dramatic turning point. Unbeknownst to either man, these two comrades in arms, who spent so much time together during the Indian Wars of 1774 and most recently renewed their friendship in Boston, will never see each other again.

---

446 Anthony DePalma, Here: A Biography of the New American Continent (New York: PublicAffairs, 2001),191–2.
447 National Archives, "From John Adams to James Warren, 18 February 1776," accessed December 9, 2017, https://founders.archives.gov/documents/Adams/06-04-02-0008.
448 Thomas Desjardin, Through A Howling Wilderness: Benedict' Arnold's March to Quebec, 1775 (New York: St. Martin's Griffin, 1907), 50.
449 On December 31, 1775, at the Battle of Quebec, the British pushed back the colonists and captured and imprisoned Daniel Morgan. During Morgan's imprisonment, Washington promoted the Virginia rifle captain to the rank of colonel. Through a prisoner exchange, Daniel Morgan was released in 1776. Morgan later led the Eleventh Virginia Regiment, consisting of the five hundred men who played an important role in the winning of the Battle of Saratoga in October 1777. The British general Burgoyne wrote about the riflemen after the battle: "The enemy had with their army a great number of marksmen, armed with rifle-barrel pieces; these, during an engagement, hovered upon the flanks in small detachments, and were very expert in securing themselves, and in shifting their ground. In this action, many placed themselves in high trees in the rear of their own line, and there was seldom a minute's interval of smoke in any part of our line without officers being taken off with single shot." This colonial victory over the British persuaded France to back the American cause with the signing of the 1778 Treaty of Alliance. In October 1780, General Washington promoted Morgan to the rank of brigadier general. In January 1781, Morgan's leadership again helped win in the south at the Battle of Cowpens in South Carolina, defeating Colonel Tarleton. Cowpens was an important strategic victory that came soon after the Continental army's disastrous loss at Camden. This rallied America's will to continue the fight, giving the colonials one voice and a renewed spirit that led to Washington's October 1781 victory at the Battle of Yorktown. Jeremy Black, War for America: The Fight for Independence, 1775–1783 (Phoenix Mill, GB: Sutton Publishing Limited, 1991), 61.

CHAPTER 15

Days of Glory

Cambridge, Massachusetts
September 10-17, 1775

ON SEPTEMBER 10, CAPTAIN CRESAP marches his rifle company from Roxbury to attend a church service in the nearby town of Dorchester. That Sunday, Private Daniel McCurtin, who serves in Captain Price's Maryland rifle company, records his impressions of the church service in his journal: "This being the Sabbath day our Rifle Company were marched to Dorchester Meeting house where we had a fine sermon, but the appearance of us as well as many other Companys seemed something strange to me, where I could see nothing else but men loaded with the ministers of death [guns], going to hear God's word. Every company had their [fifers] and drums, and marched into the House of God under arms."[450] Even in church, Cresap's men are armed and ready. The riflemen are on high alert in case the British regulars decide to charge across Boston Neck and attack Washington's army on this day of worship.

If granted the opportunity to reflect in church, Captain Michael Cresap may come upon the realization that all military involvement in the events of his past—the French and Indian War, Pontiac's War, and Lord Dunmore's War—has prepared him for this critical moment in time to lead this elite group of Maryland riflemen at the dawn of the American Revolution. His company's role is to help protect General Washington's fledgling army when it is most vulnerable. Cresap answers his mission and purpose with boldness and confidence. There is nothing timorous or tepid in his response to his calling.

Perhaps during the church service, a few of Cresap's men say a prayer of thanks for the successful completion of the fort at Lamb's Dam on Boston Neck. On this Sunday, September 10, Washington's colonials finish the construction of the fortification at Lamb's Dam. The fort has the distinction of being the closest to the enemy of any fabricated stronghold along Washington's siege line. The fortification construction began on August 23, just prior to the arrival of Cresap's Rifles at Roxbury on August 25. Since reporting in for duty, members of Cresap's riflemen have been posted near Lamb's Dam to protect and secure the men working on the building of the fort.

McCurtin records the following in his journal about events of this past week: "This and every day they [the British] fired off their...guns [at sunset], like other false tyrants, they fired another in among us, but did no damage."[451] In the past weeks that they have been in Roxbury, the men of the southern rifle companies have apparently become hardened, or at least impervious, to the cannonballs hurled at them each day by the British. An observer present at the time records this phenomenon: "The enemy fire their cannon shot into Roxbury and several have passed through the church; but little damage has yet been sustained and our soldiers become so familiarized to the sight of cannon shot rolling among them, that they manifest little or no fear of their consequences."[452]

---

450 Balch, *Journal of the Times at the Siege of Boston Since Our Arrival at Cambridge, Near Boston*, 16.
451 Balch, *Journal of the Times at the Siege of Boston Since Our Arrival at Cambridge, Near Boston*, 16.
452 Thacher, *Military Journal During the American Revolutionary War*, 37.

Amazingly, near their advanced post on Boston Neck, British regulars create little or no interference with the work of the men constructing the Lamb's Dam fortifications, even though the colonials are well within musket-shot range during this risky activity. Perhaps the British regulars hesitate to poke their heads out to take aim knowing that Cresap's men, along with men from other rifle companies, are nearby observing their every move.

Since the work of colonials in the placement of an artillery battery at Lamb's Dam, the effectiveness of this fortification will soon become apparent. Around October 6, from this fort, colonials will fire on the nearby British fortifications also located on Boston Neck while British regulars are changing watch guards. This assault will kill one British corporal with a cannonball.[453]

On September 11, in the same week that Captain Morgan departs from Cambridge with Benedict Arnold's twelve-hundred-man force to begin the Canadian campaign, Washington meets with his war council to discuss the second part of his plan: to carry out an amphibious assault on the British army in Boston. Not only would this plan put Cresap's rifle company at great risk, but also any tactical blunder at this time could possibly place Washington's entire army in danger.

The relative inactivity of the siege throughout the summer tries Washington's patience. The general was not successful at enticing the British to take the bait when he seized Ploughed Hill. The British army is not strong enough to break the colonial siege line, and Washington's forces do not possess the military might to make a general attack on the British army. Washington feels the weight of high expectations from Congress and the American people, which compel him to make another tactical military move to break the ongoing stalemate.

Washington is not yet that victorious Yorktown heroic figure known from present-day history books. In fact, in 1775, he is still inexperienced as a military commander. Even though he is an officer and a veteran of the French and Indian War, Washington has never commanded an army of this size.

Fearing that the expense will make maintaining his army during the scourge of a cold New England winter virtually impossible, Washington reasons that a decisive stroke must occur soon. Perhaps because he himself is a farmer, he is concerned that in their desperate search for fuel with which to keep warm, his men will destroy the nearby fences and orchards of innocent citizens. Further concerned that he will not be able to hold his army together as morale declines when winter sets in, the general acknowledges the possibility that men will abandon the fight for liberty. In addition, over the long run, Washington could lose the resolve of Congress to continue to sanction the rising costs of materials needed to support his army and the means with which to pay his men their promised wages.

After much contemplation and strategic planning, Washington has devised a plan. He will attack British-fortified Boston, his designated colonials crossing over the Back Bay in flat-bottomed boats, each of which will hold about fifty men. He will equip the boats with artillery, and they will fire rounds upon Boston while floating his army across the bay, a one-mile distance. Once his men have landed, they will carry out a musket assault in Boston.

Envisioning the success of this plan, Washington knows he will have to defeat the British army as quickly as possible. His next step will be to disband his own army and return the men to their homes. Caught in the vise of this building pressure cooker in the summer of 1775, Washington proposes this plan to his war council. The war council, made up in part of Charles Lee and Artemas Ward, rejects his plan unanimously "for the present at least."[454]

---

453 Balch, Journal of the Times at the Siege of Boston Since Our Arrival at Cambridge, Near Boston, 15–7; Bell, "Lt. Colonel Kemble's Catalogue of Deserters."
454 David McCullough, 1776 (New York: Simon and Schuster, 2005), 54.

111

In this instance, rejection is a good thing. Many things could go wrong with Washington's proposal. If the tide is not just right or if the wind direction changes, the boats could become stuck in mud one hundred yards from shore, and the men would be forced to walk in muck toward land while the British fire on them. Any action involved in such a plan could produce slaughter on a grand scale, worse than the mayhem the British recently perpetrated at Bunker Hill. For Washington to make a fatal error in judgment that would ultimately destroy his army and end the rebellion is exactly what the British are hoping for.[455]

While the British are, perhaps foolishly, wishing that Washington will simply give up, Captain Cresap is experiencing his own unique set of problems. Along with the growing knowledge that something is not quite right with his health, and in spite of the bedlam that ensues in nearby camps, Cresap manages to maintain discipline and order in his camp.

On September 10, Private Daniel McCurtin records in his journal that the men in the rifle companies have lost their "pass" and freedom to move about camp freely due to "our Riflemen's misbehavior."[456] However, in that journal, the private does not mention which rifle company or group of riflemen has caused the trouble. Historians have identified the troublemakers to be thirty-three riflemen in Colonel Thompson's First Pennsylvania Rifle Company. General Washington charges men in this Pennsylvania rifle unit stationed at Prospect Hill with "disobedient and mutinous Behaviour."[457]

Colonel Thompson is not a strict disciplinarian. Twice this summer, riflemen in Thompson's Pennsylvania regiment have broken into the camp guardhouse to release a number of men confined for misconduct or minor crimes. Once, the men of that unit even foolishly challenged the authority of their superior officers for disciplining a subordinate, verbally damning the officers in their presence "with great insolence."[458] The conduct of these few men in the Pennsylvania rifle company has embarrassed riflemen in other rifle companies. The men feel that the Pennsylvania riflemen's misdeeds reflect poorly on all riflemen who represent the southern states.

This is not to imply that riflemen wearing hunting shirts and moccasins are angels. At times, some men in the two Maryland rifle companies found themselves in predicaments. The day before the mutiny incident, on September 9, Samuel Mance from Captain Price's rifle company deserted. Also around the same time, two of Price's men, Jacob Smith and a man named Finby, managed to get themselves into such trouble that they were confined to a guardhouse for a week.[459]

For reasons sometimes not clear but definitely frowned upon by his superiors, Colonel Thompson seems to overlook the insubordinate conduct of some of his men, who apparently get away with their antics without consequence.

On September 18, a friend of Cresap's named Jesse Lukens, an eyewitness to these events, writes the following account of the mutiny that unfolds before him: "Once when an offender was brought to the post to be whipped, it was with the utmost difficulty [that the soon to be mutineers] were kept from rescuing [the offender] in the presence of all their officers. The [insubordinate soldiers] openly damned [the officers] and behaved with great insolence. However...colonel [William Thompson] was pleased to pardon the man and all remained quiet."[460]

---

455 Ibid., 53–4.
456 Balch, Journal of the Times at the Siege of Boston Since Our Arrival at Cambridge, Near Boston, 16.
457 Fitzpatrick, The Writings of George Washington from the Original Manuscript Sources, vol. 3, 490.
458 John A. Nagy, Rebellion in the Ranks: Mutinies of the American Revolution (Yardley, PA: Westholme Publishing, 2008), 3
459 Balch, Journal of the Times at the Siege of Boston Since Our Arrival at Cambridge, Near Boston, 16.
460 Nagy, Rebellion in the Ranks, 3; John B. Linn and William H. Egle, "Col. William Thompson's Battalion of Riflemen: June 25, 1775–July 1, 1776," in Pennsylvania Archives. 2nd series, vol. 10, (Harrisburg, PA: Clarence M. Busch, 1895), 8–10; National Archives, "To George Washington from Brigadier General Nathanael Greene, 10 September 1775," accessed December 10, 2017, https://founders.archives.gov/documents/Washington/03-01-02-0341.

Some men in the Continental army are jealous because Washington gives the sharpshooters preferential treatment. In fact, in an arrangement that further bolsters this notion, the general has segregated the southern rifle units in camps a short distance away from the camps of regulars. Furthermore, officers have excused the riflemen from "all working parties, camp guards, [and] camp duty."[461]

The musketeers cannot help but notice Washington's high regard of the southern rifle companies, sometimes referred to by New Englanders as "over-the-mountain men." The perception that their superiors favor riflemen over musketeers causes resentment and morale problems within the Continental forces. However, the next incident of misbehavior that blows up within Colonel Thompson's Pennsylvania rifle companies is something too big for even General Washington to ignore.

On Sunday, September 10, authorities confine a sergeant from Thompson's company for neglect of duty. "Murmuring"[462] among themselves, men in Thompson's unit speak of their plans to break the sergeant out of confinement. Adjutant officer Lieutenant David Zeigler learns of these plans and arrests a grumbling conspirator, confining the discontented person in the same guardhouse as the confined sergeant.

In the warmth of a September evening, the murmuring escalates. Sitting inside a house with several officers who have just finished their meal near Prospect Hill, Jesse Lukens and others at the supper table hear a disturbance coming from outside. As the officers pause to gauge the source of the ruckus, they hear cheers of "Huzzah!" that rise like cries of victory just outside their dining quarters. When the officers hurriedly file out to see what all the fuss and great commotion is about, they discover a raucous celebration led by an all-too-merry band of men who have just released the murmuring mutineer from the guardhouse. Not only has the zealous group released their fellow soldier from captivity, but the prisoner they freed is now standing in the midst of his rescuers!

The officers quickly seize the mutineer from the mob "without violent opposition."[463] They then seek out the nearest guard to escort the prisoner to the main guardhouse at Cambridge. However, officers soon realize that the incident is by no means finished.

After a short period, thirty-three men from James Ross's Pennsylvania company make their appearance and storm the camp with loaded long rifles. The mob of men swears by God that they will go to the Cambridge guardhouse and "release the man or lose their lives."[464] Having declared their intentions, Ross's men set off with much fervor from Prospect Hill to Cambridge.

Lukens writes to a friend on September 18 that it was in "vain trying to stop them."[465] That night, officers remain in camp to keep the others quiet but not before they send a messenger to General Washington in Cambridge to inform him about the mutiny that has just occurred before their eyes.

When Washington learns about the ongoing mutiny, he immediately assigns "500 men with fixed bayonets and loaded pieces [artillery]" to protect the Cambridge guardhouse.[466] Washington also orders Colonel Nathaniel Greene's and Colonel Hitchcock's units to arms to suppress the rebellion, not yet knowing the breadth of the insurrection or how widespread it is.[467]

The mutineers travel only half a mile out of Prospect Hill before Washington intercepts them. When the mutineers arrive near the guardhouse and see that they are greatly outnumbered, they run into the nearby woods for

---

461 Linn and Egle, Pennsylvania, War of the Revolution: Battalions and Line, 9.
462 Linn and Egle, Pennsylvania, War of the Revolution: Battalions and Line, 9.
463 Ibid.
464 Ibid.
465 Ibid.
466 Linn and Egle, Pennsylvania, War of the Revolution: Battalions and Line, 9.
467 J. L. Bell, "Lt. Ziegler and 'Our Thirty-Two Mutineers,'" Boston 1775, February 21, 2009, June 6, 2013, http://boston1775.blogspot.com/2009/02/lt-ziegler-and-our-thirty-two-mutineers.html.

cover. Generals Washington, Lee, and Greene, backed with men armed with fixed bayonets, quickly appear on the scene and order the mutineers to lay down their arms.

Seeing that they are greatly outnumbered, the troublemakers immediately surrender without a shot being fired. Washington commands Captain Nagel's Pennsylvania rifle company to surround the insolent men with loaded weapons and orders the ringleaders of the mutiny bound in irons and sent to confinement at Cambridge. Officers deliver the remaining insubordinate men to the quarter guard at Prospect Hill, where all are charged with mutiny.[468]

On September 12, in a general court martial in Cambridge, Washington brings to trial the thirty-three malcontents of Colonel Thompson's rifle battalion. The ill-doers get off relatively easily, considering the seriousness of their crimes. One soldier is punished for being "disobedient," and another man is charged with "mutinous Behaviour." The court deems that each man must pay a sum of twenty shillings (about one pound sterling) with the exception of one "John Seamon," who, "over and above his fine, is to suffer six days imprisonment."

Jesse Lukens believes that Washington's benevolence was "mitigated no doubt on account of their having come so far to serve the cause and it being their first crime."[469] This action ends the first mutinous act under General Washington's reign during the American Revolution.[470]

The first mutiny of the American Revolution occurs not long after Cresap's rifle company arrives at Roxbury. The initial early weeks were truly golden ones for the riflemen. During this time, they enjoyed privilege, respect, and admiration. The recent debacle has changed all that.

The recent mutiny by Thompson's Pennsylvania rifle company has further agitated and soured the frame of mind of the officers in command at Cambridge. Since the mutiny, a dark cloud hangs over each member of every rifle company participating in the Siege of Boston. At headquarters in Cambridge, Washington's, Lee's, and Gates's close proximity to Thompson's riflemen on Prospect Hill likewise spoils their view of the mutinous Pennsylvania rifle company and the other rifle companies in general.

Perhaps no comments are harsher toward the riflemen than those made by General Lee. On October 10, 1775, Charles Lee writes to Benjamin Rush regarding the rifle companies, "I once was of the opinion, that some Batallions from the Southward wou'd be necessary—but I have alter'd my opinion. I am now perswaded you have not to the Southward so good material for common soldiers. Your Riflemen have a good deal open'd our eyes

---

468 Martyn, The Life of Artemas Ward, 179; Fitzpatrick, The Writings of George Washington from the Original Manuscript Sources, vol. 3, 490; Linn and Egle, Pennsylvania, War of the Revolution: Battalions and Line, 8–10; Nagy, Rebellion in the Ranks, 4.

469 Linn and Egle, Pennsylvania, War of the Revolution: Battalions and Line, 10.

470 Fitzpatrick, The Writings of George Washington from the Original Manuscript Sources, vol. 3, 490–1. This will not be General Washington's only personal intervention in the breaking up of a fracas involving riflemen. Even after the recent mutiny, there is evidence of a culture clash that still exists between the southern rifle companies and New England militia units. A newly recruited rifle company from the backwoods and mountains of Virginia had recently arrived at Cambridge "in a uniform dress totally different from the regiments raised on the seaboard and the interior of New England, [and] excited the curiosity of the whole army, particularly the Marblehead Regiment, who were always full of fun and mischief." Not-so-kind utterings were no doubt exchanged when the Virginia men crossed paths with the men from the Marblehead regiment at Harvard Yard. A ten-year-old bystander named Israel Trask later records for posterity what happens next: "The [Marblehead] men looked on scorn on such a rustic uniform when compared to their own round jackets and fisher's trousers [and they] directly confronted from fifty to a hundred of the riflemen who were viewing the college buildings [that were converted to army barracks]. It being winter, the men began throwing snowballs at each other. In five minutes, the situation attracted a massive crowd to the Harvard yard site. The teasing quickly escalated into a full-blown tumult of fist fighting and jostling "worthy of the days of Homer. "At this juncture Washington made his appearance, whether by accident or design I never knew…I only saw him and his colored servant, both mounted. With the spring of a deer [Washington] leaped from his saddle, threw the reigns of his bridle into the hands of his servant, and rushed into the thickest of the melee [and] with an iron grip seized two tall, brawny, athletic, savage looking riflemen by the throat, keeping them at arm's length, alternately shaking and talking to them. In this position the eye of the belligerents caught sight of the general. Its effect on them was instantaneous flight at top of their speed in all directions from the scene of the conflict. Less than fifteen minutes time elapsed from the commencement of the row before the general and his two criminals were the only occupants on the field of action. J. L. Bell, "Snowball Fight in Harvard Yard," Boston 1775, September 21, 2015, http://boston1775.blogspot.com/2007/12/snowball-fight-in-harvard-yard.html; Washington Irving, The Life of George Washington, vol. 1 (London: Henry G. Bohn, 1855), 436; Bell, 2007.

upon the subject, th' to do justice to their officers, they are unexceptional; their privates are a general damn'd riff raff-dirty, mutinous, and disaffected."[471]

On October 30, 1775, Artemas Ward will write to John Adams that the officers "do not boast so much as the riflemen as heretofore. Gen' Washington has said he wished they had never come; Gen' Lee has damned and wished them all in Boston; Genl. Gates has said, if any capital movement was about to be made, the Riflemen must be moved from this camp."[472]

Ward, who directly supervises Cresap's rifle company at Roxbury, has nothing negative to say about the riflemen. Ward merely parrots the views of the other officers posted near Colonel Thompson's company. Perhaps Ward has nothing cynical to report regarding the riflemen because the companies he oversees at Roxbury have had nothing to do with the recent mutiny. In spite of the unflattering aspersions now cast on all riflemen, Cresap's reputation remains untarnished. Still, his men are assigned camp duties and fatigue, thus rendering them unwitting victims of the scandal.

On September 11, 1775, George Washington writes general orders signaling that the preferential treatment the riflemen have previously enjoyed is over. His new dictates concerning the duties of the riflemen read as follows: "Colonel Thompson's Battalion of Rifle-men posted upon Prospect Hill, to take their share of all duty of Guard and Fatigue, with the Brigade they encamp with…The Riflemen posted at Roxbury, and toward Letchmore's Point, are to do duty with the Brigade they are posted with."[473] The riflemen are no longer exempt from work assignments such as tedious routine guard duty or the hard, physical labor of camp fatigue. These fiercely independent and proud riflemen, who were born and raised in the wilderness, must now follow their superiors' orders to work alongside regular musketeers constructing protective barricades and forts as well as labor on any other tedious assignments handed down to them.

Daniel McCurtin's journal entry of September 16 confirms that a shake-up has resulted from the announcement of General Washington's September 11 general order. At Roxbury, the riflemen are "ordered to work," the first time McCurtin uses that phrase in his journal since his arrival in the Boston area a month ago.[474] Now, in addition to their usual sentry-watch duties requiring their shooting skills, the riflemen must perform other work duties in camp as assigned by their superiors. The riflemen have fallen off their pedestal. All the men serving in rifle companies must now bear the consequences of the insubordination of a few men. These so-called riflemen, who until this time had enjoyed light duty, now must perform camp duty like soldiers in any other regiment.[475]

Word spreads quickly throughout the camps that Captain Cresap is ill. What is the cause of Cresap's illness? It is not too much of a stretch to believe that Michael Cresap contracted malaria sometime during the summer of 1774, while he led a Virginia rifle company against the Shawnee Indians during Lord Dunmore's war. This confrontation occurred primarily along the low, mosquito infested bottomlands of the Ohio River Valley, near present-day Wheeling, West Virginia.[476] The wet river bottoms along the Ohio River are breeding grounds for mosquitoes that carry disease and infection. It seems that anyone who spends much time outdoors during the late summer or fall in

---

471 Martyn, The Life of Artemas Ward, 179–80.
472 Ibid, 179.
473 Fitzpatrick, The Writings of George Washington from the Original Manuscript Sources, vol. 3, 490.
474 Balch, Journal of the Times at the Siege of Boston Since Our Arrival at Cambridge, Near Boston, 17.
475 Nagy, Rebellion in the Ranks, 4.
476 Jacob, A Biographical Sketch of the Late Captain Michael Cresap, 117–25.

the lowlands and river bottoms in this region is subject to contracting malaria. In fact, malaria is so commonplace that it produces more illness than any other disease at this time.[477]

So that farm work is not interrupted, pioneers consider themselves blessed if only one family member at a time suffers recurring chills and fever, the symptoms of malaria. Settlers call the malady "swamp-fever," "chill-fever," "fever and ague," or "the shakes," so named because of the bodily symptoms this illness inflicts upon its victims.[478]

When someone suffers from malaria, the victim knows to expect recurring attacks every two or three days prior to a temporary spell of normalcy. The attacks come so regularly that settlers know just when to schedule their time and stop their work in anticipation of the next attack. Each malarial occurrence comes with predictable symptoms, each typically lasting six to twelve hours. First, the victim begins "stretching and yawning, followed by chills until the body shivers, teeth chatter, fingers turn dead white, and fingernails turn blue. Once the attack ends, a dry fever develops, with the skull feeling hot and flush, after which the sufferer is drenched in sweat and is left weak and exhausted."[479] After each cycle, the victim experiences a sense of temporary well-being before the next episode of malarial symptoms occurs.[480]

Once a sufferer's body is plagued by cyclical malarial episodes, he or she becomes weak and is rendered vulnerable to an array of diseases, including dysentery (inflammation of the colon with frequent passage of mucous and blood), dropsy (congestive heart failure), and consumption (tuberculosis). As if this is not dire enough, the sufferer of malaria also becomes susceptible to typhoid fever, jaundice, measles, smallpox, scarlet fever, and pneumonia.[481]

Problems concerning Cresap's health are further exacerbated during this time by exhaustion and lack of sanitation in the military camps. Cresap's illness is further compounded by the close proximity of men in Washington's military camps. The Colonial army consists of sixteen thousand soldiers from more than six colonies congregated in the military camps, with most of the men exhibiting various and sundry health issues. Soldiers lack access to adequate latrines. Clean water for drinking, cooking, or bathing is practically nonexistent. Dysentery (diarrhea), undoubtedly caused by unclean or contaminated water, proves the greatest health issue soldiers endure at Washington's military camps. Aside from the unavailability of clean water, lack of proper diet, and the ill-timed physical contact of a sick man further exasperate a soldier's health.[482]

Daniel McCurtin notes in his journal that the weather has been very fine this past week both day and night, but curiously he does not mention the dark cloud that hovers over Cresap's rifle company or over Peacock Tavern at Jamaica Plains, where Captain Michael Cresap lies ill. The Peacock Tavern is a well-known inn, built in 1765 near

---

477 Dary, *Frontier Medicine: From the Atlantic to the Pacific*, 81–2.
478 Ibid., 53–4, 81–2, 323.
479 Dary, *Frontier Medicine: From the Atlantic to the Pacific*, 81–2.
480 Ibid., 53–4, 81–2.
481 Ibid., 53–4.
482 Jacob, *A Biographical Sketch of the Late Captain Michael Cresap*, 117–25; Jahntz, "A Look at Late Eighteenth Century Medical Practices."

a mineral spring, six miles west of Boston and Roxbury. Presently the tavern also serves as a hospital for patriots stationed at Roxbury.[483]

Captain Lemuel Child, keeper of Peacock Tavern, likely keeps a close day-to-day watch on Captain Cresap. On April 19, 1775, Captain Child led one of the three Roxbury minutemen companies called to arms and engaged the British at both Lexington and Concord. Cresap's association with Lemuel Child and the Peacock Tavern connects Cresap to the very beginning of the American Revolution and the shot heard round the world.

Original Road Marker with the inscription: "6 mi. from Boston 1735 P. D." located directly across the road from where the Peacock Tavern once stood, Jamaica Plain, Massachusetts.

---

483 David M. Balfour, "The Taverns of Boston in Ye Olden Time," Bay State Monthly 2(2) (November 2, 1884), 106–20, accessed December 11, 2017, http://www.ma-roots.org/suffolkcounty/tav.html. The Peacock Tavern was located at the main entrance sign of the Brigham and Women's Faulkner Hospital at the intersection of Centre Street and Allandale Street in the present-day Jamaica Plain section of Boston. The site was located near the headquarters of Artemas Ward. Today, opposite where the Peacock Tavern once stood is an old stone milepost with the following inscription: "6 mi. from Boston 1735 P. D." The initials P. D. are for Paul Dudley, who set the stone in place. In 1794, Samuel Adams (1722–1803) bought the Peacock Tavern with its forty acres. The ardent patriot Samuel Adams was an organizer of the Committee for Correspondence, the organization that linked like-minded men across the thirteen colonies, patriots like Michael Cresap's father, Thomas. Samuel Adams resided at the Peacock Tavern when he served as the second governor of Massachusetts and until 1803, the last summer of his life. Old maps show that the Peacock Tavern was still standing in the 1830s. Francis S. Drake, The Town of Roxbury: Its Memorable Persons and Places (Roxbury, MA: Francis D. Drake, 1878), 435–6.

No doubt troubled by the bad news about Cresap, a small contingent of men travels a short distance from Roxbury along the main road to the Peacock Tavern to visit the captain. One of the men who document a concern for Captain Cresap is the twenty-six-year old Jesse Lukens,[484] who shares a similar background and a true kinship with Cresap. They both come from prominent surveying families and are expert riflemen. Michael, much like Jesse, proved himself in past exploits to be "brave and daring," as well as "very popular among the young men."[485]

Lukens now serves as a gentlemen volunteer in Colonel Thompson's Pennsylvania riflemen company at Roxbury. In a letter dated September 17, Lukens mentions his visit to the ailing Captain Cresap: "Peacock, Jamaica Plains. 4 o'Clk…I came here from Roxbury with some of the Rifle Gent. of that Division to ask Capt. Cresap how he does who lies here sick."[486]

Lukens does not name the men of Cresap's company who travel with him, but it is reasonable to assume that Captain Cresap's nephews, Joseph Cresap and Daniel Cresap, Jr., are among this group. If they are not on this visit, it is likely that at another time, Cresap's fellow officers and friends, including Moses Rawlings and Otho Holland Williams, pay Cresap a visit.[487]

During this period, General Washington may also on occasion check in on Cresap to see how his captain fares while lying ill at the Peacock. After all, it is the general's habit to stop at the Peacock for refreshments after he completes his occasional inspection of the American stores of ammunition located along south Dedham Street (present-day Centre Street) near the tavern.

Also near the Peacock Tavern, Washington has stationed troops on Weld Hill at present-day Bussey Hill in the Arnold Arboretum to protect the section of Dedham Road leading to his arsenal. Early upon taking command, Washington designated Weld Hill as a rendezvous point for his army to regroup if the British succeed in storming over Boston Neck and break the siege.

A day after he visits Captain Cresap, Jesse Lukens writes in a letter to an acquaintance in Pennsylvania the following: "You cannot conceive what disgrace we all are in…and that idleness shall not be a further bane to us." The mutinous rebels who are allowed to return to camp are "exceedingly sorry for their misbehavior and promise amendment." Lukens, a member of Thompson's Pennsylvania regiment, blames the riflemen's fall from grace on Thompson and his lack of leadership. To Lukens, it is such a shame, "for this much I can say for [the riflemen]…

---

484 Jesse Lukens (1748-1775) was the son of John Lukens, who, from 1761 until the American Revolution, was the general surveyor of Pennsylvania. Presumably, John Lukens was acquainted with Michael's father. The prominent surveying professions of Maryland's Thomas Cresap and Pennsylvania's John Lukens in all probability led them to cross paths on more than one occasion. Surveyors' sons often assisted their fathers in surveying tasks—thus, the connection between Michael Cresap and Jesse Lukens. In 1769, Jesse Lukens assisted his father in conducting a survey with the well-known astronomer David Rittenhouse to determine the meridian of Norristown and Philadelphia. At another time Thomas Cresap met David Rittenhouse when the astronomer traveled west through Oldtown, Maryland.

485 F. C. Johnson, ed., The Historical Record Devoted Principally to the Early History of Wyoming Valley (Wilkes-Barre, PA: Press of Wilkes-Barre Record, 1899), 226.

486 Lindsay Swift, ed., Historical Manuscripts in the Public Library in the City of Boston, no. 1 (Boston: Trustees of the Public Library, 1900).

487 In 1785, four surveyors each were appointed from Virginia and Pennsylvania to work together to complete the Mason-Dixon survey. Andrew Ellicott was part of the four-member Virginia surveying team. Also on the Virginia team were Dr. James Madison, Robert Andrews, and John Page. John Lukens, the father of Jesse Lukens, was part of the four-member Pennsylvania surveying team. Also on the Pennsylvania team were Thomas Hutchins, Dr. John Ewing, and David Rittenhouse. Several of these individuals have connections to the Cresap family that date back to the French and Indian War and Pontiac's War. Tragically, Jesse Lukens died well before his time. Connecticut encroachers killed Lukens in Pennsylvania in a gun battle not related to the Revolutionary War. Shortly after his visit with Captain Cresap at the Peacock Tavern, Lukens "volunteered for the fun of the thing" to go with a local sheriff and magistrates to push off Connecticut intruders encroaching on Pennsylvania lands. In an encounter with the intruders on December 25, 1775, Jesse Lukens was shot and killed while attempting to enforce Pennsylvania laws and regulations. On Jesse Lukens's tombstone is inscribed the following: "To virtue thus so early snatched away, One generous tear in manly tribute pay." Johnson, The Historical Record Devoted Principally to the Early History of Wyoming Valley, 226.

that upon every alarm it was impossible for men to behave with more readiness or attend better to their duty; it is only in camp that we cut a poor figure."[488]

Despite the recent negative comments of Washington's generals, General Howe still holds respect for the riflemen. He writes to England about "the terrible guns of the rebels" and provides special instructions as to how to handle a rifleman should any of the British have the good fortune to capture one.[489] British authorities are to take the captured rifleman and his rifle and send him to England and place him on exhibition. Fortunately, even though they have been stationed the closest to the British fortifications and troops of any units along the siege line, neither Cresap nor any of his men that summer are captured or taken prisoner.

There is no question that the riflemen are influential in helping to keep the British forces at bay in Boston. If it had not been for the riflemen's intimidating presence during the summer of 1775, the British might have otherwise rushed out over Boston Neck and attacked Washington's army.

However, no matter their accomplishments, because of the mutiny, the heyday of the riflemen is over. The curtain will completely descend on the glory days of these men next month.

---
488 Linn and Egle, "Col. William Thompson's Battalion of Riflemen," 10.
489 Harrington, "Patriot Riflemen During the Ammunition Crisis at the Siege of Boston in 1775."

CHAPTER 16

The Long Journey Home

Roxbury, Massachusetts
October 3, 1775, to October 11, 1775

EARLY IN OCTOBER 1775, RUMORS run rampant around the military camps at Roxbury. One story floating around implies that the British commander, Tom Gage, might soon set off from Boston to England. Another more ominous tale Continental soldiers hear is that Gage may storm out of Boston at any moment and cross Boston Neck to attack Washington's forces. However, private Daniel McCurtin notes in his journal that "many of our old warriors [think] it will prove a difficult task [as the Boston Neck is now] surrounded with canon [sic] and fortifications."[490]

Two individuals will leave Roxbury in early October—one in shame, one in honor. Of the two, only one man's deeds evoke feelings of empathy; that sentiment blankets the camps on the day Michael Cresap becomes the victim of a robbery. This foul deed elicits a strong and quick response from headquarters and a sympathetic reaction from many men within earshot of this news, especially when they learn that the criminal perpetrates the crime while Captain Cresap lies seriously ill.

On October 9, one Nicholas Machin, a private in Captain Stephenson's Virginia rifle company, is tried and found guilty of desertion and of "breaking into Captain Cresap's house"[491] and stealing twenty dollars (the monthly pay of a captain) and some personal items.[492]

At eight o'clock on the same morning, authorities punish Machin for this most ignoble act.[493] In a somewhat harsh display of discipline before his peers, authorities whip Machin with thirty-nine stripes.[494] As if this is not correction enough, enlisted musicians drum Machin out of town with a deafening cacophony produced by fifty-two drummers and at least as many shrieking fifes, "with Thousands of Spectators" looking on.[495]

Sam Hawes, a witness to Machin's punishment, records in his journal the following: "If the infernal regions had been opened and Cain and Judas…had been present, there could have not been a bigger uproar."[496]

---

490 Balch, Journal of the Times at the Siege of Boston Since Our Arrival at Cambridge, Near Boston, 20.
491 Danske Dandridge, Historic Shepherdstown (Charlottesville, VA: Michie Company, 1910), 114.
492 Ibid.
493 Washington imposed swift punishment after the occurrence of a violation or crime as evidenced by his conducting a court martial for the mutineers the day after the mutiny.
494 Manchin's punishment of thirty-nine lashes was evidence of Washington and his officers' familiarity with the Bible as this punishment has a biblical basis. The Apostle Paul was whipped with "40 lashes less one" on five different occasions (II Corinthians 11:24, KJV). In the Old Testament, the law did not allow a culprit to be whipped more than forty stripes (Deuteronomy 25:3). The offender was not to be a victim of personal revenge or degraded. The judges were present to ensure the person assigned to carry out the punishment administered it as the court directed. Judges seldom assigned a punishment that contained more than thirty-nine stripes to avoid a mistake in counting and exceed the biblical mandate of fewer than forty lashes.
495 Tomlinson, Lyon, and Haws, The Military Journals of Two Private Soldiers, 76; Balch, Journal of the Times at the Siege of Boston Since Our Arrival at Cambridge, Near Boston, 5, 21; Dandridge, Historic Shepherdstown, 114.
496 Tomlinson, Lyon, and Haws, The Military Journals of Two Private Soldiers, 76.

Private Daniel McCurtin, another witness to the drumming, records his observations of Machin's punishment in this manner: "This is the first time that I ever heard such a number of drums beat all together. They made such a report in my ears when accompanied with such [screeching] of [fifes] that I could not hear the next man to me, or however could not hear what he said."[497]

Machin's punishment proves much more severe than the comparative wrist slapping dealt to the mutineers. Cresap, the victim of the theft and one of the most popular men in camp—having departed from Roxbury a little more than a week before—is noticeably absent.

As early as September 22, 1775, possibly anticipating Captain Cresap's furlough and departure from Roxbury due to illness, General Washington composed a general order to "settle the rank of Officers of the Rifle Companies, posted at Roxbury."[498] Following this order, headquarters places Moses Rawlings in charge of the Maryland rifle company until superiors deem Captain Cresap fit to return to camp for duty.

Sometime between September 29 and October 2, Cresap leaves Roxbury for home during the height of the New England autumn. The cool, crisp fall air is quite a contrast to the heat and humidity Cresap experienced during the August march from Oldtown. Reporters and other interested parties note that Cresap's homeward-bound journey leads him in a different direction than the route he took from Fredericktown to Boston. To the wonderment of the many who keep track of his well-being, this new course appears to be leading Cresap into the heart of New York City.

The leaves of the forest along the route are in peak color. Sugar-maple trees display golden and orange colors. The red maples are dressed in brilliant crimson. The vines of Virginia creeper, with their deep scarlet-wine-colored foliage, climb and wrap around many of the trees. The leaves of both hickory and yellow poplar are golden, as if mirroring the rays of the sun. Goldenrod and New England aster blossom and show themselves along the edge of the road. Zestful, brilliant fall colors are even more glorious when contrasted with the evergreens growing nearby along the roadways that Cresap traverses.

The captain has chosen a good time to travel, for the weather is "fine" and "elegant."[499] The sky is delightful with patches of billowy white clouds, the heavens contrasted in deep-blue shades. Brittle leaves that have fallen from the oak trees carpet the ground and crunch under the feet of small animals that scamper about.

As he proceeds along home, the Maryland rifleman looks back with satisfaction on the accomplishments his rifle company carried out during their time in Roxbury. His men engaged the British forces at Boston Neck and responded to General Washington's request for reinforcements, marching six miles to Ploughed Hill when an attack seemed imminent. Cresap's men also participated in the successful construction and completion of the fortifications at Lamb's Dam on Boston Neck.

Traveling approximately a week since leaving Roxbury, Cresap passes through New Haven, Connecticut.[500] Four to five days of "hard riding and driving" remain, covering approximately eighty miles before Cresap will reach New York City. The roads along this route are in horrible condition, being "very rough, stony, and uneven."

---

497 Balch, Journal of the Times at the Siege of Boston Since Our Arrival at Cambridge, Near Boston, 21.
498 Fitzpatrick, The Writings of George Washington from the Original Manuscript Sources, vol. 3, 515.
499 Balch, Journal of the Times at the Siege of Boston Since Our Arrival at Cambridge, Near Boston, 20.
500 History accounts are not clear if Cresap traveled by foot, horse, or stagecoach or whether he traveled alone or with others. It is not known which route Captain Cresap took to New York City. From Boston, it was possible to travel to New York City on one of three post roads: the Upper Post Road, the Middle Post Road, or the Lower Post Road. If Cresap traveled to New York by stagecoach, he most likely traveled on the Upper Post Road, the road farthest inland and containing fewer stream crossings with the best taverns of the three post roads. Historians also call the Upper Post Road the Old Bay Road, and it was the most popular road in 1775 when traveling from Boston to New York City. All three post roads from Boston to New York City join at New Haven, Connecticut.

Others who have traveled this route describe the road as "soft, rocky, and treacherous…intolerable, and most miserable." Still Cresap continues onward, sometimes slowed further by "troublesome and even dangerous ferries."[501]

After passing through a section paralleling Long Island Sound, Cresap crosses the Hutchinson River, a small stream on the north side that leads to Manhattan Island and New York City. By the time Cresap arrives in the city on October 12, he has progressed 220 miles, this leg of the return trip having taken him somewhere between ten and fourteen days.[502]

Cresap travels down the main road known today as Broadway, passing the original wall of present Wall Street and the street currently known as Fifth Avenue, as well as Trinity Church and its graveyard. If he continues south along the Post Road on Manhattan Island, Cresap will travel all the way to mile marker zero on the Old Post Road, which ends at the waterfront, near Fraunces Tavern on Pearl and Broad Streets.[503] This establishment sits on the waterfront near the ferry. To continue farther, Cresap must take a ferry across the Hudson River to reach the New Jersey shoreline, which he can see in the distance on the other side of the river.

By this time, Cresap is too sick and exhausted to continue. Weakened by a fever that has plagued him for weeks and by the rigors of this harsh ten-day journey, the captain is less than halfway through his more than 550-mile journey to Oldtown. Detrimental effects of his debilitating illness require Cresap to stop and rest in New York City before he can travel onward. Over the next six days, alone now in a city among strangers, this weary warrior must soon confront the most challenging contest he has yet encountered. This tormenting struggle with an invisible foe offers him just two possible outcomes—life or death.

---

501 Charles McClean Andrews, Colonial Folkways: A Chronicle of American Life in the Reign of the Georges (New Haven, CT: Yale University Press, 1919), 217.

502 The date of Michael's Cresap's departure from Roxbury is based on his obituary, which states that Captain Cresap arrived in New York on October 12, 1775. It took George Washington ten days to travel from Cambridge to New York in 1776. A one-way stagecoach trip from Boston to New York using the Middle Post Road took two weeks. Partridge, History of the Town of Bellingham, Massachusetts, 47–8; Nathaniel Philbrick, Bunker Hill: A City, A Siege, A Revolution (New York: Viking, 2013), 287; Whitehead Hicks, Connecticut Journal, October 23, 1775.

503 The place where Cresap stayed on Manhattan Island is still unknown. One strong candidate is the Fraunces Tavern, a gathering place for the Sons of Liberty and like-minded individuals since the 1760s. This building was also known as the Queen's Head, and that moniker might have been how Cresap referred to the tavern in 1775. This building still stands today as a restaurant, tavern, and museum featuring many artifacts, documents, and displays that pertain to the American Revolution. Built in 1719, the building is alleged to be the oldest-surviving structure still standing in Manhattan. It was here that General George Washington gave his farewell speech to his officers in 1783. James Cephas Cresap, lieutenant commander in the US Navy, traveled to the Fraunces Tavern in April 1889 to help found the Sons of the American Revolution. Interestingly, his father-in-law, a descendant of Thomas Cresap, was a prominent citizen named John McDowell Leavitt, who served as president of St. John's College in Annapolis, Maryland, from 1880 to 1884. On the Annapolis campus grew the Maryland Liberty Tree, where patriots, including Thomas Cresap, gathered in 1765 to protest the Stamp Act. Louis Henry Cornish and Alonzo Howard Clark, National Society, Sons of the American Revolution, National Register, vol. 2 (New York: Louis H. Cornish, 1902), 181; Frank Bergin Kelley, Historical Guide to the City of New York (New York: Frederick A. Stokes Company, 1909), 42.

CHAPTER 17

Beat No Drum

New York City
October 18–19, 1775

ON THE MORNING[504] OF WEDNESDAY, October 18, 1775,[505] Captain Michael Cresap succumbs to a fever at his lodgings on Manhattan Island, just six days after arriving in that city. Neither bullets nor Native American arrows brought down "this gentleman of great reputation as soldier and highly esteemed…citizen,"[506] during the four wars in which he participated: the French and Indian War, Pontiac's War, Lord Dunmore's War, and the American Revolution. As ironic as it seems in retrospect, unseen microscopic organisms to which Cresap has no resistance eventually take the captain's life.[507] City officials have a day to plan a spectacular funeral for the "First Captain in the Corps of Riflemen." They will inter Captain Cresap "tomorrow evening with the honors of war, attended by all the militia of the city."

On Thursday, October 19, New York City officials execute their elaborate funeral plans for this noted military figure. Not many who take part in the funeral have met Cresap, but many feel they know this patriot from stories they have heard or read in newspapers. Even while parade planners are busy organizing participants and

---

504 Pennsylvania Evening Post.

505 On October 15, 1775, while Michael lay ill in New York City, the seventy-year-old Benjamin Franklin had arrived at Washington's camp in Cambridge. Traveling with Dr. Franklin were two other congressional delegates, Thomas Lynch and Benjamin Harrison. This 271-mile trek from Philadelphia to Boston took the congressional delegates thirteen days, covering an average of twenty-one miles per day. The purpose of the conference was to discuss with Washington and his generals the status of the Continental army and to determine how Congress could best support the war effort. Franklin, while treated with great respect by Washington and his generals, longed to visit his native home at Boston—the soil on which he had not placed foot since 1763. Franklin quickly deemed a visit to Boston an impossibility, noting that the city was in the possession of the enemy. Like Cresap at this same time, Dr. Franklin feared that he would "never have the happiness" of seeing his home again, the place Franklin desired for his family to "lay his bones" when he died. On a note of the utmost irony, the delegates' conference with Washington and his staff occurred on October 18, 1775, the very day that Michael Cresap died. Both Cresap and Franklin were destined for burial far from their native homes. Allen B. Lincoln, A Modern History of Windham County, Connecticut, vol. 2 (Chicago: S. J. Clarke Publishing Company, 1920), 1003.

506 Pennsylvania Evening Post.

507 According to contemporary written sources from 1775 forward, Cresap died from a fever. History does not reveal what caused the fever or what caused his body to fail him when he was alone and far away from family. The writers of this narrative propose two likely candidates for Cresap's fever: the combined illnesses of malaria and dysentery, ailments that killed many of Washington's men exposed to the harsh and unsanitary conditions of Revolutionary War military encampments. Cresap probably contracted malaria during the summer and fall of 1774. Cresap had been infected with malaria, a mosquito-borne disease called during his time "swamp-fever," "chill-fever," "fever and ague," or "the shakes"—so named because of the bodily symptoms this illness inflicts upon its victims. Plasmodium falciparum is a parasite that causes malaria in humans and is transmitted to people by the Anopheles mosquito. The population of these mosquitoes has been growing and spreading worldwide for more than 12,000 years since the

Earth's climate started warming and the glaciers began receding. Cresap's lengthy and apparently untreated illness was no doubt compounded by the rigors of that weary march from Maryland to Massachusetts. As Cresap's body weakened from his bout with malaria, he may also have contracted smallpox, typhus, diphtheria, or cholera while in Washington's military camps. The cumulative effects of malaria, exhaustion, and exposure to diseases spread among soldiers weakened Cresap beyond recovery, resulting in his death at thirty-three years of age. (Jacob, A Biographical Sketch of the Late Captain Michael Cresap, 117–25; Jahntz, A Look at Late Eighteenth Century Medical Practices"; Dary, Frontier Medicine: From the Atlantic to the Pacific, 54–5, 81–2, 323; Stephen M. Rich, et al., "The Origin of Malignant Malaria," Proceedings of the National Academy of Sciences of the United States 106(35) (2009): 14902–7, accessed April 14, 2016, https://www.ncbi.nlm.nih.gov/pmc/articles/PMC2720412/.

addressing details, the growing crowd along Broadway forms into groups of spectators, all anxiously waiting for the funeral procession to begin. The column of marchers starts at the residence in which Cresap died, then travels on the principal streets toward Trinity Church. At the beginning, a faint noise arises from some distance away and out of sight of the crowd. Soon the spectators hear footfalls, like the echoing of ghost soldiers. Horses snorting and the rhythmic tramping of hooves on the street accompany a progressive clamor of other sounds. From a distance, the viewers hear the music of fifes and the beat of the drums grows louder and clearer as the funeral procession moves closer.

A sergeant major appears, leading the procession. Rows of men in perfectly formed columns follow. They are the grenadiers of the First Battalion, men of tall stature dressed in perfectly tailored uniforms and miter hats. This colorful battalion of grenadiers with their firelocks reversed consists of three hundred to four hundred men. Their defining lines bring the procession into full motion.[508]

The onlookers next see two lieutenants followed by a company of about one hundred soldiers. Four drummers, along with two fifers who play a mournful dirge, follow this stalwart company of men. Now the assemblage hears a haunting, rolling rap-tap-tap beat as the marchers step with precise timing to the staccato cadence of the drums.

Next into view comes the captain of the grenadiers, flanked by two sergeants, followed by adjutants and clergymen. A band playing patriotic music passes just as the coffin carrying the deceased comes into view. The bier sits on a caisson pulled by horses. Walking parallel to the coffin are eight captains, four men supporting either side of the pall. Immediately behind the casket follows a small group of chief mourners, most likely friends or military personnel who knew Captain Cresap personally. Behind these mourners, a major walks with sword drawn.

Following behind Cresap's coffin are three battalions, making up a total of about twelve hundred men. These lengthy yet equally striking lines consist of the First and Second Battalion soldiers, noncommissioned officers, and battalion officers. Finally, making up the end of the procession are hundreds of New York citizens who spontaneously fall into their own informal formation as they follow behind the structured ranks.[509]

An estimated two thousand mourners take part in the funeral procession that passes along Broadway and reverently wends its way toward Trinity Church. Military, clergy, and friends follow as one giant being down the street toward Trinity Church, where officials conduct a burial ceremony with full military honors for Captain Michael Cresap. Following the Anglican-Episcopal Church funeral liturgy in the Book of Common Prayer, the Reverend Samuel Auchmuty[510] offers prayers for the deceased and for the mourners. The reverend follows this by leading the attendees in the singing of a hymn, a reading from the psalms, and the recitation of the Lord's Prayer.

During the funeral service, someone who personally knows Michael likely speaks sentiments akin to those printed in Cresap's obituaries, which will appear in newspapers a few days after his funeral.

Rind's Virginia Gazette writes that Captain Cresap "was a gentleman universally esteemed by those who had the pleasure of his acquaintance, a worthy member of society, and a brave soldier. His loss is greatly lamented by every well-wisher to the liberties of this once happy country."[511]

---

508 New York Gazette and Weekly Mercury, October 23, 1775.

509 *New York Gazette and Weekly Mercury, October 23, 1775.*

510 Reverend Samuel Auchmuty (1722–1777), served as rector of Trinity Church from 1764 to 1777. Auchmuty came out on the side of the loyalists after the reading of the Declaration of Independence in 1776. Forced to avoid prayers for the welfare of the king of England, Auchmuty temporarily closed Trinity Church. The Great Fire of 1776 destroyed Trinity Church and Auchmuty's parsonage, which was constructed in 1698. The church standing at the time of Captain Cresap's burial was a simple rectangular building with a gambrel roof and a small porch. The rebuilding of the second Trinity Church began in 1788. Officials tore down the second building in the winter of 1838-1839 due to snow damage. In 1846, members of the church completed the building of the third and present Trinity Church. Reverend Charles Inglis--a British immigrant and assistant to Reverend Samuel Auchmuty, rector at Trinity Church from 1765 through 1776--was a member of the "Whig Compact" (clergy composed of Loyalists vs. Patriots) who remained openly devoted to the King and Britain. However, in spite of these loyalties, Inglis remained committed to Trinity's congregation--tending to the sick, performing baptisms, and officiating at funerals. Perhaps it was Inglis who attended--or at the very least--aided in the Liturgy at the Anglican service and burial for Michael Cresap on October 19, 1775. Trinity Church, Wall Street, Rector's Office Archives, accessed December 13, 2017; Rev. William Berrian. "A Historical Sketch Of Trinity Church, New York. (1847), 127; Wentworth and Whittaker. "The Tory Clergy of the Revolution." (1891), 117-131.

511 Rind's Virginia Gazette, 1775.

In another version of the obituary published October 23, 1775[512] in the *Connecticut Journal*, a journalist records what he probably heard about Captain Cresap at the funeral service:

> On the 12th Instant arrived here from his Provincial Camp at Cambridge and on the 18th departed this Life, of a Fever, in the Twenty-eight year of his Age, Michael Cressop, Esquire, eldest son of Col. Thomas Cressop, Esquire of Potowmack, in Virginia, departed this Life of a Fever. He was Captain of a Rifle Company now in the Continental Army before Boston. He served as a Captain under the Command of Lord Dunmore, in the late Expedition against the Indians, in which he eminently distinguished himself by his Prudence, Firmness, and Intrepid[i]ty, as a brave Officer; and in the present Contest between the Parent state and the Colonies, gave Proofs of his Attachment to the Rights and Liberties of his Country. He has left a Widow and four Children to deplore the Loss of a Husband and a Father, and by his Death, his Country is deprived of a worthy and esteemed Citizen.[513]

Original Michael Cresap tombstone (Photograph courtesy of Larry Brock)

---

512 It is possible that one of Michael Cresap's nephews, Daniel Cresap, Jr. or Joseph Cresap, traveled with the captain from Roxbury to New York. How else would the New York City mayor have known such details of his life, such as how many children Cresap had? It is doubtful that many men in his rifle company outside his family knew personal details about Captain Cresap. There was no time to contact anyone for the wording of the obituary. Mention of Cresap's role in Lord Dunmore's War clearly tried to honor the captain and quash unfounded negative rumors swirling about his role in that war. The fact that the obituary stated that Cresap had four children, not five, indicates that officials did not know at that time whether or not Cresap's fifth child had yet been born.

513 Hicks, Connecticut Journal. The original tombstone carries the following inscription: "In Memory of Michael Cresap, First Cap[t]. of the Rifle Batal[l]ions, And Son to Co[l]. Thomas Cresap, Who Departed this Life October the 18[th], 1775." Cresap's tombstone is "of the old-fashioned variety with crude angels" heads in the scalloped top. The stone is constructed from ordinary brown sandstone so "common to old cemeteries" and shows evidence of long exposure to the elements that was "working toward…[its] destruction." In 1867, by permission of the Trinity Church Corporation, officials moved the original tombstone out of the weather and to the interior of the New York Historical Society, where it resides under glass for protection. A replica of the tombstone was then made and installed at the grave of Michael Cresap at Trinity Church in New York City. "Bogus Tombstones in Trinity Church," New York Times, December 15, 1901.

As a large crowd of militia and "the most respectable inhabitants"[514] of the city crowd around the rifleman's casket, the reverend closes the service with the universal phrase of finality, "Earth to earth, dust to dust, ashes to ashes," thereby committing Cresap's body to its final resting place.[515] At this time "grenadiers of the first battalion fired three volleys over his grave."[516]

A little more than two weeks after Cresap's funeral and burial in New York City, officials in Hagerstown, Maryland, conduct a stirring second memorial service to honor Captain Cresap. One last time, a large number of friends and mourners come out on the afternoon of November 4, 1775, to "commemorate the death of the late worthy Michael Cressop, Esquire, of this county and province, and first Captain in the Corps of Riflemen." In this memorial procession, officers of each company wear dark-colored scarves on their left arms, the recognized military badge of bereavement. The drums in the procession are "muffled and covered with black …and the colours in mourning." The officers then draw their troops up into "three lines, and march…to the muster ground." After performing a series of "Manual exercises" and "evolutions," the militia then proceeds into town, again marching Indian file in three lines, all the while the musicians playing a solemn requiem on their drums and fifes. Once the procession ends and before dismissal, officers give the men orders "to beat no drum, or play no fife, but to behave in a manner suitable to the occasion."[517]

The two services in New York and Hagerstown that commemorated Michael Cresap's life and death were remarkable events. John Jacob, who later will marry Captain Cresap's widow, overheard someone who apparently witnessed the funeral in New York City say that "he would not begrudge to die if his funeral could be as honorable as Cresap's."[518] While others continue the march that will one day bring that hard fought-battle for freedom to beleaguered colonists and to future generations, for this revered son of Maryland, the drums of war are forever silenced.

---

514 Rind's Virginia Gazette, 1775, 2.

515 Although the exact location of Nathan Hale's unmarked grave is unknown, Captain Hale (1755–1776) is presumably buried not far from Captain Cresap's marked grave near Trinity Church on Manhattan Island. Cresap and Hale have at least two unfortunate circumstances in common: both patriots died young early in the American Revolution, and both were interred far from home. The leadership and intelligence work of Captain Thomas Knowlton (1749–1776) from Ashford, Connecticut, were highly prized by George Washington. Like Michael Cresap, Knowlton certainly would have received higher military honors if he had not succumbed to a premature death. Soldiers buried Knowlton with military honors in an unmarked grave at 143rd Street and St. Nicholas Avenue, New York City, on the same island holding the grave of Captain Cresap. "Lieutenant Colonel Thomas Knowlton, Connecticut's Forgotten Hero."

516 Rind's Virginia Gazette, 1775, 2; Charles Thorley Bridgeman and Clifford P. Morehouse, A History of the Parish of Trinity Church in the City of New York (New York: Putnam, 1898), 371–2; The Book of Common Prayer. Officials buried Captain Michael Cresap in the Trinity Church churchyard in New York City. For part of the twentieth century, the church lay in the shadows of the New York World Trade Center, each 110 stories tall, at one time the two tallest buildings in the world. These stately towers, constructed in the 1970s, remained a vital part of America's business trade until an act of terrorism brought them crashing down on September 11, 2001, some 236 years after the Boston Liberty Tree incident. The resulting ashes from the World Trade center's twin towers completely covered Michael Cresap's grave, gravestone, and surrounding trees, but miraculously, none of the falling debris attributed to this horrendous attack damaged the Cresap gravestone. It is as if the angels of liberty stood guard over his grave.

517 Maryland Journal. 15 November 1775

518 Jacob, A Biographical Sketch of the Late Captain Michael Cresap, 123.

CHAPTER 18

Before There Was Glory

By 1742, Thomas Cresap with his wife, Hannah; their eldest son, Daniel; their daughters Elizabeth and Sarah; and their second son, Thomas Cresap, Jr. had settled in present-day Oldtown, Maryland. Historians have written that the Cresaps were among the first settlers to build a permanent residence at this site in the "howling wilderness," at the time the westernmost English outpost established in all the thirteen colonies. On June 29, 1742, the Maryland mountain region acclaimed the news of one last child born to Thomas and Hannah Cresap. This youngest child of the pioneering couple, whom his parents christened Michael Cresap, may have been the first European American born in the Upper Potomac River Valley, geographically defined as lying just west of the juncture of the south and north branches of the Potomac River.[519]

About the mid-1700s, Thomas Cresap sent his young son, Michael, to a school within the bounds of St. Thomas Church in Baltimore County, an educational forum taught by Reverend Thomas Craddock (1718–1770). In 1743, Christopher Gist sold this tract of land so that church leaders could build this church and school. Craddock not only instructed his students using passages from the Bible, he also taught his pupils Latin and Greek as well as exposing them to classical literature. Before the age of ten, schoolboys studied the Bible and Homer's *The Iliad* and *The Odyssey*. Craddock's pupils were required to memorize parts of the text of epic stories touting the deeds of ancient war heroes, such as King David and Joshua from the Old Testament of the Bible and Achilles and Odysseus from Homer's poems. The original building, found at present-day Owings Mills, Maryland, still stands today.[520]

Saint Thomas Church, Owings Mills, Maryland

---
519 Cresap and Cresap, The History of the Cresaps, 253.
520 Ethan Allen, The Garrison Church: Sketches of History of St. Thomas Parish, Garrison Forest, Baltimore County, Maryland, 1742–1852 (New York: James Porr and Company, 1898), 22, 129, 154.

Being a backwoods boy, Michael initially had a tough time adjusting to his new school environs because the other boys saw him as an odd addition to their class—an outsider, as it were. Bullies picked on Michael; however this form of treatment toward him proved short-lived—for when Michael was still just a lad, he began to stand up for himself and fight back. Rejecting and rebuffing the actions of his tormentors, he quickly won their "good graces" and soon became their "champion."[521]

And yet the restless Michael, yearning to see his family and home, ran away - traversing 140 miles on foot back to Oldtown. However, Michael did not receive the warm reception he expected. Thomas did not approve of his son's truancy, and after giving Michael a "terrible whipping,"[522] he sent the boy back to school to complete his education.

Back in the school environment, Craddock shaped Cresap's character and imbued in him a heightened awareness of love and passion for liberty. An example of a lesson Michael and his fellow students were taught comes from a Bible passage found in Proverbs 17:22, "A merry heart doeth good like medicine." Michael heard something like the following from his instructor: "Brothers and citizens, remember who we are, from where we come, and from where we spring; that we are Britons; that we are the sons of those who valued life less than liberty; and readily gave their blood to leave that liberty to posterity… and can we then be otherwise than merry and joyful, and pour forth our whole soul in grateful acknowledgment to the Divine Being?"[523]

Two other factors outside the classroom significantly shaped the character of the person young Michael came to be as an adult: his pioneering family and life on the frontier. Michael grew up in the shadow of his father, Colonel Thomas Cresap, a resident of western Maryland well-known to both settlers and Indians. Although historic accounts do not inform us just how much time Michael spent tramping the woods with his father and brothers, opportunities to trek the wilderness with his father proved numerous. Perhaps Michael acquired these frontier survival skills as a young boy and teenager while tagging along with his pathfinder father, who blazed and opened old Indian trails for colonial travel throughout the region. In 1753, Thomas Cresap blazed Nemacolin Path from Wills Creek to the Monongahela River, and in 1758, he opened the road that stretched between Fort Frederick and Fort Cumberland. In 1759, Cresap worked on Burd Road, connecting Nemacolin Path to Fort Redstone.[524]

History discloses that Michael's brother Thomas, Jr. hunted wolves for bounty. Did Thomas take his little brother along on hunting expeditions? The answer might be a resounding yes, as records reveal that as a youth, Michael possessed accomplished shooting skills with the long rifle. In addition, Michael's knowledge of the frontier and its wooded areas from a very young age indicates that he spent much time in the field hunting with his father and older brothers.

At the age of ten, frontier child prodigy Michael traveled on a business trip from Oldtown, Maryland, to Williamsburg, Virginia, with his older brother Thomas. Also traveling with the Cresap brothers were Andrew Montour and Christopher Gist. On November 6, 1752, these four men submitted a petition for eighty thousand acres of land on the Ohio River to the Council of Colonial Virginia. The party emphasized to the officials that their petition was "not to interfere with grants already made by the Ohio Company."[525] Michael Cresap's involvement as a child made this a very unusual business transaction as the council usually only accepted petitions for land from adults.

---

521 Jacob, A Biographical Sketch of the Late Captain Michael Cresap, 47.
522 Jacob, A Biographical Sketch of the Late Captain Michael Cresap, 47.
523 Allen, The Garrison Church: Sketches of History of St. Thomas Parish, Garrison Forest, Baltimore County, Maryland, 24.
524 Ellis, History of Fayette County, PA, with Biographical Sketches of Many of Its Pioneers and Prominent Men, 421-3; Will H. Lowdermilk, History of Cumberland, Maryland (Washington, DC: James Anglim, 1878), 253-4.
525 William H. Rice, Colonial Records of the Upper Potomac, vol. 1 (Parsons, WV: McClain Printing Company, 2010), 59.

During the French and Indian War (1754–1763), Michael was thirteen years of age when he participated in his first military action. In May 1756, during a raiding party on Savage Mountain, Indians killed Michael's brother Thomas. To avenge his son's death, Thomas Cresap, Sr. organized a militia unit to pursue the marauding Indians. Thomas Cresap's military company included two of his sons, Daniel and Michael, the lad who at this very young age was already skilled in handling and firing the Pennsylvania long rifle.

During this expedition on a mountain in present-day Garrett County, Maryland, Michael's company encountered the Indian party that had killed his brother. In this skirmish Michael's father spotted three Indians who were coming up the road preparing to fire their weapons. Cresap found himself vulnerable—standing on a road without any cover. However, fate intervened, as one of the militiamen serving in Cresap's company, a free-black frontiersman whose name, unfortunately, has been lost to history, distracted the Indians from their focus on Thomas Cresap Sr. and drew attention instead to himself. Instead of firing at the elder Cresap, the Indians fired at and killed the black frontiersman. The courageous behavior of this daring volunteer allowed time for four of Cresap's men to return fire—one of the shooters possibly having been the young Michael. The riflemen killed one Indian, wounded another, and caused the third to flee.

The men in Cresap's party never forgot the bravery of the black frontiersman. Locals and visitors to the area now know the summit on which the skirmish occurred as Negro Mountain, one of the oldest place names in Garrett County, so named to honor the heroic actions of the rifleman who saved the life of Thomas Cresap Sr.[526]

On July 13, 1763, near the end of Pontiac's War, a Shawnee chief named Killbuck attacked Cresap's Fort, thus beginning a lengthy siege at Oldtown, Maryland. Michael Cresap was one of the men helping defend the settlers who had gathered at the fort for protection. The incident began when five Indians fired on six of Thomas Cresap's men while they were shocking wheat. Catching them by surprise, the Indians slightly wounded one of the workers. Several of Cresap's riflemen quickly ran out of the fort to aid those under attack, temporarily driving the Indians off. One of the fort's defenders, possibly Michael, kept firing on the assailants, his actions preventing the Indians from scalping one of the laborers in the field.

On the morning of July 14, while sixteen of Cresap's men gathered under the shade of a large tree on a lane about one hundred yards from the fort, five Indians attempted another sneak attack and fired upon the party. This time, Cresap's men were ready. They immediately returned fire, killing one of the Indians on the spot. The attackers fled, leaving behind three guns, a pistol, and various other war instruments. From the large quantities of blood found in the field, Cresap's men knew they had wounded several of the attackers. The men followed the bloodstained trail, pursuing the enemy for about one mile. About three hours into the chase, Cresap's men decided to end their pursuit and returned to Cresap's Fort.

On the morning of July 15, twenty Indians attacked a small party of men and women living three hundred yards from Cresap's Fort. Spotting the Indians rushing toward them, the group of families began hollering and ran in panic toward the fort.

Hearing the commotion from his fort, Colonel Thomas Cresap immediately dispatched Michael and some of his men to assist the settlers under attack. As the settlers approached the entrance to Cresap's Lane, the Indians opened fire with about eighteen shots, killing one of the fleeing men. A bold and daring Indian approached the murdered settler with his knife and proceeded to cut open his back and divide his ribs from the backbone. However, in the midst of this grisly act, before the Indian could take the dead man's scalp, Michael Cresap shot and killed him with his pistol. Under the arching shade of the tree at the entrance to the lane, twenty-one-year-old Michael, dealing with this frenzied melee, took the scalp of the Indian, as was the custom on the 1700s frontier.

---

526 Jacob, A Biographical Sketch of the Late Captain Michael Cresap, 36.

During a temporary lull in the siege at Oldtown, Thomas Cresap sent Michael out alone on a risky trip from the fort to seek help at Frederick Town. The *Maryland Gazette* reported this on July 19:

> On Sunday afternoon we had the pleasure of seeing Mr. Michael Cresap arrive in Town [Frederick Town]. With mokosins on his legs, taken from an Indian whom he killed and scalped, being one of those who shot down Mr. Welder, the circumstances whose much lamented murder, and the success of Colonel Cresap's family, you have no doubt received from other hands. Money has been cheerfully contributed in our town toward the support of the men to be added to Col. Cresap's present force, as we look upon the preservation of the Old Town to be of great importance to us, and a proper check to the progress of the savages.[527]

Although this custom of scalping sounds as if there might have been much ill will against all Indians of that time period, this was not always the case. Thomas Cresap, Sr. was well-known for welcoming parties of Indians who stopped at Cresap's for lengthy periods before traveling to their hunting grounds or moving on to engage in war with other tribes. These Native Americans, after being well fed by "Big Spoon," as these visitors called Thomas Cresap, carried out resounding native song and dance at Cresap's Fort to entertain themselves and any neighboring settlers who might gather for entertainment. These tribal visitors enjoyed plenty of bounty and time to rest while staying on Cresap's lands.

The tradition of taking scalps in the 1700s, as abhorrent as it now seems, was accepted as normal activity in many instances—as was the reversal, when Indians took the scalps of white settlers as trophies. The act at this time might even have been hailed as just one more heroic deed on this physically demanding and unstable frontier. Michael Cresap, having witnessed more violence than any young man of his age ought to have, was during this time mainly intent on getting on with life, seeking to settle down with a wife and children, who would also soon require real, unrelenting protection from frontier perils.

Michael Cresap and Mary Whitehead, the daughter of James[528] and Mary Whitehead, exchanged wedding vows on August 6, 1764, at the altar of "old" St. Paul's Episcopal Church in Philadelphia, Pennsylvania.[529] Mary set up housekeeping in the new home that Michael built in Oldtown for the newlyweds sometime that same year. Michael returned to his business of trading, surveying, and acquiring land in Maryland, Redstone, and the Ohio River Valley. He also was involved in clearing land to accommodate families of settlers arriving near the Ohio River. The time period from August 1764 to the spring of 1774 was probably the happiest and most peaceful time of Cresap's life.[530]

---

527   Mary Carson Darlington, History of Colonel Bouquet and the Western Frontiers of Pennsylvania: 1747–1764 (Pittsburgh, PA: privately printed, 1920), 186; John Thomas Sharf, History of Maryland: From the Earliest Period to Present-Day, 1600–1775, vol. I (Baltimore: John. P Piet, 1879), 515.

528   *James Whitehead, born circa 1696, had served his community as a workhouse keeper since he was a young man. The workhouse was an establishment sometimes known as an almshouse, originally built during hard times to help the poor and needy and now set up to board all manner of miscreants and the misplaced—even to house prisoners who had committed crimes and had been apprehended. Here, these outcasts of society ate, worked, and slept, all under the official jurisdiction of Whitehead, who had a strong faithful bent. Whitehead, who was well respected as an elder in the Presbyterian Synod of Philadelphia, died February 7, 1776, in Northern Liberties Township, Philadelphia, Pennsylvania at the age of eighty-two.* "Yardkin County and Caswell County," Rootsweb, September 21, 2017, http://wc.rootsweb.ancestry.com/cgi-bin/igm.cgi?op=GET&db=grantpinnix&id=I125610.

529   Old St. Paul's Church, the name by which it is now referred to, is located at 225 South Third Street at Walnut Street in Philadelphia, Pennsylvania. No longer a working religious establishment, as of 2017, the building stands and functions as a center for families in the region who need shelter or a temporary helping hand.

530   Linn and Egle, Pennsylvania, War of the Revolution: Battalions and Line, 441–94.

Old Saint Paul's Church, Philadelphia, Pennsylvania

Beginning in 1765, Michael Cresap served as a member of the Sons of Liberty, an underground organization whose membership roster was composed of many influential patriotic men within their respective communities. Members included Paul Revere, John Hancock, John Adams, and Samuel Adams in Massachusetts; Silas Downer in Rhode Island; Patrick Henry in Virginia; and Thomas Cresap in Maryland. They were America's first organized clandestine freedom fighters to advance the idea of resistance against oppressive British policies aimed at American colonists.

From 1765 through 1783, the Sons of Liberty were active in all thirteen colonies. To avoid attracting the attention of British soldiers or loyalists, this secretive organization met under the cover of darkness at designated liberty trees. Loyalists had other names for the protesters of British policies, calling them "sons of sedition," or "sons of iniquity,"[531] because Sons of Liberty were known to hang from liberty trees effigies of the Stamp Act tax collectors!

The French and Indian War created the war debt of 70 million pounds to the British Empire, which doubled the colonies' debt to 140 million pounds.[532] To help pay off this hefty encumbrance, the British Parliament imposed burdensome taxes on the English American colonies. Colonists were not opposed to fair taxes; however, they were opposed to unjust taxes, especially since they did not have official representation speaking for them in Parliament. The Sons of Liberty did not believe that the Stamp Act taxes directly benefited the American colonies.

---

531 Linda Alchin, "Sons of Liberty, Land of the Brave," February 8, 2017, accessed December 15, 2017, https://www.landofthebrave.info/sons-of-liberty.htm.

532 Digital History, "The Problems that England Faced After the French and Indian War," 2007, accessed December 15, 2017, http://www.digitalhistory.uh.edu/teachers/lesson_plans/pdfs/unit1_6.pdf.

Details of the repugnant Stamp Act began to appear in colonial newspapers immediately, sowing seeds of discontent that later blossomed into the American Revolution.

In response to the Stamp Act, in October 1765, Colonel Thomas Cresap organized a chapter of the Sons of Liberty in western Maryland. Serving in this chapter were Thomas's sons, Daniel and Michael. The *Maryland Gazette*[533] reported on November 21, 1765, that an effigy of a Stamp Act collector had been hanged a week before at the town square in Fredericktown, Maryland, by the Sons of Liberty. The newspaper stated that the effigy "gave up the ghost to the great joy of the inhabitants of Frederick County," the "lifeless body lay[ing] exposed to public ignominy."[534]

When the Sons of Liberty returned to Fredericktown on November 30, after the effigy of the tax collector had been hanging for a week, the newspaper reporter deemed in writing that the time had come to "dispose of the corpse to prevent public infection caused from the stench of the Stamp Act."[535]

Before the mock funeral ceremony began, Colonel Thomas Cresap and select members of the Sons of Liberty, which certainly would have included Michael and his eldest brother, Daniel, assembled at the house of Samuel Swearingen in Fredericktown. Marriage closely connected the Cresap and Swearingen families. Swearingen's two sisters, Ruth and Drusilla, were married to Colonel Cresap's sons, Daniel and the late Thomas, Jr. To further extend the relationship of the two families, a daughter of Sam Swearingen married Michael Cresap's nephew, Daniel Cresap, Jr.

At three o'clock in the afternoon, the Sons of Liberty departed the residence of Samuel Swearingen and exuberantly headed toward the town square. Witnesses of the parade that proceeded through town saw an amazing spectacle: three to four hundred Sons of Liberty led by Colonel Cresap, with Michael and Daniel Cresap among them. To add more flair to the hullabaloo, this boisterous band of men was armed with guns and tomahawks.

After the Sons of Liberty buried the effigy with great ceremony, they returned to Samuel Swearingen's home, where an "elegant supper" and a grand ball had been prepared by the women. Michael was among those who witnessed "a brilliant appearance, [where] many loyal and patriotic toasts were drunk, and the whole concluded with the utmost decorum."[536]

In December 1765, Michael Cresap and about three to four hundred other Sons of Liberty "assembled once again at Fredericktown." Led once again by Colonel Cresap, the rabble-rousers marched this time about 71 miles southeast to Annapolis, Maryland, "in order to settle disputes betwixt the two houses of assembly."[537]

Being largely outnumbered, Annapolis officials took these threats seriously. Considerable excitement was in the air as rumors flew that the Sons of Liberty were on the move toward Annapolis from western Maryland. Reports abounded that Colonel Cresap's raucous company reached as far as Elk Ridge, Maryland, south of Baltimore, near present-day Patapsco State Park, just a one-day march from Annapolis. Not long after hearing this bit of troubling news and soon after the governor had urgently called his council together to lay the matter before them,

---

533 Maryland Gazette, November 30, 1765.

534 Since 1894, via legislation established by the Maryland General Assembly, Frederick County has held a half-day bank holiday to commemorate Repudiation Day. This holiday commemorates Frederick County's role in disavowing the 1765 Stamp Act. "The twelve immortal judges," so called years later by a local historian and judge, were Thomas Price (in 1775, captain of one of the two Maryland rifle companies), Joseph Smith, David Lynn, Charles Jones, Samuel Beall, Joseph Beall, Peter Bainbridge, Andrew Hough, William Blair, William Luckett, James Dickson, and Thomas Beatty. Max Fullerton, "The Stamp Act: The Day Frederick County Rebelled," Baltimore Sunday Sun Magazine, November 21, 1965, http://www.judgedavidlynn.org/The_Stamp_Act.html.

535 Maryland Gazette, November 30, 1765.

536 Ibid.

537 Ibid.

the legislature repealed the Stamp Act in Maryland. Historians credit Colonel Cresap's leadership of the Sons of Liberty with having a part in the repeal of the Stamp Act in Maryland.[538]

Michael Cresap House (north side), Oldtown, Maryland

In 1767, Michael partnered with his father to develop a town at Oldtown, Maryland. In an article they placed in the *Maryland Gazette*, father and son described their plans to develop land that was

---

538 Annapolis, Maryland, House of Records, 1765; Sharf, History of Maryland: From the Earliest Period to Present-Day, 549. On November 23, 1765, twelve Frederick County judges, including Thomas Price, repudiated the Stamp Act, the twelve judges refusing to enact the Stamp Act in Maryland. This bold action of judicial heroism made Maryland the first colony to declare the Stamp Act null and void as well as the first to rule against an act of the British Parliament. The Sons of Liberty, led by Colonel Thomas Cresap, presumably with his son Michael, followed the court's action soon afterward by conducting a public funeral for the Stamp Act in Fredericktown. At the funeral these men and other citizens symbolically buried the Stamp Act and hanged an effigy representing the Maryland's tax collector, Zachariah Hood, at the Fredericktown courthouse square at present Council Street, Frederick, Maryland.

commodiously situated for a Town, as lying on the main Road that leads to Pittsburgh and Redstone from Virginia, Maryland, and Pennsylvania. From the two last mentioned Places a good Waggon Road may be made as far as Fort-Cumberland without crossing any Mountain. And whereas it is expected the South Branch of Patowmack River will be the Boundary between Lord Baltimore and Lord Fairfax, by which Means all the Land to the North of the said Branch, so far as the Temporary Line, which is 15 Miles from this Place will be Maryland and that the town now proposed is nearest the Centre, therefore most proper for a County Town. 539

Michael and Thomas Cresap not only mentioned the advantages of having a good road passing through the town, they also spoke of the benefits of the Potomac River that was located nearby: "the River Patowmack is for 4 Months in a Year, and at sundry other Times, passable for Battoes [flat boats] and Canoes. Vessels of also 10 and 15 Tons Burden may pass and repass at some Seasons of the Year as far as Old-Town but no farther by Reason of the South Branch…coming in there unless at some particular Times, when they may go as high as Cumberland with small Loads."540

By the year 1769, Michael Cresap had established a trading post at Fort Redstone. Historians consider Michael Cresap to be the first permanent European American to settle in the area of Fort Redstone, present-day Brownsville, Pennsylvania. In 1759, Colonel Thomas Cresap accompanied Colonel James Burd in the blazing of a trail from Nemacolin Path to Fort Redstone. Had school not been in session at this time, the fifteen-year-old teenager most likely would have journeyed with Colonel Burd and his father while working on the Burd Trail. Whatever early influences attached him to this area, Michael Cresap obviously recognized Fort Redstone as an ideal place to establish a trading business with Indians and pioneers who passed through the area.541

In the spring of 1774, a war broke out between the Indians and the pioneers living along the Ohio River Valley near present-day Wheeling, West Virginia. Michael Cresap was drawn into this war, being a pioneer who claimed land in this area along the nutrient-rich, alluvial soils of the Muskingum River at the mouth of Middle Island Creek near present-day Sistersville, West Virginia.542

At present-day Parkersburg, West Virginia, George Rogers Clark, a surveyor who would later distinguish himself as the "highest ranking American military officer on the northwestern frontier during the American Revolutionary War," with about eighty to ninety men, arranged to meet Cresap after he finished his work near Middle Island Creek. Cresap then planned to join Clark's party and descend from Parkersburg down the Ohio River to establish a settlement in Kentucky.

While waiting for Cresap and other individuals to arrive at the agreed-upon meeting point, a hunting party sent out by Clark was besieged by a band of Indians, who began firing upon them. To Clark's way of thinking, this reprehensible attack—and his knowledge that a number of other regional hostilities had recently occurred—convinced him to "believe that the Indians were determined on War."543

Clark knew that his group needed to organize at once into a military unit to serve as a line of frontier defense against further Indian attacks. After a brief discussion, the men agreed among themselves that Cresap should be their leader. Clark later wrote, "Who was to command was the question…Few of us had experience in Indian warfare…we knew of Capt. Cresap…He had been experienced in the former war [French and Indian War]. He

---

539 Michael Cresap and Thomas Cresap, "The Subscribers Having a Piece of Ground at Old-Town," Maryland Gazette, March 19, 1767, 2.
540 Michael Cresap and Thomas Cresap, "The Subscribers Having a Piece of Ground at Old-Town."
541 Ellis, History of Fayette County, PA, with Biographical Sketches of Many of Its Pioneers and Prominent Men, 421–3.
542 Paul S. Clarkson and Samuel R. Jett, Luther Martin of Maryland (Baltimore: The Johns Hopkins Press, 1970), 172.
543 Clarkson and Jett, Luther Martin of Maryland, 308–9.

was proposed; and it was unanimously agreed to send for him to command the party…We now thought our army, as we called it, complete, and the destruction of the Indians sure."[544]

When Cresap learned of Clark's plans to confront the Indians, he traveled in haste to Clark's camp in an attempt to persuade Clark to change his mind, stating that such an action would only cause more unrest in the region. The spot where Cresap cleared land was located just a few miles from major Indian villages of various tribes, such as the Delaware and Shawnee. Cresap had no desire or motivation to make war or enemies with the Indians.[545]

Cresap persuaded Clark's men to regroup at Wheeling and wait a few weeks to see how events unfolded before they tried to establish a settlement in Kentucky. Upon Clark agreeing to comply with Cresap's request, on April 16, 1774, Michael committed himself to leading this detachment of frontiersmen—thus for the first time forming Cresap's rifle company.[546]

Cresap led his men north toward present-day Wheeling, West Virginia. For safety, settlers gathered around Michael Cresap's newly formed company. Rogers writes, "On our arrival to Wheeling (the country being pretty well settled thereabouts) the whole of the inhabitants appeared to be alarmed. They flocked to our camp from every direction and all we could say would not keep them from under our wings."[547] Cresap encouraged the people to return to their homes, promising that his men would patrol near their settlements, but the settlers would not depart. In the meantime, Cresap's company continued to grow in size, as hunters and single young men volunteered to serve under his leadership.

On April 25, 1774, Lord Dunmore, governor of Virginia, issued a proclamation requesting Virginia militia to protect settlers on the frontier from Indian attacks. During this time, Cresap—called by Clark "the most influential man"[548] among the frontiersmen—scouted with his rifle company up and down the Ohio River on foot and in canoes. Several of the incidents involved open skirmishes, during which time men on both sides sustained wounds or were killed.[549]

In late April 1774, Cresap received scouting reports that hostile Indians were camped at Yellow Creek, thirty miles upstream from present-day Wheeling, West Virginia. It turned out that this was the site of Logan's camp. Logan was a Mingo, a tribe formed of Lenape, Seneca, and Cayuga living in the Ohio River Valley. On April 28, Cresap marched his men toward Yellow Creek, hoping to stop any violence before it began. Follow-up reconnaissance by Cresap's men showed that the camp at Yellow Creek was just a peaceful hunting party consisting of men, women, and children. Upon this news, Cresap changed his plans and decided to march his men instead to Redstone.[550]

After traveling about thirty miles eastward from present Wheeling, West Virginia, on April 29, Cresap's party of men arrived at Catfish Camp, located midway between Wheeling and Redstone at present-day Washington, Pennsylvania. On litters, Cresap's men carried with them a mortally wounded person and two other men who had suffered gunshot wounds following a recent skirmish with the Indians.[551]

---

544 Ibid., 172.
545 Ibid., 172–3.
546 Ibid., 173–5; Robert E. McGinn, "Cresap's Rifles," The Hearthstone Collection, May–June 1987.
547 Clarkson and Jett, Luther Martin of Maryland, 173.
548 Ibid.
549 Thwaites and Kellogg, Documentary History of Dunmore's War, xiv, 11-2, 14, 29, 115, 155, 185, 260, 304.
550 Jacob, A Biographical Sketch of the Late Captain Michael Cresap, 113, 154.
551 Boyd Crumrine, The Courts, Bench, and Bar of Washington County, Pennsylvania (Chicago: Lakeside Press, 1902), 9; Clarkson and Jett, Luther Martin of Maryland, 175.

On April 30, 1774, the massacre of Logan's family occurred at Yellow Creek, near present-day Steubenville, Ohio. Yellow Creek is a small tributary that enters into the Ohio River approximately twenty-six miles upriver from present-day Wheeling, West Virginia. Several contemporary accounts based on hearsay or second-hand or third-hand reports incorrectly blamed Michael Cresap for the Yellow Creek Massacre. However, other reliable first-hand historical accounts indicate that during this time period, Cresap was many miles away at Catfish Camp, thus vindicating Cresap and those traveling with him of any wrongdoing regarding the massacre of Logan's family.[552]

In June of 1774, Cresap returned home. Upon his arrival at Oldtown, he was surprised to find Lord Dunmore, governor of Virginia, waiting at his house. Spending the next few days engaged in friendly conversation, Cresap apprised Dunmore of events concerning the ongoing Indian War, and perhaps in the act of answering Dunmore's questions, he likely offered the governor counsel. At this time Dunmore presented to Cresap a letter dated June 10, 1774, commissioning Cresap to the rank of captain to head the militia of Hampshire County.[553]

In this letter, Dunmore praised Cresap for his extraordinary conduct of valor in the Indian War. Dunmore went on to tell Cresap that the governor was "assailed by petition after petition, from almost every section of the western country praying, begging, and beseeching [Cresap] to come to their assistance."[554]

At this time Cresap exercised all his "power and influence to assist the distressed inhabitants of the western frontier."[555] Cresap renewed his determination to utilize his time, talents, and treasure for the remainder of the summer to continuing to fight in the Indian War. He went about organizing another rifle company. Men desiring to serve under Cresap's banner flocked to him in such large numbers that it became necessary to place the overflow of recruits in a company under the command of Hancock Lee.[556]

By July 10, 1774, Cresap and his rifle company returned to Redstone and the Monongahela River Valley, where he again patrolled the Ohio River region. Throughout the rest of the summer and early fall of 1774, Cresap and his men continued to patrol and protect the settlements along the Ohio River.[557]

During the summer of 1774, Lord Dunmore organized a military campaign that he planned to lead himself. He assigned General Andrew Lewis to organize a separate unit of four regiments and volunteers to lead a Southern Division, while Dunmore, heading the Northern Division, would eventually meet Lewis at the conjunction of the Kanawha River and Ohio River. From this time forth, the event that involved the hostilities that occurred on the Ohio River became known as Lord Dunmore's War.

---

552 In the ensuing years, historians have based their erroneous claims on Logan's untrue statements that Cresap murdered Logan's family, a report later widely circulated by none other than Thomas Jefferson in his book Notes on Virginia. However, overwhelming evidence stated by eyewitness accounts reveals that Daniel Greathouse (1752–1775) was the ringleader of the massacre of Logan's family. Luther Martin, who married Michael Cresap's daughter, said the following about the Yellow Creek Massacre: "No man who really knew the late [Captain] Cresap could have believed the [Logan] tale. He was too brave to be perfidious or cruel. He was a man of undaunted resolution; a man of whom it might be said, which I believe was ever said of man, 'that he knew not fear.'" J. F. Everhart and A. A. Graham, History of Muskingum County, Ohio (Columbus, OH: J. F. Everhart & Co, 1882), 32; "The Greathouse Family of Ohio Country (West) Virginia, and Brown County, Ohio," last revision by Marjorie, July 9, 2007, accessed January 6, 2017, https://web.archive.org/web/20080212203527/http://home.earthlink.net/~leota_m/grathous.html.
553 Brantz Mayer, Tah-Gah-Jute; or, Logan and Michael Cresap (Baltimore: Maryland Historical Society, 1851), 114.
554 Jacob, A Biographical Sketch of the Late Captain Michael Cresap, 69.
555 Ibid.
556 Ibid.; Mayer, Tah-Gah-Jute; or, Logan and Michael Cresap, 114.
557 Clarkson and Jett, Luther Martin of Maryland, 310; Mayer, Tah-Gah-Jute; or, Logan and Michael Cresap, 95.

At this time Captain Cresap's company served with Major Angus McDonald as part of Lord Dunmore's advance guard.[558] On July 24, McDonald's troops of about four hundred men rendezvoused with Cresap's company at Fort Fincastle, present-day Wheeling, West Virginia. Historians later called this offensive action the Wappatomica Campaign. The area known as Wappatomica consisted of a group of Shawnee towns located along the Muskingum River, not far from present-day Dresden, in Muskingum County, Ohio. These Native American habitats were the closest villages to the pioneer homes along the Ohio River and were considered the most hostile to new Anglo-American settlements in their region.

Some of the most courageous men of the west at that time served under McDonald's command as captains. Besides Captain Michael Cresap and his nephew, Michael Cresap, Jr., a few historically notable names stand out, such as James Wood, the future governor of Virginia; Daniel Morgan; and Hancock Lee. George Rogers Clark served as a scout in this expedition.

While General Lewis's army carried out his mission to approach Shawnee territory along the Ohio River from the southeast, Dunmore's army entered the Shawnee territory from the northeast. When Dunmore arrived at Fort Fincastle on September 30, he attached Captain Michael Cresap's company to his command.

As Dunmore's army descended the Ohio River, what a sight Captain Cresap and his company must have witnessed, as more than twelve hundred men with one hundred swimming cattle and 250 packhorses splashed across the Ohio River toward the mouth of Hocking, near the present-day site of Hockingport, Ohio. Up to this time, no one in the region had ever seen a troop force this large. This massive caravan turned out to be the largest military campaign assembled since 1755, when General Braddock marched against the French at Fort Duquesne. When Lord Dunmore's troops were combined with the southern unit under Lewis, Dunmore's numbers were twice as large as those of Braddock's campaign. At the conjunction of Hock Hocking and the Ohio River, Dunmore's men built a stockade that Dunmore named Fort Gower.[559]

On October 10, the Battle of Point Pleasant, involving Lewis's military forces, occurred at the conjunction of the Kanawha and Ohio Rivers. This turned out be the only major battle of Lord Dunmore's War. Chief Cornstalk and the Shawnee Indians were defeated in this battle. Perhaps much to his chagrin, Captain Cresap did not personally participate in the Battle of Point Pleasant as he was assigned to Lord Dunmore's unit at Fort Gower.

On October 11, Dunmore departed Fort Gower and began marching up the Hocking River toward the Indian towns upstream, hoping to get between the Indian villages and the Indians who had attacked Lewis's men at Point Pleasant. Like MacDonald two months before, Dunmore was taking the fight to the Indians in their territory.

---

558 An interesting anecdote from McDonald's campaign survives that tells of the expert shooting skills of Cresap's Rifles: "When McDonalds' little army arrived on the near bank of the Muskingum, and while lying there, an Indian on the opposite shore got behind an old log or tree, and was lifting up his head occasionally to view the white men's army. One of Captain Cresap's men, of the name John Hargiss, seeing this, loaded his rifle with two balls, and placing himself on the bank of the river, watched the opportunity when the Indian raised his head, and firing at the same instant, put both balls through the Indian's neck and laid him dead, which circumstance, no doubt, had great influence in intimidating the Indians." Another example of the precise shooting skills exhibited by Cresap's riflemen that occurred during Dunmore's War involved three men of Captain Cresap's company camped at Redstone. The story goes that as a buzzard sailed high over their heads, Daniel Cresap, Jr., Joseph Cresap, and William Ogle all raised their rifles and pointed their sights at the bird. The frontiersmen fired three shots simultaneously. The bird dropped out of the sky like a rock. Each of the men claimed that his shot had brought down the bird. Upon close inspection by bystanders, it was determined that each of the three balls fired by the men fired had pierced the vulture, much to the amazement of all who witnessed this remarkable display of expert marksmanship. The Shain brothers, members of Cresap's Rifles, further elevated the reputation of this elite group of riflemen. The two men could hit a mark the size of a cent from a distance of twenty to twenty-five yards—no small feat for what frontiersmen referred to as "offhand shooting," meaning from a standing position without a rest for the rifle. Jacob, A Biographical Sketch of the Late Captain Michael Cresap, 26-7, 70.

559 Virgil. A. M. Lewis, History of the Battle of Point Pleasant: Fought between White Men and Indians at the Mouth of the Great Kanawha River (Charleston, SC: The Tribune Printing Company, 1908), 23; Fort Gower Resolutions, 2017; Bill Sullivan, "Lord Dunmore: Beneath the Kilt," Making History, April 20, 2016, accessed January 9, 2017, http://makinghistorynow.com/2016/04/lord-dunmore-beneath-the-kilt/; Jim Glanville, "Fort Gower: Forgotten Shrine of Virginia History," Augusta Historical Bulletin 46 (2010), 74–90, accessed January 9, 2017, http://www.holstonia.net/files/FortGower2011.pdf.

Other frontiersmen, aside from Michael Cresap, who traveled with Dunmore up Hocking River toward the falls in Shawnee territory near present-day Athens, Ohio, were scouts Simon Kenton, Simon Girty, and George Rogers Clark. Dunmore established his new headquarters at Camp Charlotte near Chillicothe, Ohio.[560]

On October 19, Chief Cornstalk of the Shawnee Indians, along with eight other chiefs, came to Camp Charlotte to talk with Dunmore, and interpreters introduced the Indian leader to him. At the conference, Cornstalk and the other chieftains sat face to face with Lord Dunmore and his officers. Here Captain Cresap—accompanied by his peers, including Lord Dunmore, Colonel Adam Stephen, Colonel William Crawford, Major Angus McDonald, Captain George Rogers Clark, and Captain Daniel Morgan—sat across from Cornstalk in "the known center of the American wilderness."[561]

During the week of October 18, the two opposing sides drafted and finalized the Camp Charlotte Treaty, which effectively ended the Indian War. The Indians agreed to return all the white and Negro prisoners as well as the horses they took during the war. They also agreed to pay compensation for all the property they destroyed. The Indians also agreed that they would no longer hunt on or visit the land south of the Ohio River except for the sole purpose of trading goods with white people and that they would not molest boats navigating the Ohio River. Settlers were now free to settle safely in present-day Kentucky and Tennessee without harassment from the Indians.

In return, Governor Dunmore guaranteed the Indians that he would not permit white people to hunt on the northern side of the Ohio River. Cornstalk, surrounded by Lewis and Dunmore's forces, had no other option than to submit to the terms offered by Lord Dunmore. By doing so, Cornstalk saved his Shawnee people from certain annihilation from an overpowering army.[562]

On October 31, Dunmore broke camp and started his return trip to Fort Gower. Chief Cornstalk and his sister, the Grenadier squaw Nonhelema, traveled with Lord Dunmore's army as far as the Hocking River, probably as temporary hostages. More remarkably, during this time, Chief Cornstalk and his sister were under the direct care of Captain Cresap and stayed with him in his tent. Captain Cresap had the monumental responsibility of ensuring the safety of Cornstalk and his sister. If any harm came to either one of them during this time, any agreements made in the treaty of Camp Charlotte would surely become null and void. If Cresap had participated in the massacre of Chief Logan's family or started the Indian War, as Logan and some Pennsylvanians claimed, certainly Chief Cornstalk would not have trusted Cresap for his safekeeping, nor would he have camped with Cresap in his tent.[563]

Dunmore's army arrived at Fort Gower on November 5, 1774. Upon their return to Fort Gower, Cresap and the other officers of Lord Dunmore first heard about the results of the meeting of the First Continental Congress, which met between September 5 and October 26 that year.[564] The troops learned that the Continental Congress sent to King George III of England a declaration of rights and grievances, in part stating that the colonists had

---

560 Lewis, History of the Battle of Point Pleasant, 55–6; Thwaites and Phelps, Documentary History of Dunmore's War, 246.

561 Lewis, History of the Battle of Point Pleasant, 55–6.

562 Ibid., 55–7.

563 Jacob, A Biographical Sketch of the Late Captain Michael Cresap, 73; Mayer, Tah-Gah-Jute; or, Logan and Michael Cresap, 124; Thwaites and Kellogg, Documentary History of Dunmore's War, 308.

564 In the summer of 1774, while Captain Michael Cresap was engaged in the Ohio River Indian War, Thomas Cresap and eight hundred residents of Frederick County, Maryland, met at Elizabethtown, Maryland, [present Hagerstown, Maryland] to discuss their concerns about the loss of their natural and constitutional rights. At the top of their list of concerns was the British Parliament's support of the blockade in the harbor surrounding Boston. The colonists felt that intrusive act was a "dangerous invasion of American Liberty." At this meeting, they proposed a "General Congress of Delegates" from each colony to meet and develop a uniform plan that preserved the rightful liberties of all Americans. The colonists agreed that they would strictly follow mandates established by the representatives who protected their natural rights. As a result of similar meetings held throughout the colonies, the First Continental Congress met in Philadelphia on September 5, 1774, to address the concerns put forth by the colonies. Williams and McKensey, History of Frederick County, vol. 1, 82.

certain rights that included "life, liberty, and property; and they have never ceded to any sovereign power whatever, a right to dispose of either without their consent."[565] Members of the Congress also agreed to meet again on May 10, 1775, if the king did not correct the American colonies' grievances against Britain Parliament by that date.

Having just returned from the Indian War, Lord Dunmore's officers, a contingent that in all likelihood included Captain Cresap, immediately called a meeting at Fort Gower. The officers drew up resolutions stating that they were "ready at all times, to the utmost of [their] power, to maintain and defend [their] just rights and privileges." They would be loyal to King George III so long as he delighted "to reign over a brave and free people." The officers also stated that "love of liberty and the attachment to the real interests and just rights of America outweigh every other consideration and [that they will] exert every power within [them] for the defense of American Liberty and for the support of her just rights and privileges, not in any precipitate, riotous, or tumultuous manner, but when regularly called forth by the unanimous voice of our countrymen."[566]

Thus the officers who fought under Lord Dunmore were among the first military units to support the First Continental Congress, essentially declaring their independence on the banks of the Hocking and Ohio Rivers eighteen months before the signing of Declaration of Independence.

In *The Winning of the West*, Theodore Roosevelt wrote that great benefits to the newly formed nation resulted from the mighty success of Lord Dunmore's War, which defeated the confederated Indian tribes, and resulted in the Chillicothe Treaty. Roosevelt declared that had it not been for the successes of Lord Dunmore and his backwoodsmen during the struggle, the United States could quite possibly have been cooped up between the sea and the mountains.

Roosevelt stated, "Certainly, in all the contests waged against the northwestern Indians during the last half of the eighteenth century, there was no other where the whites inflicted so great a relative loss on their foes. Its results were most important. It kept the northwestern tribes quiet for the first three years of the Revolutionary struggle; and above all it rendered possible the settlement of Kentucky, and therefore the winning of the west. Had it not been for Lord Dunmore's War, it's more than likely that when the colonies achieved their freedom, they would have found their western boundary fixed at the Allegheny Mountains."[567]

---

565 History.org, "Declaration and Resolves of the First Continental Congress, October 14, 1774," accessed December 2017, http://www.history.org/almanack/life/politics/resolves.cfm.

566 American Archives: Documents of the Revolutionary Period, 1774–1776, "Resolutions Adopted at a Meeting of Officers Under the Command of Lord Dunmore, November 5, 1774," accessed December 15, 2017, http://amarch.lib.niu.edu/islandora/object/niu-amarch%3A99267.

567 Theodore Roosevelt. Theodore Roosevelt's "The Winning of the West": A Modern Abridgement (New York: Hastings House Publisher, 1963), 174-5; Lewis, History of the Battle of Point Pleasant, 67.

EPILOGUE

SUMMER AND FALL OF 1775 marked the golden age of the riflemen, exemplified by the life of Michael Cresap and the contributions made by all rifle companies serving directly under Washington's command during the Siege of Boston. Captain Michael Cresap's death and funeral symbolized an end to the glory days of these backwoods marksmen. Never again would this assemblage of warriors enjoy the same acclaim and respect that Michael Cresap and his men experienced in New England at the beginning of the American Revolutionary War. On the other hand, the influence fashioned by these patriots that summer would continue to resonate throughout the war and beyond.

On October 21, 1775,[568] command promoted Lieutenant Moses Rawlings to the rank of captain, thus filling the void left by the death of Captain Cresap.[569] More organizational leadership changes soon followed involving the three rifle companies stationed at Roxbury. In January 1776, Congress authorized a new Maryland regiment under the leadership of Colonel William Smallwood and promoted Captain Price to the rank of major, placing him under Colonel Smallwood's charge. The authorities then promoted First Lieutenant Otho Holland Williams to command the Maryland rifle company formerly led by Price.

It seems that in Cresap's untimely absence, Captain Hugh Stephenson's role as senior officer not only brought him to the direct attention of General Washington but also caused his military star to ascend. With Captain Cresap's death and Captain Price's promotion, beginning in January, Stephenson began serving as senior officer over the three remaining rifle companies stationed at Roxbury.

In a letter written to Congress from Cambridge on March 23, 1776, recommending Stephenson's promotion from captain to lieutenant, General Washington stated, "In my Opinion [Stephenson] is the fittest person in the Army for [the promotion of Lt. Colonel], as [he is] the oldest Captain in the service, having distinguished himself at the Head of a Rifle Company all the last War and highly merited the approbation of his superior officers."[570]

One can presume that Cresap, who exhibited the same distinguished qualities Washington admired, would, like Stephenson, have achieved the rank of lieutenant colonel.

On March 4-5, Americans gained possession of Dorchester Heights just east of Roxbury. With its commanding view of Boston, Dorchester Heights strengthened the siege line considerably. The line also overlooked Boston Harbor, where patriots placed artillery they had seized at Ticonderoga in the colony of New York, an incredibly successful operation coordinated by Henry Knox, who became General Washington's chief artillery officer of the Continental Army throughout the American Revolutionary War. The two Maryland rifle companies under Price and Rawlings and Stephenson's Virginia rifle company were stationed near the knoll to help defend the hill should the British decide to attack. However, the attack never came, for a spring tempest played havoc with Howe's boats,

---

568 Francis B. Heitman, *Historical Register of the Officers of the Continental Army: April 1775 to December 1783.* 459
569 Hentz, *Unit History of the Maryland and Virginia Regiment*, 4
570 Fitzpatrick, *The Writings of George Washington from the Original Manuscript Sources*, vol. 4, 393–4.

forcing the British general to abort his efforts to remove the colonials from Dorchester Heights. The Americans attributed the timing of the spring storm to Divine Providence.[571] General Howe and the British army evacuated Boston between March 7 and March 17, 1776.

On March 13, 1776, General Washington wrote from his headquarters in Cambridge, "The Rifle Regiment under the command of Lieutenant Colonel Hand[572] and three rifle Companies under the command of Capt. Stephenson are to be ready to march tomorrow morning at ten O Clock—A Copy of their Route, with their orders, will be deliver'd to Lt. Col. Hand and Capt. Stephenson, this afternoon."[573]

On March 14, the riflemen left Roxbury and reported to General Washington at his headquarters in Cambridge. Anticipating that New York was the next destination General Howe planned to occupy, the British utilizing their force of both naval ships and army, Washington ordered the three rifle companies from Maryland and Virginia to march to Staten Island in order to reinforce the Colonial army already present and to help build up fortifications.

The following day, March 15, 1776, the three rifle companies marched off from Cambridge bound for New York. On March 28, the riflemen from Virginia and Maryland marched across King's Bridge, arriving on the north end of Manhattan Island, New York. On April 13, General Washington followed the rifle companies when he moved the largest part of his Continental forces from Boston to New York.

On April 7 on Staten Island, Rawlings' and Stephenson's men skirmished with twenty-five British soldiers whom authorities had sent ashore to obtain water to bring back to their ships, the *Savage* and the *James*. In this encounter, the riflemen captured ten British soldiers and seized materials in their possession.[574]

On June 2, 1776, the main body of Howe's fleet began to appear, anchoring at Sandy Hook just east of Staten Island to begin an ambitious invasion of the mainland.[575]

On July 4, 1776, the day the Continental Congress adopted the Declaration of Independence, General Washington wrote a letter to Congress detailing the reorganization of the four Maryland and Virginia rifle companies into one unit. His report in general seems to praise the excellent service these men provided him during the Siege of Boston:

To the President of the Congress

New York, July 4,[576] 1776

Sir:
This will be handed to you by Colo: Stephenson whom I have ordered, with the Captains of two Rifle Companies from Maryland to wait on Congress. They will point out such measures as they conceive most likely to advance the raising of a new Batallion and the Persons they think worthy of promotion that have

---

571 *Jeremy Black, War for America: The Fight for Independence, 1775–1783 (Phoenix Mill, GB: Sutton Publishing Limited, 1991),80-81.*

572 *Edward Hand (1744 -1802), a trained physician, served during the Siege of Boston as a Lieutenant Colonel for the Pennsylvania rifle battalion.*

573 Fitzpatrick, The Writings of George Washington from the Original Manuscript Sources, vol. 3, 389.

574 Hentz, Unit History of the Maryland and Virginia Regiment, 4.

575 Schlesinger, The Almanac of American History, 120–1.

576 On July 9, Washington ordered his officers to assemble their brigades at six in the evening at their respective parade grounds, and the Declaration of Independence was read aloud to them. Some formations stood not far from Cresap's less-than-one-year-old grave. Washington wrote in his general orders on this day that Congress declared "the United Colonies of North America, free and independent States…and hopes this important Event will serve as a fresh incentive to every officer, and soldier, to act with Fidelity and Courage as knowing that now the peace and safety of his country depends (under God) solely on the success of our arms." Some of the brigades assembled at Lower Manhattan, New York, were within shouting distance of Trinity Church and the grave of Captain Michael Cresap, the rifleman who was born along the banks of the Potomac River but who now rested along the banks of the Hudson River. Fitzpatrick, The Writings of George Washington from the Original Manuscript Sources 1745–1799, vol. 5, 245; Mary Stockwell, "Declaration of Independence," Digital Encylopedia, accessed December 21, 2017, http://www.mountvernon.org/digital-encyclopedia/article/declaration-of-independence/.

served with them, agreeable to the inclosed List: I am not acquainted with them, but from their report and recommendation, which I doubt not is just, and if Congress will please to enquire of them, they will mention other proper persons as officers.

Only about 40 of the three Old Companies have reinlisted, which I will form into one for the present and place under an Officer or two, 'till a further and complete Arrangement is made, of the whole Battallion.[577]

Apparently, Washington sent Virginia rifle company's Captain Stephenson and the Maryland rifle companies' Captain Price and Captain Rawlings to be the small delegation traveling from New York to Philadelphia to deliver the general's message to Congress concerning the reorganization of the units of men.[578]

Congress authorized General Washington to expand the three original rifle companies, Maryland's two units and Virginia's one unit, with the addition of two rifle companies from Maryland and four from Virginia. Congress named this newly organized brigade of nine companies "the Maryland and Virginia Rifle Regiment." Only forty men reenlisted from the three original Maryland and Virginia companies that had marched to Boston during the summer of 1775.[579] Because Washington needed more riflemen, the general sent several officers home to recruit more men, stressing his orders to fill their companies as quickly as possible and return with their new recruits to Bergen, New Jersey, to rendezvous and receive instructions.

By early July, the three original rifle companies left their posts on Staten Island and were reassigned to the west side of the Hudson River in New Jersey, away from the main body of the Continental army stationed on Long Island and Manhattan. Historical records indicate that until these officers returned from their recruiting duties, headquarters stationed some men at Fort Lee and placed others temporarily under the command of Brigadier General Hugh Mercer, commander of the Flying Camp at Amboy, New Jersey. The riflemen who remained behind while their officers were away recruiting other men were engaged in activities such as scouting and the gathering of intelligence and information.[580]

Some riflemen whose enlistment had expired may have been privileged to hear the reading of the Declaration of Independence from the steps of Independence Hall as they passed through Philadelphia on their journey home, including Lieutenant Joseph Cresap, who did not reenlist after serving a year.[581]

In August, George Washington promoted Rawlings to the rank of colonel and gave him command over the battalion of Virginia and Maryland rifle companies, replacing Colonel Stephenson, who died in August of camp fever, perhaps brought on by dysentery that he may have contracted in the military camps at Roxbury. Unfortunately, as happened in so many other cases, Stephenson's well-being more than likely declined, as did Cresap's health, from exposure to the unsanitary conditions of military camp life.

---

577 Fitzpatrick, The Writings of George Washington from the Original Manuscript Sources, vol. 5, 216-7.

578 Hentz, Unit History of the Maryland and Virginia Regiment, 2–4.

579 In 1776, recommended to serve in Captain Hugh Stephenson's company of riflemen were men who revered Michael Cresap: Abraham Shepherd, captain; Samuel Finlay, first lieutenant; William Kelly, second lieutenant; and Henry Bedinger, third lieutenant. Recommended to serve in Captain Rawlings' company were Richard Davis, captain; Daniel Cresap, Jr.; Nieman Tannehill, second lieutenant; and Rezin Davis, third lieutenant. Recommended to serve in Captain Williams's company were Philmon Griffith, captain; Thomas Hussey Luckett, first lieutenant; Adamson Tannehill, second lieutenant; and Henry Hardman, third lieutenant.

580 Hentz, Unit History of the Maryland and Virginia Regiment, 7–8; National Archives, "To George Washington from Brigadier General Hugh Mercer, 26 July 1776," accessed August 21, 2017, https://founders.archives.gov/documents/Washington/03-05-02-0349; Richard Baker, "A Successful Failure," US Army Military Institute (2010), accessed August 21, 2017, https://www.army.mil/article/41948/A_Successful_Failure.

581 Danske Dandridge, George Michael Bedinger: A Kentucky Pioneer (Charlottesville, VA: The Mische Company Printers, 1909). General John Smallwood departed Maryland on July 9, 1776, in command of nine Maryland companies of the First Maryland Regiment. John Sullivan commanded them until Smallwood arrived. Smallwood missed the Battle of Long Island but arrived in time for the Battle of Fort Washington.

From August 27 through August 30, 1776, the Battle of Brooklyn and the Battle of Brooklyn Heights occurred, the first major confrontation between the British and American forces since the signing of the Declaration of Independence. Stationed at this time across the Hudson River on the New Jersey shore, the riflemen under Rawlings' command did not participate directly in this battle.

Veteran riflemen and new recruits began to rendezvous in the fall at Bergen, New Jersey. From here, the men, with new orders in hand, marched north to Fort Lee on the New Jersey side. From Fort Lee, Rawlings' riflemen crossed the Hudson River to assist in the defense of Fort Washington, located at the highest point on Manhattan Island.

At the Battle of Fort Washington on November 16, 1776, remnants of Cresap's celebrated rifle company fought courageously alongside new recruits in one last gallant and daring stand under the command of Colonel Moses Rawlings, a leader whom his men called "a very worthy and brave officer."[582] This contest illustrates how command used the riflemen—as they had at Ploughed Hill and Dorchester Heights during the Siege of Boston—as a frontline defense. This confrontation at New York echoed a geographic scenario similar to Bunker Hill, Ploughed Hill, and Dorchester Heights in Boston. At each of these sites, the colonists, in an adult game of King of the Hill, had possessed control of the summit. As for the British, if they were to beat their rivals on these occasions, the redcoats must climb to the top and capture the premier position—but not before first facing the riflemen.

On the morning of the battle, General William Howe, who commanded eight thousand troops, sent one of his officers to offer the soldiers defending Fort Washington the opportunity to surrender. Colonel McGaw, who commanded the fort, refused this offer, remarking that his men would defend the fort "to the last extremity."[583]

Colonel Moses Rawlings and Major Otho Holland Williams, who commanded the now-combined Maryland and Virginia regiment made up of about 350 men, led into battle four companies from the Pennsylvania Flying Camp. Rawlings, using trees and rock outcrops that overlooked a steep bank, situated his men on a ridge about a half mile north of Fort Washington. From this post, the riflemen were able to overlook both the Hudson and East rivers. Here the riflemen could gaze with eagle eyes into the great valley below and see Hessian soldiers readying for their assault on Fort Washington.

Holding their fire until the Hessian soldiers made it almost to the top of the summit, the riflemen finally cut loose, firing such deadly rounds upon them that this barrage of bullets forced the Hessian soldiers to scramble back down the hill to regroup five different times during the battle.

Because of their overwhelming numbers, the Hessians eventually succeeded in ascending the summit, where for one hour, a great battle occurred, resulting in much carnage. Eventually, the British, whose men outnumbered the colonists about four to one, managed to bring artillery and more reinforcements to the hill and establish themselves on the summit.

The smoke from the discharge of many rifles lay so thick and heavy on the ridge that visibility was greatly reduced, the wind blowing smoky vapors back into the faces of the riflemen. At the same time, the men of the Virginia and Maryland regiment also struggled with their rifles, which became fouled with overuse, rendering the weapons nonfunctional. To complicate things even further, both Colonel Rawlings and Major Williams suffered injuries during the battle.

After it was clear that resistance had proved futile, Rawlings gradually withdrew his regiment until all his men reached the interior of Fort Washington but only after contesting every inch of ground while at the same time wreaking great havoc upon the enemy. By late afternoon, the British had established a clearly defined line within one hundred yards of the fort.

---

582 Dandridge, Historic Shepherdstown, 148.
583 Ibid., 156.

A participant in the fighting recorded a glowing report of the men whom Michael Cresap had trained. It is a report that would have made the Maryland captain proud: "All the glory that was going [in the battle of Fort Washington] had in my idea of what had passed, been engrossed by the regiment of Rawlings, which had been actively engaged, killed a number of the enemy, and lost many themselves."[584] Of Rawlings' 274 men, "52 officers and soldiers were killed or wounded" while riflemen of Rawlings' regiment "killed or wounded upwards to 600 men."[585]

The British offered conditional surrender to the defenders of the fort, who consisted of 2,763 colonial men and 210 officers. Just before sunset, the riflemen and their officers marched out and laid down their arms only to quickly discover that the British did not intend to honor the surrender agreement. The redcoats seized everything the men possessed, and the prisoners were treated as "Rebels to the King and Country."[586]

While under captivity, Rawlings, Williams, and the other surviving officers were marched to New York, where they were detained for "two months and four days,"[587] after which time British authorities sent them to Long Island on parole. Suffering from the consequences of improper treatment, Lieutenant Daniel Cresap, the nephew of Captain Michael Cresap, and Captain Thomas Beall, the future founder of Cumberland, escaped.[588] The British detained the other officers who served under Rawlings for more than four years[589] before releasing them. Soon thereafter, the British released Moses Rawlings and Otho Holland Williams to General Washington in a prisoner exchange.

The enlisted men who served under Rawlings suffered a much crueler fate. During imprisonment, these men died within three or four months[590] from the results of excessive inhumane treatment. A few of these men were privates who served with Captain Michael Cresap during the Siege of Boston; however, most of these unfortunate men were new recruits who had joined Rawlings' regiment during the summer of 1776. A congressional report stated that Rawlings' regiment of Virginia and Maryland riflemen were "literally destroyed, never again [to be] reinstated or recruited."[591] This report concludes, "The state of Maryland neglected to provide for most of her officers thus thrown out of their command [after the Battle of Fort Washington]."[592]

The state's records for Maryland veterans of the Revolutionary War were poorly kept and in most cases are non-existent. Men who had marched to Boston with Captain Michael Cresap had difficulty collecting their pensions

---

584 Danske Dandridge, American Prisoners of the Revolution (Charlottesville, VA: The Mische Company of Printers, 1911), 73-4.
585 Moses Rawlings, "Regarding the Actions of Rawlings and His Men at the Siege of Washington," Papers of the War Department, accessed December 18, 2017, http://wardepartmentpapers.org/docimage.php?id=42259&docColID=45686&page=1.
586 Dandridge, American Prisoners of the Revolution, 16-7.
587 US House of Representatives, Heirs of Captain Thomas Beall, Report #128 to Accompany Bill H.R. No. 806, Second Session, Thirtieth Congress, February 28, 1849.
588 Ibid.
589 Ibid.
590 Ibid.
591 US House of Representatives, Heirs of Captain Thomas Beall.
592 Ibid.

in their senior years for by the 1820s, no formal records existed of the soldiers who served with Captain Michael Cresap's 1775 rifle company.[593]

For example, John Lazear—who lived in the Town Creek-Murley Branch area near Oldtown, Maryland—appeared in court in 1820 in Bedford County, Pennsylvania, at the age of sixty-five. The court records that the deponent enlisted under Captain Michael Cresap for one year and marched to Boston. In 1776 Lazear marched to New York and Staten Island at a place called Amboy where the deponent was honorably discharged, having served in the military of the United States under the said enlistment one year and to the end of his enlistment. Captain Cresap died before the year was out, and Captain Moses Rawlings was appointed in his place. Lazear filed for a pension through Maryland in 1818 but was denied "as there was no formal record of his Company's existence."[594] Perhaps Cresap's missing roster is one more reason why history has overlooked the lives, legends, and contributions of these Maryland soldiers who sacrificed so much in the founding of our country. Confirming the testimony of John Lazear was Joseph Cresap, a lieutenant in Captain Cresap's company. Because of Joseph Cresap's testimony, Lazear's pension application was ultimately approved.[595]

Certainly remembering the fear that the rifle companies instilled in the British army during the Boston siege, General Washington in 1777 advised an officer in one of his ranger companies to dress his men like riflemen. Washington wrote, "To dress a Company or two of true Woods Men in the right Indian Style and let them make the Attack accompanied with screaming and yelling as the Indians do, it would have very good consequences."[596]

During the American Revolution, British officers ridiculed the open formation of fighting employed by rifle companies such as that commanded by Captain Cresap. In fact, the redcoats berated the riflemen who in their estimation fought like "a race of bush fighters."[597] The truth of the matter was that when it came to the reputation of these "pioneer sharpshooters of the world"—the British soldier, like the Indians[598]—feared the riflemen "like the devil."[599]

---

593 The majority of men who marched with Captain Cresap to Boston did not reenlist when their one-year enlistment period ended in June 1776. Records indicate that after the trials and hardships the riflemen experienced during the summer of 1775 and following the loss of their esteemed leader, most of Michael Cresap's company did not reenlist, including Captain Michael Cresap's nephew, Lieutenant Joseph Cresap. Those few privates who did reenlist—numbering a few more (or possibly less) than ten men from Cresap's original rifle company—were taken captive and held on British prison ships after the Battle of Fort Washington. Many of these men sadly died due to cruel and inhumane treatment while aboard those prison hulks. These heroes might have saved themselves by simply changing their allegiance to the British crown, but they refused. Because the rosters of these patriots were poorly kept, their names are lost to posterity. These unfortunate souls who were personally trained and imbued with the spirit of liberty by Michael Cresap are just a few of the many unknown soldiers from the period of the American Revolutionary War who suffered in captivity on prison ships. The remains of a few of Cresap's riflemen may lie today at the Prison Ship Martyrs Monument in the New York City borough of Brooklyn along with the 11,500 other men who suffered and died on British prison ships in New York Harbor. Officers such as Daniel Cresap, Jr. and Moses Rawlings, who the British imprisoned along with the other regular enlistees, were blessed with somewhat better fates. Daniel Cresap, Jr. escaped his prison confines while the British released Moses Rawlings and Otho Holland Williams in a prisoner exchange. Douglas Martin, "Resurrecting Patriots and Their Park: Shrine to Revolution Martyrs Is Part of the Fort Greene Renewal," New York Times, September 23, 1995, http://www.nytimes.com/1995/09/23/nyregion/resurrecting-patriots-their-park-shrine-revolution-s-martyrs-part-fort-greene.html.
594 Richard Perrin Day, "A Perrin History: The Lazear Family," Perrin History (2016), accessed August 21, 2017, http://www.perrinhistory.net/Narrative/SectBLazear/lazear.html.
595 Day, "A Perrin History."
596 Higginbotham, The War for American Independence, 4.
597 William Waller Edwards, "Morgan and His Riflemen," William and Mary Quarterly 23, 1914, 104–5, https://archive.org/details/jstor-1915109.
598 British General John Burgoyne noted that Indians allies did not help them when they knew riflemen were present. Burgoyne stated, "Not a man of [the Indians] was to be brought within the sound of a rifle shot." Black, War for America: The Fight for Independence, 1775–1783, 61.
599 Edwards, "Morgan and His Riflemen," 105.

The rifleman's method of fighting baffled the British, who continued their antiquated order of fighting all the way through the war until their surrender of Cornwallis at Yorktown. The British army did not adopt the long rifle as a military weapon until 1794.[600]

Despite the death of his son, Colonel Thomas Cresap continued to remain active in supporting the Revolutionary War effort, running supplies to George Rogers Clark at Fort Pitt. War records show that, starting in 1778 and continuing through 1779, Thomas Cresap was involved with the Continental Boat Service. The operation started at the Conococheague, at present-day Williamsport, Maryland, the home of Daniel Cresap - Colonel Cresap's oldest son. From the Conocochaegue, the Continental Boat Service floated supplies upriver on the Potomac River, to Oldtown, Maryland, where Colonel Cresap resided.

Daniel Cresap, Sr., the father of Daniel Cresap Jr., likely assisted the army at Williamsport at the "storehouse' located "near the Point of the Hill on the bank of the Conococheague" [601] and helped coordinate boat operations and the delivery of supplies to his father at Oldtown.

Continental forces stationed armed guards to protect the storehouse and boats from "the depredations of Tories" at Conococheague and Oldtown and "to keep off the Indians."[602] Captain John Lee and Lieutenant Stockton commanded these flotillas that consisted of seventy-two armed men, who were suitably armed to prevent Tories from gaining possession of these supplies before they reached Washington's western army of the United States.

From Oldtown, the supplies were then shipped over land by packhorses and wagons to the western army at Fort Pitt, a frontier military stronghold commanded by Lieutenant Colonel George Rogers Clark, who served with Michael Cresap during the Ohio Indian wars of 1774.

The operation involving the Continental Boat Service and Colonel Thomas Cresap in the backwoods of the western frontier proved to help present a significantly positive outcome to the Revolutionary War effort. Lieutenant Colonel Clark believed that the best strategy to stop the British-incited Indian attacks in the west was to directly attack British forts and outposts situated on the frontier northwest of the Ohio River. From Fort Pitt, supported in part with supplies provided by Thomas Cresap and the Continental Boat Service, Colonel Clark led 175 men deep into the Ohio and Illinois wilderness, where they conquered several Indian villages and British outposts.

In February 1779, Clark took Vincennes from the British, a victory that made him an instant American military champion to the colonies, who celebrated Clark's success. General Washington used this victory to help negotiate support from France while Virginia used Clark's conquest to claim the Illinois territory, a move that eventually secured the Northwest Territory for America.

---

600 In 1777 at Valley Forge, officers and soldiers followed a set of army guidelines developed by Baron Von Steuben. In 1779, Baron Von Steuben's instructions were published as the Regulations for the Order and Discipline of the Troops of the United States. Since paper was scarce, officials printed these regulations on blue paper, known as the Blue Book. The US Army applied the Blue Book ordinances in the field until 1814. These procedures affected military drills and tactics until the Mexican War of 1846. Influenced by the riflemen he observed in battle during the early part of the American revolution, and totally contrary to combat procedures the baron had learned in the old world, Baron Von Steuben incorporated into the Blue Book "the open skirmish formation line," so the rifleman adopted this Indian method of fighting for survival on the frontier, making it an established military tactic. Edwards, "Morgan and His Riflemen," 105; Brian M. Shay, "After 230 Years, The 'Blue Book' Still Guides NCOs," US Army Military Institute (2009), accessed August 22, 2017, https://www.army.mil/article/29717/.
601 Southern Campaign American Revolution Pension Statements and Rosters, Pension Application of John Black, March 13, 1834, http://revwarapps.org/r887.pdf.
602 Ibid.

By 1777, the widow of Captain Michael Cresap, Mary Whitehead Cresap, had married David Rogers. A native of Ireland, Rogers came to America early in his life and settled at Oldtown, where he made his living as a merchant. In 1775, Rogers established a settlement five miles outside present-day Wheeling, West Virginia.

Rogers served as a member of the Virginia state legislature. After he married Mary Cresap, Rogers located their home in Hampshire County, Virginia, just across the Potomac River from Oldtown, Maryland. In an operation much like the Continental Boat Service in Maryland, Virginia governor Patrick Henry appointed David Rogers to lead a boating expedition to New Orleans to pick up "military stores [and] munitions of war."[603] Recruiting a small company of about thirty men around Old Fort Redstone, Colonel Rogers began an extensive expedition down the Ohio and Mississippi rivers on two flatboats. After a harrowing trip, Rogers arrived around September 20 in New Orleans.

Completing his business and securing the military goods, Rogers departed New Orleans for the journey up the Mississippi and Ohio Rivers to deliver the goods to Fort Pitt. By August 5, he had gone as far north as St. Louis, where he stopped and rested. Rogers met George Rogers Clark at Louisville, where Clark assigned twenty-three of his men to accompany Rogers to Fort Pitt. Sometime on October 4 or 5, Rogers was attacked and killed by a party of Indians led by Simon Girty, the infamous renegade, and all the supplies Rogers had transported were seized by the enemy.

News of Rogers's death traveled slowly back to Williamsburg, Virginia. As late as November 8, Thomas Jefferson, the new Virginia governor who had succeeded Patrick Henry, anxiously awaited information of Rogers's success delivering military supplies to Fort Pitt. Jefferson would have surely been disappointed regarding the loss of the supplies. And as if that debacle was not tragedy enough, Mary Whitehead Cresap Rogers was soon stricken with grief after learning that she was now a widow for the second time.[604]

After Michael Cresap's death, John Jeremiah Jacob (1757–1839) not only managed the Cresap family affairs but also took over all business affairs relating to what had been Cresap's stores at Oldtown and Redstone. In the same fashion as he had spent most of his early years, he focused the remainder of his days caring for Michael's surviving family, only giving up the business portion of things in summer of 1776, when he entered military service, probably around the same time that Mary Cresap made a commitment to become the wife of David Rogers.

Jacob's military career began at seventeen years of age as a private. During Lord Dunmore's War of 1774, Jacob served a little more than two months under the command of Captain Michael Cresap's nephew, also named Michael Cresap (1750–1788), the son of Daniel Cresap, Sr. During the American Revolution in 1776, Jacob served in the rank of ensign in the company of the Maryland militia commanded by Colonel Henry Shryock of the Flying Camp. Although officials discharged the company at Philadelphia on December 5, 1776, Jacob continued serving in the military as a second lieutenant with the sixth Maryland regiment under the command of Colonel Otho Holland Williams.

For the remainder of his time in the military, Jacob served as paymaster, except during times of battle, when he took his place as an officer on the line. Before the end of the American Revolution, officials promoted Jacob to first lieutenant and eventually captain—designated, by rule of seniority, the same rank held by his mentor, Michael Cresap, at the time of Cresap's death.

Jacob participated in battles at Hillsborough, Brandywine, Germantown, and Monmouth, and Camden, the latter bringing an end to his active military service.[605]

---

603 Louis Phelps Kellogg, Frontier Retreat on the Upper Ohio, 1779–1781 (Madison, WI: Wisconsin Historical Publications, 1917), 88.
604 National Archives, "From Thomas Jefferson to Bernardo De Galvez, 8 November 1779," accessed August 22, 2017, https://founders.archives.gov/documents/Jefferson/01-03-02-0174.1789; Kellogg, Frontier Retreat on the Upper Ohio, 1779–1781, 17–8, 78–94, 104–6, 115, 123, 185, 192.
605 Warren Skidmore and Donna Kaminsky, Lord Dunmore's Little War of 1774 (Rocky Mount, NC: Heritage Books, Inc., 2002), 31; John Jeremiah Jacob, "Pension Statement of John Jeremiah Jacob," Southern Campaign American Revolution Pension Statements and Rosters (May 27, 1818), December 18, 2017, http://revwarapps.org/w11930.pdf.

In 1781, Mary Cresap Rogers (circa 1750–1821) married a third time to Jacob, the young protégé of Michael Cresap. To accommodate his wife and stepchildren, Jacob built an addition to the house that Michael had constructed for his family at Oldtown, Maryland, in 1764. Today, this house is known as the Irvin Allen/Michael Cresap Museum, the oldest surviving structure in Allegany County, Maryland.

Michael Cresap Museum, Oldtown, Maryland

In 1785, Jacob moved his family across the Potomac River from Oldtown and served as a minister and sheriff in Hampshire County, Virginia (present-day West Virginia). Francis Asbury, the famous traveling Methodist preacher, stayed with Mary and John Jacob at their home when he passed through the area. In 1813, Asbury ordained John J. Jacob as a Methodist preacher.

In September 1826, Jacob—a staunch defender of Cresap's innocence in the Yellow Creek/Logan family massacre—penned a biography titled *Biography of the Late Captain Michael Cresap*, which proved instrumental in clearing malicious and unjust charges regarding his former employer and friend.[606]

After Mary Cresap Rogers Jacob died in 1821, Jacob married a second time to Susan McDavitt. A nephew of Captain Michael named Joseph Cresap performed Jacob's remarriage in Joseph's home at Cresaptown, Maryland. Jacob raised a second family, including a son and namesake, John J. Jacob, Jr. (1829–1893), who became the fourth governor of West Virginia. Following Jacob's death, family members buried him at Mound Hill Cemetery, Romney, West Virginia.

Joseph Cresap (1755–1827) was the son of Daniel Cresap, Sr. and a nephew of Captain Michael Cresap. During his life, Joseph Cresap served in several roles as a farmer, soldier, Maryland state senator, and Methodist pastor. Joseph married on four separate occasions. His first wife, Deborah Whitehead, and his second wife, Sarah Whitehead, were sisters of Mary Whitehead Cresap, the wife of Captain Michael Cresap.

Joseph was an original member of Captain Michael Cresap's company of riflemen. When he was just nineteen years of age, led by his uncle Michael, Joseph participated in Dunmore's War at the Shawnee Indian conflict of 1774. In 1775

---

606   Jacob, A Biographical Sketch of the Late Captain Michael Cresap.

during the revolutionary period, Lieutenant Joseph Cresap marched again with Michael Cresap's rifle company en route to join General George Washington near Boston. After completing a one-year enlistment with Cresap's rifle company, Joseph returned home to civilian life. People who knew Joseph remembered him as a skillful rifleman who was a good shot.

Joseph is described in a 1788 list of settlers as having located in "lands west of Fort Cumberland," where he acquired a large tract of land known as Upper Oldtown, which came to include present day Cresaptown, Maryland.[607]

Joseph Cresap attended the first meeting at John Graham's house in Cumberland, Maryland, to establish Allegany as the county seat. This meeting initiated the first of many civic duties he was to perform for the state of Maryland. In December 1790, the legislature appointed Joseph Cresap, along with two other men, as commissioners for tax in Allegany County. Joseph often represented the county in the legislature and became a member of the Maryland state senate. He served as a member of the House of Delegation in 1800, 1801, and 1802.

Joseph was instrumental in the formation of the first Methodist church in Allegany County, those first meetings being held in his home at Cresaptown. Methodist preachers known as circuit riders began making their rounds in Allegany County in 1783. These preachers were appointed by the first Methodist Bishop in America, Francis Asbury. As early as June 30, 1784, Asbury lodged at Joseph Cresap's and preached at Cresap's Mill. Sometime during this period, Bishop Asbury dedicated the first Methodist Church in Cresaptown and appointed Joseph Cresap as a "first-class Methodist leader."[608]

The house Joseph built in Cresaptown in 1793 became a prominent Allegany County landmark. Joseph constructed this dwelling as an eight-room, two-story log structure, which saw numerous additions, and at some later point, he covered the structure with native stone. The home stood along Darrow's Lane in Cresaptown, now the site of the general vicinity of third base at Weber Little League Baseball Field in present-day Cresap Park. Unfortunately, this once influential house was destroyed by fire in the winter of 1929.

In the early 1800s, because Maryland poorly maintained American Revolutionary War military records in the state, officials depended on Joseph Cresap, one of the last surviving members of Captain Michael Cresap's rifle company, to authenticate and verify soldiers' pension claims. After his death, family members buried Joseph Cresap on a knoll adjacent to the North Branch overlooking the Potomac River, located on the estate where Joseph had lived at Cresaptown.[609]

Daniel Cresap, Jr. (1753–1794) was the son of Daniel Cresap, Sr. and nephew of Captain Michael Cresap. Lieutenant Daniel Cresap, like his brother Joseph, served in the rifle company under the command of his uncle, Captain Michael Cresap, in both Lord Dunmore's War in 1774 and the Siege of Boston in 1775. After his uncle Michael died, Daniel served under the command of Captain Moses Rawlings for the remainder of his time participating in the Siege of Boston. Unlike Joseph, Daniel Cresap reenlisted after his first year of enlistment ended. Officials promoted Daniel to first lieutenant of the rifle company under the command of Captain Richard Davis on July 9, 1776.

In November 1776, after the Battle of Fort Washington, the British took Daniel Cresap, Jr. as a prisoner of war. He escaped imprisonment with Thomas Beall, whom historians call the founder of Cumberland, Maryland.

In 1788, by authority of an act, Daniel Cresap, David Lynn, and Benjamin Brookes were appointed as commissioners to establish land values and settle land disputes in the distribution of military lots "west of Fort Cumberland" in Allegany County. These lands at this time included present-day Allegany and Garrett Counties.

---

607 Nina Cresap, "Joseph Cresap's Cresaptown," Rootsweb, accessed August 24, 2017, http://www.rootsweb.ancestry.com/~mdallegh/Cresaptown.htm.
608 Ibid.
609 Cresap, "Joseph Cresap's Cresaptown."

Daniel Cresap, Jr. and several other surveyors worked with the chief surveyor, Mr. Deacon, to establish survey lines of individual tracts of land.[610]

In 1790, Daniel Cresap, Jr. and Thomas Beall served together with two other delegates representing western Maryland in the state House of Delegates. Daniel Cresap, Jr. also served in the House of Delegates in 1791 and 1792.[611]

During the Whiskey Rebellion of 1794, Colonel Daniel Cresap, Jr. led a regiment under the command of Major-General Henry "Light-Horse Harry" Lee III, the father of Confederate General Robert E. Lee. In December 1794, Daniel contracted pneumonia and died in Uniontown, Pennsylvania, while returning home from quelling the Whiskey Rebellion. This former member of Cresap's Rifles received a glowing eulogy at the time of his death, sentiments similar to those that were also certainly spoken after Michael Cresap's passing. According to the eulogy, Daniel Cresap, Jr. "served in the late war which secured liberty and independence for this country, and was ever ready to vindicate these rights so gloriously obtained whenever they appeared to be in the least bit endangered. To the character of a soldier he united that of a patriot. In him were also blended and social virtues of a loving husband, indulgent father, and a sincere friend. His death is regretted, not only by his relatives, but by an extensive circle of friends and acquaintances."[612]

Colonel Moses Rawlings (1745–1809), the son of Aaron Rawlings, a wealthy tobacco planter, and Susannah Beard Rawlings, was born in Anne Arundel County Maryland in 1745. Early in life, Rawlings moved to the Oldtown area, where Michael Cresap was born and raised. Rawlings acquired large tracts of land along Oldtown Creek, present day Town Creek near the Bull Ring Ranch at Green Ridge State Forest.[613]

Moses served in the Continental army from 1775 to 1779, first earning the rank of lieutenant colonel on June 27, 1776, as commander of a new regiment incorporating soldiers from Captain Michael Cresap's rifle company. After Michael Cresap's death in October 1775, Rawlings took command of his former rifle company, which until about June 1776 had remained in the same form as Cresap would have known it. After this date, army commander George Washington ordered Rawlings and fellow riflemen Colonel Hugh Stephenson and Otho Holland Williams to raise a new regiment that would incorporate five Virginia companies and four Maryland companies.

In mid-October, Rawlings received orders to bring up the riflemen to defend Fort Washington, New York, where he positioned the new regiment about a half mile north of Fort Washington on Manhattan Island. On November 16 the British attacked Fort Washington, killing or wounding most of Rawlings' regiment, forcing its leaders to surrender. The melee caused injuries to officers Rawlings and Williams. Witnesses of the occasion recorded that Rawlings suffered a fractured leg.

Alexander Graydon, a witness to the battle, related that "Rawlings fought with great gallantry and effect as the [enemy] were climbing the heights, until the arms of the riflemen became useless from the foulness they contracted from the frequent repetition of their fire. From this incident, and the great superiority of the enemy, Colonel Rawlings was obliged to retire into the fort."[614]

George Washington spoke of Rawlings in a letter to John Augustine Washington dated November 19, 1776: "By General Greene's account, the enemy suffered greatly on the north side of Fort Washington. Colonel Rawlings' regiment was posted there, and behaved with great spirit."[615]

---

610 Connie Beachy. "Early Settlers of Allegheny Co., Maryland," Our Family Histories (1998), accessed August 24, 2017, http://www.ourfamilyhistories.com/hsdurbin/other-states/earlySettlersMD.html. Daniel Cresap, Sr. was sixty years of age in 1788. The authors presume that Daniel Cresap, Jr. is the "Daniel Cresap" elected to the Board of Allegany County Commissioners in 1789 and the House of Delegates in 1790.

611 Edward C. Papenfuse, "Historical List of House of Delegates, Allegany County, Maryland, 1790–1974," Maryland State Archives (1990), accessed August 24, 2017, http://msa.maryland.gov/msa/speccol/sc2600/sc2685/house/html/alhouse.html.

612 Bowen's Virginia Centinel and Gazette, December 29, 1794.

613 Irvin G. Allen, Historic Oldtown, Maryland (Oakland, MD: Garrett Historical Society, 1983), 9.

614 Alexander Graydon. Memoirs of His Own Time (Philadelphia: Lindsay and Blakiston, 1846), 200.

615 Ibid., 194.

Rawlings was captured by the British and likely imprisoned on the prison ship *Whitby*, the first prison ship to arrive at Wallabout Bay, off the coast of Long Island, in October 1776. On this prison hulk, Rawlings suffered severe indignities, as did all colonial prisoners held captive on prison ships during the war.

While under captivity, Rawlings, Williams, and other surviving officers were marched to New York, where soldiers detained them for "two months and four days,"[616] after which time British authorities sent them to Long Island on parole. After a period of nearly fourteen months from the time of his capture, Rawlings was exchanged on January 16, 1778.[617]

On January 12, 1777, just days before Rawlings was exchanged, Washington promoted the Maryland captain to the rank of Colonel over one of the sixteen additional continental regiments.[618] General Washington first ordered Rawlings to Fort Pitt "to take charge of the prisoners confined there. Rawlings resigned on June 2, 1779 [619]after he was denied command of a German regiment posted at Fort Pitt.

At the end of three years, some Maryland officers obtained commissions in other regiments; however, higher command did not promote Colonel Rawlings to lead another unit even though fellow rifleman Major Otho Holland Williams obtained a Maryland regiment. Although not on the battlefield, Rawlings continued to serve the colonies by performing other important functions. On October 2, 1779, command appointed Rawlings to deputy assistant quartermaster general of the army, overseeing prisoners confined at Fort Frederick in Washington County on the western shore of Maryland.

Fort Frederick, Fort Frederick State Park, Big Pool, Maryland (Photograph courtesy of Steve Dean)

---

616 US House of Representatives, Heirs of Captain Thomas Beall.
617 Hentz, Unit History of the Maryland and Virginia Regiment.
618 *Francis B. Heitman, Historical Register of the Officers of the Continental Army: April 1775 to December 1783. 459*
619 *Ibid, 459*

During the Siege of Yorktown in the fall of 1781, Rawlings procured one hundred head of cattle for the purpose of supplying Washington's army with beef.

In April 1788, at the Annapolis Convention, Rawlings served as one of the representatives for Washington County (now Allegany County) and cast a vote in favor of ratifying the federal Constitution.

In 1797, while anticipating a possible war with France, President George Washington appointed Rawlings to the rank of brigadier general. In 1801, when Thomas Jefferson ran for president of the United States, Rawlings served as an elector.

Moses Rawlings died in May 1809, on the plantation he purchased in later life at the mouth of Patterson's Creek overlooking the Potomac River in Hampshire County (present West Virginia). His grandson, William Rawlings, removed his remains and reburied Moses Rawlings at Rose Hill Cemetery, Cumberland, Maryland. From all accounts, Moses Rawlings was a close friend of Michael Cresap. In his brief life, it would appear that Cresap admired Rawlings, who had obviously been a trustworthy and soldierly companion.[620]

Otho Holland Williams (1749–1794) was orphaned at the age of thirteen. He spent his early years on the Springfield farm in present-day Williamsport, Maryland, where Daniel Cresap, Sr., older brother of Michael Cresap, also owned a home. During his childhood years, Williams apparently developed a close relationship with the family members of Daniel Cresap, Sr., and by the age of twenty-six, Williams had acquired considerable skills as a rifleman.

During the summer of 1775, Lieutenant Williams marched with Captain Price's Maryland rifle company from Hagerstown, Maryland, to Cambridge, Massachusetts, to join George Washington during the Siege of Boston.

During the summer of 1776, Washington reorganized the rifle companies into the Maryland and Virginia Rifle Regiment. Here Williams served as a major under Colonel Stephenson and Lieutenant Colonel Moses Rawlings.

At the battle of Fort Washington in November 1776, after Rawlings suffered severe but nonfatal wounds, Williams took command of the rifle regiment. British troops overwhelmed the Colonial army, forcing them to surrender.

Williams was wounded in the fighting, taken prisoner, and held captive, first in Sugar Ware House and then on a British prison ship. Williams remained a prisoner of war for fifteen months until he was exchanged for a British officer on January 16, 1778.[621]

General Washington promoted Williams to the rank of colonel and gave him command of the Sixth Maryland Regiment. Williams served with distinction and honor as deputy adjutant general under both Generals Horatio Gates and Nathaniel Greene during the Southern Campaign.

By the end of the war, Williams was promoted to the rank of brigadier general. Even though he was held prisoner for fifteen months during the war, Williams took part in many of the key moments of the American Revolutionary War, including the Siege of Boston and the battles of Fort Washington, Camden, Monmouth, Guilford Courthouse, Hobkirk's Hill, Eutaw Springs, and Cowpens. Immediately after the war, Williams moved to Baltimore, Maryland, and served as a customs collector for the Port of Baltimore.

---

620 Dandridge, American Prisoners of the Revolution, 52; Rawlings, "Regarding the Actions of Rawlings and His Men at the Siege of Washington"; Maryland State Archives, "Annapolis Convention to Ratify the Federal Constitution, April 21–29, 1788," 205–11, accessed October 13, 2017, http://msa.maryland.gov/msa/speccol/sc2600/sc2685/html/fedconst.html; Dale J. Schmitt, "The Capture of Colonel Moses Rawlings," Maryland Historical Magazine 7(2) (1976), 205–11; Emily Emerson Lantz, "Lineage of the Rawlings," Baltimore Sun, May 14, 1905. A quaint locale in Maryland originally called Hickory Flats, Rawlings, Maryland—named for Moses Rawlings—became entrenched in history when officials established a post office close to a railroad near the community on March 7, 1856. Officials of the Maryland Historical Trust recorded that Moses Rawlings built a part of the original stone structure of the old Daniel Cresap Stone Home at Rawlings. The structure burned to the ground on July 24, 1982.

621 Hentz, Unit History of the Maryland and Virginia Regiment.

In 1787, Colonel Thomas Cresap died, and his oldest son, Daniel Cresap, Sr., moved from the Springfield Farm to Upper Oldtown and that year built a new home at present-day Rawlings, Maryland. In that same year, Otho Holland Williams purchased the Springfield farm and soon after purchased a tract near the farm along Conococheague Creek and established the town of Williamsport, which officials named for him.

In 1792, after President George Washington first offered the position of brigadier general of the US Army to Daniel Morgan and he declined, Washington next offered this position to Otho Holland Williams. Due to his declining health, caused by injury and illness incurred during the war, Williams turned down this position, which would have made him second in command of the army. It is evident that George Washington held in high regard the officers who commanded the rifle companies. The general's evident high regard for riflemen Morgan, Rawlings, and Williams hints at the promising future that would have likely been in store for Captain Michael Cresap had he lived.

Otho's close connection to the Cresap family is indicated by an original document found in Williams's personal papers regarding a deed from Lord Baltimore to Thomas Cresap mentioning Cresap's management of Lord Baltimore's property around present-day Williamsport, Maryland. Otho became very close to Daniel Cresap, Jr. This is indicated by the fact that Daniel Cresap, Jr. named his first son Edward Otho Cresap. The Cresaps would pass down Williams's name to succeeding generations of their family, including General Edward Otho Cresap Ord (1818–1883), who later would make a name for himself during several battles of the Civil War and who would make an appearance on scene at the surrender that took place in Wilmer McLean's parlor at Appomattox Village, Virginia. Williams died in 1794 at the age of forty-six and is buried at the highest point of the Williamsport town cemetery overlooking the Potomac River. In 1905, Congress allotted $20,000 for a suitable monument to honor "this brave soldier."[622]

Richard Davis, Jr. (1750–1801) served in 1775 on the Committee of Observation with Colonel Thomas Cresap and Moses Rawlings. Davis assisted Michael Cresap in recruiting his celebrated troop of riflemen. During the summer of 1775, Lieutenant Davis marched to Boston, serving as a lieutenant in Captain Michael Cresap's company, and he reenlisted in 1776. In November 1776, after the Battle of Fort Washington, Davis became one of the many prisoners the British took into custody. By mid-1778, Davis resigned his commission after the British exchanged him for another prisoner the colonials were holding. Davis died at the age of fifty-one on July 26, 1801, and was buried with full military honors at the old Episcopal church in Hagerstown, Maryland. "He had a reputation for being a brave soldier and honorable man."[623]

Historians credit the officers of these rifle companies with several distinctions. First, the captains of the rifle companies from the three colonies of Pennsylvania, Virginia, and Maryland were the first to receive military commissions from Congress. Second, the captains of the rifle companies were the first to "recruit, organize, train, and lead men into combat" under the command of General Washington.[624] This in essence was the birth of the US Army—June 14, 1775. Cresap's Independent Maryland Rifle Company has earned one additional significant place in military history. Records hail Cresap's Rifles as the first military unit from the Alleghenies, including the upper Potomac River, Ohio River, and Mississippi River watershed basins, to join the newly formed American

---

622 John Thomas Chew Williams. A History of Washington County, Maryland, vol. 1 (Hagerstown, MD: Higginson Book Company, 1906), 78–9.
623 Ibid., 128
624 Hannum, "America's First Company Commanders," 12–9.

army. At the start of the American Revolution, these geographical locations constituted the farthest outreaches of the colonial western frontier.[625]

Gun historians note that "with the wide acceptance" of the long rifle "by the American backwoodsmen as an indispensable part of existence and its unerring accuracy in the hands of…skilled marksmen, it was inevitable that these men and their rifles would play a significant role in the…development of our country. These patriots, inured to a hard existence, were a natural source of…manpower for the defense of the country. Their rifles represented a superior form of weaponry surpassing any employed by American foes."[626]

These frontiersmen with their long rifles did indeed help win a series of the country's early wars, including the French and Indian War, the American Revolution, and the Battle of New Orleans in the War of 1812, thus significantly contributing to the development and success of America.

On a cold November 14 in 1908, United States President William Howard Taft traveled to the Prison Ship Martyrs Monument in Brooklyn, New York, for an official ribbon-cutting dedication ceremony. This confirms the fact that, even after such an extended length of time, many leaders have paid and will continue to pay allegiance to those who fight and die for their country. Whether the weathered bones of soldiers have languished on abandoned beaches or on battlegrounds around the globe, along vast rows in military graveyards, or buried in the ocean deep, or in quaint church cemeteries, therein lie heroes who gave their all for liberty.[627]

Michael Cresap never had the opportunity to reveal his story or his feelings regarding the events, some contradictory, that occurred in his much-too-brief life span. The Maryland frontiersman's body and its secrets—encased in ancient soil in Trinity Church cemetery, guarded by the vigilant eye of the Goddess of Liberty herself—remain shrouded in intrigue.

---

625 Ibid.
626 Kentucky Rifle Association, The Kentucky Rifle: A True American Heritage in Picture.
627 A. Gustafson, "Presidential Visits to the Brooklyn Navy Yard," (February 15, 2013), retrieved December 19 2017, http://turnstiletours.com/presidential-visits-to-the-brooklyn-navy-yard/.

REFERENCES

Abbott, William. "The Relation of New Hampshire Men to the Siege of Boston." *Magazine of History with Notes and Queries* 6(2) (August 1907): 63–85. Accessed December 20, 2014. https://books.google.com/books?id=WfEOAAAAYAAJ&pg=PA76&lpg=PA76&dq=Ploughed+Hill&source=bl&ots=tBxOus5gom&sig=oTLZV4ybhsSw2dd73DLIRmoab0Y&hl=en&sa=X&ei=kgWVVOn_M_H_sATziIKwCQ&ved=0CFIQ6AEwCw#v=onepage&q=Ploughed%20Hill&f=false.

Adams, Charles Francis. *Familiar Letters of John Adams and His Wife Abigail Adams during the Revolution*. Cambridge, MA: Riverside Press, 1876. https://books.google.com/books?id=fYEEAAAAYAAJ&pg=PA65&lpg=PA65&dq=%E2%80%9Ca+peculiar+kind+of+musket,+called+a+rifle.%E2%80%9D+%2B+John+adams&source=bl&ots=nfSvw7ddgT&sig=X-u-lIBcwgpeeOOkLUbODV_SQoE&hl=en&sa=X&ved=0ahUKEwjj1qj-0KzXAhUBLSYKHSw0C3cQ6AEIKDA.

Alchin, Linda. "Sons of Liberty." Land of the Brave, February 8, 2017. Accessed December 15, 2017. https://www.landofthebrave.info/sons-of-liberty.htm.

Aldrich, A. Owen. "The Poetry of Thomas Paine." (January 1955). https://journals.psu.edu/pmhb/article/viewFile/41002/40723.

Allen, Ethan. *The Garrison Church: Sketches of History of St. Thomas Parish, Garrison Forest, Baltimore County, Maryland, 1742–1852*. New York: James Porr and Company, 1898.

Allen, Irvin G. *Historic Oldtown, Maryland*. Oakland, MD: Garrett Historical Society, 1983.

American Archives: Documents of the Revolutionary Period, 1774-1776. "Frederick County (Maryland) Committee: June 21, 1775." Accessed November 8, 2017. http://amarch.lib.niu.edu/islandora/object/niu-amarch%3A95917.

———. "Resolutions Adopted at a Meeting of Officers under the Command of Lord Dunmore: November 5, 1774." Accessed December 15, 2017. http://amarch.lib.niu.edu/islandora/object/niu-amarch%3A99267.

American History from Revolution to Reconstruction and Beyond. "Aaron Burr Jr. (1756–1836)." Accessed November 21, 2017. http://www.let.rug.nl/usa/biographies/aaron-burr-jr/.

American Long Rifles. "William Henry, Sr., Patriot and Gunsmith—A Life to Remember," November 2, 2009. Accessed November 10, 2017. http://americanlongrifles.org/forum/index.php?topic=7305.0;wap2.

The American Pioneer: A Monthly Periodical Devoted to the Objects of the Logan Historical Society. Cincinnati, OH: John S. Williams, 1884. https://archive.org/stream/americanpioneerm01cinc#page/n10/mode/1up.

"Americans Fortify Lamb's Dam in Roxbury." Boston 1775, October 6, 2007. Accessed February 27, 2013. http://boston1775.blogspot.com/search?q=Lamb%27s.

Ancestry.com. "Public Service Claims—Romney and Winchester (1775)."Accessed January 15, 2015. http://boards.ancestry.com/thread.aspx?mv=flat&m=18&p=topics.Military.amerrev.va.

———. "Robert Levers Family." 2009. Accessed November 14, 2013. http://boards.ancestry.com/thread.aspx?mv=flat&m=49&p=surnames.levers.

Andrews, Charles McClean. *Colonial Folkways: A Chronicle of American Life in the Reign of the Georges*. New Haven, CT: Yale University Press, 1919. https://books.google.com/books?id=GW3YAAAAMAAJ&pg=PA217&lpg=PA217&dq=soft,+rocky,+and+treacherous%E2%80%A6.intolerable,+and+most+miserable.&source=bl&ots=Gu2-psCxZ2&sig=788rzYSl3e3_HoP1gESdtDdGvCA&hl=en&sa=X&ved=0ahUKEwjIn-va8oTYAhVSkeAKHZIWBWcQ6AEIKzAA#v.

Bailey, Kenneth P. *Thomas Cresap: Maryland Frontiersman*. Boston: Christopher Publishing House, 1944.

Baker, Richard. "A Successful Failure." US Army Military Institute (2010). Accessed August 21, 2017. https://www.army.mil/article/41948/A_Successful_Failure.

Balch, Thomas, ed. *Journal of the Times at the Siege of Boston Since Our Arrival at Cambridge, Near Boston: August 9, 1775*. Philadelphia: Seventy-Six Society, 1857. https://books.google.com/books?id=uHh9AAAAIAAJ&pg=PA1&lpg=PA1&dq=%E2%80%9CJournal+of+the+Times+at+the+Siege+of+Boston+since+our+Arrival+at+Cambridge#v=onepage&q&f=false.

Balch, Thomas, ed. Papers Relating Chiefly to the Maryland Line during the Revolution: Daniel McCurtin. Journal of the Times at the Siege of Boston. Philadelphia: T.K. and P.G. Collins, Printers, 1857. https://books.google.com/books?id=uHh9AAAAIAAJ&pg=PA1&lpg=PA1&dq=%E2%80%9CJournal+of+the+Times+at+the+Siege+of+Boston+since+our+Arrival+at+Cambridge#v=onepage&q&f=false.

Balfour, David M. "The Taverns of Boston in Ye Olden Time." *Bay State Monthly* 2(2) (November 2, 1884): 106–20. Accessed December 11, 2017. http://www.ma-roots.org/suffolkcounty/tav.html.

Barber, John W., and Henry Howe. *Historical Collections of the State of New Jersey*. New York: P. S. Tuttle, 1844. https://archive.org/stream/historicalcollec00john#page/n1/mode/2up.

Barber, John Warner. *Connecticut Historical Collections*. New Haven, CT: Durrie and Peck and J. W. Barber, 1836. https://archive.org/stream/connecticuthisto00inbarb#page/n26/mode/1up.

Barclay, David. *Old Houses and Historic Places in the Vicinity of Newburgh, NY*. Newburgh: NY: Historical Society of Newburgh Bay and the Highlands, 1909. https://books.google.com/books?id=_V1KAAAAYAAJ&pg=PA131&lpg=PA131&dq=Barclay,+David.+1909.+Old+Houses+and+Historic+Places+in+the+Vicinity+of+Newburgh,+NY.&source=bl&ots=5uJm8JpFm2&sig=Rl9Q5ImBejF-a1Dt0EGIkop9Fck&hl=en&sa=X&ved=0ahUKEwj4vu2Z8crXAhWpiFQKHRTYBVgQ6AEIKDAA#v=onepage&q=Barclay%2C%20David.%201909.%20Old%20Houses%20and%20Historic%20Places%20in%20the%20Vicinity%20of%20Newburgh%2C%20NY.&f=false.

Bartleby. "The Fundamental Orders of Connecticut, 1639." Accessed May 13, 2014. http://www.bartleby.com/43/7.html.

Bayles, Richard M. *History of Windham County, Connecticut*. New York: W. W. Preston and Company, 1889. https://archive.org/stream/historyofwindham00bayl#page/n4/mode/1up.

Beachy, Connie. "Early Settlers of Allegheny Co., Maryland." Our Family Histories (1998). Accessed August 24, 2017. http://www.ourfamilyhistories.com/hsdurbin/other-states/earlySettlersMD.html.

Beckius, Kim Knox. "Wander Around an Ancient Burial Ground: Here Lies William Knox." TripSavvy. Last revised May 16, 2017. http://gonewengland.about.com/od/hartfordattractions/ig/Ancient-Burying-Ground/Here-Lies-William-Knox.htm.

Bedinger, Doug. "Battle of Fort Washington." Bedinger Family History and Geneology. Accessed August 20, 2017. http://www.bedinger.org/battle-of-fort-washington.html.

———. "A Boy in Prison." Bedinger Family History and Geneology. Last revised September 2, 2015. Accessed August 20, 2017. http://www.bedinger.org/a-boy-in-prison.html.

Beers, J. H. *Commemorative Biographical Record of Dutchess County, New York*. Chicago: J. H. Beers and Co., 1897. https://archive.org/stream/commemorativebio00beers#page/424/mode/2up/search/vanderburgh.

Bell, J. L. "An Earlier Allusion: Beneath the Venerable Elm…" Boston 1775, July 18, 2010. http://boston1775.blogspot.com/2010/07/earlier-allusion-beneath-venerable-elm.html.

———. "How Many Cannons Did Washington Have in 1775?" Boston 1775, January 21, 2013. Accessed December 6, 2017. http://boston1775.blogspot.com/search/label/Richard%20Gridley.

———. "It Has Stood Like a Watchman." Boston 1775, July 5, 2010. December 12, 2014. http://boston1775.blogspot.com/2010/07/it-has-stood-like-watchman.html.

———. "Lt. Colonel Kemble's Catalogue of Deserters." Boston 1775, May 15, 2012. Accessed January 21, 2015. http://boston1775.blogspot.com/2012/05/lt-col-kembles-catalogue-of-deserters.html.

———. "Lt. Ziegler and 'Our Thirty-Two Mutineers.'" Boston 1775, February 21, 2009. Accessed June 6, 2013. http://boston1775.blogspot.com/2009/02/lt-ziegler-and-our-thirty-two-mutineers.html.

———. "Snowball Fight in Harvard Yard." Boston 1775, December 2, 2007. Accessed September 21, 2015. http://boston1775.blogspot.com/2007/12/snowball-fight-in-harvard-yard.html.

Bennett, Maria Ventresca. "A History of Roslindale." Roslindale Historical Society. Accessed Accessed May 22, 2013. http://www.roslindalehistoricalsociety.org/history.htm.

Best, Frank E. *The Amidon Family*. Chicago: Frank E. Best, 1904. https://archive.org/stream/amidonfamilyreco00best#page/n3/mode/2up.

Bethlehem, Pennsylvania Online. "History of South Bethlehem, Pennsylvania, Previous to Its Incorporation." 1913. Accessed November 14, 2017. http://www.bethlehempaonline.com/sbethhistory.html.

Black, Jeremy. *War for America: The Fight for Independence, 1775–1783*. Phoenix Mill, GB: Sutton Publishing Limited, 1991.

Black, John. "Pension Statement of John Black." *Southern Campaign American Revolution Pension Statements and Rosters*. (March 13, 1834.) Accessed December 18, 2017. http://revwarapps.org/r887.pdf.

Bloom, Robert L. *History of Adams County, Pennsylvania: 1700–1990*. Gettysburg, PA: Adams County Historical Society, 1992.

"Bogus Tombstones in Trinity Church." *New York Times*, December 15, 1901.

Bonnell, Robert O., Edgar T. Bennett, and John J. McMullen. *Report of State Roads Commission for Fiscal Years 1957–1958*. Baltimore: State Road Commission, 1958. Accessed September 25, 2017. https://archive.org/stream/reportofstateroa1957mary#page/n5/mode/2up/search/monocacy+road.

Boston Tea Party Ships and Museum. "Uniforms of the American Revolution." Accessed May 16, 2014. http://www.bostonteapartyship.com/uniforms-of-the-american-revolution.

Boutell, Lewis Henry. *The Life of Roger Sherman*. Chicago: A. C. McClurg and Company, 1896. https://archive.org/stream/lifeofrogersherm00boutiala#page/n11/mode/2up.

Bowen's Virginia Centinel and Gazette. December 29, 1794.

Brandegee, Arthur M., and Eddy H. Smith. *Farmington, Connecticut: The Village of Beautiful Homes*. Farmington, CT: Arthur M. Brandegee and Eddy H. Smith, 1906. https://archive.org/stream/farmingtonconnec00bran#page/198/mode/1up.

Bridgeman, Charles Thorley, and Clifford P. Morehouse. *A History of the Parish of Trinity Church in the City of New York*. New York: Putnam, 1898. https://books.google.com/books?id=pmAEAAAAYAAJ&pg=PA372&d

q=church+service+of+Michael+Cresap&hl=en&sa=X&ei=wRnqVMXLJMyrggTgg4LgDA&ved=0CDQQ6AEwBA#v=onepage&q=church%20service%20of%20Michael%20Cresap&f=false.

"The Brobst Chronicles: A History of the Early Brobst/Probst Families in Pennsylvania." Rootsweb. Accessed November 17, 2013. http://homepages.rootsweb.ancestry.com/~brobst/chronicles/chap3.htm.

Brooks, A. B. "Story of Fort Henry." *West Virginia History* 1(2) (1940): 110–8. Accessed January 7, 2017. http://www.wvculture.org/hiStory/journal_wvh/wvh1-2.html.

Brumbaugh, Gaius Marcus. Maryland Records: Colonial, Revolutionary, County, and Church from Original Sources, vol. 1. Baltimore: Williams and Wilkens Company, 1915.

Burlington Historical Society. "A Brief History of Burlington, Connecticut." Accessed March 28, 2014. http://www.burlington-history.org/historyof.html.

Byars, William Vincent, and M. Gratz. *1754–1798*. Jefferson City, MO: Hugh Stephens Printing Company, 1916.

"Cambridge, August 31." *Hartford Courant*, September 4, 1775.

Cannon, Timothy L., Tom Corsline, and Nancy F. Whitmore. *Pictorial History of Frederick, Maryland: The First 250 Years, 1745-1995*. Key Publishing, 1995

Chalkley, Lyman. "Chronicles of the Scotch-Irish Settlement of Virginia, vol 2." *US Gen Web Archives* (1999). Accessed November 8, 2017. http://files.usgwarchives.net/va/augusta/court/2court23.txt.

Chapin, Henry. *Address Delivered at the Unitarian Church, Uxbridge, Mass., in 1864*. Worcester, MA: Press of Charles Hamilton, 1881. https://archive.org/stream/addressdelivered1864chap#page/n3/mode/2up.

City of Easton, Pennsylvania. "General Info: A Brief History and Architectural Tour." Accessed November 13, 2017. http://www.easton-pa.com/history.html.

City of Frederick, Maryland. "History of Frederick-Town." Accessed October 4, 2013. https://www.cityoffrederick.com/306/History.

Clare, Israel Smith. *A Brief History of Lancaster County*. Lancaster, PA: Argus Publishing Company, 1892.

Clark, David B. "Five Brothers: Two Loyalists—The Green Family." United Empire Loyalists' Association of Canada, December 9, 2013. http://www.uelac.org/Loyalist-Info/extras/Green-Adam/Green-Adam-story-Dave-Clark.pdf.

Clarkson, Paul S., and Samuel R. Jett. *Luther Martin of Maryland*. Baltimore: The Johns Hopkins Press, 1970.

Claghorn, Charles Eugene III. "Washington's Travels in New England: A Chronological Itinerary." Florida Society, Sons of the American Revolution. Last revised August 4, 2003. Accessed November 21, 2017. http://archive.today/wOpmB.

"Cogswell Tavern." RevolutionaryCT.com, March 25, 2014. http://www.revolutionaryct.com/cogswell-tavern-private-residence/.

Condit, Uzal W. *A History of Easton, Pennsylvania: The Earliest Times to the Present, 1738–1885*. Easton, PA: George W. West, 1885. https://archive.org/details/historyofeastonp02cond.

Connecticut American Revolution. "Ethan Allen: The Green Mountain Boys and the Arsenal of the Revolution." Accessed March 24, 2014. http://www.ctamericanrevolution.com/maps/1_Ethan_Allen_January_2013.pdf.

Connecticut Courant, August 7, 1775. Newspapers.com

Connecticut History. "The Charter Oak Fell—Today in History: August 21." Accessed May 13, 2014. http://connecticuthistory.org/the-charter-oak-fell/.

———. "George Washington Slept Here (Just Perhaps Not Well)." Accessed May 16, 2104. http://connecticuthistory.org/george-washington-slept-here-just-perhaps-not-well/.

Connecticut History Illustrated. "Moses Butler Tavern, Hartford, October 2, 1893." Accessed May 19, 2014. http://www.cthistoryonline.org/cdm/singleitem/collection/cho/id/829/rec/6.

———. "Old Red Tavern on Park Street, Hartford." Accessed May 19, 2014. http://connecticuthistoryillustrated.org/islandora/object/40002%3A19983.

Connecticut Military Department. "Connecticut Military History: Israel Putnam." Accessed May 16, 2014. http://www.ct.gov/mil/cwp/view.asp?a=1351&q=258410.

Connecticut Society of the Sons of the American Revolution. "Governor Oliver Wolcott Branch #10." Accessed March 25, 2014. http://www.connecticutsar.org/branches/wolcott.htm.

Constitutional Gazette. August 9, 1775. Newspapers.com

Cornish, Louis Henry, and Alonzo Howard Clark. *National Society, Sons of the American Revolution, National Register*, vol. 2. New York: Louis H. Cornish, 1902. https://archive.org/stream/nationalregister00sons#page/n9/mode/2up.

Costello, Don. "The Settling of Bolton." Bolton Historical Society, October 1995. May 19, 2014. http://www.boltoncthistory.org/specialedition.html.

Coughlin, Bill. "The Spirit of 1775." Historical Marker Database, April 15, 2011. Accessed September 9, 2014. http://www.hmdb.org/marker.asp?marker=41708.

Crawford, Mary Caroline. *Among Old New England Inns*. Boston: Colonial Press, 1907. http://books.google.com/books?id=_Qc1AAAAIAAJ&pg=PA378&lpg=PA378&dq=Perkins+Tavern+%2B+AShford&source=bl&ots=zqZ1yL4Yn5&sig=O7HRNTtQk2pTAgiDL0qvMswxkkw&hl=en&sa=X&ei=mpBWU5-tJK7jsASQhIDgDA&ved=0CGMQ6AEwBw#v=onepage&q=Perkins%20Tavern%20%2B%20AShford&f=false.

Cresap, Joseph Ord, and Bernarr Cresap. *The History of the Cresaps*. Gallatin, TN: The Cresap Society, 1987.

Cresap, Michael, and Thomas Cresap. "The Subscribers Having a Piece of Ground at Old-Town." *Maryland Gazette*, March 19, 1767.

Cresap, Nina. "Joseph Cresap's Cresaptown." Rootsweb. Accessed August 24, 2017. http://www.rootsweb.ancestry.com/~mdallegh/Cresaptown.htm.

Crumrine, Boyd. The Courts, Bench, and Bar of Washington County, Pennsylvania. Chicago: Lakeside Press, 1902.

Cummins, George Wyckoff. *History of Warren County, New Jersey*. New York: Lewis Historical Publishing Company, 1911. https://archive.org/stream/cu31924010411118#page/n7/mode/2up.

Dandridge, Danske. *American Prisoners of the Revolution*. Charlottesville, VA: The Mische Company Printers, 1911. https://archive.org/stream/cu31924093960825#page/n7/mode/2up.

———. *George Michael Bedinger: A Kentucky Pioneer*. Charlottesville, VA: The Mische Company Printers, 1909. Accessed August 21, 2017. https://archive.org/stream/georgemichaelbed00dand#page/n5/mode/2up.

———. *Historic Shepherdstown*. Charlottesville, VA: Michie Company, 1910. https://babel.hathitrust.org/cgi/pt?id=mdp.39015013136166;view=1up;seq=7.

Darlington, Mary Carson. *History of Colonel Bouquet and the Western Frontiers of Pennsylvania: 1747–1764*. Pittsburgh, PA: privately printed, 1920. https://archive.org/details/historycolonelh00darlgoog.

Dary, David. *Frontier Medicine: From the Atlantic to the Pacific*. New York: Alfred A. Knopf, 2008.

Day, Richard Perrin. "A Perrin History: The Lazear Family." Perrin History (2016). Accessed August 21, 2017. http://www.perrinhistory.net/Narrative/SectBLazear/lazear.html.

Dedham Historical Society. "A Capsule History of Dedham." Accessed September 10, 2014. http://web.archive.org/web/20061006081231/http://www.dedhamhistorical.org/history.php.

DePalma, Anthony. *Here: A Biography of the New American Continent*. New York: PublicAffairs, 2001.

DePold, Hans. "225th Anniversary of Rochambeau's March through Bolton." Bolton Historical Society, June 2006. Accessed May 19, 2014. http://www.boltoncthistory.org/rochambeaumarch.html.

———. *Bolton Historic Tales: America Chronicles.* Charleston, SC: History Press, 2008.

———. "Bolton's Historical Moments During the American Revolution." Bolton Historical Society. Last revised September 2013. Accessed May 15, 2014. http://www.boltoncthistory.org/historicmoments.html.

———. "The Changing Face of Bolton's Heritage Farm House." Bolton Historical Society, October 2007. Accessed November 25, 2017. http://www.boltoncthistory.org/heritagefarmhouse.html.

———. "The Oliver White Tavern." Bolton Historical Society, February 2006. Accessed May 19, 2014. http://www.boltoncthistory.org/oliverwhitetavern.html.

———. "Rediscovering the Minister's House." Bolton Historical Society, December 2005. Accessed May 19, 2014. http://www.boltoncthistory.org/ministershouse.html.

Desjardin, Thomas. *Through A Howling Wilderness: Benedict' Arnold's March to Quebec, 1775.* New York: St. Martin's Griffin, 1907.

Devine, Joseph. "Mastadons of Orange County, New York." Accessed January 28, 2014. http://home.roadrunner.com/~montghistory/The%20Mastodons%20of%20Orange%20County%20042809.pdf.

Digital History. "The Problems That England Faced after the French and Indian War," 2007. Accessed December 15, 2017. http://www.digitalhistory.uh.edu/teachers/lesson_plans/pdfs/unit1_6.pdf.

Digital Maryland. Cator Print 163: Fountain Inn. Accessed September 26, 2017. http://collections.digitalmaryland.org/cdm/ref/collection/cator/id/65.

Donovan, Francis D. *The New Grant: A History of Medway.* New York: Mill River Press, 1976.

———. *The Middle Post Road.* Medway, MA: Francis D. Donovan, 1991.

Drake, Francis S. *The Town of Roxbury: Its Memorable Persons and Places.* Roxbury, MA: Francis D. Drake, 1878. https://archive.org/stream/townofroxburyits00drak#page/n7/mode/2up.

DuPont, Ronald J. Jr. *Vernon 200: A Bicentennial History of the Township of Vernon, New Jersey, 1792–1992.* McAfee, NJ: The Friends of Dorothy E. Henry Library, 1992.

Durham, J. Lloyd. "Outfitting an American Revolutionary Soldier." NCpedia, 1992. Accessed May 16, 2014. http://ncpedia.org/history/usrevolution/soldiers.

"Early Hotels of the Town of Newton." *New Jersey Herald,* February 27, 1919. http://bergencountyhistory.org/forums/index.php?topic=45.0.

Edwards, William Waller. "Morgan and His Riflemen." *The William and Mary Quarterly* 23 (1914): 73-105. https://archive.org/details/jstor-1915109.

Electric Scotland. "The Glengarry McDonalds of Virginia: Angus McDonald (Emigrant)." Accessed January 7, 2017. http://www.electricscotland.com/webclans/m/macdonald/glengarry2.htm.

Ellis, Franklin. *History of Fayette County, PA, with Biographical Sketches of Many of Its Pioneers and Prominent Men.* Philadelphia: L. H. Everts and Co., 1882. https://archive.org/stream/historyoffayette00elli#page/n5/mode/2up.

Ellis, George Edward. *March 17, 1876: Celebration of the Centennial Anniversary of the Evacuation of Boston by the British Army, March 17, 1776.* Boston: By order of the City Council, 1876. http://archive.org/stream/marchthcelebrat00edwagoog#page/n181/mode/1up/search/Lamb's+Dam.

Elson, Louis C. *The History of American Music.* New York: MacMillan Company, 1904. https://babel.hathitrust.org/cgi/pt?id=mdp.39015054365468;view=1up;seq=16.

Emerson, William A. *History of the Town of Douglas, Massachusetts.* Boston: Frank W. Bird, 1879. https://archive.org/stream/historyoftownofd00emer#page/n7/mode/1up.

Everhart, J. F., and A. A. Graham. *History of Muskinghum County, Ohio.* Columbus, OH: J. F. Everhart & Co, 1882. https://archive.org/details/cu31924028848673.

"Extract from a Letter from Cambridge." *Pennsylvania Packet*, August 28 1775, 6.

"Extract from a Letter from Fredericktown, Aug. 1." *Pennsylvania Gazette*, August 16, 1775.

"Extract of a Letter from a Gentleman in Frederick-town to his Friend in Baltimore, dated July 19." *Pennsylvania Packet*, August 7, 1775.

"Extract from a Letter from Prospect Hill, August 31." *Pennsylvania Gazette,* September 21, 1775.

Family Search. "First Pennsylvania Regiment (Revolutionary War)." Accessed September 11, 2013. https://familysearch.org/learn/wiki/en/1st_Pennsylvania_Regiment_(Revolutionary_War.

FamilyHart. "Garrett County Revolutionary War Veterans." Rootsweb (2013). Accessed August 21, 2017. http://midatlantic.rootsweb.ancestry.com/MD/garrett/revwarvets.html.

Find a Grave. "Captain Israel Seymour." Accessed May 13, 2014. http://www.findagrave.com/cgi-bin/fg.cgi?page=gr&GRid=10485534.

Fischer, David Hackett. *Liberty and Freedom: A Visual History of America's Founding Ideas.* New York: Oxford University Press, 2005. http://books.google.com/books?id=uc8KP_QtW-sC&pg=PA99&lpg=PA99&dq=Pillar+of+Liberty+%2B+Dedham+%2B+Massachusetts&source=bl&ots=vu-44P1CEc&sig=9xLYVkZ4xD1SDKY_V4EXIF2HyTE&hl=en&sa=X&ei=a-_9U77iDfLfsASD0oGICg&ved=0CDUQ6AEwAg#v=onepage&q=Pillar%20of%20Liberty%20%2B%20Dedham%20%2B%20Massachusetts&f=false.

Fitzpatrick, John C., ed. *The Writings of George Washington from the Original Manuscript Sources 1745–1799*, vol. 3. Washington, DC: US Government Printing Office, 1931. https://catalog.hathitrust.org/Record/000366819.

———. *Writings of George Washington*, vol. 4. Washington, DC: US Government Office, 1931. https://catalog.hathitrust.org/Record/000366819.

———. *Writings of George Washington*, vol. 5. Washington, DC: US Government Office, 1932. https://catalog.hathitrust.org/Record/000366819.

Foote, William Henry. 1850. "Cornstalk, The Shawnee Chief." *Southern Literary Messenger* 16(9) (1850): 533–40. http://www.newrivernotes.com/topical_books_1850_virginia_cornstalk_shawneechief.htm.

Force, Peter. *Peter Force's American Archives*, 4th series, vol. 4. n.d. http://archive.org/stream/AmericanArchives-FourthSeriesVolume4peterForce/AaSeries4VolumeIv#page/n836/mode/1up.

Frassett, James. "Daniel Morgan—The Early Years." *Lock Stock and Barrel Living History Newsletter and Event Calendar* 3(4) (2000). Accessed March 4, 2013. http://www.revolutionarywararchives.org/morganearlyyears.html.

Frazza, Al. "Revolutionary War Sites in Newton, New Jersey." Revolutionary War New Jersey, 2017. Accessed November 14, 2017. http://www.revolutionarywarnewjersey.com/new_jersey_revolutionary_war_sites/towns/newton_nj_revolutionary_war_sites.htm.

———. "Revolutionary War Sites in Oxford, New Jersey." Revolutionary War New Jersey, 2013. Accessed November 14, 2017. http://www.revolutionarywarnewjersey.com/new_jersey_revolutionary_war_sites/towns/oxford_nj_revolutionary_war_sites.htm.

Freeman, Douglas Southall. *Planter and Patriot*, vol. 3 of *George Washington: A Biography.* New York: Scribner, 1951.

French, Allen. *The Siege of Boston.* New York: MacMillan Company, 1911.

Frothingham, Richard, Jr. *History of the Siege of Boston.* Boston: Charles C. Little and James Brown, 1851. https://archive.org/stream/historysiegebos01frotgoog#page/n5/mode/2up.

Fullerton, Max. "The Stamp Act: The Day Frederick County Rebelled." *Baltimore Sunday Sun Magazine*, November 21, 1965. http://www.judgedavidlynn.org/The_Stamp_Act.html.

Gage, General. "Extract of a Letter From General Gage to Lord Dartmouth." *American Archives: Documents of the American Revolution, 1774-1776.* June 25, 1775. http://amarch.lib.niu.edu/islandora/object/niu-amarch%3A90144 (Accessed January 30, 2018).

Galvin, James. "Washington Rides Through." Farmington Historical Society, March 29, 2014. http://farmington-historicalsociety-ct.org/1780/09/washington-rides-through/.

Genealogy.com. "My Family: Information About John Evans." Accessed September 16, 2013. http://familytreemaker.genealogy.com/users/k/o/z/Mary-Evelyn-Kozlov/WEBSITE-0001/UHP-0278.html.

George Washington's Dates and Places. Accessed March 29, 2014. https://sites.google.com/site/gwdatesplaces/dates.

George Washington's Mount Vernon. "Nelson (Horse)." Accessed March 24, 2014. http://www.mountvernon.org/educational-resources/encyclopedia/nelson.

Glanville, Jim. "Fort Gower: Forgotten Shrine of Virginia History."*Augusta Historical Bulletin* 46 (2010): 74–90. Accessed January 9, 2017. http://www.holstonia.net/files/FortGower2011.pdf.

Goodrich, Charles A. *Lives of the Signers to the Declaration of Independence.* Hartford, CT: R. G. H. Huntington, 1841.

Gorecki, Larry. "The Necessary Considerations of Emulating an American Rifleman During the American Revolutionary War." The Continental Line, 2001. Accessed September 9, 2014. http://www.continentalline.org/articles/0103/010301.htm.

Grady, Richard. "Mendon Walking Tour." Blackstone Daily, July 23, 2014. http://www.blackstonedaily.com/mendon.pdf.

———. "Now and Then—The Ammidon Inn." Mendon, Massachusetts, July 2014. http://hope1842.com/mendonntammidon.html.

Grady, Richard, and John Trainor. "Patriots Day: Mendon's Role in the American Revolution." Mendon, Massachusetts, July 23, 2014. http://hope1842.com/mendonamerrev.html.

Graydon, Alexander. *Memoirs of His Own Time.* Philadelphia: Lindsay and Blakiston, 1846. https://books.google.com/books?id=HjIEAAAAQAAJ&printsec=frontcover&source=gbs_ge_summary_r&cad=0#v=onepage&q=rawlings%20fought%20with%20&f=false.

"The Greathouse Family of Ohio Country (West) Virginia, and Brown County, Ohio." Last revision by Marjorie, July 9, 2007. Accessed January 6, 2017. https://web.archive.org/web/20080212203527/http://home.earthlink.net/~leota_m/grathous.html.

Griggs, Susan J. *Folklore and Firesides in Pomfret, Hampton, and Vicinity (1950).* Salem, MA: Higginson Book Company, 1992. https://archive.org/stream/earlyhomesteadso00grig#page/n0/mode/1up.

Guelzo, Allen C. *The American Revolution.* Chantilly, VA: The Teaching Company, 2008.

"Gunmakers along the Wyomissing Produced Arms for Reading Riflemen Who Aided Washington: Local Troops Rushed to Commander's Assistance When War Started." *Reading Eagle*, September 23, 1934. http://news.google.com/newspapers?nid=1955&dat=19340922&id=4PIwAAAAIBAJ&sjid=k-EFAAAAIBAJ&pg=3724,4534628.

Gustafson, A. "Presidential Visits to the Brooklyn Navy Yard." (February 15, 2013). Retrieved December 19 2017. http://turnstiletours.com/presidential-visits-to-the-brooklyn-navy-yard/.

Halbrook, Stephen P. *The Founders' Second Amendment: Origins of the Right to Bear Arms.* Chicago: Ivan R. Dee, 2008. https://books.google.com/books?id=1DWSBAAAQBAJ&pg=PA99&lpg=PA99&dq=placed+their+balls+in+poles+of+seven+inches+diameter,+fixed+up+for+the+purpose+at+a+distance+of+two+hundred+and+fifty+yards&source=bl&ots=VJVI46Ag8t&sig=Hy-IDud16mIm44YFcEAAME85UpU&hl=en&s.

Hale, Edward Everett. "Captain Nathan Hale (1755–1776)." The Connecticut Society of the Sons of the American Revolution. Accessed May 15, 2014. http://www.connecticutsar.org/patriots/hale_nathan.htm.

Hamilton, Schuyler. *History of the National Flag of the United States of America*. Philadelphia: Lippencott, Grambo, and Company, 1852.

Hamwey, Ken. "Bellingham Historical Museum Could Use a Helping Hand." *Bellingham Bulletin*, November 2009. Accessed November 26, 2017. http://www.bluetoad.com/display_article.php?id=253829.

Hannum, Patrick H. "America's First Company Commanders." *Infantry* 4 (2013): 12–9. Accessed December 19, 2017. http://www.benning.army.mil/infantry/magazine/issues/2013/Oct-Dec/pdfs/Hannum.pdf.

Hanover Area Chamber of Commerce. "Hanover's History." Accessed September 25, 2017. http://hanoverchamber.com/wp-content/uploads/2014/10/HanoversHistory.pdf.

Hanover (York County, PA) Centennial Committee. *Official Program of the Centennial of Incorporation of the Borough of Hanover*. Hanover, PA: E. L. Koller, 1915. Accessed November 10, 2017. https://archive.org/stream/cu31924028862402#page/n27/mode/2up/search/tavern.

Harrington, Hugh T. "Patriot Riflemen During the Ammunition Crisis at the Siege of Boston in 1775." AmericanRevolution.org." 2000. Accessed January 21, 2013. http://www.americanrevolution.org/riflemen.html.

Harrison, Hugh T. "Patriot Riflemen During the Ammunition Crisis at the Siege of Boston in 1775." AmericanRevolution.org, 2000. Accessed January 21, 2013. http://www.americanrevolution.org/riflemen.html.

Harrity, William Francis. *Journal of Captain William Hendricks: From Carlisle to Boston, Thence to Quebec, 1775*, 2nd series, vol. 15. Harrisburg, PA: E. K. Meyers, 1890. https://books.google.com/books?id=LA5JAQAAMAAJ&pg=PA22&lpg=PA22&dq=Archives+%2B+Journal+of+Captain+William+Hendricks&source=bl&ots=747gRoBP6p&sig=ZIA6B24oSmCVy9glXYrXJv4XTpc&hl=en&sa=X&ved=0ahUKEwjSl_XulrnXAhUJ3SYKHXldBg4Q6AEIKDAA#v=onepage&q=Archives%20%2B%20Journal%20of%20Captain%20William%20Hendricks&f=false.

Hart, J. Percy. *Hart's History and Directory of Three Towns: Brownsville, Bridgeport, and West Brownsville, Pennsylvania* (Cadwallader, PA: J. Percy Hart, 1904.

Hartford Courant, September 11, 1775.

Harwinton Historical Society. "The Stage Coach Ride from Hartford to Litchfield." Accessed March 25, 2014. http://www.harwintonhistory.com/Stagecoachroad.html.

Hasbrouk, Frank. *History of Dutchess County, NY*. Poughkeepsie, NY: S. A. Matthieu, 1909. https://archive.org/stream/cu31924028853327#page/n9/mode/2up/search/upper+road.

Haskell, Albert L. 2013. *Haskell's Historical Guide of Somerville, Massachusetts*. Somerville, MA: Albert L. Haskell, n.d. Accessed March 4, 2013. http://www.somervillema.gov/sites/default/files/documents/HaskellsHistoricalGuideBook.pdf.

Haskell, Caleb. Caleb Haskell's Diary: May 5, 1775–May 30, 1776: A Revolutionary Soldier's Record before Boston and with Arnold's Quebec Expedition. Edited by Lothrop Withington. Newburyport, MA: William H. Huse & Company, 1881.

Headley, Russel. *History of Orange County, New York*. Middletown, NY: Van Deusen and Elms, 1908. https://archive.org/details/historyoforangec00head

Hearn, Donna P. "Brief Overview of the Town of Dover's History." Town of Dover, New York. Accessed January 30, 2014. http://townofdoverny.us/Town_History.cfm.

Heart, Jonathan, Wilshire Butterfield, John Dickinson, and Josiah Harmar. *Journal of Captain Jonathan Heart on the March with His Company from Connecticut to Fort Pitt.* Albany, NY: Joel Munsell's Sons, 1885.

Heitman, Francis B. *Historical Register of the Officers of the Continental Army: April 1775 to December 1783.* Washington, DC: The Rare Book Shop Publishing Company, 1914. https://archive.org/stream/franheitmanreg00bernrich#page/148/mode/2up/search/Chambers.

Helfenstein, Ernest. *Historical Notes of All Saints Parish, Frederick, MD, 1742–1908.* Frederick, MD: Marken and Bielfeld, 1908. http://books.google.com/books?id=CaA9AAAAYAAJ&printsec=frontcover&source=gbs_ge_summary_r&cad=0#v=onepage&q&f=false.

Hentz, Tucker F. *Unit History of the Maryland and Virginia Regiment (1776–1781): Insights from the Service Record of Capt. Adamson Tannehill.* Richmond: Virginia Historical Society, 2007. http://www.vahistorical.org/research/tann.pdf.

Hentz, Tucker F. "Unit History of the Maryland and Virginia Rifle Regiment (1776-1781): Insights from the Service Record of Capt. Adamson Tannehill." *Military Collector and Historian, Vol. 58, No.3., 129-144.* Fall 2006. www.military-historians.org/company/journal/58-3/58-3.pdf (accessed February 9, 2018).

Hickman, Kennedy. "American Revolution: Brigadier General Daniel Morgan." ThoughtCo. Accessed April 4, 2017. https://www.thoughtco.com/brigadier-general-daniel-morgan-2360604.

———. "American Revolution: Siege of Boston." ThoughtCo, May 8, 2015. http://militaryhistory.about.com/od/americanrevolution/p/siege-of-boston.htm.

Hicks, Whitehead. *Connecticut Journal*, October 23, 1775. Newspapers.com

Higginbotham, Don. *Daniel Morgan: Revolutionary Rifleman.* Chapel Hill: Omahundro Institute of Early American Culture and the University of North Carolina Press, 1979.

———. *The War for American Independence: Military Attitudes, Policies, and Practices, 1763–1789.* New York: The Macmillan Company, 1971.

Historic Buildings of Connecticut. "Elm Tree Inn (1655)." August 25, 2009. Accessed March 24, 2014. http://historicbuildingsct.com/?p=1938.

———. "Oliver White Tavern (1743)." March 3, 2010. Accessed May 15, 2014. http://historicbuildingsct.com/?p=3160.

———. "Rose Farm House, Bolton (1725)." March 8, 2010. Accessed May 15, 2014. http://historicbuildingsct.com/?p=3169.

———. "Sheldon's Tavern (1760)." July 8, 2008. Accessed March 31, 2014. http://historicbuildingsct.com/?p=859.

"Historic Downtown Lancaster Self-Guided Walking Tour." Lancaster City Visitor Center, 2011. Accessed October 24, 2013. http://freepages.genealogy.rootsweb.ancestry.com/~hanksplace/Files/TourBooklet.pdf.

Historical and Genealogical Record of Dutchess and Putnam Counties, NY. Poughkeepsie, NY: The A.V. Haight Co., 1912. https://archive.org/stream/historicalgeneal01oxfo#page/22/mode/2up.

Historical Maps of Pennsylvania. "1775–1779 Pennsylvania Maps." Accessed November 15, 2013. http://www.mapsofpa.com/18thcentury/1777fadenatlaspa.jpg.

———. "Faden 1777 Colonial Map of New York and Connecticut." Accessed January 30, 2014. http://www.mapsofpa.com/18thcentury/1777fadenmontresor.jpg.

"History of the Grosvenor Family." Ohio University Alumni. Accessed May 16, 2014. http://www.ohioalumni.org/grosvenor-family.

History.org. Declaration and Resolves of the First Continental Congress, October 14, 1774." Accessed December 2017. http://www.history.org/almanack/life/politics/resolves.cfm.

"History's Headlines: Highway to the Past: The 18th Century Road Between Easton and Reading Was Once the Pathway to Patriots." WFMZ-TV 69 News, May 27, 2016. Accessed November 13, 2017. http://www.wfmz.com/features/historys-headlines/historys-headlines-highway-to-the-past-the-18th-century-road-between-easton-and-reading-was-once-the-pathway-of-patriots/18286679.

Hooker, David J. "Colonel James Ross." September 9, 2014. http://www.djhooker.com/26/10990.htm.

Hueneke, Chris. "The Abrahams." Umstead Family Genealogy Central, 2007 Accessed. September 14, 2014. http://www.umstead.org/abraham%20md%20time%20line.html.

Hurd, D. Hamilton. *History of Norfolk County, Massachusetts, with Biographical Sketches of Many of Its Pioneers and Prominent Men.* Philadelphia: J. W. Lewis and Co., 1884. https://archive.org/stream/historyofnorfolk00hurd#page/n5/mode/2up.

Hurley, Joe. "New Milford Loses Historic Oak." *Danbury News-Times*, April 4, 2003. http://www.gaylordsville.org/DNT_APR16_TREE.html.

Hurst, Neal Thomas. "Fringe on American Hunting Shirts, CA 1775–1815." N. Hurst Historic Tailoring. Accessed May 16, 2014. http://www.nhursttailor.com/N.Hurst_Tailor/Research_files/Fringe.pdf.

———. "'Kind of Armour Being Peculiar to America': The American Hunting Shirt." BA thesis, College of William and Mary, 2013. Accessed May 13, 2014. http://www.academia.edu/3336557/_kind_of_armour_being_peculiar_to_America_The_American_Hunting_Shirt.

Hutchinson, Paul. "George Washington's Presidential Trail." Accessed July 23. 2014. http://www.paulhutch.com/brv_nhc/gw_presidential_trail.htm.

———. "Photo Album. Places. Blackstone River Valley National Heritage Corridor, Mendon." Accessed July 23, 2014. http://www.paulhutch.com/images/photowebs/Places/Blackstone_River_Valley_National_Heritage_Corridor/Mendon/slides/IMGP5157.html.

Irving, Washington. *The Life of George Washington*, vol. 1. London: Henry G. Bohn, 1855.

Jacob, John J. A Biographical Sketch of the Late Captain Michael Cresap. Cincinnati, OH: John F. Uhlhorn, 1866.

Jacob, John Jeremiah. "Pension Statement of John Jeremiah Jacob." *Southern Campaign American Revolution Pension Statements and Rosters* (May 27, 1818). December 18, 2017. http://revwarapps.org/w11930.pdf.

Jacob Rohrbach Inn. "The Farmsteads of Antietam: Joshua Newcomer Farm." August 9, 2017. https://jacob-rohrbach-inn.com/blog/2017/08/the-farmsteads-of-antietam-joshua-newcomer-farm/.

Jahntz, David C. 2012. "A Look at Late Eighteenth Century Medical Practices." BAHR No Products, 2012. Accessed April 11, 2016. http://www.bahrnoproducts.com/PDF/A%20LOOK%20AT%20LATE%2018TH%20CENTURY%20MEDICAL%20PRACTICES.pdf.

James, James Alton. *George Rogers Clark Papers, 1771–1781*, vol. 3. Springfield, IL: Trustees of the Illinois Sates Historical Library, 1912. Accessed August 22, 2017. https://archive.org/stream/georgerogerscla00jamegoog#page/n13/mode/1up.

Jameson, E. O. *The History of Medway, 1713–1885*. Providence, RI: J. A. and R. A. Reid, 1886. https://archive.org/stream/historyofmedwaym00jame#page/n55/mode/2up.

Jefferson County Historical Society. "Historic Figures of Jefferson County." Accessed January 21, 2013. http://jeffersonhistoricalwv.org/thepeopleb.html.

"Joe Volz: Remembering Repudiation Day in Frederick." Gazette.Net, November 25, 2010. http://ww2.gazette.net/stories/11252010/fredcol182434_32534.php.

Johnson, F. C., ed. *The Historical Record Devoted Principally to the Early History of Wyoming Valley.* Wilkes-Barre, PA: Press of Wilkes-Barre Record, 1899. https://archive.org/stream/historicalrecordv8john#page/n3/mode/2up/search/Lukens.

Johnston, Henry P. *The Campaign of 1776 Around New York and Brooklyn*. Brooklyn, NY: Long Island Historical Press, 1878. https://archive.org/stream/campaignof1776ar00john#page/n7/mode/2up/search/cresap.

Jordon, Francis Jr. *The Life of William Henry of Lancaster, Pennsylvania (1729–1786)*. Lancaster, PA: New Era Printing Company, 1910.

Kelley, Frank Bergin. *Historical Guide to the City of New York*. New York: Frederick A. Stokes Company, 1909. https://archive.org/details/historicalguidet00citya.

Kellogg, Louis Phelps. *Frontier Retreat on the Upper Ohio, 1779–1781*. Madison, WI: Wisconsin Historical Publications, 1917. https://archive.org/stream/frontierretreato00kellrich#page/16/mode/2up/search/roger.

———. "The Recognition of George Rogers Clark." *Indiana Magazine of History* 25(1) (1929): 40–46. Accessed August 22, 2017. https://scholarworks.iu.edu/journals/index.php/imh/article/view/6485/6691.

Kentucky Rifle Association. *The Kentucky Rifle: A True American Heritage in Picture*. Washington, DC: The Forte Group, 1985.

Kollen, Richard. "Washington's Dinner at Munroe Tavern." Lexington Historical Society, March 2011. Accessed May 16, 2014. http://lhsoc.weebly.com/uploads/6/5/2/1/6521332/washingtons_dinner_at_munroe_tavern-d.pdf.

Kummel, Henry B. "Map Showing Direction of Ice Movement in Northern New Jersey." Rutger's University Cartography Services, 2013. Accessed November 15, 2017. http://mapmaker.rutgers.edu/HISTORICALMAPS/IceMovement_1902.jpg.

Kutztown Historical Committee. *The Centennial History of Kutztown, Pennsylvania*. Kutztown, PA: Kutztown Publishing Company, 1915. https://archive.org/stream/cu31924028863490#page/n63/mode/2up/search/swan.

Laidley, W.S. "Captain Michael Cresap and the Indian Logan." *The West Virginia Historical Magazine Quarterly* 3-5 (1903): 159. https://books.google.com/books?id=6_QxAQAAMAAJ&pg=PA159&lpg=PA159&dq=experienced+officers%E2%80%A6the+very+best+men+that+can+be+procured%E2%80%A6to+honor+the+Maryland+Province.&source=bl&ots=4IbdIt017P&sig=O2G4at0yehVg3oumK5ajlPWweRs&hl=en&sa=X&ved=0ahUKE.

Lancaster County Historical Society. *Papers Read Before the Lancaster County Historical Society*, vol. 25–26. Lancaster, PA: Lancaster County Historical Society, 1921. http://books.google.com/books?id=-tUwAQAAMAAJ&pg=PA128&lpg=PA128&dq=1775+Lancaster+North+American+Hotel&source=bl&ots=e_d_ljDR4D&sig=dXonZ1XCGT5zg2CIAB4TaYrdydo&hl=en&sa=X&ei=TtxOUpf0HeKnigLixIEY&ved=0CEUQ6AEwAg#v=onepage&q=1775%20Lancaster%20North%20.

LancasterHistory.org. "Sketch of Joseph Simon." October 24, 2013. http://www.lancasterhistory.org/images/stories/JournalArticles/vol3no7pp165_172.pdf.

"Lancaster's Ancient Inns: Taverns Which Have Stood Since the American Revolution." *New York Times*, August 27, 1888. http://query.nytimes.com/mem/archive-free/pdf?res=F00E12F9395413738DDDAE0A94D0405B8884F0D3.

Lantz, Emily Emerson. "Lineage of the Rawlings." *Baltimore Sun*, May 14, 1905.

Lee, Richard Henry. *The Letters of Richard Henry Lee: Volume 1, 1762-1778*. New York: The Macmillan Company, 1911. https://books.google.com/books?id=Sb8KAQAAIAAJ&pg=PA131&lpg=PA131&dq=%E2%80%9CEvery+shot+is+fatal.%E2%80%9D+%2B+Richard+Henry+Lee+%2B+rifle&source=bl&ots=kUQQjokWk7&sig=2DEWxHSmtYNauuKARfnRT7riQuk&hl=en&sa=X&ved=0ahUKEwi0s-nL4MrXAhWLMSYKHfZADC8Q6AEIKzAB#v.

Lehigh County Historical Society. *Proceedings of the Lehigh County Historical Society*, vol. 5. Allentown, PA: Lehigh County Historical Society, 1921. http://books.google.com/books?id=pJUyAQAAMAAJ&pg=PA27&lpg=PA27&dq=July+18++%2B+1775+%2B+%22George+Nagle%22+%2B+Rifle&source=bl&ots=x1tNVvbXvt&sig=VUpkMz5uFXkZgkMW_xUkKfIgZQc&hl=en&sa=X&ei=UrzvU5isHoyLyATo54DIBA&ved=0CB0Q6AEwAA#v=onepage&q=July%2018%20%20%2B%201775%20%2B%20%22George%20Nagle%22%20%2B%20Rifle&f=false.

Levering, Joseph Mortimer. *A History of Bethlehem, Pennsylvania: 1741–1892*. Bethlehem, PA: Times Publishing Company, 1903. https://archive.org/details/historybethlehem00leve.

Lewis, J. W. *History of Litchfield County, Connecticut*. Philadelphia: J. B. Lippincott and Co., 1881. https://archive.org/stream/historyoflitchfi00jwle#page/n1/mode/2up.

Lewis, Virgil. A. M. *History of the Battle of Point Pleasant: Fought between White Men and Indians at the Mouth of the Great Kanawha River*. Charleston, SC: The Tribune Printing Company, 1908. https://archive.org/stream/historybattlepo01lewigoog#page/n8/mode/2up.

Library of Congress. "The Province of New Jersey, Divided into East and West, Commonly Called the Jerseys." Accessed December 9, 2013. http://www.loc.gov/resource/g3810.ct000079/.

Lincoln, Allen B. *A Modern History of Windham County, Connecticut*, vol. 2. Chicago: S. J. Clarke Publishing Company, 1920.

Linn, John B., and William H. Egle. "Col. William Thompson's Battalion of Riflemen: June 25, 1775–July 1, 1776." In *Pennsylvania Archives*. 2nd series, vol. 10, 8–10. Harrisburg, PA: Clarence M. Busch, 1895. https://archive.org/stream/pennsylvaniaser210harruoft#page/8/mode/2up.

———. *Pennsylvania, War of the Revolution: Battalions and Line*. Harrisburg, PA: Lane and Hart, 1880. https://archive.org/stream/pennsylvaniainwa01linniala#page/5/mode/1up.

Litchfield Historical Society. "Oliver Wolcott." Accessed March 28, 2014. http://www.litchfieldhistoricalsociety.org/library/families/wolcott_oliver.php.

Little, James. "Ancestors of Elizabeth 'Betsy' Collier Little." California Littles. Accessed May 13, 2014. http://www.californialittles.com/betsycollier/a8.htm#i751.

"London Intelligence." *London Public Advertiser*, August 5, 1775.

London Public Advertiser, September 12, 1775. Newspapers.com

London Public Advertiser, November 3, 1775.

Lossing, Benson J. *The Diary of George Washington from 1789–1791*. New York: Charles B. Richardson and Company, 1860. https://archive.org/stream/diaryofgeorgewas01wash#page/48/mode/2up/search/thompson.

———. "Pictorial Field Book of the Revolution." 1850. Rootsweb. Accessed January 7, 2015. http://freepages.history.rootsweb.ancestry.com/~wcarr1/Lossing1/Chap22.html.

"Lost City: Local Taverns and Big Breweries." Underbelly, February 18, 2016. Accessed September 25, 2017. http://www.mdhs.org/underbelly/2016/02/18/lost-city-local-taverns-and-big-breweries/.

Loucks, Augusta. "History of York Rifle Company." USGenWeb Archives, 1908. Accessed September 11, 2014. http://files.usgwarchives.net/pa/york/military/rifles1.txt.

Love, William DeLoss. *The Colonial History of Hartford*. Hartford, CT: William DeLoss Love, 1914. https://archive.org/stream/colonialhistoryo00hart#page/n9/mode/2up.

Lowdermilk, Will H. *History of Cumberland, Maryland*. Washington, DC: James Anglim, 1878. https://archive.org/stream/historycumberla00lowdgoog#page/n8/mode/2up.

"Lt. Colonel Thomas Knowlton, Connecticut's Forgotten Hero." The Connecticut Society of the Sons of the American Revolution. Accessed May 15, 2014. http://www.connecticutsar.org/patriots/knowlton_thomas.htm.

Lukens, Herman Tyson. "Are You a Descendant of Jan Lucken, One of the Founding Fathers of Germantown, PA in 1683?" Rootsweb. Accessed May 13, 2014. http://freepages.genealogy.rootsweb.ancestry.com/~lukens/jan4/d0/i0001032.htm.

Maass, John R. "June Fourteenth: The Birthday of the US Army." US Army Center of Military History. (2013). Accessed September 24, 2017. http://www.history.army.mil/html/faq/birth.html.

Mackesy, Piers. *The War for America: 1775–1783*. Cambridge, MA: Harvard University Press, 1964.

Martin, Brooke E. "History of Farmington, Parts 1–3." Farmington Historical Society, March 24, 2014. http://www.farmingtonhistoricalsociety-ct.org/fh_histsources.html.

Martin, Douglas. "Resurrecting Patriots and Their Park: Shrine to Revolution Martyrs Is Part of the Fort Greene Renewal." *New York Times*, September 23, 1995. http://www.nytimes.com/1995/09/23/nyregion/resurrecting-patriots-their-park-shrine-revolution-s-martyrs-part-fort-greene.html.

Martyn, Charles. *The Life of Artemas Ward*. New York: Artemas Ward, 1921.

Maryland Gazette, November 30, 1765.

Marx, Walter H. "Werewolf in Jamaica Plain." *Jamaica Plain Gazette*, October 21, 1994. Accessed May 22, 2013. https://www.jphs.org/colonial-era/werewolf-in-jamaica-plain.html.

Mary Warren Chapter, Daughters of the Revolution. "Glimpses of Early Roxbury," 1805. Accessed May 22, 2013. http://dunhamwilcox.net/ma/roxbury_ma_glimpse.htm.

"Maryland Has a Stamp Act Anniversary." *New York Times*, November 26, 1893. http://query.nytimes.com/mem/archive-free/pdf?res=F0091FFA3E5A1A738DDDAF0A94D9415B8385F0D3.

Maryland Historical Society. "Otho Holland Williams Papers, 1744–1839, MS. 908." Accessed November 21, 2017. http://www.mdhs.org/findingaid/otho-holland-williams-papers-1744-1839-ms-908.

Maryland Journal, November 15, 1775

Maryland State Archives. "Muster Rolls and Other Records of Service of Maryland Troops in the American Revolution." *Archives of Maryland Online*. n.d. http://msa.maryland.gov/megafile/msa/speccol/sc2900/sc2908/000001/000018/html/am18--28.html (Accessed February 9, 2018).

Maryland State Archives. "Annapolis Convention to Ratify the Federal Constitution, April 21–29, 1788." Accessed October 13, 2017. http://msa.maryland.gov/msa/speccol/sc2600/sc2685/html/fedconst.html.

———. Early State Records Online: MSA SC M 3195, p. 1957, December 11, 1765. Accessed December 15, 2017. http://aomol.msa.maryland.gov/megafile/msa/speccol/sc4800/sc4872/003195/html/m3195-1957.html.

———. "Maryland Manual." Accessed December 17, 2013. http://msa.maryland.gov/megafile/msa/speccol/sc2900/sc2908/000001/000156/pdf/am156--329.pdf.

Masiello, Carol. "Uxbridge Breaks Tradition and Makes History: Lydia Chapin Taft." *Blackstone Daily*, July 26, 2014. http://blackstonedaily.com/Journeys/cm-lt.htm.

Mason, Orion T. *The Handbook of Medway History: A Condensed History of the Town of Medway, Massachusetts*. G. M. Billings, 1913. https://archive.org/stream/handbookofmedway02maso#page/78/mode/2up.

Massachusetts Historical Society. "The Sons of Liberty, August 14, 1769." 2001. Accessed December 10, 2013. http://www.masshist.org/objects/cabinet/august2001/august2001.html.

May, Fred T. "German Patriots in the Revolutionary War." (2003). Accessed October 29, 2013. http://mayhouse.org/family/essays/German-Patriots/Index.html.

Mayer, Brantz. *Tah-Gah-Jute; or, Logan and Michael Cresap.* Baltimore: Maryland Historical Society, 1851. https://archive.org/stream/tahgahjuteorloga00mayeiala#page/n3/mode/2up/search/Cresap.

McCullough, David. *1776.* New York: Simon and Schuster, 2005.

———. "A Man Worth Knowing." *Imprimis* 35(5) (2006).

McDowell, Donald R. "Those Tall American Patriots and Their Long Rifles." Revolutionary War Archives, 1988. Accessed July 25, 2014. http://www.revolutionarywararchives.org/longrifle.html.

McGinn, Robert E. "Cresap's Rifles." *The Hearthstone Collection*, May–June 1987.

McGrath, Roger D. "The American Riflemen in the Revolutionary War." New American, September 3, 2010. http://www.thenewamerican.com/culture/history/item/4786-the-american-rifleman-in-the-revolutionary-war.

McIntyre, James. "Separating Myth from History: The Maryland Riflemen in the War of Independence." *Maryland Historical Magazine,* June 2009: 101–19. http://msa.maryland.gov/megafile/msa/speccol/sc5800/sc5881/000001/000000/000415/pdf/msa_sc_5881_1_415.pdf.

Miles, Lion G. "The Mohicans of Stockbridge." BerkShares, Inc., March 4, 2014. http://berkshares.org/heroes/mohican.

Military History Now. "The Shot That Set the World On Fire: How George Washington Started History's First 'World War.'" February 17, 2016. Accessed December 7, 2017. http://militaryhistorynow.com/2016/02/17/the-shot-that-set-the-world-on-fire-how-george-washington-started-the-first-world-war/.

Miller, John Allen. "The Flying Camp Batallion." Emmittsburg Area Historical Society, October 4, 2013. http://www.emmitsburg.net/archive_list/articles/history/rev_war/flying_camp_batallion.htm.

Montgomery, Thomas Lynch. *Colonel William Thompson's Battalion of Riflemen,* in *Pennsylvania Archives*, vol. 2. Harrisburg, PA: Harrisburg Publishing Company, 1906. https://archive.org/stream/musterrollsetc1700mont#page/6/mode/2up.

Moore, Frank. "Boston Liberty Tree Cut Down." History Carper, September 9, 1775. May 3, 2013. http://www.historycarper.com/1775/09/09/boston-liberty-tree-cut-down/.

———. *Diary of the American Revolution from Newspapers and Original Documents.* New York: Charles T. Evans, 1858. http://scans.library.utoronto.ca/pdf/2/3/diaryofamericanr01mooruoft/diaryofamericanr01mooruoft.pdf.

Morrissey, Brendan. *Boston 1775: The Shot Heard Around the World.* Oxford: Osprey Publishing, 1993.

Nagy, John A. Rebellion in the Ranks: Mutinies of the American Revolution. Yardley, PA: Westholme Publishing, 2008.

National Archives. "Diary Entry: 7 November 1789." Accessed May 16, 2014. http://founders.archives.gov/documents/Washington/01-05-02-0005-0003-0007.

———. "From George Washington to Richard Henry Lee, 29 August 1775." November 21, 2014. http://founders.archives.gov/documents/Washington/03-01-02-0270.

———. "From John Adams to James Warren, 18 February 1776." Accessed December 9, 2017. https://founders.archives.gov/documents/Adams/06-04-02-0008.

———. "From Thomas Jefferson to Bernardo De Galvez, 8 November 1779." Accessed August 22, 2017. https://founders.archives.gov/documents/Jefferson/01-03-02-0174.

———. "To George Washington from Brigadier General Horatio Gates, 22 June, 1775." Accessed November 14, 2103. http://founders.archives.gov/documents/Washington/03-01-02-0011.

———. "To George Washington from Brigadier General Hugh Mercer, 26 July 1776." Accessed August 21, 2017. https://founders.archives.gov/documents/Washington/03-05-02-0349.

———. "To George Washington from Brigadier General Nathanael Greene, 10 September 1775." Accessed December 10, 2017. https://founders.archives.gov/documents/Washington/03-01-02-0341.

———. "Washington Papers: Diary Entry 1 July, 1791." Accessed September 25, 2017. https://founders.archives.gov/documents/Washington/01-06-02-0002-0006-0001#GEWN-01-06-02-0002-0006-0001-fn-0002.

National Registry of Historic Places Inventory. "General Gates House and Golden Plough Tavern." July 1971. Accessed November 10, 2017. http://www.dot7.state.pa.us/CRGIS_Attachments/SiteResource/H001123_01H.pdf.

Neumann, George C. *The History of the Weapons of the American Revolution*. New York: Bonanza Books, 1967.

New York Gazette and Weekly Mercury, October 23, 1775.

Pennsylvania Evening Post, Saturday, October 21, 1775. Newspapers.com

Pennsylvania Packet. August 16, 1775. Newspapers.com

———. September 4, 1775. Newspapers.com

"Pennsylvania Rifles are Born In Lancaster." *Lancaster PA Changed America*. 2018. http://visithistoriclancaster.com/history_art/pennsylvania_rifles (accessed January 17, 2018).

Philbrick, Nathaniel. *Bunker Hill: A City, A Siege, A Revolution*. New York: Viking, 2013.

Pittar, Henry Hamilton. "Map of Frederick City, Frederick County, Maryland." Baltimore: Henry Hamilton Pittar, 1853.

Powell, Allan. *Maryland and the French and Indian War*. Baltimore, MD: Gateway Press, Inc., 1998.

Prats, J. J. "Campsite of Lord Dunmore, 1774." Historical Marker Database, August 30, 2008. Accessed January 10, 2017. http://www.hmdb.org/Marker.asp?Marker=10892.

Prowell, George R. *Continental Congress at York, Pennsylvania: York County in the Revolution*. York, PA: York Printing Company, 1914. https://archive.org/stream/continentalcongr00prow#page/160/mode/1up/search/Doudel.

Ptacek, Kathryn. "The Oxford Furnace Incident." New Jersey Skylands, December 9, 2013. http://www.njskylands.com/hsoxfordfurnace.htm.

Purdue's Virginia Gazette, "PostScript Number 27," August 4, 1775, 7. Newspapers.com

Rawlings, Moses. "Regarding the Actions of Rawlings and His Men at the Siege of Washington." Papers of the War Department. Accessed October 12, 2017. http://wardepartmentpapers.org/docimage.php?id=42259&docColID=45686&page=1.

Rebuilding Freedom. "The Liberty Tree." May 3, 2013. http://rebuildingfreedom.org/educate-yourself/history/the-liberty-tree/. Reichel, William C. *The Crown Inn Near Bethlehem, Pennsylvania: A History*. Philadelphia: King and Baird, 1872.

Revolutionary War and Beyond. "The Olive Branch Petition." Accessed July 22, 2014. http://www.revolutionary-war-and-beyond.com/olive-branch-petition.html.

Rice, William H. *Colonial Records of the Upper Potomac*, vol. 1. Parsons, WV: McClain Printing Company, 2010.

———. *Colonial Records of the Upper Potomac, 1748–1750*, vol. 3. Parsons, WV: McClain Printing Company, 2013.

Rich, Stephen M., Fabian H. Leendertz, Guang Xu, Matthew LeBreton, Cyrille F. Djoko, Makoah N. Aminake, Eric E. Takang, Joseph L. D. Diffo, Brian L. Pike, Benjamin M. Rosenthal, Pierre Formenty, Christophe Boesch, Francisco J. Ayala, and Nathan D. Wolfe. "The Origin of Malignant Malaria." *Proceedings of the National Academy of Sciences of the United States* 106(35) (2009): 14902–7. Accessed April 14, 2016. https://www.ncbi.nlm.nih.gov/pmc/articles/PMC2720412/.

Richards, Henry Melchior Muhlenberg. "The First Defenders of the Revolution," in *The Pennsylvania German in the Revolutionary War, 1775–1783*. Lancaster, PA: Pennsylvania-German Society, 1908. https://archive.org/stream/pennsylvaniager1718rich_0#page/n65/mode/2up/search/Bethlehem.

Richardson, Gary. "Richardson Tavern, Millis, Massachusetts." Rootsweb, 2005. Accessed July 24, 2014. http://archiver.rootsweb.ancestry.com/th/read/RICHARDSON/2005-06/1117744546.

Rind's Virginia Gazette. November 9, 1775. Newspapers.com

Roosevelt, Theodore. *Theodore Roosevelt's "The Winning of the West": A Modern Abridgement.* New York: Hastings House Publisher, 1963.

Rose, Alexander. *American Rifle: A Biography.* New York: Random House Publishing, 2008. Royster, Charles. A Revolutionary People at War: The Continental Army and the American Character, 1775–1783. Chapel Hill: University of North Carolina Press, 1979.

Rutgers University Cartography Services. "Historical Maps of New Jersey." December 11, 2013. http://mapmaker.rutgers.edu/MAPS.html.

Ruttenber, Edward M. *History of the Town of New Windsor.* Newburgh, NY: Historical Society of Newburgh Bay and the Highlands, 1911. https://archive.org/stream/historyoftownofn00rutte#page/32/mode/2up/search/rifle.

Ruttenber, Edward Manning, and Lewis H. Clark. *History of Orange County, NY.* Philadelphia: Everts and Peck, 1881. https://archive.org/details/cu31924028832693.

Sam Houston State University. "Black Americans in Defense of Our Nation." 1985. Accessed March 26, 2014. http://www.shsu.edu/~his_ncp/AfrAmer.html.

Sargent, Winthrop. The History of an Expedition against Fort Du Quesne in 1755 under Major General Edward Braddock. Lewisburg, PA: Wennawoods Publishing, 1997.

Sarudy, Barbara Wells. 2014.

Schlesinger, Arthur M. Jr. *The Almanac of American History.* New York: Bramhall House, 1983.

Schmitt, Dale J. "The Capture of Colonel Moses Rawlings." *Maryland Historical Magazine* 7(2) (1976): 205–11. http://msa.maryland.gov/megafile/msa/speccol/sc5800/sc5881/000001/000000/000282/pdf/msa_sc_5881_1_282.pdf.

Schrader, Arthur F. *American Revolutionary War: Songs to Cultivate the Sensations of Freedom.* Folkway Records no. FH 5279, 1976, album. Includes "The Rebels" and "The Liberty Tree."

Schultz, Edward T. *First Settlements of Germans in Maryland.* Frederick, MD: D. H. Smith, 1896. http://archive.org/stream/firstsettlements00schuitz#page/n113/mode/2up/search/tavern.

Scudder, Horace E. *A History of the United States of America.* New York: American Book Company, 1901.

Sealsfield, Charles. *Life in the New World.* New York: J. Winchester, 1844.

Sharf, John Thomas. *History of Maryland: From the Earliest Period to Present-Day, 1600–1775*, vol. I. Baltimore: John P Piet, 1879. http://books.google.com/books?id=CGU1AAAAIAAJ&pg=PA528&dq=Sharf+Western+Maryland+%22sons+of+liberty%22&hl=en&sa=X&ei=J1OZT_bBKMbq0QGg36mmCg&ved=0CEQQ6AEwAg#v=onepage&q=thomas%20Cresap&f=false).

Shay, Brian M. "After 230 Years, The 'Blue Book' Still Guides NCOs." US Army Military Institute (2009). Accessed August 22, 2017. https://www.army.mil/article/29717/.

Sibley, John Langdon. *Biographical Sketches of Graduates of Harvard.* Cambridge, MA: Charles William Sever, 1873.

Sigal Museum. "Bachmann Publick House." Accessed October 7, 2017. https://sigalmuseum.org/bachmann/.

Silas Deane Online. "Letter from Silas Deane to Elizabeth Deane, 3 June 1775." Accessed November 24, 2017. http://www.silasdeaneonline.org/documents/doc12.htm.

Skidmore, Warren, and Donna Kaminsky. *Lord Dunmore's Little War of 1774*. Rocky Mount, NC: Heritage Books, Inc., 2002.

Smith, Philip H. *History of Dover, New York: General History of Dutchess County, 1609–1876*. Pawlings, NY: published by the author, 1877. https://archive.org/details/generalhistoryof00smituoft.

Snell, James P., and W. W. Clayton. *History of Sussex and Warren Counties, New Jersey*. Philadelphia: Everts and Peck, 1881.

Stockbridge-Munsee Community. "Origin and Early Mohican History." Accessed November 17, 2014. http://www.mohican.com/originearlyhistory/.

Stockwell, Mary. "Declaration of Independence." *Digital Encyclopedia*. Accessed December 21, 2017. http://www.mountvernon.org/digital-encyclopedia/article/declaration-of-independence/.

Strozier, Mark. "Morgan and Virginians Arrive in Cambridge on August 8, 1775." Sons of the American Revolution, San Antonio, Texas, Chapter, September 9, 2014. http://sarsat.org/HistoricalAccounts/17750808MorganandVirginiansarriveinCambridge.htm.

Sullivan, Bill. "Lord Dunmore: Beneath the Kilt." Making History, April 20, 2016. Accessed January 9, 2017. http://makinghistorynow.com/2016/04/lord-dunmore-beneath-the-kilt/.

Sweetman, Jennie. "Early Surgeon Remembered." *New Jersey Herald*, n.d.

———. "Hinchman Clan Has Vernon Ties." *New Jersey Herald*, June 8, 1980.

———. "Sussex County Inns: Taverns Served Many Purposes." KWWL.com, December 10, 2013. http://www.kwwl.com/story/20512513/2013/01/05/sussex-county-inns-taverns-served-many-purposes.

Swift, Lindsay, ed. *Historical Manuscripts in the Public Library in the City of Boston*, no. 1. Boston: Trustees of the Public Library, 1900.

"Taft Visits Homes of His Ancestors: Meets Many of His Rural Kin in Mendon and Uxbridge and Names a Taft Baby; Covers with Gov. Draper Route Which Washington Traveled 131 Years Ago." *New York Times*, August 20, 1910. http://hope1842.com/taftvisit.html.

Taft, Ernest A. *Bellingham: Images of America Series*. Charleston, SC: Arcadia Publishing, 2003.

Taurasi, Liz. "Historical View of Westwood: Ellis Tavern." Westwood Patch, July 25, 2012. Accessed July 23, 2014. http://westwood.patch.com/groups/goodnews/p/historical-view-of-westwood-ellis-tavern.

Thacher, James. *Military Journal During the American Revolutionary War*. Boston: Richardson and Lord, 1823. https://archive.org/stream/jamesthachermil00revorich#page/37/mode/1up.

Thomas Jefferson Foundation. "Hanover, Pennsylvania." 1991. Accessed September 25, 2017. https://www.monticello.org/site/research-and-collections/hanover-pennsylvania.

Thwaites, Reuben Gold, and Louise Phelps Kellogg. *Documentary History of Dunmore's War*. Madison, WI: Wisconsin Historical Society, 1905. https://archive.org/stream/documentaryhisto00kelluoft#page/xxiv/mode/2up/search/Boston.

Tiffany, Osmond. *A Sketch of the Life of and Services of Otho Holland Williams*. Baltimore: John Murphy and Co., 1851. http://www.gutenberg.org/files/27293/27293-h/27293-h.htm.

TimeandDate.com. Calendar for Year 1775 (United States). Accessed December 6, 2017. http://www.timeanddate.com/calendar/index.html?year=1775&country=1.13.

Tomlinson, Abraham, Lemuel Lyon, and Samuel Haws. *The Military Journals of Two Private Soldiers: 1758–1775*. Poughkeepsie, NY: Abraham Tomlinson, 1855. https://archive.org/stream/militaryjournals00tomliala#page/n7/mode/2up.

Town of Burlington, Connecticut. "Burlington, Connecticut: A Town History." Accessed April 18, 2015. http://burlingtonct.us/our-town/history.php.

Town of Litchfield, Connecticut. "Town of Litchfield History." Accessed March 29, 2014. http://www.townoflitchfield.org/Pages/LitchfieldCT_WebDocs/hist.

Town of Millis, Massachusetts. "Historical Geography of Millis." Accessed July 26, 2014. Accessed http://millispd.net/index.cfm?pid=12334.

"The Tree of Liberty—Boston, Massachusetts." The Planet Prisoner, December 14, 2011. Accessed May 3, 2013. http://theplanetprisoner.wordpress.com/2011/12/14/the-tree-of-liberty-boston-ma/.

Trinity Church, Wall Street. Rector's Office: Archives. n.d. Accessed December 13, 2017. https://www.trinitywallstreet.org/about/history.

Trumbull, J. Hammond. *Collections of the Connecticut Historical Society*. Hartford, CT: Press of Case, Lockwood, and Brainard, 1870.

———. *The Memorial History of Hartford County, Connecticut: 1633–1884*. Boston: Edward L. Osgood, 1886. https://archive.org/details/memorialhistoryo02trum.

"Unveiling of Cresap Tablet: Logan Elm Park, October 1916." *Ohio Archaeological and Historical Publications* 26 (1916): 123–45. https://books.google.com/books?id=gvwKAAAAIAAJ&pg=PA127&lpg=PA127&dq=Benjamin+O.+Cresap&source=bl&ots=yqpdfR_DkX&sig=iGJ_PBK93OiujqVIj2FUOTnYDsE&hl=en&sa=X&ei=sbmtVI3WFM-vogT8oYK4DA&ved=0CDMQ6AEwCA#v=onepage&q=Benjamin%20O.%20Cresap&f=false.

US Department of the Treasury. "Resource Center: Portraits and Designs." Last revised December 5, 2010. July 22, 2014. http://www.treasury.gov/resource-center/faqs/Coins/Pages/edu_faq_coins_portraits.aspx.

US Geologic Survey. "Feature Detail Report for Hocking River," July 12, 1979. Accessed January 10, 2017. https://geonames.usgs.gov/apex/f?p=gnispq:3:0::NO::P3_FID:1076055.

US House of Representatives. Heirs of Captain Thomas Beall, Report #128 to Accompany Bill H.R. No. 806. Second Session, Thirtieth Congress. February 28, 1849. https://books.google.com/books?id=HBwZAAAAIAAJ&pg=RA5-PA31&lpg=RA5-PA31&dq=Regiment+of+bergen+%2B+1776+%2B+new+York+%2B+Thomas+beall&source=bl&ots=3teUpw7h_6&sig=iTu_B1RW5cnvTEdU31IIMAk_6II&hl=en&sa=X&ved=0CBwQ6AEwAGoVChMInev3-peGyQIVgTQ-Ch09cAlD#v=onepage&q=Regiment%20of%20bergen%20%2B%201776%20%2B%20new%20York%20%2B%20Thomas%20beall&f=false.

US National Park Service. "Date in History: 1775." Accessed May 3, 2013. http://www.nps.gov/revwar/revolution_day_by_day/1775_main.html.

———. "Roxbury during the Siege of Boston: April 1775–March 1776." Boston National Historical Park. Accessed February 27, 2013. http://www.nps.gov/bost/forteachers/upload/roxbury.pdf.

Valuska, David L. Thompson's Rifle Company." The Continental Line, September 11, 2014. http://www.continentalline.org/articles/article.php?date=0602&article=060204.

Waldo, Loren P. *An Early History of Tolland, Connecticut*. Hartford, CT: Press of Case, Lockwood, and Company, 1861. https://archive.org/stream/earlyhistoryofho00wald#page/n6/mode/1up.

Wallace, Paul. A. W. *Daniel Boone in Pennsylvania*. Harrisburg, PA: Commonwealth of Pennsylvania Historical and Museum Commission, 1967. http://books.google.com/books?id=hiXwK-_8DRkC&pg=PA17&lpg=PA17&dq=%22daniel+morgan%22+cousin+%22daniel+boone%22&source=bl&ots=3MDhBjpaOq&sig=2-YHvXhaBTdS7RuFqbsBK8lovaU&hl=en&sa=X&ei=WiltVJCELM-pyATIqoDoDg&ved=0CCsQ6AEwAQ#v=onepage&q=%22daniel%20morgan%22%20cousin%20%22daniel%20boone%22&f=false.

Warner, Richard B. "A Band of Cousins." Connecticut Society of the Sons of the American Revolution, March 24, 2014. https://www.connecticutsar.org/patriots/cousins.htm.

Warner, Sam Bass Jr. *Street Car Suburbs: The Process of Growth in Boston (1870–1900).* Boston: President and Fellows of Harvard College, 1978.

"Watertown, August 28." *Pennsylvania Gazette*, September 6, 1775.

Waymarking.com. "Captain Michael Doudel's Company, York, PA: US Revolutionary War Memorials." Posted by Math Teacher, April 2, 2013. Accessed September 10, 2014. http://www.waymarking.com/waymarks/WMGR0M_Captain_Michael_Doudels_Company_York_PA.

Webb, Edward A. *The Historical Directory of Sussex County, New Jersey.* Andover, NJ, 1872. https://archive.org/stream/historicaldirect00webb#page/n5/mode/2up.

Weinberger, Jill Knight. "Touring the Quiet Corner." *New York Times*, June 2, 2002. http://www.nytimes.com/2002/06/02/travel/touring-the-quiet-corner.html.

West Virginia Division of Culture and History. "'Manufactured History': Refighting the Battle of Point Pleasant." *West Virginia History* 56 (1997): 76–87. Accessed January 9, 2017. http://www.wvculture.org/history/journal_wvh/wvh56-5.html.

"Westwood Public Library Historic Photograph Collection." *Historic Photographs of Westwood, Massachusetts.* Scrapbook, March 2015.

Whitney, H. B. "History of the Town of Sheldon." Rootsweb, 2004. Accessed March 24, 2014. http://www.rootsweb.ancestry.com/~vermont/FranklinSheldon.html.

Wikipedia, The Free Encyclopedia, s.v. "Alexander Scammell." *Wikipedia*. Accessed July 23, 2014. http://en.wikipedia.org/wiki/Alexander_Scammell.

———. "Bernat Mill." Accessed July 22, 2014. http://en.wikipedia.org/wiki/Bernat_Mill.

———. "Boston Post Road." Accessed August 6, 2013. http://en.wikipedia.org/wiki/Boston_Post_Road.

———. "Boston Post Road Map." Accessed August 7, 2017. http://upload.wikimedia.org/wikipedia/commons/e/e7/Boston_Post_Road_map.png.

———. "The Charter Oak, Charles de Wolf Brownell." Accessed May 13, 2014. http://en.wikipedia.org/wiki/File:The_Charter_Oak_Charles_De_Wolf_Brownell_1857.jpeg.

———. "History of Dedham, Massachusetts, 1635–1792." Accessed September 10, 2014. http://en.wikipedia.org/wiki/History_of_Dedham,_Massachusetts,_1635%E2%80%931792.

———. "Jamaica Plain." Accessed May 22, 2013. http://en.wikipedia.org/wiki/Jamaica_Plain.

———. "King's Highway: Charleston to Boston." August 7, 2013. http://en.wikipedia.org/wiki/King%27s_Highway_(Charleston_to_Boston).

———. "List of Continental Army Units (1775)." Accessed September 10, 2017. http://en.wikipedia.org/wiki/List_of_Continental_Army_units_(1775).

———. "Maryland and Virginia Rifle Regiment." Accessed August 20, 2017. https://en.wikipedia.org/wiki/Maryland_and_Virginia_Rifle_Regiment#Primary_references_.28books.

———. "Prison Ship Martyrs' Monument." Accessed August 5, 2017. https://en.wikipedia.org/wiki/Prison_Ship_Martyrs%27_Monument.

———. "Samuel Taft House, Photograph." Accessed July 22, 2014. http://en.wikipedia.org/wiki/Samuel_Taft_House#mediaviewer/File:Samuel_Taft_House,_Natonal_Historic_Site,_Uxbridge,_MA.jpg.

———. "Seth Reed House Uxbridge Photograph." Accessed July 22, 2014. http://en.wikipedia.org/wiki/File:SethReadHouseUxbridge.gif.

———. "Suffolk Resolves." Accessed September 10, 2014. http://en.wikipedia.org/wiki/Suffolk_Resolves.

———. "Yankee Doodle." Accessed December 15, 2014. http://en.wikipedia.org/wiki/Yankee_Doodle.

Williams, Thomas John Chew. *A History of Washington County, Maryland*, vol. 1. Hagerstown, MD: Higginson Book Company, 1906. https://books.google.com/books?id=Q9AwAQAAMAAJ&pg=PA128&lpg=PA128&dq=Hagerstown+%2B+riflemen+%2B+1775&source=bl&ots=hV_tLTJ66D&sig=vIFKcwcM9rvvLkgYtykOJz75BFo&hl=en&sa=X&ei=G6CSVe-XF8bp-AGftI3QCg&ved=0CB0Q6AEwADgU#v=onepage&q=Hagerstown%20%2B%20riflemen%20%2B%201775&f=false.

Williams, Thomas John Chew, and Folger McKensey. *History of Frederick County*, vol. 1. Baltimore: L. R. Titsworth and Co., 1910. https://books.google.com/books?id=2ud-8Kr70DAC&pg=PA22&ots=1u-ZxPIUBq&dq=Cresap+%2B+%22Sons+Of+Liberty%22&sig=IoP4LqMu2JDacKkG7RzFRuYYvqo#v=onepage&q=Cresap%20&f=false.

Works Progress Administration. *Massachusetts: A Guide to Its Places and People*. Cambridge, MA: The Riverside Press, 1937. https://archive.org/stream/massachusettsgui00federich#page/n4/mode/1up.

Works Progress Adminsitration, Federal Writers Project. *American Guide Series: Connecticut: A Guide to Its Roads, Lore, and People*. Boston: Houghton Mifflin Company, 1938. https://archive.org/stream/connecticut00federich#page/570/mode/1up.

Works Progress Administration, Federal Writers' Project. *New Jersey: A Guide to Its Present and Past*. New York: Viking Press, 1939. https://archive.org/stream/newjerseyaguide00fedemiss#page/456/mode/2up

Works Progress Adminstration. *Pennsylvania: A Guide to the Keystone State*. New York: Oxford University Press, 1940.

Wright, Kevin W. "Anderson House: 1785." NewtonNJ.net, 2000. Accessed December 10, 2013. http://www.newtonnj.net/Pages/andersonhse.htm.

———. "Sussex Courthouse." NewtonNJ.net, 2000. Accessed December 10, 2013. http://www.newtonnj.net/Pages/sussexcourthse.htm.

Yale Law School. "A Declaration by the Representatives of the United Colonies of North America, Now Met in Congress at Philadelphia, Setting Forth the Causes and Necessity of Their Taking Up Arms." http://avalon.law.yale.edu/18th_century/arms.asp.

"Yardkin County and Caswell County." Rootsweb. Accessed September 21, 2017. http://wc.rootsweb.ancestry.com/cgi-bin/igm.cgi?op=GET&db=grantpinnix&id=I125610.

Young, Henry J., ed. "The Spirit of 1775: A Letter of Robert Magaw, Major of the Continental Riflemen to the Gentlemen of the Committee of Correspondence in the Town of Carlisle, Dated at Cambridge, 13 August 1775, with an Essay on the Background and Sequel." *John and Mary's Journal* 1 (1975).

APPENDIX A

Route Traveled By Cresap's Rifles: Towns and Corresponding Daily Mileage			
Date	Day	Place	Miles
May 1775		Near Ashland, Kentucky	
June 1775		Wheeling, West Virginia (about 8 days travel)	200
June 1775		Catfish Camp (Washington), Pennsylvania	30
June 1775		Redstone (Brownsville), Pennsylvania	24
June 1775		Great Meadows (Farmington, Pennsylvania), Pennsylvania	23
June 1775		Little Meadows (Grantsville), Maryland	25
June 1775		Cumberland, Maryland	25
July 1775		Oldtown, Maryland	15
July 1775	Monday	Fredericktown (Frederick) Maryland (3 days of travel)	85
August 1, 1775	Tuesday	Taneytown, Maryland	25
August 2, 1775	Wednesday	Hanover, Pennsylvania	16
August 3, 1775	Thursday	York, Pennsylvania	20
August 4, 1775	Friday	Lancaster, Pennsylvania	25
August 5, 1775	Saturday	Lancaster, Pennsylvania	
August 6, 1775	Sunday	Lancaster, Pennsylvania	
August 7, 1775	Monday	Adamstown, Pennsylvania	24
August 8, 1775	Tuesday	Kutztown, Pennsylvania	28
August 9, 1775	Wednesday	Allentown, Pennsylvania	18
August 10, 1775	Friday	Easton, Pennsylvania	18
August 11, 1775	Saturday	Oxford, New Jersey	18
August 12, 1775	Sunday	Johnsonburg, New Jersey	15
August 13, 1775	Monday	Newton, New Jersey	10
August 14, 1775	Tuesday	Vernon, New Jersey	23

August 15, 1775	Wednesday	Blooming Grove, New York	22
August 16, 1775	Thursday	New Windsor, New York	11
August 17, 1775	Friday	Wingdale, New York	27
August 18, 1775	Saturday	Roxbury, Connecticut	25
August 19, 1775	Sunday	Harwinton, Connecticut	29
August 20, 1775	Monday	Hartford, Connecticut	22
August 21, 1775	Tuesday	Coventry, Connecticut	25
August 22, 1775	Wednesday	Thompson, Connecticut	33
August 23, 1775	Thursday	Mendon, Massachusetts	21
August 24, 1775	Friday	Woodbury, Massachusetts	23
August 25, 1775	Saturday	Roxbury, Massachusetts	10
		Total miles Cresap's Rifles walked from Fredericktown, Maryland to Roxbury, Massachusetts.	487
		Total miles Cresap's Rifles walked starting from Redstone, Pennsylvania to Roxbury, Massachusetts.	660
		Total miles Michael Cresap walked from Ashland, Kentucky to Roxbury, Massachusetts since May 1775	914

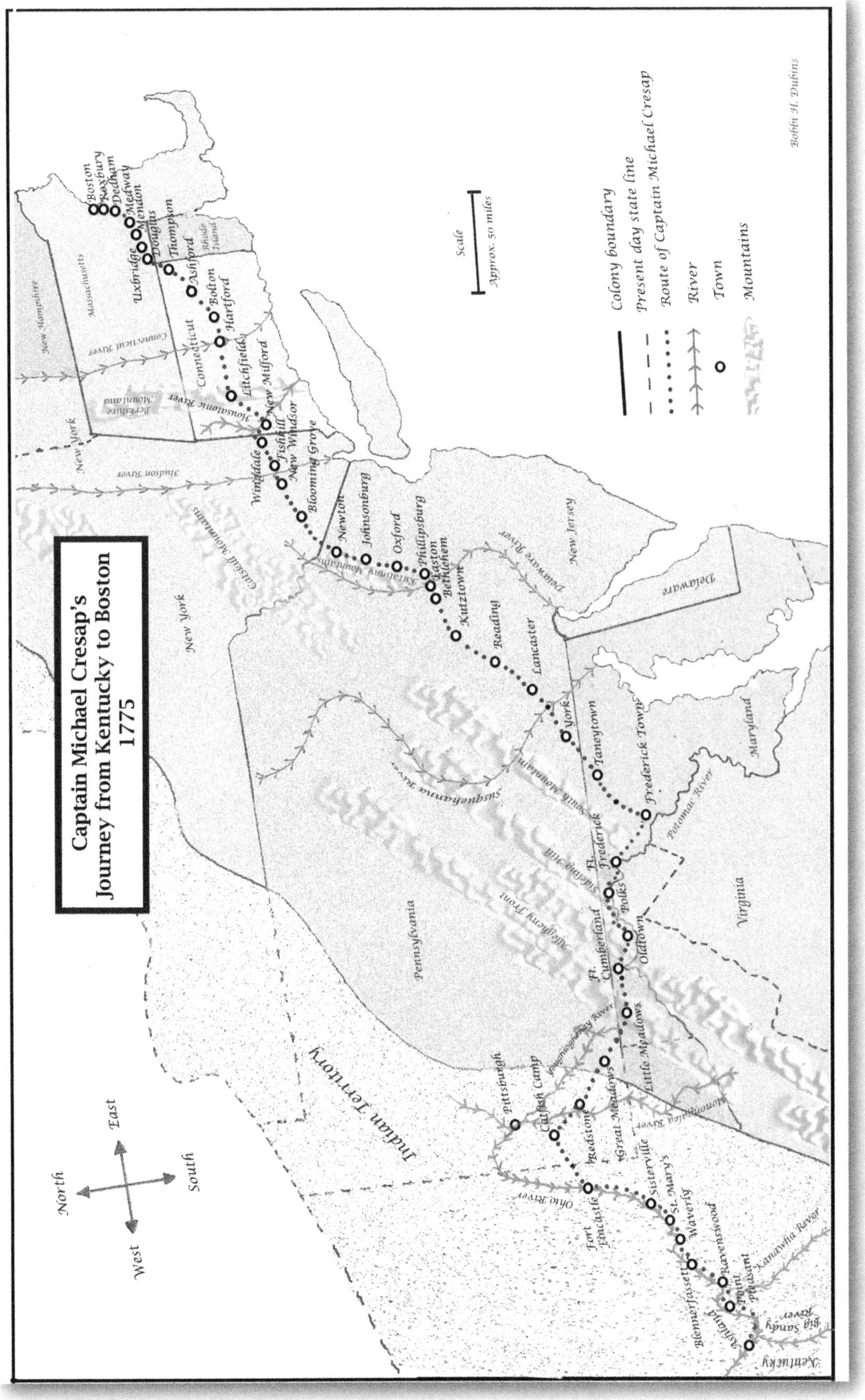
Captain Michael Cresap's
Journey from Kentucky to Boston
1775
North
East
West
South
Indian Territory
New York
New Hampshire
Massachusetts
Connecticut
Rhode Island
Pennsylvania
New Jersey
Delaware
Maryland
Virginia
Kentucky
Hudson River
Connecticut River
Housatonic River
Berkshire Mountains
Catskill Mountains
Kittatinny Mountains
Susquehanna River
Delaware River
Allegheny Front
Sideling Hill
South Mountain
Potomac River
Youghiogheny River
Monongahela River
Ohio River
Kanawha River
Big Sandy River
Boston
Roxbury
Dedham
Medway
Mendon
Uxbridge
Douglas
Thompson
Ashford
Bolton
Hartford
Litchfield
New Milford
Wingdale
Fishkill
New Windsor
Blooming Grove
Newton
Johnsonburg
Oxford
Phillipsburg
Easton
Bethlehem
Kutztown
Reading
Lancaster
York
Taneytown
Frederick Town
Ft. Frederick
Polks
Oldtown
Ft. Cumberland
Little Meadows
Great Meadows
Redstone
Catfish Camp
Pittsburgh
Fort Fincastle
Sisterville
St. Mary's
Waverly
Blennerfassett
Ravenswood
Point Pleasant
Ashland
Scale
Approx. 50 miles
Colony boundary
Present day state line
Route of Captain Michael Cresap
River
Town
Mountains
Bobbi H. Dubins

APPENDIX B

"As Americans we hail with delight any attempt to rescue from oblivion the words or actions of those whose names we have been taught to revere."
Quoted from *"Military Journal during the American Revolutionary War,"* by James Thacher, 1823
1775 Roster of Cresap's Riflemen (partial list)[628]

Captain Michael Cresap (MD State Archives)
Lieutenant Moses Rawlings (Heitman)
First Lieutenant Thomas Warren, (MD State Archives)
Second Lieutenant Joseph Cresap, (MD State Archives)
Lieutenant Daniel Cresap, Jr., (Cresap & Cresap)
Ensign Richard Davis (MD State Archives)
Samuel Blackburn (Pension File # S.35194)[629]
Sparling Bowman (Pension (File # S.3048)
William Boyd (Pension File # S.35197)
John Chenowith (Pension File # W.9787)
John Clarke (Pension File # S.3158)
Martin Claubaugh (Pension File # W.3222)
Walter Clabbaugh (Linn & Egle)
Henry Dugan (Pension File # S.35792)
John Eichelberger (Pension File # W.9424)
Robert L. English (Pension File # R.3354)
Terrance Finnegan (Journal of Henry Bedinger)
Thomas Hallam (Henderson vs. Cresap Heirs Deposition)
Shadrack Hiatt (Pension File # S.13361)
John Lazier (Pension File # S.40075)
George Miller (Pension File # W.9570)
William Moody (Pension File # S.38246)

---
628 *Sources listed in parenthesis next to a name can be found in "References." Pension records can be found in the footnote below."*
629 *Southern Campaigns Revolutionary War Pension Statements and Roster . n.d. http://revwarapps.org/. Accessed 6 February 2018.*

George Moore (Pension File # W.14620)
Nathan Peak (Pension File # S.35550)
Benjamin Power (Pension File # S.5945)
Jacob Shade (Pension File # S.6082)
Jonathan Sheppard (Pension File # S.38365)
Michael Smith (Pension File # W.6088)
James Turner (Pension File # S.3841)

Pension applications and other sources have revealed the identities of a few of the men who marched with Captain Michael Cresap to Boston in 1775. While approximately one hundred men's names are missing from this roster, the names of the riflemen verified with documentation are listed above. As information published in books and magazines over the ensuing years has been at the very least confusing, and in some cases misleading, research to identity the names of all the men who marched with Captain Cresap to Boston is ongoing.